LITERACY AND MOTIVATION

Reading Engagement
in Individuals and Groups

LITERACY AND MOTIVATION

Reading Engagement in Individuals and Groups

Edited by

Ludo Verhoeven
Nijimegen University

Catherine E. Snow
Harvard University

STICHTING LEZEN

LAWRENCE ERLBAUM ASSOCIATES, PUBLISHERS
2001   Mahwah, New Jersey   London

Lawrence Erlbaum Associates, Inc., Publishers
10 Industrial Avenue
Mahwah, New Jersey 07430

Cover design by Kathryn Houghtaling Lacey

Library of Congress Cataloging-in-Publication Data

Verhoeven, Ludo Th.
    Literacy and motivation : reading engagement in individuals and groups / edited by
Ludo Verhoeven, Catherine E. Snow.
        p. cm.
    Includes bibliographical references.
    ISBN 0-8058-3193-2 (cloth : alk. paper) – ISBN 0-8058-3194-0 (pbk. : alk. paper)
        1.   Reading—Social aspects. 2. Group reading. 3. Literacy. I. Snow, Catherine E. II.
Title.

LB1050.2 . V47 2001
302.2'244—dc21
                                                                                                00-051393

Printed in the United States of America
10   9   8   7   6   5   4   3   2   1

Contents

Acknowledgments

The purpose of this volume is to open new perspectives in the study of reading engagement by bringing together research findings from psychology, linguistics, sociology, anthropology, and education. The initiative for this volume was supported by the Stichting Lezen (Dutch Platform for Reading Promotion), the Expertisecentrum Nederlands (National Language Education Center) at the University of Nijmegen, and the Harvard Graduate School of Education. The editors would like to thank the Stichting Lezen, the Netherlands Ministry of Education and Sciences, and the Faculty of Social Sciences of the University of Nijmegen for their financial support. They also wish to thank all contributors to this volume for their cooperation.

Ludo Verhoeven
Catherine E. Snow

Literacy and Motivation: Bridging Cognitive and Sociocultural Viewpoints

Ludo Verhoeven
Nijmegen University

Catherine E. Snow
Harvard University

There is an increasing societal concern about the development of literacy. The notion that a literacy crisis exists is fairly generally subscribed to, but the specific definition of the crisis being referred to varies enormously, as a function of the discourse community where the crisis is being discussed. For those concerned primarily with the developing world, the term *literacy crisis* invokes the crucial role of literacy in economic development combined with restricted literacy skills in the population, limited access to schooling, and the challenges of implementing universal schooling and adult literacy programs simultaneously. In countries with generally high literacy rates, including those in North America and Europe, the term *literacy crisis* refers to severe inequities in the distribution of literacy skills—to the fact that members of immigrant and minority groups and children attending the schools that serve these groups are at enormously higher risk of failure than the population as a whole. In yet other developed nations with close to universal literacy, *literacy crisis* is used to refer to the fact that the literacy skills members of the workforce possess are insufficient to meet the new challenges associated with the increasingly sophisticated technical, electronic, and computer-based demands of even blue-collar jobs. Finally, another sense in which literacy crisis is used refers to the aliteracy of technically literate individuals. Examples cited in this regard are varied: Children progressing satisfactorily through school nonetheless spend much less time reading than did children of 50 years ago; best-selling books for adults are more likely to be how-to books or "trash" fiction than good literature;

I

and widely shared conversation about the products of great authors has been replaced by shared conversations about television programs and computer software. The chapters of this book address an issue that is often ignored in discussing literacy, in an attempt to promote a new way of thinking about literacy crises of all these various sorts. The central issue in this volume is how a world of engaged readers can be created. Literacy engagement involves the integration of cognitive strategies and motivational goals during literate activities. Promoting literacy acquisition requires interventions that address attitudes and beliefs as much as interventions that assure cognitive changes in the learners. In fact, chapters of this book argue, coming to grips with the notion of engagement in literacy requires redefining literacy itself to acknowledge the degree to which it is a social activity and an affective commitment, in addition to being a cognitive accomplishment. In seeking answers to the question of how a world of engaged readers can be created, the authors focus on the affective side of literacy, the enjoyment that readers derive from reading, the motivations that impel them to learn to read and that impel them to spend time reading, the wide variety of social and cultural factors that influence motivation to read, and the array of forms that literacy can take and roles that it can play.

One might think that deriving joy from reading is only relevant to the last definition of literacy crisis just given—the aliteracy of competent readers. In fact, though, we argue (and various of the chapters demonstrate) that enthusiasm for reading is a prerequisite to learning how to read; nurturing enthusiasm for literacy is thus an indispensable component of adequate early prevention and intervention programs, a crucial aspect of good reading instruction in the elementary school years, and a serious challenge in adult literacy programs. We present here a view of literacy in which motivation for reading is as important as orthographic knowledge or comprehension strategies; indeed, we argue that without some level of motivation, neither orthographic knowledge nor comprehension strategies are likely to develop optimally. In order to promote universal literacy, cognitive and sociocultural perspectives on literacy development must be integrated with one another.

CREATING A WORLD OF ENGAGED READERS

Literacy Development

There is now general consensus, after 40 years of controversy and conflicting results, about the processes that skilled readers engage in while reading. First, it is clear that skilled reading involves attention to the marks on the page—that visual processing of a very high proportion of the graphic symbols, not a sparse sampling, occurs. Second, it seems that readers engage in a process of phonological representation of those graphic symbols—even when reading nonalphabetic orthographies. This process of phonological recoding makes possible the identification (i.e., access to pronunciation, not necessarily to meaning) of novel words, even of nonsense words. The recoding process as engaged in by skilled readers is rapid, automatic, and seemingly effortless for the vast majority of words—certainly for frequently encountered words, for words that include frequently encountered sequences of letters (e.g., for nonce words like *confrequation*), and for words that are spelled regularly. If this process of phonological recoding is relatively effortless, word identification is rapid and accurate, access to word meaning is straightforward, and comprehension of sentence and text meaning is possible. To the extent that word identification becomes more effortful, comprehension is likely to be disrupted. Of course, skilled readers also utilize various comprehension strategies (e.g., rereading; self-monitoring; and using information from organizational markers, from pictures, from world knowledge and genre familiarity, from syntactic analysis, etc.) to support their reading, in particular when the decoding process is somewhat less automatic than usual (e.g., when reading a novel full of Russian names, or an article with many pharmaceutical terms).

Where is there room in this model of skilled reading for motivation, enthusiasm, and enjoyment? One key link here has to do with the need for rapid and effortless translation of the graphic symbols into phonological representations if comprehension is to occur. Rapidity and effortlessness in this process are the products of practice. Only with many hundreds of hours of actual reading, and only after having encountered and identified millions of written words, can the effortless processing of adult-level reading material be assured. Thus, we argue that opportunities for practice are a crucial part of any reading instructional program, as the practice, combined with the learner's understanding of the principles underlying the orthography that he or she is learning, ensures rapid processing.

Engaging in enough practice to ensure fluency presupposes a number of factors are in place:

- Children approach reading instruction understanding the uses, purposes, and value of literacy. This expectation typically reflects having been exposed to adult literacy practices during the preschool years—having seen adults read for pleasure and for information, write lists and letters, and rely on literacy for a variety of functions (see Barton, chap. 1).

- Children approach reading instruction enthusiastic about learning to read. This expectation often reflects having had affectively positive experiences with reading in the preschool years, from being read to in the context of cherished relationships (see Bus, chap. 2).

- Children approach reading instruction expecting to succeed. Children who enter formal instructional contexts already able to recognize a few words (STOP on a sign, their own first names, *hamburger* on a MacDonald's menu) think of literacy as a game they too can play, and are motivated to expand their skills.

- Children have access to reading materials of a level that they can read successfully and that they want to read. Teachers play a crucial role in designing excellent environments for children to practice their developing reading skills. They need to know precisely what literacy skills each child has mastered, in order to pick books of the right level, and they need to know each child's interests and preferences, in order to suggest books that will be optimally engaging. Of course, as children's skills mature and as their interests shift, teachers must be able to track these changes and keep up, while supplying lots and lots of attractive books (see Elley, chap. 11).

Clearly, then, our view of skilled reading and of reading development incorporates a central place for engagement in literacy practice, a factor that is likely only if joy is part of the experience. Equally important, of course, is the prior motivation to become a reader, which presupposes an understanding of the functions that reading can play and/or participation in a community in which literacy activities are characteristic of membership.

Literacy and Motivation

Motivation can be seen as an active process in which children construct ideas about language and literacy as they communicate. Learners are engaged in selecting activities, in attending to specific parts of these activities, and in applying strategies for problem solving. Learning can be defined as a process in which new information is linked to prior knowledge. Learners integrate new information with what they already know. While being engaged in conversations, or in reading texts, learners continuously make predictions, monitor the outcome of these predictions, and seek a solution to problems they encounter. As such, literacy can be seen as an instrument to foster children's thinking and concept development (see Guthrie & Knowles, chap. 8).

Literacy, thinking, and motivation cannot easily be separated. Literacy is crucial for thinking. Through literacy, children are able to construct meaning, to share ideas, to test them, and to articulate questions. A high level of literacy helps children to collaborate with others in learning new concepts. Children can be taught to draw inferences from their personal knowledge and to actively link their knowledge schemata to new ideas that are introduced in a text or in a lesson. The task for the teacher is to engage children by introducing concepts that can modify and expand students' existing knowledge schemes. Students must learn how to use new knowledge as a basis for developing higher level skill in comprehension and thinking. Effective teachers help children select relevant study topics, model their own way of using comprehension strategies, and prompt students to make inferences from the text.

A reciprocal relationship between motivational variables and development of literacy and thinking can be established. Engagement, intrinsic motivation, personal interest, and other motivational factors enhance learning, and are also affected by it (Alexander, 1998; Schunk & Zimmerman, 1994). Engaged readers activate prior knowledge to construct new understandings, and use cognitive strategies to regulate comprehension in order to satisfy personal interests. Motivations to read range widely, including interest in specific topics, aesthetic goals, escape, solving specific problems, and academic purposes. Engaged readers often participate in social contexts to complete a task, to gain knowledge, to interpret an author's perspective, or to escape into the world of literature, approaching these literate activities as ones that can be carried out with social support and mediation (see Baker, Afflerbach, & Reinking, 1996).

The notion of literacy engagement is closely linked to views of children as having an active role in their own development. The child as a novice is continually attempting to make sense of new situations and to acquire the skills necessary to function in those situations. The teacher's role is to help the child by arranging tasks and activities in such a way that they are more easily accessible. *Intersubjectivity,* shared understanding based on a common focus of attention, is seen by adherents of literacy engagement as a crucial prerequisite for successful communication between teacher and child. Teachers also have the role of creating settings in which children's engagement is maintained, such as cooperative peer groups. Small groups have proven to be quite effective in increasing language learning opportunities for young children. In small groups, children have the opportunity to negotiate meaning, to transfer information, and to observe a variety of communicative strategies. Research on the ethnography of communication has shown that children working in small groups with minimal teacher assistance learn subject matter, solve problems, and develop social skills, and that differences in child ability or sociocultural background do not impede the group functioning.

Another critical factor in literacy engagement is access to books. Many public service efforts to help promote reading success focus on making books more widely available, in particular to low-income and minority families, and on encouraging families to read to their young children. Examples of such efforts include the work in the United States of Reading Is Fundamental (RIF), an organization that gives books to children, or of Reach Out and Read (ROR), a network of pediatricians who prescribe book reading to parents and give children age-appropriate books at regularly scheduled infant and toddler checkup and vaccination visits. Public libraries play a central role in ensuring access to books, and often initiate programs of story reading, book clubs, and so on to encourage participation. Public service announcements aired by the major television broadcasters in the United States (see McKenna, chap. 7, for another example) include messages about the value of reading to children. These examples could be multiplied. Central to them all, though, is the focus on books serving as the vehicle for resolving the literacy crisis (see Elley, chap. 11).

We enthusiastically endorse the value of efforts like these, but note as well that books are only one part of the picture. Even the wonderfully attractive, well-illustrated, charmingly written, and often relatively inexpensive children's books now available are not sufficient to lure every child into literacy, nor are they sufficient to lure every parent into optimal support for their children's literacy development. As just noted, learning to read is a complex process involving knowledge of often tiny, and confusable, visual symbols, of the principles underlying an orthography, and of strategies for comprehension. Although a few children figure these things out by themselves and become precocious, untaught readers, the vast majority need well-designed instruction from talented and informed teachers. Books help, but the crucial contribution comes not from having the books, but from reading the books—the end result of instruction.

Literacy Education

Research on literacy education has sought answers for the question of how the development of spoken and written language can be fostered from their origins in early infancy to their mastery as systems of representation for communication with others and for the inner control of thinking and feeling. For children, the transition from oral to written language can be thought of as a critical and challenging process. From research on parent input to young children, we know that interactive activities, such as storybook reading, have a great impact on children's oral and written language development (see Sulzby & Teale, 1991). Conditions that strengthen the relevance and purpose of literacy for learners turned out to be quite important for the development of literacy. The most important facilitator of literacy development turns out to be the extent to which parents are sensitive to their children's literacy attempts, and their endeavors to extend the conversation while taking such attempts as a starting point (see Snow, Barnes, Chandler, Goodman, & Hemphill, 1991; Leseman & de Jong, chap. 4). Thus, parental responses to young children's interest in books, letters, and written words on signs or labels soon function to facilitate literacy learning in the same way that the semantic connectedness of adult utterances to the child's language promotes language development (see De Temple & Snow, chap. 3).

An important general conclusion of the research on emergent literacy was that the attainment of literacy could be stimulated by offering children a school environment where valid understandings about literacy could continue to emerge. In such an environment, children have the opportunity to build on the positive literacy experiences they have had prior to school. The development of a broad literacy curriculum in which language experiences are highly emphasized has therefore been widely promoted. Although it is now clear that a language experience approach to literacy acquisition is appropriate prior to formal reading instruction, it is also generally accepted that a naturalistic model that relies exclusively on exposure and immersion does not ensure universal success at the complex task of learning to read and write. Accumulated research evidence indicates that many children need and most benefit from sequentially structured activities that are mediated by a teacher or by skilled peers in order to become fluent readers (Adams, 1989; Perfetti, 1998; Snow, Burns, & Griffin, 1998). Our endorsement of formal and structured reading instruction does not conflict, though, with our conviction that children are active learners who need to participate meaningfully in literacy to progress optimally (see Verhoeven, chap. 6). Children with low abilities in particular benefit if they believe they can control their academic progress through effort. Instruction must thus teach students to use strategies to accomplish literacy tasks, and at the same time persuade them that their successes and failures on literacy tasks are due to their efforts to use appropriate strategies (Borkowski, Carr, Rellinger, & Pressley, 1990).

Learning to read and write involves much more than the ability to decode print to speech and to encode speech in print. Registers of written language require a different selection and organization of ideas than those of oral language. In written communication, logical and ideational functions are primary, whereas oral communication typically has a more informal, interpersonal character. In oral communication, the listener has access to a wide range of contextual cues, whereas in written communication such cues are almost completely absent. A basic assumption of literacy education is therefore that gaining power in all modes of language must take place in all courses at varying school levels (cf. Pressley, 1998; Verhoeven, 1996). Literacy learning should be viewed as inherently integrative. As children participate in classroom activities, they are naturally able to connect the different modes of language use to learning. Besides the learning of literacy, children learn how to use literacy as an effective learning device. Given the close connection between literacy and thinking, literacy can be viewed as an instrument to develop higher order cognitive skills. In order to support children's motivations toward literacy, it is important to focus on meaningful experiences, and to stimulate critical thinking in reading and creative expression in writing.

Literacy in the later school years can be fostered by planning socially purposeful lessons that have a clear conceptual focus (see Langer, 1991; Rogoff, 1990). Students should be given time to reflect, to practice relevant strategies, and to achieve depth of meaning and understanding. Instruction should focus on principles and ideas that help children make connections between prior knowledge and the new information in the text. However, from observational studies we know that very little time is devoted to explicit or direct instruction of reading and writing strategies. Teachers spend a lot of time in assessment activities, and in preparing children for externally imposed assessments. They listen to students' oral reading or check their writing products for spelling and formulation errors. Traditional teachers tend to impart knowledge and strategies in a structured way, following a predefined sequence of reading and writing lessons on a fixed schedule. In such a teacher-directed approach, the role of the students is by and large a passive one.

In a learner-centered approach the teacher fills the role of a coach who shares control with the students. In this approach, the teacher encourages discussion and provides detailed explanations about the identity, scope, and relevance of different strategies. Children are offered opportunities to build on their own strategies for acquiring and using knowledge independently. Learning occurs interactively, and classroom formats include small-group experimentation, small- and large-group discussions, and reading and writing conferences. In such groupings, disagreement about textual inferences will provoke genuine questions that may generate new ideas (see Langer, chap. 9). In this way children learn to share ideas and to check the validity and appropriateness of these ideas. Strategies, such as comprehension monitoring, using graphic organizers, and activating prior knowledge, are taught not just as recipes for learning but as flexible learning devices. Students come to realize that they can use language as a foundation for building new concepts and new structures of meaning. They thus gain more internal control, become less dependent on others, and gain confidence in their own strategies for reading and writing. Introducing students to new concepts within problem-solving situations provides them with the opportunity to experience changes in their own thinking and to elaborate on the new information. A technique that has been suggested to enhance students' conceptual development is *anchored instruction* (cf. Bransford, Vye, Kinzer, & Risko, 1990; Kinzer & Risko, 1998). Anchored instruction prescribes rich and cohesive informational contexts that enable students to identify and define problems, to specify reasons for problem solution, to generate strategies for solving identified problems with minimal teacher guidance, and to observe quickly the result of their attempted solutions.

Literacy instruction that fully acknowledges the importance of engagement extensively integrates literature into the curriculum. Given its aesthetic potential, the use of literature can be seen as an important teaching tool. A climate that motivates children to explore the meaning of human experience through the language of literature generates learning of many sorts. Literature has the power to enhance the intrinsic motivation of students to read because of its appeal to their natural curiosity and aesthetic involvement. Such intrinsic motivations help children to activate their conceptual knowledge as well as their cognitive strategies. Cognitive accomplishments such as increased vocabulary, more rapid processing of complex syntax, control over the devices of literary language, increased reading speed, and improved reading comprehension are the natural consequence of integrating engaging literature into the curriculum.

By using literature in the classroom, meaningful encounters with the most effective sources of human expression can be devised (see Cox & Zarrillo, 1993). Good literature provides an in-depth study of universal values and needs, and it captures students' interests and challenges them to explore new avenues of meaning. *Literature* as we are using the term includes picture books, novels, folklore, poems, biographies, and nonfiction. By using trade books, print media, and electronic media across the curriculum, children can be offered a broad variety of text structures and contexts to be explored. A program that incorporates literature should be grounded in the ideas and interests of children. Surveys of children's interests have made clear that there are age-related differences, as well as individual preferences for topics and genres. Young children see reading as entertainment. They typically prefer stories about animals, nature, and folk and fairy tales. Children in the middle grades start to show interest in adventures and real-life stories. As they grow older, children more and more come to see reading as a way of extending their knowledge. Informational books, historical novels, and biographies are then preferred. Children's engagement with the literature used in reading instruction is enhanced if some of that literature reflects their world outside of school; attending to the cultural and linguistic diversity of the class in selecting literature to study expands the curriculum for all children, while deepening the potential for reflective responses. At the same time, of course, literature is a source of knowledge about the other, and as they get older and their reading skills improve, children are increasingly capable of processing literature that introduces them to novel settings, situations, and characters.

Literature groups in which books of interest to the group are read and discussed constitute models of social participation in literacy activities (see McKenna, chap. 7). Social interaction can be key to understanding and to enhancing the meanings in literary works. Students in groups that read and discuss a chosen book, and perhaps report on it to the entire class, learn to share opinions and resolve differing interpretations of their reading naturally. Such literature groups constitute the context for much reading by highly literate adults–their introduction in elementary classrooms may well help prepare children for a lifetime of engagement in literacy. Teachers can contribute by setting up the groups, encouraging participation based on interest rather than reading skill, and modeling receptivity to others' ideas as a discussion participant.

Literacy education is not just an end in itself. Literacy is at the center of the school curriculum because written language is used to learn across the curriculum. The cognitive processes involved in literacy learning can also be applied to other curriculum areas. Integrated literacy strategies can be used in curriculum domains such as science, social studies, mathematics, and art, extending to these domains the opportunities for children to construct a social identity, develop multifaceted personal relationships, learn to deal with cultural and linguistic diversity, and construct meanings from different perspectives (cf. Hiebert, 1991).

Literacy Across Cultures

Literacy can be seen as a highly culture-specific type of activity. Heath (1982, 1983) presented the now classic description of how differently literacy can be defined and can function within different social groups in one community. Within the Black community Heath studied, literacy was predominantly a group activity involving the reading aloud of written text by an expert and interpretation by a group of people. Families showed little orientation toward literate language use, preferring to exploit the advantages of shared social, physical, and historical knowledge to enrich their oral language. In the middle-class White community, on the other hand, solitary reading was considered to be a legitimate activity and children were oriented toward literate ways of thinking at an early age. The working-class White children Heath studied were taught to revere but not question the text. Heath's study makes clear that different communities in a society show different motivations to use written language, and are accordingly engaged in different literacy practices.

The kinds of differences Heath pointed out may be even more extreme in multicultural societies, within which minority groups often must juggle the sociolinguistics of more than one language as well as several different literacy practices (Durgunoglu & Verhoeven, 1998). Turkish immigrants in the Netherlands, for example, read and write Dutch, the written code with the highest status, primarily in societal institutions including schools. Written Turkish can be used for intragroup communication, communication with friends and family in Turkey, and expressing Turkish ethnicity. Yet another written code, Arabic, may be used for religious identification. In order to do justice to the literacy motivation of minority groups, their literacy needs should be defined in terms of their multilingual and multicultural realities. Au (1993, 1998) claimed that the literacy achievement gap between cultural groups in a society can be largely explained by linguistic and cultural behavior patterns that conflict with mainstream education (see Serpell, chap. 12). Following a social constructivist perspective, she argued that poverty and school failure are both manifestations of historical and systemic conditions rooted in discrimination, in that the conditions of low-income students' lives and communities, as well as the material circumstances in their schools, lead to severe inequalities in educational opportunity. Others have argued that the differing levels of achievement of different social groups reflect real differences in access to an optimal preparation for literacy rooted in home as well as school experiences, and reflect the fact that groups that have been discriminated against have generally received education from less well prepared teachers and thus have themselves developed language and literacy skills to lower levels (Jencks & Phillips, 1998).

Discussing the notion of literacy engagement across cultures, we should be aware of the fact that there is a great diversity in both the distribution and degree of (il)literacy in different parts of the world (see Elley, chap. 11; Verhoeven, 1994; Wagner, 1995). The numbers of illiterates and the consequences of being illiterate for personal life have gained attention. Literacy policies initiated by the local authorities in various countries have brought about literacy campaigns, including basic education, in order to reduce the proportion of illiterates (see Wagner, chap. 15; Weber, chap. 13). Initiatives have begun to focus on the functional dimensions of, and the personal needs for, literacy. It has now been widely acknowledged that literacy programs should recognize the different realities of diverse groups of learners, although procedures for incorporating this acknowledgement into actual teaching practice are not widely implemented.

Evaluation research has shown that the most successful basic education programs have focused on well-identified needs, provided training to special interest groups on request, or combined income-generating programs with literacy education. Not only can literacy be seen as a lifelong continuum, it must also be seen as deeply involved in social practice and cultural tradition. Within a local community, the ability to read and write can be seen as a crucial means to communicate one's own views and to have access to cultural institutions and scientific resources. Beyond one's immediate community, literacy leads to participation in the world, providing access to alternative sources of information and means to express one's views and beliefs on the basis of informed choices.

The provision of basic education can be seen as a primary task in improving chances for universal literacy. Universal access is the first requisite. Schools have to be available to children, within walking distance of their homes. Furthermore, school participation by all children, of both genders, should be ensured. Especially among poor and rural families there is an underrepresentation of girls in educational programs, mainly due to the sexual division of labor that assigns domestic tasks to women (Kelly & Elliott, 1982). From a broad variety of studies, it has become clear that the participation of children from rural populations, urban slums, and marginalized groups, such as refugees and minorities, is often minimal. An important question is whether literacy education for language minorities should be provided in the mother tongue or the second language. Research findings generally favor mother-tongue programs (e.g., Okedara & Okedara, 1992). However, these types of programs are fraught with constraints, such as disagreement about the standard form of the language and absence of an accepted orthography. Finally, a functional level of literacy achievement should be guaranteed. In order to prevent a relapse in literacy skills after basic education, learners should have the opportunity to use literacy in a variety of postliteracy activities (see Dave, Ouane, & Perera, 1988; Easton, 1989). Concepts of literacy that are sensitive to varying local cultural settings are needed to define such activities. Literacy education would ideally be integrated into programs addressing human resource development more broadly, such as those designed to resolve health care inequities, provide adequate shelter in large cities, and counter acute un- and underemployment (see Lawrence, 1992).

Literacy campaigns are often regarded as the best remedy in overcoming illiteracy. However, a fast expansion of basic schooling in developing societies does not necessarily result in a rise of literacy levels. Fuller and Heineman (1989) made clear that in many cases the unbridled expansion of schooling has resulted in an erosion of the capacity of the school to provide enduring levels of functional literacy to the students. Policymakers in developing societies usually face limited resources, limited educational expertise, and a limited organizing and coordinating capacity. Moreover, their work is carried out in a fragile state environment characterized by such contradictory forces as relentless popular pressure to expand basic schooling but scarce public resources, or centrifugal cultural pluralism coexisting with hierarchical control and routinized forms of local administration. As a result, effective responses by the authorities to inefficiencies of local teaching are unavailable, leading to erosion of the quality of education (Fuller, 1992). In recent documents, policymakers have shown themselves to be increasingly attentive to eroding levels of school quality, while focusing on the provision of incentives for classroom and school-level improvements (Lockheed et al., 1991).

The work of Gray (1956) was very influential in defining an engagement perspective on literacy for developing societies. It articulated a shift from a work-oriented economic view toward a broader sociocultural and political perspective on literacy. The concept of literacy was no longer an end in itself, but was seen as an instrument for social transformation and socioeconomic progress. Due to the work of Paolo Freire, the Brazilian sociologist, the concept of literacy education in developing societies has been broadened to incorporate education for freedom and independent decision making. According to Freire's view, reading and writing are instruments that can be used to express one's identity, to affect one's environment, and to set in a motion a process of change. Depending on societal and personal needs, literacy can be addressed as an integral component of development programs, along with nutrition, health, and other life-improvement knowledge (cf. Giere, Ouane, & Ranaweera, 1990; see also Street, chap. 14).

THIS VOLUME

The chapters in this volume address from a variety of perspectives the necessary link between literacy and motivation. An attempt is made to show how the development of spoken and written language can be fostered from their origins in early infancy to their mastery as systems of representation for communication with others and for the inner control of thinking and feeling. Acknowledging the value of cross-national and cross-cultural comparisons, we include chapters discussing the promotion of literacy engagement in different parts of the world. The chapters collected in this volume address factors influencing literacy development during the preschool as well as the school years, motivation to read and ways to enhance it, cultural and social meanings associated with reading in different settings and at different points in history, and factors that may interfere with reading, as well as considerations about how reading may change through and in a world dominated by the new technologies. We give here a brief preview of the organization of the book and the various chapters.

Part I focuses on the social and affective context of literacy development. The chapters in this part all start from the assumption that the traditional characterization of literacy as cognitive rather than affective, and as solitary rather than social, is misguided. Barton's introductory chapter reveals the degree to which, even for successfully literate adults, much literacy activity involves social support and is connected to the important agendas of daily life, and the chapters that follow describe how differences among families in the social and the affective contexts they create around literacy have consequences for the literacy development of their children—a theme that is reintroduced later in the volume, in Serpell's chapter. Van der Voort's chapter explores the impact of technological change—the universality of television—on the uses of literacy within the home, and thus also presages the discussion by Reinking in section II, on reading in a media-saturated world.

Part II focuses primarily on somewhat older children, and shifts from a discussion of naturally occurring variation in literacy environments to a description and analysis of prevention programs and educational interventions. These interventions were all designed to improve reading outcomes, not by the traditional means of enhancing literacy instruction, but by enhancing the learner's experience of joy while reading, by shifting the conditions of learning from solitary to social, by directly affecting attitudes rather than skills, and by displaying the wide array of contexts in which literacy is relevant and of uses to which literacy can be put. The interventions described range from changing teaching methods to increasing the supply of attractive reading materials—but all are effective because they recognize the inherently social and affective nature of literacy.

Part III steps back to present more explicitly macroanalytic perspectives on literacy—perspectives from cross-national and historical standpoints, perspectives based in social and cultural conceptions of literacy, and perspectives that recognize the importance of incorporating notions of engagement into literacy policy initiatives. These chapters both document successes in local and national literacy programs, and define the challenges to future efforts to promote equity in access to literacy.

I: The Social and Affective Context
of Literacy Development

The first part of the book opens with the study of literacy in everyday contexts. In his chapter, David Barton shows how varied the meanings and uses of literacy in the home and community can be. He also claims that people treat literacy along with other media in an integrated way, and that much literacy learning takes place outside school. To back up these claims, he draws on a detailed ethnographic study of literacy practices in Lancaster, England. He defines the engagement of adults in a variety of literacy practices embedded in the textually mediated world of everyday life, thus setting the stage for the following chapters in this section, which present analyses of the social and emotional contexts for literacy in homes where young children are starting to learn to read.

In the next chapter, Adriana Bus reviews book reading through the lens of attachment theory. She starts out with a discussion of the effects of book reading. She then embeds early book reading in the context of the broader parent–child relationship, showing how differences in the history of interactive experience that parents and children share affect the frequency and quality of parent–child book reading. She proclaims the need for family programs that support parents in responding to their children's motivations and understandings of literacy.

In the following chapter, Jeanne De Temple and Catherine Snow present a close examination of conversations about literacy in the family. They claim that literacy stimulation involves the social mediation of psycholinguistic activity. Personal literacy and public, socially mediated literacy are shown to be two sides of the same coin. The authors argue that social, conversational activity that occurs around literacy must be incorporated into our notions of what reading is. From an analysis of literacy practices in various groups of mother–child dyads, they show that conversations between mothers and children can be seen as an organic part of literacy activity, and that these conversations are as gradable as more autonomously displayed literacy skills are in beginning, independent, or fluent readers.

The next chapter starts out with the question how important home literacy is for acquiring literacy in school. Paul Leseman and Peter de Jong try to answer this question, first of all, by means of a review of previous studies. In addition, they report on a home and school literacy study carried out in the Netherlands. In this study, the effects of several facets of informal education in the home environment, including literacy, on children's language, literacy, and math development were assessed. The facets of home informal education were also related to the family's sociocultural context. They conclude that there are probably more routes of preparation for schooling than home literacy in a narrow sense. Enhancing opportunities for and quality of play and problem-solving interactions, conversations, and storytelling all contribute to preparing young children for academic achievement.

The final chapter in this section deals with the impact of television on children's reading behavior. Tom van der Voort makes an attempt to answer the question of whether television is contributing to the decline in reading. Moreover, he goes into the effects of television on the development of reading skills. Specific attention is given to the role of watching subtitled foreign programs, a frequent opportunity in small language communities. He comes to the conclusion that reading is indeed on the decline due to television. He also argues that television has a small negative impact on children's reading comprehension. Watching subtitled foreign programs, however, may result in a positive effect on the development of decoding skills. Given the dominance and ubiquity of the visual media in our world, promoting reading engagement requires considering ways of using television to support and supplement literacy.

II: Prevention and Instruction Programs
That Promote Literacy Engagement

Part II of the volume focuses on educational programs that have emerged from the social-affective view of literacy this volume proposes. Linking to the previous section describing contexts for the early development of literacy skills, the first chapter, by Ludo Verhoeven, presents methods shown to help prevent literacy problems in young children. Taking Vygotsky's work on the mediation of human thought as a starting point, Verhoeven examines the role of scaffolding in early literacy education. Within a Vygotskian approach to development, it is claimed that cultural tools such as language and literacy are best learned through social interaction with others, and that the child's repertoire can be gradually expanded in guided participation with skilled partners. Vygotsky's theory was the basis for designing scaffolded literacy instruction for children at risk. Verhoeven reports on two empirical studies in which the role of scaffolded instruction in early literacy education was assessed. In the first study, a transactional kindergarten curriculum based on storybook reading as a routinized activity is described, and its effect on the language and literacy development of low socioeconomic status (SES) children examined. The role of small-group instruction in this program was also examined. In the second study, the effect of a literature-based one-to-one tutoring program for children with reading difficulties was investigated. The results show that programs in which content-based literacy, cognitive strategies, and motivation are centrally integrated optimally facilitate the transition from oral language to written language.

The next two chapters deal with aspects of motivation for reading in somewhat older children. Michael McKenna's chapter describes ways to promote positive reading attitudes in the context of the relation between attitudes and motivation. He starts with an overview of current theories of attitude formation, resulting in a model in which three principle factors are distinguished: the direct impact of reading, beliefs about reading outcomes, and beliefs about cultural norms on reading. He suggests that intervention strategies that help students to actively process their beliefs and reasoning will enhance engagement. McKenna also presents findings of reading attitude research, showing that reading attitudes tend to worsen over time, more rapidly so for poor readers, and for boys as compared to girls. Finally, he evaluates the benefits of different intervention techniques, such as incentive programs, peer interactions, cross-age interactions, bibliotherapy, and electronic text.

In the subsequent chapter, John Guthrie and Kaeli Knowles extend the topic of how to promote reading motivation from the perspective of reading engagement. They start by distinguishing among intrinsic motivation, extrinsic motivation, interest, and attitude, and show how these aspects of motivation contribute to the cognitive and conceptual processes in reading comprehension. Then they define dimensions of the instructional and school contexts that facilitate reading motivation, resulting in the following principles for promoting reading motivation: conceptual themes, real-world interactions, support for self-direction, use of interesting texts, cognitive strategy instruction, social collaboration, and support of students' self-expression.

The following chapter deals with the connection between literacy and literature in education. Judith Langer describes ways in which literary imagination can provoke problem solving and mutual understanding in classrooms. Narrative is seen as the linguistic form that invites readers to participate in the events and ideas of a piece of writing as an insider, bringing into play history, desires, and conflicts. In search of the real story, people create scenarios, take multiple perspectives, and seek motives and relationships. From insider perspectives, people explore horizons of possibilities, raising questions for the moment, and rethinking the shape of future issues.

David Reinking discusses multimedia and engaged reading in a digital world. He reviews theoretical perspectives that capture the uniqueness of digital texts across several dimensions aimed at improving their quality, their effectiveness in promoting learning, and their contribution to enhancing literacy education. He argues that electronic texts as multimedia artifacts may be inherently more engaging to readers than are conventional printed texts. He illustrates the potential for exploiting the capabilities of electronic text by describing a research project in which teachers and students create multimedia book reports.

III: Policy Perspectives on Promoting Literacy Engagement

The final section of this volume focuses on contrasting varying views of literacy, and on extracting from them their implications for policy. Warwick Elley opens this section with a global perspective on literacy. First of all, he uses the UNESCO statistics on adult literacy to identify major trends and high-priority needs for policymaking. The data show that the vast majority of illiterates live in developing countries, that two-thirds of them are women, and that the rate of illiteracy is higher in the older age groups. In addition, Elley describes the major findings of the International Educational Achievement (IEA) study concerning literacy scores in more than 50 countries. The results provide further evidence for the enormous gap between rich and poor countries. Children in Third World countries by the middle of high school have on average attained the same level of reading ability as students in middle primary grades in industrialized societies. Factors that appear to differentiate between good and poor readers in virtually every country include access to reading materials, captioned television, pupils' attitudes, and home language. Elley then describes intervention programs premised on the importance of access to books for children learning to read. He reviews empirical studies of such programs carried out in Fiji, Indonesia, Singapore, Sri Lanka, and South Africa, and concludes that book-distribution programs are extremely helpful in supporting the literacy development of children in Third World schools if accompanied by instructions to teachers concerning how to use the books in the classroom.

In the next chapter, Robert Serpell proposes a subculturally contextualized conception of literacy development in a society, and discusses its implications for the design of educational practices. According to Serpell, becoming literate involves acquiring membership in a community of practice, and a sense of ownership of the cultural meaning system that informs the literate activities of the community. He suggests that the process through which an individual becomes literate can be illuminated by considering development as participatory appropriation. Different literacy (sub)-cultures can be defined, reflecting not only particular language and writing systems, but also distinctive sociocultural practices. Reflecting on the findings in the Baltimore Early Childhood Project, Serpell proposes that the filter of intimate culture determines which elements of cultural traditions are able to influence children's literacy development. In the engagement perspective, he advocates programs designed to enhance the effectiveness of home–school communication, and the promotion of peer support and cooperative learning, as well as the acknowledgment of a wider range of (sub)cultural activities as valued educational outcomes.

In the following chapter, Rose-Marie Weber describes the efforts that the early Soviet government made to further the revolution by bringing literacy to the entire population of the former Russian Empire, in an attempt to close the gap between Soviet Russia and the prosperous industrialized West. She sketches the mobilization of the campaign as an aspect of the Soviet political agenda, while at the same time commenting on the practicalities that the new state faced in developing literacy across different languages and cultures. Weber concludes that the campaign mobilized the population on a massive scale in a brief period of time, propelled by enormous political will. It succeeded in engaging urban and rural populations, and established relevance to both European and Asian traditions of literacy. In the beginning, the climate for literacy fostered a cultural ideal of readers engaging with print, but from the 1930s onward, greater controls were imposed on what could be read or written.

The subsequent chapter, by Brian Street, emphasizes the social context of literacy by taking into account sociocultural aspects of development and the concerns of different communities and individuals. Street contrasts the "autonomous" with an "ideological" view of literacy. The autonomous view defines literacy in terms of universal cognitive or technical skills that can be learned independently of specific contexts or cultural frameworks. The ideological view, on the other hand, defines literacy practices from the perspective of cultural and power structures in society. According to Street, many of the claims made by those who hold the autonomous view of literacy can only be understood as part of an effort to maintain and justify the dominance of those in power.

In the final chapter, Daniel Wagner discusses a series of polarizing interdisciplinary and ideological debates that have troubled the field of adult literacy education over the past decades: literacy versus literacies, supply versus demand, quantity versus quality, mother tongue versus second language. He comes up with several recommendations and policy directions that may guide future work, such as increased focus on standards, professional development, quality improvement, and program accountability. The chapter concludes with comments on the increased importance of improving the dialogue among literacy constituencies. The focus on engagement with literacy exemplified in this volume reveals clearly the importance to children's literacy development of their participation in meaningful literacy practices with parents, and thus the centrality of attention to the literacy capacities of all adults in society. Thus this final chapter links back to the issues raised in the first section of the volume, concerning the importance of interactions in the home in preparing children for literacy engagement and literacy success.

REFERENCES

Adams, M. J. (1989). *Beginning to read: Learning and thinking about print*. Cambridge, MA: MIT Press.

Alexander, P. A. (1998). The nature of disciplinary and domain learning: The knowledge, interest, and strategic dimensions of learning from subject-matter text. In C. Hynd (Ed.), *Learning from text across conceptual domains*. Mahwah, NJ: Lawrence Erlbaum Associates.

Au, K. H. (1993). *Literacy instruction in multicultural settings*. Orlando, FL: Holt, Rinehart & Winston.

Au, K. H. (1998). Social constructivism and the school literacy learning of students of diverse backgrounds. *Journal of Literacy Research, 30*, 297–319.

Baker, L., Afflerbach, P., & Reinking, D. (Eds.). (1996). *Developing engaged readers in home and school communities*. Mahwah, NJ: Lawrence Erlbaum Associates.

Borkowski, J. G., Carr, M., Rellinger, E. A., & Pressley, M. (1990). Self-regulated strategy use: Interdependence of metacognition, attributions, and self-esteem. In B. F. Jones (Ed.), *Dimensions of thinking: Review of research* (pp. 53–92). Hillsdale, NJ: Lawrence Erlbaum Associates.

Bransford, J., Vye, N., Kinzer, C., & Risko, V. (1990). Teaching thinking and content knowledge: Toward an integrated approach. In B. F. Jones & L. Idol (Eds.), *Dimensions of thinking and cognitive instruction* (pp. 381–414). Hillsdale, NJ: Lawrence Erlbaum Associates.

Cox, C., & Zarrillo, J. (1993). *Teaching reading with children's literature*. New York: Macmillan.

Dave, R., Ouane, A., & Perera, P. (1988). *Learning strategies for post-literacy and continuing education: A cross-national perspective*. Hamburg: UNESCO Institute of Education.

Durgunoglu, A. Y., & Verhoeven, L. (1998). *Literacy in a multilingual context*. Mahwah, NJ: Lawrence Erlbaum Associates.

Easton, P. (1989). Structuring learning environments: Lessons from the organization of postliteracy programs. *International Review of Education, 35*(4), 389–408.

Fuller, B. (1992). Raising literacy under fragile state institutions. *Annals AAPSS, 520*, 133–142.

Fuller, B., & Heineman, S. (1989). Third World school quality: Current collapse, future potential. *Educational Researcher, 18,* 12–19.

Giere, U., Ouane, A., & Ranaweera, M. (1990). Literacy in developing countries: An annotated bibliography. *Bulletin of the International Bureau of Education, 35/36,* 254–257.

Gray, W. S. (1956). *The teaching of reading and writing.* Chicago: Scott Foresman.

Heath, S. B. (1982). What no bedtime story means: Narrative skills at home and at school. *Language in Society, 11,* 49–76.

Heath, S. B. (1983). *Ways with words: Language, life and work in communities and classrooms.* Cambridge, MA: Harvard University Press.

Hiebert, A. H. (1991). *Literacy for a diverse society.* New York: Teachers College Press.

Jencks, C., & Phillips, M. (1998). *The Black–White test score gap.* Washington, DC: Brookings Institution.

Kelly, G., & Elliott, C. (Eds.). (1982). *Women's education in the Third World: Comparative perspectives.* Albany: State University of New York Press.

Kinzer, C. K., & Risko, V. J. (1998). Multimedia and enhanced learning: Transforming preservice education. In D. Reinking (Ed.), *Handbook of literacy and technology* (pp. 185–202). Mahwah, NJ: Lawrence Erlbaum Associates.

Langer, J. A. (1991). Literacy and schooling: A sociocognitive perspective. In A. H. Hiebert (Ed.), *Literacy for a diverse society* (pp. 9–27). New York: Teachers College Press.

Lawrence, J. E. S. (1992). Literacy and human resources development: An integrated approach. *Annals AAPSS, 520,* 42–53.

Lockheed, M., Rodd, A., & Verspoor, A. (1991). *Improving primary schools in developing countries: A review of policy options.* New York: Oxford University Press.

Okedara, J. T., & Okedara, C. A. (1992). Mother tongue literacy in Nigeria. *Annals AAPSS, 520,* 91–102.

Perfetti, C. (1998). Two basic questions about reading and learning to read. In P. Reitsma & L. Verhoeven (Eds.), *Problems and interventions in literacy development* (pp. 15–48). Dordrecht, Dordrecht: Kluwer.

Pressley, M. (1998). *Reading instruction that works: The case of balanced teaching.* New York: Guilford.

Rogoff, B. (1990). *Apprenticeship in thinking.* New York: Oxford University Press.

Schunk, D., & Zimmerman, N. J. (Eds.). (1994). *Self-regulation of learning and performance: Issues and educational applications.* Mahwah, NJ: Lawrence Erlbaum Associates.

Snow, C. E., Barnes, W., Chandler, J., Goodman, I., & Hemphill, L. (1991). *Unfulfilled expectations: Home and school influences on literacy.* Boston: Harvard University Press.

Snow, C. E., Burns, M. S., & Griffin, P. (1998). *Preventing reading difficulties in young children.* Washington, DC: National Academy Press.

Sulzby, E., & Teale, W. (1991). Emergent literacy. In R. Barr & D. Pearson (Eds.), *Handbook of Reading Research* (Vol. 2, pp. 727–757). New York: Longman.

Verhoeven, L. (1994). *Functional literacy: Theoretical issues and educational implications.* Philadelphia: John Benjamins.

Verhoeven, L. (1996). Language in education. In F. Coulmas (Ed.), *Handbook of sociolinguistics* (pp. 389–404). London: Basil Blackwell.

Wagner, D. A. (1995). Literacy and development: Rationales, myths, innovations, and future directions. *International Journal of Educational Development, 15,* 341–362.

THE SOCIAL AND AFFECTIVE CONTEXT OF LITERACY DEVELOPMENT

1

Literacy in Everyday Contexts

David Barton
University of Lancaster

The study of literacy in everyday contexts can be seen as a starting point for any endeavor aimed at reading promotion. I want to make three basic claims as a result of examining people's everyday reading and writing. The first of these is that the meanings and uses of literacy in the home and community are many and varied. This means that a starting point for education can be to reflect on everyday literacy practices, understanding how they are often distinctive to a particular time and place. Educators, researchers, students and parents can increase their understanding of literacy by researching their own practices. Second, studies of everyday reading and writing emphasize that reading is increasingly one of a variety of ways in which people make sense of the world; also, people treat different media in an integrated way, not necessarily distinguishing reading print from other forms of sense making. The teaching of reading needs to be in the context of a range of media. Third, it can be seen that most learning about literacy takes place outside schools; it starts in the home before children go to school, it continues alongside schooling, and it carries on in the home and community right through adulthood into old age. School learning needs to be located within the broader context of learning in the home and the community, and homes can be seen as important sites for learning, both for adults and for children.

To back up these claims, I draw on a detailed study of reading and writing carried out in Lancaster, a town in northwest England. In this chapter I summarize the findings of this study of local literacies and demonstrate the complex ways in which adults are engaged readers in their daily lives. I argue that viewing reading as a cultural practice helps understand the engagement of adult readers in the textually mediated world of everyday life. The focus is on adults, but, crucially, the home is where children first experience reading and writing and it is where they lay the foundations of their learning of literacy. This chapter draws heavily on Barton and Hamilton (1998), where the study is described in more detail.

The Lancaster study involved a wide range of research methods. The central form of data collection was a detailed study of life in one neighborhood. This included repeated in-depth interviews with people in their own homes, some covering a period of more than a year. The interviews were complemented by observations of events such as shopping, cooking, participating in local community groups, visiting the library, and visiting the doctors. There was extensive photography of the visual literacy environment and the collection of documents such as letters, newspapers, leaflets, and notices. Most interviews were recorded and transcribed, and the study resulted in a large amount of data. It is very difficult to bring together and to summarize such a diverse study. I do this by drawing on the concept of *vernacular literacy practices,* as way of understanding the reading and writing that people do in their everyday lives. This concept provides a useful summary term for much of the reading and writing that our study uncovered.

This research can act as particular case demonstrating the three claims made earlier: that the meanings and uses of literacy in everyday life are many and varied; that reading is integrated with other forms of meaning making; and that much learning takes place outside of schools. It shows the ways in which adults are engaged readers in their everyday lives and how adults' practices provide an important context for children's first exposure to literacy practices. The study also provides an example of what can be gained in understanding the engagement of readers from examining reading as a cultural practice and which we have referred to elsewhere as a *situated literacy* (Barton, Hamilton, & Ivanic, 2000). It can then provide a framework for examining other contexts and seeing the sorts of comparisons and generalizations that can be made in different contexts and across different cultures.

THE RANGE OF LITERACIES IN EVERYDAY CONTEXTS

The first point to make from our study is that there was a great deal of reading and writing in people's everyday lives. In all areas of people's home and community lives there was reading and writing. We were also struck by the variety of reading and writing, the many different ways in which people participated in literate activity. As a way of summarizing people's reading and writing, we found it useful to concentrate on six areas of everyday life. These are areas of life in which people are active, and we identify the ways in which they bring reading and writing into their everyday or vernacular activities. It is these vernacular literacy practices that we are focusing on; they are essentially ones that are not regulated by the formal rules and procedures of dominant social institutions and that have their origins in everyday life. Rather than go into the definition more fully at this point, I first describe these six areas of vernacular activity and provide examples of the range of literacy practices in them. I then go on to discuss more fully what is meant by the term and to examine the fusion of dominant and vernacular practices.

   The first three areas of everyday practice where there was considerable reading and writing are ones that in a general sense are unsurprising; the point of the study was to develop them with examples and with greater detail. These areas are *organizing life, personal communication,* and *private leisure.* To these three areas of everyday practice we add three further ones: *documenting life, sense making,* and *social participation.* These are areas whose significance we came to realize during the study, in the process of collecting and analyzing the data. In this chapter I go through these six areas one at a time, linking examples from people's individual lives to broader social practices.

Organizing Life

Much day-to-day activity involves literacy. People structure their lives, and they use literacy to do this. They have notice boards for details of appointments and social activities; they also use calendars and appointment diaries, address books, and lists of phone numbers. Within the home there is regular organization: There are places where letters, pens, and scrap paper are kept; different sorts of books are kept in different rooms, and the order of books on the shelves may be important, reflecting particular classification systems. Many people keep complex records of weekly finances. Transient hand-written notes are also important for organizing life, whether they are common ones such as shopping lists and lists of things to do, or whether they are more individual examples such as lists of people to pray for. There are often records kept of cards and letters that are sent and received, and lists of Christmas cards sent. Many of these activities are the literacy chores of everyday life, and they are gendered just as the carrying out of other household chores is gendered. Some organization is done by individuals for themselves, whereas other aspects are for the family, the household, or other group.

Personal Communication

People send cards and letters to relatives and friends. All sorts of letters are sent and received, and letters come in various forms. We came across examples of letters for family news, to start or end relationships, to invite, to thank, to celebrate, and to congratulate. They included fan mail to pop stars, and enquiries to unknown people. They could be friendly or threatening, signed or anonymous, serious or jocular; some were collaboratively written and read, and some were recorded on video or audio tape. They were especially important for people at times when they were isolated from family and friends; they were also used to maintain relationships that were kept secret from others. Personal letter writing seems to be a particularly accessible from of writing for people and can be seen as a basic genre from which other genres develop, as explored in Barton and Hall (2000).

There are many sorts of personal communication. People also sent and received a range of cards for birthdays, Christmas, and anniversaries, as well as ones for occasions when someone was ill, an exam was passed, or a baby was born. Some were commercial, and some were individually made at home; often they were mixed, with hand-written words added to the printed message. In addition, personal communication is not just letters and cards. People leave notes of all sorts for each other—for example, on the stairs just inside the front doors of their houses, so that they are seen when someone comes home; in the kitchen concerning shopping or meals; stuck on other people's doors; or slipped through the letter slot. These may be functional; they may be expressing relationships of affection or anger. Some messages are privately circulated; others are designed to be declared and displayed publicly within the home, such as birthday cards on the mantelpiece or wall. As a more public display, in Lancaster people put up signs announcing birthdays, babies, and engagements on the traffic roundabout; this is another form of personal communication. People also pay to put details of births, birthdays, and marriages in the local newspaper. These are sometimes humorous, as when a 50th birthday announcement is accompanied by a photograph of the person at age 5 years. Personal communication takes many forms and serves many purposes, and the literacies used are equally varied and wide ranging.

Private Leisure

Not unexpectedly, we found that people read books and papers for leisure, as ways of relaxing and passing the time. There are patterns in people's reading: Some people read books and magazines every evening, and some only do this when traveling or when on vacation. Children and adults can be "lost in a book." Equally, they can be lost in a map, in a magazine, in the local paper, or in the mail-order catalogue. Some of this involves fantasy consumption. People sometimes do this when they are alone, and sometimes in order to be alone; in this case, reading creates a way of being private in a public space. People often read particular sorts of books and avoid others. One man, an avid reader of wartime stories, was vehement in his hostility to fiction and only wanted to read things based on "real life." In discussions of the promotion of reading, book reading is often taken as the only form of reading, and fiction is taken as the only form of book reading. Our study highlighted how book reading is located in other activities and how fiction is only one form of book reading.

Most of the private leisure we came across was reading, but several people also wrote as a leisure activity, for themselves or for others. In particular, we were surprised at the number of people who reported writing poetry as a leisure activity; it seemed a particularly accessible form of personal writing for them. This, like other examples, fits several of these categories, as sometimes poetry was written for other people, as in the personal communication of a card with a hand-written poem sent to someone in hospital. Other people did different forms of creative writing as leisure activities. Many leisure pursuits are mediated by literacy. Some leisure activities, such as being a fan, involved a range of literacy activities, spanning reading books and magazines and writing notes and letters, and incorporating other media, including television. People varied in the extent to which they used literacy for private leisure; nevertheless, many seemingly straightforward leisure interests, such as hobbies or sport, drew on a complex range of literacies.

These three forms of vernacular practices were starting points; they were in a sense expected and predicted at the beginning of our study and are commonly reported uses of reading and writing. As the study developed, with repeated interviews and further observation we uncovered more activities where reading and writing were important. These three further activities were less expected and were derived from the data. Nevertheless, once identified, they may seem familiar to people across a range of contexts.

Documenting Life

We found that people maintain records of their lives in many ways, through keeping documents such as birth certificates and school reports, and from cutting out reports of their lives such as weddings and sporting achievements from the local newspaper, sometimes organizing them in scrapbooks. They also keep souvenirs from holidays, festivals, and other family events. Some people take photos as records of their lives, and have albums. Many people make and keep recipe books; individually, we found that people keep records of a wide variety of activities, including records about car maintenance, gardening diaries, and notes about health and development, as well as records of finances. People write diaries at various points in their lives, and then keep the diaries; they keep some letters for years, but not others; people keep old address books. There are points when these documents are reread and sorted through. Some of these documents are passed on across generations.

For a few people this activity develops into writing a full-fledged autobiography. Certain people write their life histories; others intend to. This can be an example of the changing practices throughout a person's life. We had an example of a man in his seventies, who had done no personal writing in his life, deciding to write his life history. This documenting aspect of vernacular literacy may be for oneself, for one's family, or for a broader community. We came across people keeping records of their broader families and communities and investigating their family and local history, topics popular enough to have their own national magazines in the neighborhood newspaper shop. Local history courses are among the most popular of adult education courses.

SENSE MAKING

People consciously carry out their own research. In the simplest sense, this involves reading instruction booklets and guarantees to see how household items are used or to get them repaired. It includes devotional reading of religious and other inspirational books for personal development and understanding. Beyond this, there were deliberate investigations of unknown topics, such as where people investigated further a family illness, their child's difficulties at school, or a legal grievance. Again, these could be personal interests, family concerns, or issues covering the whole neighborhood. People pursued these topics by carrying out research: reading, writing, talking to people, and piecing together information from a range of sources. We found that people become local experts on particular topics and others turn to them for help and advice. There can be a tenacious imperative to learn, to find out more, and to solve a problem by trespassing into areas of expertise and tackling literacies normally reserved for others. For example, people may read complex medical or legal books written for professionals in these areas. People have to learn how to do this, and, as adults, they learn how to learn and to find out where and how to get the resources they need. To do this, they draw on and create vernacular knowledge. Less pressingly, as mentioned earlier, people may have interests and hobbies that they pursue and where they become known as experts; this can be on topics as diverse as bird watching, making clothes, car repairs, and travel. This can lead to great differences in what individuals know about. It is revealing to look across a community and to investigate the vernacular funds of knowledge that exist and to understand the ways in which people utilize this knowledge.

Social Participation

People participate in a wide range of social activities. We were surprised at the large number of groups and clubs that exist in the town, and at the fact that everyone in our study seems to have connections to at least one such organization and several people are or have been officers of organizations. There are clubs and associations concerned with animals, nature, sports, religion, music, politics, care for the sick and elderly, and much more. They range from small short-lived campaigning groups to long-established local branches of national organizations. We estimate that there are well over a thousand such groups in Lancaster, a medium-size town. Participation in groups can involve literacy in many ways. People read and contribute to notices and newsletters, participate in meetings, raffles, and jumble sales, and design posters. People write to local newspapers as members of associations and send in reports of activities and achievements. Records of memberships and finance are kept, and there may be complex funding applications. There are different modes of participation; even when people are not actual members of associations, they may still go to meetings, and they may read about the activities of neighbors and friends in the local paper and display notices in their front windows.

As a form of social participation, a minority of people can be described as politically active and, in fact, they describe themselves in these terms; many others, nevertheless, participate in local political activity by signing petitions, attending public meetings, writing letters, and going on marches and demonstrations. In this context, literacy is being used a transformative tool, to effect change. It is noteworthy that at both the demonstrations we have details of, the first anti-poll-tax march and a demonstration against the smell in one part of the town, there were people who said they had never been on demonstrations before. People may participate socially in different ways at particular points in their lives and may move in and out of being active. Sometimes such activity is thrust on people. We documented an example where local land was being sold off to developers and people had to organize themselves quickly into a group, drawing on local knowledge and developing new expertises; many people found that they were engaging in literate worlds of law, campaigning, and local government that they were unfamiliar with.

The six categories just given were identified by starting from individuals' lives, but they may also serve group functions. It is important not to identify reading and writing as just something that individuals do. Rather, groups of various sorts may use reading and writing in different ways. This is important in understanding ways in which reading can be promoted and supported. In identifying the domain of these literate activities, we have moved between different terms, at times ascribing them to families, to households, to neighborhoods, and to communities. We found that all four of these terms were useful and they all had a role in understanding some aspects of people's literacy. Nevertheless, families, household, neighborhoods, and communities may support literacy in different ways.

Whether or not the people in a house are related, there are some functions of *households* that are carried out anyway. These involve reading and writing to do with practical household management and communication. *Families* were important when people talked about their informal learning of literacy and some networks of support and obligation. People used a broad notion of family; often they referred to relatives, who in some cases lived nearby, on the same street or round the corner, and in other cases who lived elsewhere in Lancaster or in nearby towns. The practice of letter writing was very important for families maintaining communication when they are separated by distance. The extended families were important when people talked about supporting their children's learning of literacy. The physical *neighborhood* had some salience in more public literacy activities, where people relied on neighbors for support, and where common local issues, such as traffic problems and street lighting, were addressed. Some of these topics were initiated by local people, and others by the local residents' association, the city council, or the police.

In these neighborhood issues, local people identified a common interest, but they were not the most important determinants of people's sense of social identity: People also had networks and communities of interest that stretched way beyond the boundaries of the neighborhood we studied. Some issues that linked people, such as the poll tax, were of common interest city-wide. The notion of *community* is an amorphous one, but people nevertheless identified with particular communities of interest, such as the clubs and associations mentioned earlier, or as parents of children attending particular schools; literacy often had a significant specialized place holding these communities together as textually mediated worlds. In another sense of community, the neighborhood we studied was largely a monolingual English-speaking community. Nevertheless, the people in the Gujarati-speaking Moslem households were part of a strong Gujarati Muslim community in Lancaster and the northwest of England. Similarly, Polish-speaking Catholics in the neighborhood were part of broader communities. In both cases, the communities were held together by religion and language.

VERNACULAR LITERACIES

Having identified a range of everyday activities where people use reading and writing, I want to turn to the ways in which people participate in these activities to see the extent to which we can define a set of vernacular practices that are distinct from other practices, such as more dominant educational practices. The basis of vernacular literacy practices is that they are rooted in everyday experience and serve everyday purposes. We find that they draw on and contribute to vernacular knowledge. Often they are less valued by society and are not particularly supported, nor regulated, by external social institutions.

The first point in identifying vernacular literacy practices is that they are learned informally. They have their roots in people's homes and in their upbringing, and can be seen as part of what James Gee (1990) has referred to as people's primary discourses. In the activities covered earlier there are examples of people's vernacular learning. An important distinction between vernacular learning and other learning, such as that within an educational or training context, is that vernacular learning is learning not systematized by an outside authority (Howard, 1991). The relations between the learner and the expert are different, and these roles are not fixed, but shift from context to context. There is an acceptance that people will engage in vernacular practices in different ways, sometimes supporting, sometimes requiring support from others.

Second, literacy learning in the home is rarely separated from use; rather, home literacy practices are integrated. This is true in several senses: In home literacy events, written and spoken language are often integrated in the ways that Shirley Brice Heath (1983) demonstrated in her work. In addition, different media are integrated; literacy is also integrated with other symbolic systems, such as numeracy, and visuals; and different topics and activities can occur together. This can be contrasted with some of the practices of schools, where learning is separated from use, divided up into subject areas, disciplines, and specialisms, and where knowledge is often made explicit, reflected on, and open to evaluation. At home it often remains implicit and is not reflected on or evaluated.

These are some of the ways in which vernacular literacy practices can be contrasted with other, more dominant literacy practices. Dominant literacies are those associated with institutions such as education, law, religion, and the workplace. To the extent that we can group these dominant practices together, they are more formalized than vernacular practices and they are given high value, legally and culturally. They are more standardized and they are defined in terms of the formal purposes of the institution, rather than in terms of the multiple and shifting purposes of individual citizens and their communities. In dominant literacies there may be experts and teachers through whom access to knowledge is controlled. Because of their relative freedom from formal institutional control, vernacular practices are more likely to be voluntary and self-generated, and are not imposed externally (see Ivanic & Moss, 1991). They may also be a source of creativity, invention, and originality, and the vernacular can give rise to new practices—improvised and spontaneous—which embody a different set of values from dominant literacies.

Literacy in Networks

One of the ways in which social institutions work is by means of the networks they sustain, and people's literacy practices are located in their networks of support. Much of people's reading and writing involved other people and was located in reciprocal networks of exchange. Many of these were personal networks of friends, neighbors, and family in the neighborhood, and in Lancaster more generally. Everyone we talked to had such personal networks of support and advice that they could draw on and contribute to, although they were more extensive for some people than for others. We found that people participate in networks in a variety of ways, taking on more or less active and publicly visible roles in them. Sometimes people experience these networks as constraining and oppressive rather than supportive. Networks also have limitations: They may break up as a result of people falling out with each other or moving away, and they may not provide expertise in the ways that are needed at a particular time. A further point is that changes in people's networks can result in changes in the support people have for literacy activities. This is particularly acute for adults with problems reading and writing, and it is often changes in their networks that lead them to address such problems and to seek help in basic education classes. Personal networks are important when people want to make changes of all sorts in their lives, and networks can both support and constrain such changes.

Support for reading and writing is not just as the level of educational provision but includes help is dealing with public bureaucracies. Although everyone is forced into contact with official bodies, whether paying taxes, for instance, or dealing with the medical or educational systems, people in our study varied a great deal as to whether or not they had networks that extended into these more public arenas. We found that personal networks have a particular importance when people confront official bureaucratic worlds, and the literacy demands of these areas are ones that could be supported more by external agencies.

Looking more generally at people's networks, we found a further sort of activity going beyond a simple dichotomy of activities being either self-generated or imposed. Helping other people with a reading or writing activity, for example, involves reciprocity and obligations that are not imposed. Doing things for other people, or on behalf of others, is a way of being collaborative that is often closely tied into people's sense of identity and self-worth among family, friends, and neighbors. We found that in addition to the categories of self-generated and imposed literacies, we need a notion of negotiated literacies; these are ones that are not necessarily reciprocal but that are nevertheless integral to the social relationships people develop in their local lives. To summarize the discussion of networks, we have confirmed their importance in people's lives and we can also sketch out some of their complexities. Reciprocal networks of support are widespread, but the links between people are not always positive. Networks can also act as constraints, within both personal networks and the semi-institutional ones that people participate in associated with work, school, and official bureaucracies. Often these are experienced as having elements of imposition and compulsion.

Dominant and Vernacular Literacies

Although our study was primarily an investigation of local literacies, we inevitably came across the many ways in which dominant literacies impinge on local lives. This happens in various ways, including the range of bills people have to pay, the demands of schooling, medical encounters, and legal activities. In the home there can be a range of practices from other domains, including bureaucratic government practices, such as those associated with choosing schools, claiming benefits, and filling in the electoral register; commercial practices, such as dealing with advertisements, shopping, and junk mail; and work practices of many sorts. The range of official encounters people have varies a great deal. Many people encountered much complex imposed literacy associated with dealing with the state, whether they were elderly, ill, unemployed, poor, or a combination of these. It struck us that often those who are least able to cope have the most literacy demands of this sort placed on them.

It is useful in this discussion to contrast dominant and vernacular practices, but the divide is not clear-cut. Some of the documenting of life, for example, which we have classified as a vernacular literacy, is required by outside agencies making tax returns or claiming benefits, where people have to keep records of their activities. This involves participation in dominant literacy practices, and people are incorporated into these bureaucratic practices by means of legal and financial penalties. Similarly, sense making and social participation can involve participation in dominant practices, although often in the sense of trespassing across the social boundaries of appropriate reading and writing. A simple example of the mix of dominant and vernacular practices (pursued in Barton & Hamilton, 1998, chap. 1) is that of making and keeping recipes for cooking; this is an area that is partly institutional, with recipe books and magazines, catering courses in colleges, and cookery demonstrations on television. Nevertheless, it is also partly vernacular, in that people have their own practices around making and keeping recipes, and often they create individual and personal texts that may be passed on across generations.

Another way in which dominant and vernacular practices overlap is that there can be a distinction between the intentions of the producer of the text, on the one hand, and what people actually do, their vernacular practices, on the other hand. There may be official texts, like a letter from the council, or commercial texts, like a newspaper or a catalogue. The texts are official, but what people do with them, the practices themselves, can be vernacular. People develop their own practices around these texts. Vernacular practices can be responses to imposed literacies. Some vernacular responses to official literacy demands disrupt the intentions of those demands, either functionally or creatively, to serve people's own purposes; sometimes they are intentionally oppositional to and subversive of dominant practices. Writing graffiti and defacing notices would be an example of this, especially where it is used to challenge official public messages. What is interesting here is how people make literacies their own, turning dominant literacies to their own use, by constant incorporation and transformation of dominant practices.

The fusion of dominant and vernacular can be seen in the variety of texts we came across. There is a wide range of very different texts within the areas of social practice we identified. Organizing life, for instance, can involve notes, notices, diaries, and address books. Social participation can bring in notices, newsletters, and minutes. The range of books we encountered covered a broad spectrum from fiction through many different types of nonfiction. A particular literacy event can utilize a range of texts ranging from informal transient hand-written notes through to official published public documents. Having identified particular types of texts, we then find that they contain great diversity. The diaries that people write, for example, can include a mixture of genres, including fantasy, poetry, and record keeping; they serve many different purposes for the writers.

Some of the texts we have identified in our study, such as the diaries and local newsletters, are vernacular texts, generated in the course of everyday activities. Others are more dominant texts, having their origins outside the community. Often a text is part commercial, as in bought address books, or prewritten greetings cards. People act on these texts, making them their own. In addition, some of the ways in which commercial practices have supported the development of a text may not be obvious. Letter writing, for example, has been supported and shaped by the postal service since Victorian times, as has sending Christmas cards, holiday postcards, birthday cards, and Valentines cards; these practices, along with using the telephone, are now intermittently supported by direct television advertising. For commercial reasons, there is currently a battle over our vernacular communication practices.

PROMOTING READING IN TIMES OF CHANGE

Any contemporary discussion of reading promotion has to address the fact that we are in the midst of great changes in media and communication. This was apparent in our study; here I want to draw attention to some of these changes and discuss their relation to the promotion of reading. Some of the changes we were beginning to see in our study were related to the spread of new technologies and the increasing number of homes with computers. This can potentially have great effects on people's everyday literacy practices. At the same time, institutions have changed their practices through introducing new technologies, and people have had to respond to these changes—by using automatic bank tellers or computerized library catalogues, for example. Although many of the developments around computing were not aimed at everyday literacies but for more specialized working practices, people have turned them to their own uses. One publicly visible difference that has resulted from the coming of computers in the home has been changes in the way people have produced newsletters, advertisements, and flyers for clubs and associations.

The new technological knowledge associated with computers, telephones, and video recorders can change relationships within families, because people acquire this knowledge at different rates. Children often develop expertise around new technologies that their parents do not have. Children's funds of technological knowledge can threaten teachers, too, especially as such knowledge, unlike some other areas of vernacular knowledge, is valued by schools, and teachers themselves may not have the expertise. The phenomenon of children possessing knowledge that is of value to families is also apparent in bilingual homes in Britain, where children sometimes know more English, or have greater familiarity with everyday practices, than their parents. This is probably true wherever families are dislocated and where children have greater access to education than their parents. Nevertheless, the changing relationships within families caused by technological disparities are particularly apparent at this point in history.

Increased literacy demands have also affected social participation in local groups. The closure of a local housing project when government funding was withdrawn is an example of something happening more generally throughout the public sector in Britain. Like many other initiatives, it had been a short-term, experimental project, dependent on continual renewal of funds through a bidding process to local and central government. Support for such activities is now haphazard and unpredictable, with groups bidding against one another for resources. Even long-term established communal resources, such as libraries, are having to compete for ever scarcer public funds. Many sorts of funding now demand complex applications and, to be successful, organizations need someone who knows how to fill in the forms. Such a process places new literacy demands on the officers of such organizations, and it is not clear how this expertise is to be acquired. With declining trade union membership, opportunities for training in this are now available to fewer people. Nevertheless, the local adult college has recently put on courses for officers of associations, and this is one of the ways in which educational provision can support people in activities they already do.

Looking more broadly at social change, there is greater regulation and surveillance of social practices, especially in terms of the encroachment of the professional into the private realm of the family. This is apparent in shifting literacy practices—for instance, in the practices surrounding children's emergent reading, where there is more state intervention in children's preschool lives. There have been moves to increase the regulation of literacy practices in households as family literacy programs are promoted by the government, along with suggestions about what parents should do to improve their children's reading and writing, and certificated courses are developed for parents themselves. This regulation is generally rooted not in an appreciation of vernacular practices, but in the views of schools and policymakers about the kind of support that families should provide their children with. Our work supports the belief that children can learn a great deal about literacy by observing and participating in the literacy activities of the home. There is a great deal that parents and others in the home and community can do to support children's literacy development. However, as I have argued elsewhere (Barton, 1995), that does not necessarily mean that parents should take on the practices of formal education and be expected to act as school teachers, as some of the rhetoric of family literacy programs seems to be demanding.

Changes in the relation of home and school are part of broader shifts that are happening in attitudes to schooling and education. There has been greater media and political attention paid to education as it has become a focus for policy debate between political parties. In relation to vernacular literacies, our impression is that although schools may have the potential to introduce children to a wider variety of voices than that experienced in the home, the spread of the National Curriculum in Britain has reduced the variety of texts and the number of possible ways of reading and writing in the classroom. Education has become a disputed territory and part of this is in the range of variation of voices permitted (see the discussion in Hamilton, 1996).

The changes described here are in some ways eroding the literacy practices that bind communities together, and are making older practices obsolescent. In other ways, they present opportunities to reshape and strengthen the power of literacy in community life and to rethink ways of supporting children's literacy development. New demands keep literacy practices constantly on the move for people organizing and controlling their everyday lives. This results in changes in a complex balance of relationships involving resources, expertise, and needs for support. The context of change needs to be kept in mind when discussing ways of promoting reading. It is important to document and understand contemporary changes without prejudging change as a threat to reading and literacy. The results of our study do not support the gloom and doom of there being less reading today; rather, there is a range of reading embedded in people's lives. We would encourage a greater reflection on the complexity of existing everyday practices as a starting point for promoting reading.

REFERENCES

Barton, D. (1995). Exploring family literacy. *Reading, 29*(3), 2–4.

Barton, D., & Hall, N. (Eds.). (2000). *Letter writing as a social practice.* Amsterdam: John Benjamins.

Barton, D., & Hamilton, M. (1998). *Local literacies: reading and writing in one community.* London: Routledge.

Barton, D., Hamilton, M., & Ivanic, R. (Eds.). (2000). *Situated literacies.* London: Routledge.

Gee, J. (1990). *Social linguistics and literacies.* London: Falmer Press.

Hamilton, M. (1996). Keeping alive alternative visions. In J. P. Hautecoeur (Ed.), *Alpha 97: Basic education and institutional environment* (pp.). Hamburg: UNESCO Institute for Education.

Heath, S. B. (1983). *Ways With Words.* Cambridge, MA: Cambridge University Press.

Howard, U. (1991). Self, education and writing in nineteenth century English communities. In D. Barton & R. Ivanic (Eds.), *Writing in the community* (pp. 78–108). Newbury Park, CA: Sage.

Ivanic, R., & Moss, W. (1991). Bringing community writing practices into education. In D. Barton & R. Ivanic (Eds.), *Writing in the community* (pp. 193–223). Newbury Park, CA: Sage.

2

Parent–Child Book Reading Through the Lens of Attachment Theory

Adriana G. Bus

Leiden University

Book reading plays an important role in becoming literate and in preparing preschoolers and kindergartners for success in school. This chapter starts with a discussion of the effects of book reading. Outcomes of a series of studies carried out in European and American families indeed support the role of book reading as the single most important family routine for building understandings and skills essential for reading success (International Reading Association & National Association for the Education of Young Children, 1998). I doubt, however, that book reading fits with every pattern of parenting. Sharing books and stories may be a cognitive stimulus, but, assuming that conversations accompanying the reading of text are a key to the literacy-stimulating function of book reading (De Temple & Snow, chap. 3, this volume; Snow, Tabors, Nicholson, & Kurland, 1995; Whitehurst et al., 1988), book reading may simultaneously be an expression of how parents interact with young children. We have therefore begun to conduct a series of studies that look at book reading in the perspective of the broader relationship context. We examine how differences in the history of interactive experience that parents and children share affect the frequency and quality of parent–child book reading.

EFFECTS OF BOOK READING

Book-reading routines in literate families are an important stimulus for young children's language and literacy development. A quantitative meta-analysis that we carried out a few years ago gives straightforward support for the importance of book reading (Bus, van IJzendoorn, & Pellegrini, 1995). In selecting the studies to be included in this meta-analysis, we focused on studies examining the frequency of parental book reading to preschoolers. Combining almost 30 studies from which pertinent data could be derived about the effects of parent–preschooler reading, we found that a lack of reading experiences may put children at risk in becoming literate. Book reading appeared to be related to outcome measures such as language growth, emergent literacy, and reading achievement. We hardly found any studies with negative effects.

The overall effect size of $d = 0.59$ indicates that book reading explains about 8% of the variance in outcome measures. In contrast to other researchers (see, e.g., Adams, Treiman, & Pressley, 1998; Scarborough & Dobrich, 1994), I argue that this is not a modest but a notable effect size. The binomial effect size displays for different variables in Fig. 2.1 (Rosenthal, 1991) show that the strength of the association between book reading and literacy skills is even somewhat greater than the strength of the association between the nonword reading deficit and dyslexia.

The nonword reading deficit is one of the most powerful predictors of reading disabilities; dyslexic children are better in reading real words than nonwords, even after several years of reading experience, suggesting that dyslexics have difficulty with alphabetic skills (Snowling, 1987). A meta-analysis including all available studies testing the nonword reading deficit confirmed this hypothesis; among dyslexics, the nonword reading deficit is present in 61.5% of all cases of dyslexia (van IJzendoorn & Bus, 1994). The association between book reading and children's reading development is even somewhat stronger. In a group of children performing at a low level of (emergent) reading skills, 64% belong to the group of not-well-read-to chil-

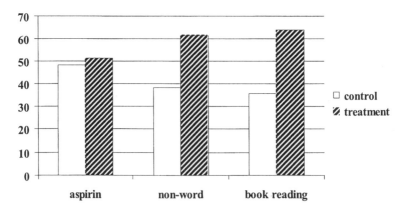

FIG. 2.1. Binominal effect size displays for aspirin, non-word reading deficit, and book reading.

dren. In a group with normal language and reading skills, more children belong to the well-read-to group than to the not-well-read-to group.

Note that in the medical field, much lower effect sizes justify interventions on a broad scale. Aspirin, for example, is prescribed to people who are at risk to develop cardiovascular problems. The binomial effect size display of aspirin in Fig. 2.1 shows that less people develop a cardiovascular problem when they use aspirin. However, a difference as small as 3% between the control (no prescription of aspirin) and intervention group (prescription of aspirin) is the justification for this intervention.

SOCIAL CONTEXT AS A DETERMINER OF THE SUCCESS OF THE BOOK-READING INTERACTION

In spite of the finding that book reading is strongly related to children's language and reading development, I doubt that reading to children can be viewed solely as an intellectual proposition (see, for a personal account that supports this notion, an interview of Hillary Clinton; Clinton, 1997). We have therefore begun to test the hypothesis that book reading is not an isolated technique to stimulate early learning in the domain of literacy but a profoundly social process, embedded in parent–child relationships, and that the frequency and quality of book reading are strongly related to the history of other interactive experiences that children share with their parents and other caregivers. To test the hypothesis that book-reading routines depend on the broader relationship context, our ongoing research program focuses on the association between the affective bond of parents and children on the one hand and quality and frequency of book reading on the other. This long-term research program in collaboration with Marinus van IJzendoorn, an attachment researcher, has revealed strong evidence for the role of the broader relationship context. The rest of this chapter presents some outcomes of this research program.

Our research focuses on children with varying histories of interactive experience. In a series of studies, we have begun to compare children who have a positive history of interactive experiences with children who have a negative history. We hypothesize that a positive history of interactive experience with the parent (typical of so-called securely attached children) fosters more and more productive book-reading interactions and that a negative history (so-called insecurely attached children) limits the occurrence of book reading and its learning potential. On the base of their interactive experiences, children develop a mental representation of their interactions with the parent; they anticipate that the parent's future behavior will be similar to the past interactions on which the child's representations are based.

To assess the broader relationship context of the book-reading process, we measure parent–child security. In several studies, we used Ainsworth's well-known Strange Situation to reveal differences in attachment security (Ainsworth, Blehar, Waters, & Wall, 1978). With the younger children participating in our studies, this procedure (consisting of eight episodes, including two separation and two reunion episodes) is administered according to the guidelines of Ainsworth and her colleagues. With older children, we used a slightly adapted procedure that is similar to Ainsworth's procedure: A stressful situation was created by bringing the child in an unknown environment with a stranger, and by separating the mother and child twice.

The attachment categories are scored during the reunion. *Secure* children seek proximity; after being cuddled they explore the environment again. *Insecure-avoidant* children avoid the mother, and *insecure-resistant* children seek proximity but are at the same time resistant to contact. We assume that children's responses to the parents during the reunion session reflect their internal models of parental responses and their relationship with the parent. It is assumed that attachment security is also a good predictor of parental sensitivity toward children's interest and knowledge level.

Effect of the Parent–Child Relationship on Book-Reading Routines

The idea that a child who is interested in literacy-related activities will evoke more reading seems a plausible explanation for early differences in reading frequency (see, e.g., Scarborough & Dobrich, 1994). We, on the other hand, hypothesize that interactive book reading more strongly depends on the quality of the parent–preschooler relationship than on child characteristics such as temperament or interest. A main assumption of our research into book reading is that parents and children who share a positive history of interactive experiences are more inclined than pairs with a negative history of interactive experiences to engage with unknown aspects of their environment, including written material (Bus, 1993, 1994). To test the hypothesis that book reading is indeed based on a social-construction principle, we started to study the frequency of bookreading as a function of the broader relationship context.

We selected infrequently reading mother–child pairs and pairs who had developed a daily book-reading routine (Bus & van IJzendoorn, 1995). The pairs with a book-reading routine read at least once a day. Many mothers felt offended by the question of whether or not they had already started reading to their child. Answering our questions, they emphasized that they had read books to their child from a very early age on and that they looked on book reading as a part of daily routines. Infrequently reading mothers, on the other hand, reported that they read to their child but that they do not manage to read every day. These mothers mostly acknowledged the importance of book reading but indicated that they did not always have time to read to their child. Only one Dutch mother included in this study told us that she had not started to read to her 3-year-old son because he did not like books. In sum, almost all mothers participating in this study seemed to value book reading as a family activity and as a cognitive and emotional stimulus for 3-year-old children. However, they differed in the time spent on sharing books with their child. I expect that beyond a certain threshold level, differences in the quantity of this activity may have little bearing (Adams et al., 1998). Given the complexity of learning processes that result from book reading, my best guess would be that book reading matters if it is part of daily recurrent routines in the family, and that book reading is not effective as an incidentally occurring event.

We compared the emotional bond between mother and child in three groups with 15 dyads in each group: (a) infrequently reading dyads, low socioeconomic status (SES); (b) frequently reading dyads, low SES; and (c) frequently reading dyads, high SES. The results clearly confirm the hypothesis that a group at risk in becoming literate, namely, children who are infrequently read to, indeed have a less trusting and close relationship with their mother. Insecurely attached mother–child pairs indeed are less inclined to develop daily book-reading routines than secure ones. Comparing frequently reading pairs (reading at least once a day) with infrequently reading pairs (reading at most twice a week), we found some striking differences. In the group of infrequently reading pairs from a low SES, children with a negative history of interactive experiences (the insecure ones) were strongly overrepresented (73%) compared to the group of frequent readers from a low SES (33%) or frequent readers from a high SES (13%).

Because of the correlational nature of the results, security may be a key factor or a consequence of book reading. However, the latter option is not very plausible. As another outcome of the present study (Bus & van IJzendoorn, 1992) we also revealed support for a positive relation between the reunion score and an interview measuring the mother's mental representation of her own childhood attachment experiences. The Adult Attachment Interview developed by Main and her colleagues (Main, Kaplan, & Cassidy, 1985) is a semistructured interview in which questions about general characteristics of the mother's relationship with her own parents are supplemented with questions about specific childhood events and about the current relationship with her parents. Given a positive relation between the interview and the reunion score, it is plausible that the child's behavior in the reunion session refers to a fundamental characteristic of the mother–child relationship, deeply rooted in the mother's own biography.

Differences in the Process of Reading

The book-reading paradigm assumes that parental *scaffolding* techniques determine the success of the interaction. Scaffolding means that parents offer support that allows children to engage in an activity in a more sophisticated way than they could on their own. Verbal scaffolding of book reading refers to the adult being responsive to what the child says and does nonverbally in a way that keeps the child engaged and elicits cohesive language and behavior in response to the book and the adult's language. I argue that when the mother–child relationship is less secure, the parent may be less successful in creating a context that fosters engagement and enjoyment on the side of the children. In a series of studies, we tested the idea that an insecure bond between parents and children is related to a situation in which children are hard to engage in bookreading sessions and in which children do not seem to enjoy the book and the interactions surrounding the reading of the book.

To test this assumption, we have begun to study interactive parent–child book-reading sessions. Characteristic of these studies is that book reading is not observed in its naturally occurring form in the home. In our laboratory or at home, parents and children were invited to share a book supplied by the researcher. Although parents were left free to choose a form that might be appropriate to engage their child, the sessions may not be fully valid representations of the meaning and purpose of such interactions in actual life experience. However, we preferred such a design to actual life observations because "laboratory" observations are more likely to be comparable from one participant to the next and are more likely to contain the kinds of interactive behavior that are of interest to us.

All studies so far support the hypothesis that the atmosphere during parent–child book reading is related to children's history of interactive experience with the parent. Comparing securely and insecurely attached mother–child pairs, children's engagement and enjoyment in the book reading appeared to be one of the most striking differences among book-reading sessions with securely versus insecurely attached children. Children with a negative history of interactive experience with the parent (insecurely attached children) appeared to be less easy to engage in book-reading sessions than children with a positive history (the secure ones), as shown by child attentiveness, maternal interventions to control the child's behavior, and child responsiveness (Bus & van IJzendoorn, 1988, 1992, 1995, 1997; Bus, Belsky, van IJzendoorn, & Crnik, 1997).

From the very start of book reading, the insecure children are less attentive (Bus & van IJzendoorn, 1997). In one study, for example, we observed mothers and their 44- to 63-week-old infants in our laboratory. Among other tasks, the mother–child pairs shared a simple expository book typical for this age range with thematically ordered pictures: on each page a setting characteristic of a farm with a one-sentence text. The insecurely attached children were less attentive than the secure ones: They often looked at other objects in the environment or made attempts to escape from the mother's lap. Insecurely attached children responded less to the book content by referencing: They were less inclined to make animal sounds, touch the pictures (e.g., caressing an animal on a picture), or make movements to represent an object in a picture (like horse riding in response to a picture of a horse). Their mothers were more inclined to control the child's behavior; they restricted the infant's movements by putting an arm around the child or by keeping the book out of reach.

Studies involving older children show similar patterns, although distraction and disciplining emerged in somewhat different forms (Bus & van IJzendoorn, 1988, 1992). From a cross-sectional study of interactive reading with 18-, 32-, and 66-month-old children (Bus & van IJzendoorn, 1988), for example, it appeared that the atmosphere surrounding the interaction of securely attached dyads was more positive than that of the anxiously attached dyads. In securely attached dyads, there was less need to discipline; these children were less distracted than in anxiously attached dyads.

Book-Reading Strategies

None of our studies involving White Dutch and American parent–child dyads supports the idea that parental book-reading behaviors per se determine the success of the interaction. The studies led us to believe that one cannot judge the kinds of reading per se as either facilitative or nonfacilitative; rather, the context must be considered. As children are younger and less experienced, it may, for example, be better to discuss details of pictures instead of initiating more demanding meaning-based conversations surrounding the reading of the text.

In one study (Bus & van IJzendoorn, 1995), we observed mothers using a variety of strategies ranging from labeling to just reading. In this study with Dutch 3-year-olds, we observed mothers while reading a picture-storybook with all the characteristics of written language: full story scheme, inferential passages, and book language. Interactive readings appeared to be a sequence of reading and talk episodes, combining a variety of strategies rather than a seamless whole. However, there were differences in emphasis. We found mothers mainly name or label the pictures with the younger children. Alternatively, with older children who had been read to a lot, we saw the parent often demonstrate uninterrupted reading and pause only when the child initiated a topic or asked a question. Which patterns of interaction are most accentuated seems to differ as a consequence of children's age and past book-reading experience (see also Martin, 1998). As the child becomes older and more experienced, general background knowledge, language use, knowledge of the nature of the activity of reading itself, and knowledge of the activity of storybook reading all grow (Sulzby & Teale, 1987). Such changes affect the language and social interaction of individual reading episodes. Mother–child pairs seem to be on a continuum, ranging from mainly listening to the literal text like an audience, to discussing the pictures and mostly neglecting the text.

In a study mentioned before focused on 1-year-old infants (Bus & van IJzendoorn, 1997), we observed differences in the pattern of interaction as a function of children's level of referencing. Around the first birthday, infants seem to make a shift from acting on the book to higher levels of referencing. The younger children in this sample, 12 to 13 months old, were grasping, touching, reaching, and "eating" the book, whereas the 14- to 15-month-old children were responding in more sophisticated ways, such as making sounds or gestures and looking and laughing at the pictures. These older children are also responding more to comments and questions by the mother. Although the data are not longitudinal and the age range is small, the cross-sectional differences suggest a growing understanding that books are referential media and that they contain pictures and symbols that stand for things. The behavior of these infants suggests that they are beginning to appreciate the symbolic features of picture books.

All mothers evoked, supported, and extended the referencing behavior of their child by using (proto)symbols such as animal sounds, gestures, or labels, by evoking responses ("touch the kitty"), and by pointing at the pictures. However, there was evidence that mothers adapt their behavior to the infant's responses and that they become more demanding as their infant's level of referencing is growing more mature; as infants become more responsive to the mothers and as they start to use protosymbols, mothers extend their referencing behavior by pointing at the pictures and by evoking responses ("pet the baa-lamb"). More than in the previous stage, mothers make attempts to teach labels through pointing, evoking responses, and labeling at the same time. However, although there seems to be a relationship between a child's age, book-reading experiences, and the appropriateness of certain scaffolding behaviors, parents typically move freely among these scaffolding behaviors in response to their children's interest and understanding of the book content (see also Kaderavek & Sulzby, 1998).

Successful Use of Scaffolding

Our research on the quality of book reading focused on the mothers' success in strategically scaffolding book language in order to make reading a meaningful event for their children. Just as a secure relationship may foster productive book-reading interactions, insecure parents producing behaviors that are interpreted negatively by the child may obstruct the child's enjoyment of the storybook interaction and thus limit the learning potential of parent–child bookreading. I focus here on the match between the parent's and child's level of understanding of the book as determiner of the "successful use of scaffolding" (Kaderavek & Sulzby, 1998). The elements of such context include the individual behavioral repertoire of both the infant and the mother, and the reciprocity that develops as both partners in an interaction respond and adapt to each other.

A recent study involving 1-year-old Caucasian American boys, all very similar in age and book-reading experiences, confirmed the hypothesis that insecure pairs were less likely to constitute an interactional context that fosters children's engagement and thus proved less rewarding and less informative (Bus et al., 1997). We did a microanalysis of the book-reading behaviors involving toddlers and their parents. The mother–child pairs were observed when the children were 18 months old. The father–child pairs were observed 2 months later when the children were 20 months old. Both parents read from a book that included a series of pictures with babies making faces, crawling, staying, walking, playing, eating, drinking, being dressed or bathed, and sleeping. Each page also contained a few sentences printed over two pages.

Most children in this study mainly responded to the pictures in a book by pointing and labeling, and their mothers tried to initiate such actions by following predictable routines (Ninio & Bruner, 1978). Typically, mothers initiated interactions by motivating ("look here"), pointing at pictures, questioning ("look, what's that?"), labeling ("see, a rabbit!"), commenting ("it's the same color as yours"), and positive feedback ("yes, it's a rabbit"). Children initiated interactions and responded to parental questions and comments by pointing, labeling, commenting, and nonverbal responses. The following fragment illustrates a typical interaction.

M: (turning the page) ooh, look
C: (points at a picture of a baby) Michael (sounds excited)
M: yeah, he looks like Michael
M: look, what's that? (pointing to another picture at the same page)
C: a ball
M: good boy, you're right, it's a ball

Other, less frequently occurring behaviors on the side of the mothers were nonverbal responses (e.g., imitating drying as if the child comes out of the bath), negative feedback ("no, that's not a ball"), correcting the child's behavior (the parent turns the page back after the child has spontaneously turned the page), verbatim reading of the text, and disciplining ("don't look at that"). Infrequently occurring behaviors on the side of the children were low-level responses (e.g., hitting the book), aggression toward the mother (pinching the parent or pushing aside the hand of the parent), and distraction (walking around the room).

The profiles of the maternal and children's behaviors during the interactive sessions strongly differed as a function of the attachment category. One group of insecure pairs—the *insecure-avoidant* group—seemed unable to merge their unique styles into a contingent and reciprocal relationship. We had the impression that mothers did not succeed in creating an age-appropriate interaction with their children. Instead of evoking interactive routines around the pictures, these mothers often just read the verbal text, thus ignoring the child's limited ability to understand story and pictures on his or her own. On the one hand, these mothers may have been responding to their children's distracted behavior. The children were inclined to be more unresponsive to the book content and to be more distracted than the children of both other groups. The mothers created the impression that they wanted to reach the finish line as soon as possible and that they wanted to terminate the unproductive and unsatisfactory interaction. On the other hand, book reading is a reciprocal process, and these insecure-avoidant children may have been more unresponsive to the book content and more distracted than other children because of the lack of support from their mothers in understanding the book and in maintaining their motivation. Just like in the Strange Situation during the reunion, these children do not seem to expect support and help from the mothers during a difficult task such as reading a book, and they run away. The mothers were unable to break through their children's expectations and to support their understandings and motivations.

The other insecure group—the *insecure-resistant* children—was superficially more engaged, but a better look at the sessions revealed several problems. The mothers initiated labeling routines to the same extent or even more so than secure mothers. However, more than secure mothers, these mothers were inclined to direct attention ("look at that") and to correct the child's behavior. Overstimulating and overcontrolling behavior by the mother seemed to relate to ambivalence on the part of the children. The children were not obviously disengaged, but they explored the book somewhat less than other children (lower scores on nonverbal responses). They also differed from the rest by showing aggression toward the mother (pushing or hitting her) and by responding at a low level to the book (e.g., hitting the book). Just as in the Strange Situation, these children did not run away, but they were unable to explore the book because of their preoccupation with the mother. By encouraging book orientation, these mothers may have been attempting to circumvent their children's aggressive responses. We had the impression that because these mothers stressed dialogic reading so much, they may have increased children's behaviors such as being aggressive toward the mother and showing low-level responses such as hitting the book.

It must be noted that in the case of father-child dyads, no attachment-group differences emerged with respect to book reading. Although on average the fathers reported being involved in book-reading routines to the same extent as mothers, the expected association with father-child attachment security did not emerge. Despite their self-reports, it may be that fathers, on average, are less experienced in reading to their children and, as a result, their book-reading style may be more determined by situational factors than by interactive patterns developed over a longer history of book reading. In fact, many fathers may not have a notion of how to adapt the reading session to their child's comprehension and motivation level.

PARENT-CHILD INTERACTION ACROSS CULTURES

The research discussed so far supports the hypothesis that book reading depends on the parental ability to involve the child in a book and to support and sustain the child's curiosity and exploratory behavior during the reading session. Since early parent-child interactions may also vary as a function of cultural background, we expect that the quality of support offered by the parent during activities such as book reading may explain differences in literacy education across ethnic groups as well. In addition to facets such as parental literacy (Leseman & de Jong, 1998), culturally specific child-rearing patterns may influence how parents respond to and support their children during activities such as book reading (cf. Baker, Scher, & Mackler, 1997). We have therefore begun to test the hypothesis that culturally specific forms of parenting may influence the quality of parental support and inhibit interactive routines that offer literacy learning opportunities (Bus, Leseman, & Keultjes, 2000). We controlled for confounding variables such as SES by matching the ethnic groups participating in this study on educational attainment level and job status.

In-depth analyses of how Turkish, Surinamese (South America), and Dutch parents read a simple narrative text to their 4-year-old child indeed reveal differences in parental behaviors such as supportive presence, respect for the child's autonomy, structure and limit setting, and quality of instruction (Erickson, Sroufe, & Egeland, 1985). The findings also support the hypothesis that culturally specific child-rearing patterns are basically at the root of the observed lower quality of parental support, and not other differences across the three ethnic groups, such as parental literacy. The dimension that provides the best separation among the least literate group (the Turkish) and the other two groups relates to characteristics of the reading process, such as the degree to which parents start conversations accompanying the reading of text, but not to the quality of parental support. Just like previous research into the parenting style of ethnic minorities (Riksen-

Walraven, Meij, Hubbard, & Zevalkink, 1996; van IJzendoorn, 1990), the present results indicate that in particular Surinamese mothers are less responsive during activities such as book reading than the Dutch or Turkish low-SES parents. Van IJzendoorn (1990) suggests that Surinam–Dutch parents waver between complete adaptation to the Dutch norms, and their own somewhat stricter criteria for controlling the child's behavior. This ambivalence of complete adaptation to the dominant Dutch culture versus strong adherence to their own culture may result in less responsive behavior, especially in culturally less integrated families.

Too much checking on children's understanding, for example, may be one parental behavior that appears to contribute to the nonsuccess of the parent–child interactions. The following fragment of a protocol (code number 174114) illustrates such maternal behavior. After having read the page, the mother starts to check on the child's understanding ("what did mamma read?"). When the child appears unable to answer her questioning, she simply repeats her questions and, eventually, she rereads the text without any adaptations to the child's level of understanding.

M: (reads) Liesbeth is ill
M: (reads) she has been in the hospital
M: (reads) she has to stay in bed
M: what did mamma read?
(C: shakes no)
M: tell mama?
M: what did I read?
C: I don't know
(C: shakes no)
M: no?
M: what did mama just read?
M: (reads) Liesbeth is ill
(C: points)
M: good
M: (reads) she has been in the hospital

In spite of less responsive parental behavior, some children appeared to remain engaged in the session and seemed to enjoy the bookreading all the way through the book (see for similar results Kaderavek & Sulzby, 1998). Even when the parent does not do anything "good" from a didactic perspective, the interactive session may evoke enjoyment and engagement in the storybook reading and support children's interest in books and their understanding of stories and book language (see also Neuman, 1996; Neuman & Roskos, 1993). Further research seems therefore warranted to test the possibility that, in spite of a less rewarding book-reading process, dyads may develop reading routines and children may build understandings and skills essential for reading success.

CONCLUSIONS AND DISCUSSION

Although book reading has appeared to be most effective in stimulating the early socialization of literacy, the provision of books and encouragement to read together actually may not produce meaningful conversations around text in every parent–child dyad. Our studies so far reveal evidence for the hypothesis that the development of literacy is a profoundly social process, embedded in the parent–child emotional relationship. Examining parent–child book reading through the lens of attachment theory, our studies illustrate how the emotional relationship between parent and child can embrace or inhibit interactive routines that offer literacy learning opportunities. Book-reading sessions of insecure pairs prove less rewarding and instructive, and this may explain why such dyads may not develop book-reading routines to the same extent as secure pairs. Many insecurely attached children indeed belong to a group at risk in becoming literate, namely, children who are infrequently read to. Culturally specific child-rearing patterns can embrace or inhibit interactive bookreading routines that offer optimal literacy learning opportunities, as well. This finding indeed supports Serpell's statement (chap. 12, this volume) that interactive routines typical of "high-quality" book reading may fit best with the perspective of the mainstream European and American culture.

Our research findings suggest that, without helping the participants to change their reading habits, literacy programs encouraging book reading at home might have a counterproductive effect. As many parents have problems in engaging their young children in activities such as shared readings or similar literate activities, we might need family literacy programs that support these parents in responding to their child's motivations and understandings and in dealing with their child's negative responses. However, we should avoid assuming that specific activities such as book reading must occur in preconceived ways. Because there is cultural variation in literacy-related practices, we should avoid precipitous recommendations to parents about best practices. Each parent–child interaction is a reflection of the participants' unique interpersonal style, history of storybook readings, and sociocultural norms. Also, bookreading or similar literate activities, such as dinner-table conversations (De Temple & Snow, chap. 3, this volume), may not hold a monopoly on the socialization of early literacy. However, appealing descriptive accounts of alternative literate practices such as oral storytelling or guided television watching (Serpell, 1997) are to my best knowledge still missing.

REFERENCES

Adams, M. J., Treiman, R., & Pressley, M. (1998). Reading, writing, and literacy. In I. E. Sigel & K. A. Renninger (Eds.), *Handbook of child psychology, Fifth Edition, Vol. 4: Child psychology in practice* (pp. 275–355). New York: Wiley.

Ainsworth, M. D. S., Blehar, M. C., Waters, E., & Wall, S. (1978). *Patterns of attachment: A psychological study of the Strange Situation.* Hillsdale, NJ: Lawrence Erlbaum Associates.

Baker, L., Scher, D., & Mackler, K. (1997). Home and family influences on motivation for reading. *Educational Psychologist, 32,* 69–82.

Bus, A. G. (1993). Attachment and emergent literacy. *International Journal of Educational Research, 19,* 573–581.

Bus, A. G. (1994). The role of social context in emergent literacy. In E. M. H. Assink (Ed.), *Literacy acquisition and social context* (pp. 9–24). New York: Harvester Wheatsheaf.

Bus, A. G., Belsky, J., van IJzendoorn, M. H., & Crnik, K. (1997). Attachment and bookreading patterns: A study of mothers, fathers, and their toddlers. *Early Childhood Research Quarterly, 12,* 81–98.

Bus, A. G., Leseman, P. M., & Keultjes, P. (2000). Joint bookreading across cultures: A comparison of Dutch, Surinam-Dutch, and Turkish-Dutch parent–child dyads. *Journal of Literacy Research, 32,* 53–76.

Bus, A. G., & van IJzendoorn, M. H. (1988). Mother–child interactions, attachment, and emergent literacy: A cross-sectional study. *Child Development, 59,* 1262–1273.

Bus, A. G., & van IJzendoorn, M. H. (1992). Patterns of attachment in frequently and infrequently reading dyads. *Journal of Genetic Psychology, 153,* 395–403.

Bus, A. G., & van IJzendoorn, M. H. (1995). Mothers reading to their three year olds: The role of mother–child attachment security in becoming literate. *Reading Research Quarterly, 40,* 998–1015.

Bus, A. G., & van IJzendoorn, M. H. (1997). Affective dimension of mother–infant picturebook reading. *Journal of School Psychology, 35,* 47–60.

Bus, A. G., van IJzendoorn, M. H., & Pellegrini, A. D. (1995). Joint book reading makes for success in learning to read. A meta-analysis on intergenerational transmission of literacy. *Review of Educational Research, 65,* 1–21.

Clinton, H. (1997, February 10). Comfort and joy. *Time,* p. 59.

Erickson, M. F., Sroufe, A., & Egeland, B. (1985). The relationship between quality of and behavior problems in preschool in a high-risk sample. *Monographs of the society for research in child development, 50,* 147–166.

International Reading Association & National Association for the Education of Young Children. (1998). Learning to read and write: Developmentally appropriate practices for young children. *Reading Teacher, 52,* 193–216.

Kaderavek, J. N., & Sulzby, E. (1998). Parent–child joint bookreading: An observational protocol for young children. *American Journal of Speech-Language Pathology, 7,* 33–47.

Leseman, P. M., & de Jong, P. F. (1998). Home literacy: Opportunity, instruction, cooperation, and social-emotional quality predicting early reading achievemen. *Reading Research Quarterly, 33,* 294–319.

Main, M., Kaplan, N., & Cassidy, J. (1985). Security in infancy, childhood, and adulthood: A move to the level of representation. *Monographs of the Society for Research in Child Development, 50,* 66–104.

Martin, L. E. (1998). Early book reading: How mothers deviate from printed text for young children. *Reading Research and Instruction, 37,* 137–160.

Neuman, S. B. (1996). Children engaging in storybook reading: The influence of access to print resources, opportunity, and parental interaction. *Early Childhood Research Quarterly, 11,* 495–513.

Neuman, S. B., & Roskos, K. (1993). Access to print for children of poverty: Differential effects of adult mediation and literacy-enriched play settings on environmental and functional print tasks. *American Educational Research Journal, 30,* 95–122.

Ninio, A., & Bruner, J. S. (1976). The achievement and antecedents of labelling. *Journal of Child Language, 5,* 1–15.

Riksen-Walraven, J. M., Meij, J. T., Hubbard, F. O., & Zevalkink, J. (1996). Intervention in lower-class Surinam–Dutch families: Effects on mothers and infants. *International Journal of Behavioral Development, 19,* 739–756.

Rosenthal, R. (1991). *Meta-analytic procedures for social research* (rev. ed.). Newbury Park, CA: Sage.

Scarborough, H. S., & Dobrich, W. (1994). On the efficacy of reading to preschoolers. *Developmental Review, 14,* 245–302.

Serpell, R. (1997). Literacy connections between school and home: How should we evaluate them? *Journal of Literacy Research, 29,* 587–616.

Snow, C., Tabors, P., Nicholson, P., & Kurland, B. (1995). SHELL: Oral language and early literacy skills in kindergarten and first-grade children. *Journal of Research in Childhood Education, 10,* 37–48.

Snowling, M. (1987). *Dyslexia. A cognitive developmental perspective.* Oxford: Basil Blackwell.

Sulzby, E., & Teale, W. H. (1987). *Young children's storybook reading: Longitudinal study of parent–child interaction and children's independent functioning* (Final report to the Spencer Foundation). Ann Arbor: University of Michigan Press.

Van IJzendoorn, M. H. (1990). Attachment in Surinam–Dutch families: A contribution to the cross-cultural study of attachment. *International Journal of Behavioral Development, 13,* 333–344.

Van IJzendoorn, M. H., & Bus, A. G. (1994). Meta-analytic confirmation of the nonword reading deficit in developmental dyslexia. *Reading Research Quarterly, 30,* 266–275.

Whitehurst, G. J., Falco, F. L., Lonigan, C., Fischel, J. E., DeBaryshe, B. D., Valdez-Menchaca, M. C., & Caulfiels, M. (1988). Accelerating language development through picture-book reading. *Developmental Psychology, 24,* 552–558.

CHAPTER

3

Conversations About Literacy: Social Mediation of Psycholinguistic Activity

Jeanne M. De Temple
Catherine E. Snow
Harvard University

The term *literacy* has come to be used to refer to an ever wider domain of activities, from media literacy and computer literacy to citizenship literacy, many of them only tangentially related to the traditional core of the concept of literacy, namely, reading. Even when confined to the domain of print, the term *literacy* is systematically ambiguous, in much the way words for literacy artifacts like *book* or *poem* are systematically ambiguous between reductionist and constructionist meanings. As Reddy (1979) pointed out many years ago, the word *book* can refer both to the physical object (it was a book of 300-plus pages, he used the book to prop open the window) and to the message or content, independent of its physical packaging (Kuhn's book changed our view of science, I need a book that will keep me amused on a long plane ride). Somewhat analogously, *literacy* can be used to refer to the psycholinguistic capacity to read (Finnish high school students score first in the world in literacy, nationwide literacy assessments demanded by the president) as well as the social practices associated with reading (Guillaume's impeccable taste and literacy amazed us all; youth literacy is threatened by MTV). Historical discussions of literacy, which contrasted it with orality and generated much discussion of the features that distinguished literate from oral modes of communication (see, e.g., Gee, 1988; Scollon & Scollon, 1981; Tannen, 1985; and many others), left unclear whether the personal, psychological, or the social, cultural sense of literacy was being invoked. Similarly, discussions concerning the cognitive consequences of literacy (e.g., Goody & Watt, 1963; Olson, 1977; Ong, 1977) fail in general to specify whether they are asking if cognitive consequences of literacy derive from becoming literate, in the individual, psycholinguistic sense of literate, or from access to literate cultures, in the social, constructivist sense of literate.

We argue in this chapter that the distinction between psycholinguistic and social definitions of literacy is blurred because these two are, in fact, two sides of the same coin. Personal literacy and public, socially mediated literacy are, we demonstrate, equally central to any serious notion of *literate*, and thus the social, conversational activity that occurs around literacy must be incorporated into our notions of what reading is. This is an insight that is abundantly supported by observation of literacy activities engaged in by preschool-aged children. Participation in literacy events for a child younger than 5 years typically means engaging in a conversation about a book or another literate artifact. These conversations have been amply documented, and hypothesized to be the source of many of the documented benefits of reading books with children (Bus, van IJzendoorn, & Pellegrini, 1992; Scarborough & Dobrich, 1994), but have typically not been seen as intrinsically literate activities. Analyzing how such conversations go on across three different groups of mother–child dyads, we have come to see the conversations as an organic part of the literacy activity, and as "gradable" in much the way more autonomously displayed literacy skills are gradable as typical of beginning, independent, or fluent readers.

The most common way of thinking about literacy, of course, puts the autonomous reading of a text at a higher developmental level than being read to, reading with help, or discussing the pictures in a book. The definition of literacy we espouse in this chapter, in contrast, places conversations about books at the center of literate activities—for adults as well as for children. Of course, the character of those conversations may change with age and developmental level, and they certainly achieve greater temporal disconnectedness from the actual event of obtaining meaning from print for older readers, but nonetheless we see "participation in literate conversation" both as a metaphor for being literate and as a very literal context for developing literacy skills, knowledge, and motivation.

A Conversation-Enhanced View of Literacy. Typically, literacy skills are assessed and graded in a way that reflects how independently one can read a particular text, or conversely the complexity level of the texts that one can read independently. Although this view of assessment has its place, we instead, for the purposes of this chapter, explore the notion that literacy can be graded or assessed on the basis of the quality of the conversation in which one's literacy skills enable one to participate. Consider the following conversations of four African American mothers living in different urban areas of the United States. Each conversation occurred with her preschool-aged child during a shared reading of *The Very Hungry Caterpillar* (Carle, 1969):

Example 1: Tyrone (age 47 months)

Mother:	"One Sunday morning the warm sun came up and *pop* out of the egg came a *tiny* and a very large caterpillar." Look Tyrone! See the sun (points to sun)?
Tyrone:	(nods)
Mother:	What's this (points to caterpillar)?
Tyrone:	I *saw* that (points to caterpillar)!
Mother:	Caterpillar.
Tyrone:	Caterpillar.
Mother:	"He started to look for some food."
Mother:	"On Friday he ate through five oranges but he was still hungry." How many?
Tyrone:	Two one three four.
Mother:	How many? Start here!
Tyrone:	One two three four five (Mother points to oranges as Tyrone counts).
Mother:	Right.

Example 2: Jasmine (age 46 months)

Mother:	What are these?
Jasmine:	Apples.
Mother:	No those are not apples!
Jasmine:	That's an apple.
Mother:	No that's oranges! All those are oranges. Oranges have leaves too and stems. They just break them up before they get to the store.

Example 3: Keisha (age 45 months)

Mother:	"One cupcake and one slice of watermelon."
Keisha:	One watermelon.
Mother:	And guess what? Later that night do you know what happened to him? The caterpillar? "That night he had a stomachache." Eating all that food that's why.
Keisha:	Eating all that food!
Mother:	See? See how he's looking so sad and pitiful? Guess what Keisha? "The next day was Sunday again. The caterpillar ate through one nice green leaf. He ate through one nice green leaf and after that

he felt much better." Why'd he feel much better I wonder. Hmmm, let's find out.

Keisha: Let's find out.

Mother: Okay.

Example 4: Charles (age 57 months)

Mother: Okay let's read. "The next day was Sunday again. The caterpillar ate through one nice green leaf and after that he felt much."

Charles: Mom look at face. (points to the cocoon)

Mother: Why you think um after he ate that leaf that he felt much better? Can you tell me about that and why he ate that leaf he felt much better? After eating all this food and he felt like he was full and tired and worn out. Why you think he ate this leaf and he felt much better than the food?

Charles: He feel much better right here.

Mother: Why?

Charles: Big leaf?

Mother: No what I'm saying why did he felt much better after eating the big green leaf?

Charles: He hungry?

Mother: No he wasn't hungry because he ate all the fruits and all the food.

Charles: He got the food . . .

Mother: Okay okay wait a minute. I'll explain it to you. The reason why he felt better after he ate the green leave, big leaf, because it's light. It's not full with all the heavy food because he couldn't take that. That's why he look the way he was looking when I showed you back here. Let's go back a few pages. See how he look? See all this food he went through? That's why he lookin' like that. It was too full for his stomach. He couldn't hold all that. And then that's why that night he had a stomachache.

Charles: He ate that. (points to the pickle)

Mother: He went through everything you see. I showed it you. Even these fruits I showed you. We went through that. But when he ate that great big old leaf, it was so light to him. That's why he felt much better.

Charles: Look. (points to the caterpillar on the leaf)

Mother: Mmhm. And even though he have another expression on his face. It's like a happy face. Okay let's go on.

One way of seeing the differences among these conversations focuses on developmental change—that the conversations centered around naming pictures were being carried out with younger children, or children less familiar with the content of the book. Another way of seeing them is as representing distinct notions about literacy—literacy interpreted as a mechanism for discovering and rehearsing facts by Tyrone's mother, and as involving opportunities to explore one's personal reactions to and interpretation of facts by the other three mothers. Both these views are, in fact, correct—that the conversations with a high proportion of talk that goes beyond naming pictures and repeating the text, which we characterize as incorporating more *nonimmediate* talk, are more likely to occur with older children, and do reflect in the oral mode processes of inference and evaluation that are more frequent in advanced than beginning readers. At the same time, though, there are stable individual styles of book-reading conversation chosen by different mother–child pairs, despite similar child ages and experience with the book in question. One question that has motivated our work is the effect on the child's development of language and literacy skills of engagement in these different types of conversation. We present here some data showing what conversations during book reading look like, how they differ across different social groups, and what relationships can be found between the nature of such conversations and children's progress toward more autonomous participation in challenging forms of literacy activity.

The Value of Nonimmediate Talk. Our previous analyses of the incidence of nonimmediate talk during book reading have focused on a longitudinal sample of low-income children studied as part of the Home School Study of Language and Literacy Development (Snow, 1991). Because of the longitudinal nature of that study, we have been able to trace relationships between use of nonimmediate talk and later child outcomes on tasks assessing language and emergent literacy skills (Beals & De Temple, 1993; De Temple, 1994; De Temple & Beals, 1991).

In this study a mother's use of nonimmediate talk during book reading when her child was 3 years old was strongly associated with the child's scores 2 years later, in kindergarten, on measures of story comprehension, receptive vocabulary, skill in giving definitions, superordinates, and emergent literacy ($r = .31$ to $.46$). Not only did the mothers' use of nonimmediate talk prove to be a good predictor of children's later language and literacy skills, but also the use of immediate talk also predicted the children's outcomes; however, this type of talk predicted negatively their later skills. The percentage of immediate talk used by the mother during book reading at each annual visit was negatively associated with the measures of language and literacy in kindergarten ($r = -.26$ to $-.46$). Mothers whose talk during book reading focused relatively more on information immediately available from the illustrations or text had children who scored lower on kindergarten measures of language and literacy; those who devoted little of their talk to immediate topics had children who scored higher. This is somewhat surprising because a behavior such as labeling objects in an illustration would seem to be a useful preparation for some of the outcome measures we used, such as the Peabody Picture Vocabulary Test, a test of receptive vocabulary.

The total amount of nonimmediate talk during book reading was relatively low, and most of the mothers' comments and questions were coded as immediate talk. However, the amount of immediate talk decreased over time, as did the total amount of talk. The amount of nonimmediate talk did not increase over time, but it accounted for an increasingly higher proportion of the total talk engaged in.

These findings led us to explore the question of variability across subgroups within the population of low-income, high-risk mothers in the nature of the conversations engaged in during book reading. The sample of families that participated in the Home School Study, although of low income and of limited parental education, nonetheless constituted a relatively stable, limited-risk population. Half the mothers had completed high school, and some had pursued further vocational and educational training. Half the families were two-parent families in which both parents were employed. None of the children studied were the product of an adolescent pregnancy. And the families were sufficiently financially and emotionally stable to be able to follow through on a commitment to participate in the yearly observations and test sessions required as part of the longitudinal study.

We chose, thus, to replicate the observations of mother–child book reading in much higher risk samples of welfare mothers, almost all high school dropouts, and many adolescent parents. These samples were available as part of work evaluating the effect of two different types of parent education programs designed to promote parental literacy and employability. We present here for purposes of comparison information about all three samples, and an overview of the two types of intervention delivered to the higher risk samples, before turning to the findings.

The New Chance Embedded Observational Study. As part of the larger New Chance Evaluation, the New Chance Embedded Observational Study focused on 290 young mothers receiving welfare; all were between 16 and 22 years of age at the time of observation, had given birth at age 19 years or younger, and had dropped out of high school (Zaslow & Eldred, 1998). Two-thirds of the mothers scored at ninth grade or below on a test of literacy. The mothers were mostly African American (84%) and lived in one of seven urban areas across the United States. New Chance provided a comprehensive program aimed at helping the mother complete the GED (high school equivalency) certificate and develop job skills. In addition, New Chance provided support and counseling in family planning, health education, life skills, and parenting skills. Child care was also provided so mothers could take advantage of these training opportunities.

Mothers were videotaped at home engaged in a sequence of tasks with their children, one of which involved reading and then discussing *The Very Hungry Caterpillar*. The children ranged in age from 28 to 68 months with an average age of 43.6 months. We present here data only from the conversation during reading, as that part of the observation was comparable to the Home School Study observation.

The JOBS Observational Study. The larger JOBS Evaluation was an effort to evaluate training programs designed to ensure successful transition from welfare to work for long-term welfare mothers, which involved collecting interview and child outcome data from approximately 3,000 mothers in three sites (U.S. Department of Health and Human Services & U.S. Department of Education, 1995). The JOBS Observations focused on 362 mother–child dyads who were participating in the larger study, all located in one urban area in the South of the United States. This program used a human capital development approach emphasizing education and training activities. It differed from the New Chance educational efforts in being focused entirely on job-related skills and in being less intensive. Child care was not provided, and the per-participant costs of the JOBS training efforts were less than half those of the New Chance intervention. Although 40% of the women had been teenagers at the time of their first child's birth, they were all over 20 years old at the beginning of the study, with two-thirds between 25 and 34 years old. More than half of the women were high school graduates. However, 53% scored at the lowest levels on a test of literacy (Test of Applied Literacy Skills). The mothers were almost all African American (96%). Mothers and children were visited at home and videotaped during a sequence of tasks, one of which was reading and discussing *The Very Hungry Caterpillar*. As for the New Chance study, we analyze here only the talk during the reading. The children ranged in age from 40 to 69 months. The mean age was 55.18 months.

The Home School Study of Language and Literacy. The Home School Study, some results of which were described earlier, is a longitudinal study following 83 children from age 3½ into middle school. The data reported here were collected on the first home visit, when the children ranged in age from 41 to 51 months with a mean age of 46.5 months.

A COMPARISON OF BOOK READING IN THE THREE STUDIES

Amount of Talk and Global Book-Reading Quality. Mothers in all three studies went beyond simply reading the book aloud to the child and talked about the book, making comments and asking questions (see Table 3.1). The

TABLE 3.1
Total Number of Maternal Utterances During Book Reading: Descriptive
Statistics for the New Chance Observational Study, the JOBS Study,
and the Home School Study of Language and Literacy Development

Variable	Mean	SD	Range
Total number of utterances			
New Chance	50.76	36.45	1–195
JOBS	44.53	37.85	0–286
Home School Study	38.91	26.41	1–114
Book-reading quality			
New Chance	6.54	1.48	3–9
JOBS	6.32	1.61	3–9

total number of maternal utterances included all of the mother's talk to the child beyond the reading of the text. Talk before and after was not included. The amount of talk ranged greatly in all three samples, but the teen mothers in New Chance, on average, talked considerably more than the others (De Temple & Snow, 1998). Mothers in the Home School Study added the least amount of talk beyond reading the text, although the average number of utterances was still high.

A global coding of book-reading quality was applied to the book readings from the New Chance and JOBS studies. The purpose of this code was to provide a measure of the mother's reading reflecting her comfort level with the activity, her reading fluency, and her reading intonation or animation (which may indicate both her ability to engage the child in the story and her comprehension level). Mothers who are relatively comfortable with the task of reading a picture book aloud, who read more fluently and with fewer hesitations, and who demonstrate comprehension through intonation are likely to more successfully engage their children in book reading than those who struggle in these areas. Mothers from New Chance and JOBS were rated similarly on this global measure.

Nonimmediate Talk. Although the mothers talked a great deal during the book reading, very few utterances could be coded as nonimmediate (see Table 3.2). Nonimmediate utterances were all utterances that required going beyond the here and now, beyond information that was immediately available from the text or illustrations. Nonimmediate utterances include questions, comments, or responses involving explanations, evaluations of characters, inferences, predictions, and connections to the real world or other literature. Mothers in New Chance and JOBS produced, on average, fewer than two nonimmediate utterances. Those in the Home School Study used somewhat more but still, on average, fewer than four nonimmediate utterances. However, when the use of nonimmediate talk is examined as a

TABLE 3.2
Number of Maternal Nonimmediate Utterances During Book Reading:
Descriptive Statistics for the New Chance Observational Study, the JOBS
Study, and the Home School Study of Language and Literacy Development

Study	Number of Nonimmediate Utterances		
	Mean	SD	Range
New Chance	1.94	2.64	0–17
JOBS	1.97	3.02	0–21
Home School Study 1	3.67	3.20	0–14

proportion of the total amount of talk, the mothers in the Home School Study look quite different from those in the more high-risk samples (see Table 3.3). Although the mothers in New Chance and JOBS talked the most, they used the least amount of nonimmediate talk and it made up less than 4% of their total talk. In contrast, nonimmediate talk made up 10.33% of the talk during book reading for mothers in the Home School Study.

A small percent (16.9%) of the mothers in the Home School Study used no nonimmediate talk while reading *The Very Hungry Caterpillar*. Among those mothers in the higher risk families, this type of talk was often completely absent. In the New Chance sample 41.8% and in the JOBS sample 43.8% of the mothers used no nonimmediate talk. These readers took a very literal approach to the text, and the children neither heard, nor were prompted to make, interpretations, evaluations, predictions, or connections to their lives.

Immediate Talk. Most of the comments and questions that occurred during book reading could be coded as immediate talk (see Table 3.4). This type of talk is limited to information immediately available on the page and includes labeling objects depicted in the illustrations, naming colors, counting, drawing the child's attention to an illustration, and requests to recall a familiar chunk of text. Although all three groups showed a wide range in the

TABLE 3.3
Percent of Maternal Nonimmediate Utterances During Book Reading:
Descriptive Statistics for the New Chance Observational Study, the JOBS
Study, and the Home School Study of Language and Literacy Development

Study	Nonimmediate Utterances (%)		
	Mean	SD	Range
New Chance	3.45	4.24	0–25
JOBS	3.81	5.37	0–30
Home School Study 1	10.33	8.15	0–31.25

TABLE 3.4
Percent of Maternal Immediate Utterances During Book Reading:
Descriptive Statistics for the New Chance Observational Study the JOBS
Study, and the Home School Study of Language and Literacy Development

	Immediate Utterances (%)		
Study	Mean	SD	Range
New Chance	68.30	12.87	18.5-100
JOBS	67.00	16.00	0-100
Home School Study 1	60.21	15.06	21.42-100

percent of immediate talk used, mothers in the New Chance and JOBS samples used, on average, a higher percent of immediate talk than those in the
Home School Study.

Effects of Child Age. In the Home School Study we had provided the
same book for mothers to read to their children on three annual visits and
found that over time the total number of utterances and the percent of immediate utterances decreased, but the percent of nonimmediate utterances
increased. Although mothers in the New Chance study differed from those
in the Home School Study in terms of the amount of talk used and the type
of talk, the association between the talk during book reading and the age of
the child was similar (see Table 3.5). Mothers talked more with younger
children and less with older children; they used proportionally less
nonimmediate talk with younger children and more with the older children.
A higher percent of the mothers' talk was immediate with younger children,
and a lower percent of immediate talk was used with older children.

There was a strong positive association, among those mothers in the
New Chance study, between the use of nonimmediate talk during book
reading and the global measure of book-reading quality (see Table 3.6).
Those mothers who were rated low on comfort level, reading fluency, and
reading intonation used both a smaller number of nonimmediate utter-

TABLE 3.5
Correlations Between Book-Reading Variables and Child Age

	Correlation With Child Age	
Book-Reading Variable	JOBS	New Chance
Total number of utterances	−.15**	−.25***
Nonimmediate utterances (%)		.27***
Immediate utterances (%)		−.11*

*p < .05. **p < .01. ***p < .001.

TABLE 3.6
Correlations Between Nonimmediate Talk During
Book Reading and Book-Reading Quality

	Correlation With Book-Reading Quality	
Book-Reading Variable	JOBS	New Chance
Number of nonimmediate utterances	.11*	.28**
Percent of nonimmediate utterances		.29**

*p < .05. **p < .001.

ances and proportionally a small amount of nonimmediate talk, whereas those rated higher on book-reading quality used more. This relationship was not found for the JOBS sample.

CONCLUSIONS AND DISCUSION

Literacy is, of course, a term that encompasses many different behaviors, and that can be viewed from a number of different perspectives. Literacy can be rather narrowly defined as what one does while reading, or as the capacities that make reading possible. Much more broadly, it can be defined as participation in certain kinds of social-cultural activities, typically associated with but neither limited to nor even absolutely requiring the reading of text. Our approach in this chapter has been to describe literacy as an activity involving centrally the conversation that goes on during book reading with young children. In other words, literacy practices are both constituted and enriched by relevant conversation, and dialogues about books being read or that have been read embellish the texts themselves such that they also constitute literacy practices.

During the socialization of young children into literacy, the conversation becomes crucial to literate participation, because it is the primary route by which the child gets access to the text. We have reported in this chapter striking differences among groups of low-income families in the nature of the conversation they engage in during book reading with 3-year-olds, with mothers who have lower educational achievement and higher social risk status in general producing less nonimmediate talk during such conversations. Given the relationship of nonimmediate talk during book reading to later child outcomes for the Home School Study sample, these differences across groups are alarming.

The differences seen among the Home School Study families during book reading are reminiscent of differences among them in other conversational contexts as well (Snow & Kurland, 1996). For example, one of the families with a very high incidence of nonimmediate talk during book reading had the following conversation, with its incorporation of information about a popular children's book set in Boston, at dinner:

Ethan (age 56 months)

Mother:	I got the telephone number for the parade today.
Father:	Yeah?
Mother:	And um I walked by Boston Garden I could see some ducks in there.
Ethan:	Yeah?
Mother:	Yep!
Ethan:	Were they . . .
Father:	Did you wash your hands for dinner?
Mother:	Uhoh!
Father:	Soap and water those are dirty hands.
Father:	Okay?
Ethan:	Okay.
Mother:	Well I told them Ethan says hi.
Ethan:	What did they say?
Mother:	I didn't walk right up to them because I had to rush I had a lot of things to do. But um yeah and it was kind of raining out when I went by the first time. Okay tomorrow Ethan I will call the place where you get tickets for the parade okay? And find out . . .
Ethan:	What place?
Mother:	Ah it's called the Boston Historic uh Foundation. I'll call them up and find out everything we need to know.
Ethan:	Know what Susan thought where it was?
Mother:	What?
Ethan:	Know where Susan thought it was?
Mother:	Where?
Ethan:	Um in Boston.
Mother:	Yeah.
Mother:	It's in Boston right where the duckling in the story went remember in the Boston Garden in the story? Remember how they were on the Cambridge side of the river when she had made the nest? And then remember when she had to meet Mr Mallard? And um Michael the policeman had to cross them and everything? That was in Boston.
Ethan:	And they thought um that bridge was a island?
Mother:	Yeah right but then they did find an island right underneath the bridge. If I remember correctly.

In yet another family, reference is made during the dinner table conversation to *Charlotte's Web*:

Rosalyn (age 48 months)

Sister:	I got some translucent pressed powder today at Spag's.
Father:	You got some what?
Sister:	Translucent pressed powder today at Spag's.
Father:	Rosalyn will you set that down before it spills?
Rosalyn:	I have to put it where everybody can reach it.
Father:	Oh all right.
Sister:	How does it look? (coyly)
Rosalyn:	I know mom can reach it too.
Father:	Oh I'm sorry I was paying attention to what she was saying. Translucent what?
Sister:	Pressed powder.
Father:	Pressed powder?
Father:	And where what, what is this eye shadow?
Sister:	No it's skin colored powder. Put it on my face and it covers it. Covers your zits and stuff.
Father:	Well if it's skin colored how am I supposed to know how it looks?
Sister:	Well gee!
Father:	It looks marvelous! (falsetto, playful) It looks wonderful! You're so radiant! Just like . . . What's the name of that pig in *Charlotte's Web*?
Sister:	I do not look like a pig!
Rosalyn:	Yeah she not Wilbur.
Father:	Wilbur! That's his name.

The occurrence of these conversations outside the immediate context of book-reading presupposes general familiarity among all the family members with the books being discussed or alluded to—constitutes, in other words, literate activity. In some of the Home School Study families, such talk was never observed to occur.

A recent study (Becker, 1997) of women whom most would identify as highly literate revealed a similar range in the degree to which literacy was incorporated into the women's social, conversational lives. Becker set out to study avid readers, women who read at least three books a month (most many more) and had done so for most of their adult lives. Through extensive interviews with these avid readers, Becker discovered two subgroups, differentiated most powerfully by the range of types of reading engaged in and the role of conversations about books in their social relationships. One group read, typically, for escape, tended to limit themselves to one type of fiction, and reported not knowing whether their best friends read or what kinds of things they read. These women were likely to have partners who were not frequent readers, and reported mostly limited reading in their families of origin. The other group, which read more widely and read serious literature more often, reported knowing what their partners and friends were reading, exchanging information about books regularly, participating in book groups or other contexts for the discussion of books, and selecting friends on the basis of shared reading interests. In other words, even for these skilled, frequent readers, it is possible to identify levels of literacy based on the nature of the conversations their reading enabled them to participate in.

We have studied low-income mothers of children likely to have problems with reading when they get to school. Becker was studying highly skilled and frequent readers. Within both these groups, though, we see the nexus of conversation and literacy, and we see an enormous range of engagement in conversation around literacy, and of embellishment of texts that have been read with talk about those texts. Conversation is intrinsically more accessible to young children than is reading—thus we see understanding the nature of book-based conversation and its potential to support an interest in reading and an understanding of texts read as a contribution to the improvement of reading outcomes, particularly for children at academic risk.

ACKNOWLEDGMENTS

The authors acknowledge funding from the Spencer Foundation in support of the Home-School Study of Language and Literacy Development, from the W. T. Grant Foundation, the Foundation for Child Development, and one anonymous funder in support of the New Chance Embedded Study, and from the W. T. Grant Foundation and the Foundation for Child Development in support of the JOBS Embedded Study. Robert Granger and the Manpower Demostration Research Corporation coordinated the collaborative effort that made both the New Chance and the JOBS Embedded Observational Studies possible. We are indebted to Patton Tabors, who has played a central role in conceptualizing all these three studies, to Eliza Whitbeck and Claudia Cooper for major contributions to transcription and coding, to Brenda Kurland for carrying out the New Chance analysis, and to the research team of Harvard's Projects in Language Development.

REFERENCES

Beals, D. E., & De Temple, J. M. (1993). Home contributions to early language and literacy development. In D. J. Leu & C. K. Kinzer (Eds.), *Examining central issues in literacy research, theory, and practice* (pp. 207–215). Forty-Second Yearbook of the National Reading Conference. National Reading Conference, Inc., Chicago, IL.

Becker, C. A. (1997). *Haves and Have-mores: A developmental analysis of avid women readers' literate histories.* Doctoral dissertation, Department of Psychology, Harvard University.

Bus, A. G., van Ijzendoorn, M. H., & Pellegrini, A. D. (1995). Joint book reading makes for success in learning to read. A metanalysis on intergenerational transmition of literacy. *Review of Educational Research, 65,* 1–21.

Carle, E. (1969). *The very hungry caterpillar.* New York: Philomel.

De Temple, J. M. (1994). *Book reading styles of low-income mothers with preschoolers and children's later literacy skills.* Unpublished doctoral dissertation, Harvard Graduate School of Education, Cambridge, MA.

De Temple, J. M., & Beals, D. E. (1991). Family talk: Sources of support for the development of decontextualized language skills. *Journal of Research in Childhood Education, 6*(1), 11–19.

De Temple, J. M., & Snow, C. (1998). Mother–child interactions related to the emergence of literacy. In M. J. Zaslow & C. A. Eldred (Eds.), *Parenting behavior in a sample of young single mothers in poverty: Results of the New Chance Observational Study* (pp. 114–169). New York: Manpower Demonstration Research Corporation.

Gee, J. P. (1988). Discourse systems and aspirin bottles: On literacy. *Journal of Education, 170*(1), 27–40.

Goody, J., & Watt, I. (1963). The consequences of literacy. *Comparative Studies in Society and History, 5,* 304–345.

Olson, D. (1977). From utterance to text: The bias of language in speech and writing. *Harvard Educational Review, 47*(3), 257–281.

Ong, W. J. (1977). *The presence of the word.* New Haven, CT: Yale University Press. *Interfaces of the word.* Ithaca, NY: Cornell University Press.

Reddy, M. J. (1979). The conduit metaphor—A case of frame conflict in our language about language. In A. Ortony (Ed.), *Metaphor and thought* (pp. 284–324). Cambridge: Cambridge University Press.

Scarborough, H.S., & Dobrich, W. (1994). On the efficacy of reading to preschoolers. *Developmental Review, 14,* 245–302.

Scollon, R., & Scollon, S. B. K. (1981). *Narrative, literacy, and face in interethnic communication.* Norwood, NJ: Ablex.

Snow, C. E. (1991). The theoretical basis for relationships between language and literacy in development. *Journal of Research in Childhood Education, 6,* 5–10.

Snow, C. E., & Kurland, B. F. (1996). Sticking to the point: Talk about magnets as preparation for literacy. In D. Hicks (Ed.), *Child discourse and social learning: an interdisciplinary perspective* (pp. 189–220). New York: Cambridge University Press.

Tannen, D. (1985). Relative focus on involvement in oral and written discourse. In D. R. Olson, N. Torrance, & A. Hildyard (Eds.), *Literacy, language, and learning: the nature and consequences of reading and writing* (pp. 124–147). Cambridge: Cambridge University Press.

U.S. Department of Health and Human Services & U.S. Department of Education. (1995). *The JOBS Evaluation: How well are they faring? AFDC families with preschool-aged children in Atlanta at the outset of the JOBS Evaluation.* Washington, DC: U.S. Department of Health and Human Services, Office of the Assistant Secretary for Planning and Evaluation.

Zaslow, M. J., & Eldred, C. A. (Eds.). (1998). *Parenting behavior in a sample of young single mothers in poverty: Results of the New Chance Observational Study.* New York: Manpower Demonstration Research Corporation.

CHAPTER

4

How Important Is Home Literacy for Acquiring Literacy in School?

Paul P. M. Leseman
Peter F. de Jong
University of Amsterdam

Early introduction to books and early participation in literacy-related inter-actions in the home environment are seen as most important to prepare young children for literacy instruction at school. This idea is largely undis-puted and is the starting point of present-day endeavors to raise literacy levels in the homes of young children, especially when they are at risk of later educational failure. However, considering the evidence, the impor-tance attributed to (early) home literacy can be seriously questioned.

Generally, the strength of the relationships found between home literacy and several outcome measures, including reading and writing at school, should be qualified as small. For example, in a recent review, Scarborough and Dobrich (1994) reported a median correlation of .28. Similarly, Bus, van IJzendoorn, and Pellegrini (1995), conducting a meta-analysis, found corre-lations ranging from .27 to .33. However, one could argue, as Bus (chap. 2, this volume) does, that even effects of this modest size can have large im-pact on the scale of society. Consequently, large-scale programs to enhance home literacy seem to be justified.

However, before we accept this argument in favor of home literacy pro-grams, two further problems concerning the reported relationships be-tween home literacy and school achievement should be considered. First, the estimates of the relationship between home literacy and language and literacy development are (almost) entirely based on correlational studies. Therefore, strictly speaking, no causal implication whatsoever can be de-rived from these reviews. As a matter of fact, few studies on home literacy adequately controlled for other possible explanations of the observed correlations, such as, for instance, the child's cognitive and verbal ability, which at least is partly genetic in origin and may determine the child's literacy experiences instead of being determined by them (cf. Leseman & van den Boom, 1999; Scarr, 1997).

A second problem concerns the specificity of the effects of home literacy on the various outcome measures. In most of the studies, home literacy was isolated from other aspects of the home environment, such as socioeconomic status (SES) and, more importantly, other socialization processes that in theory might influence language and literacy development without, paradoxically as it seems, any recourse to literacy in a narrow sense. The exceptions we know of are, among very few others, the studies by Wells (1985) and the Home School Language and Literacy study by Snow and Dickinson and colleagues (Snow, 1991, 1999). Typically, these studies demonstrate that also ordinary mealtime conversations and instructional talk in object play can influence language and literacy development.

In this chapter, an attempt is made to answer the question of how important home literacy is for acquiring literacy in school. First, we review previous research on informal literacy education at home and on early literacy education programs. In addition, we present a study on the effects of home literacy and related informal educational practices at home on literacy acquisition in school in a multicultural sample of low-SES and minority children as compared to middle-class children in the Netherlands.

INFORMAL LITERACY EDUCATION AT HOME

Literacy, conceived as the ability to read and write texts of a certain length and informational complexity, and also including a positive attitude toward reading and writing texts for a variety of purposes, probably is a complex skill. Following Snow (1993; Dickinson & Snow, 1987), reading (and by extension, writing) can be seen as a set of skills, each of which can be assessed independently, and all of which may have somewhat different developmental histories. At the "bottom," reading skill consists of the ability to recognize letters rapidly, to recognize words in an automatized fashion, and to access rapidly word meanings in a part of the memory system called the *mental lexicon*. At the "top," reading skill involves integration of new information with previously stored information, and the identification of authorial stance and perspective in order to form a coherent model of what the text is about (van Dijk & Kintsch, 1983).

According to Snow, the list of component skills of literacy can be divided into four broad categories: print skills in a narrow sense (e.g., knowing letters), language analysis skills (e.g., phonemic segmentation skills), vocabulary and world knowledge, and pragmatic skills. Pragmatic skills, for instance, include understanding the diverse functions of literacy, having ideas about different text genres, and understanding that reading and writing are forms of communication, like talking, yet because of the distanced nature (reader and writer are mostly not present in the same situation and often have only little knowledge of each other) they differ in important ways from oral communication. Connected to this are skills to use language appropriately in situations in which the immediate context offers no support for interpretation, as in reading and writing.

Theoretically, following this argument, the home environment may contribute in several ways to the preparation of children for reading and writing instruction. It may provide children with opportunities to get familiar with literacy and literacy technology. It may present models of literacy use and may foster positive attitudes toward literacy learning in school (cf. Bus & van IJzendoorn, 1995; Leseman & de Jong, 1998). The mere presence of literacy, for instance, in the form of print on food packages, free advertisement papers, magazines, and newspapers (so-called environmental print) pervading the home may enable young children to develop spontaneously ideas or concepts about literacy—for instance, about the representational function of script, or about the functions of literacy (e.g., writing a postcard to send someone your greetings, reading instructions to use an apparatus).

The home environment may also contribute to literacy development in a less direct way through influencing oral language development. Singing lullabies and nursery rhymes and related language games involving alliteration are, among other things, excercises in the sound structure of language, probably promoting the development of some aspects of phonological awareness, which is related to the first stages of learning to read and write (Goswami & Bryant, 1990). Similarly, drawing and painting pictures as part of children's play activities at home may be considered to be a preparation for learning the fine psychomotor aspects of writing (Pontecorvo, 1994).

The development of children's vocabulary and world knowledge is also dependent on input from the home environment (Beals, De Temple, & Dickinson, 1994; Beals & Tabors, 1993; Wells, 1985). This concerns direct instruction in word meanings but also children's spontaneous vocabulary acquisition, which depends on the richness of the vocabulary used by the parents and the informativity of the verbal context in which new words appear (Beals & Tabors, 1993). Talking about a past event, reporting on "your day," telling stories, or discussing general topics may foster receptive and productive text comprehension skills, which become important as soon as reading and writing in school concerns texts (cf. Hoff-Ginsberg, 1991).

The home environment may contribute in even less direct ways to literacy acquisition in school by learning opportunities provided in other situations that may stimulate development of general thinking and problem-solving skills, enhance world knowledge, and promote social-emotional attitudes favoring school learning (de Jong, Leseman, & van der Leij, 1997; de Ruiter & van IJzendoorn, 1993; McGillicuddy-DeLisi & Sigel, 1991; Sigel, Stinson, & Flaugherty, 1991). Besides literacy-related experiences and oral language exchanges, an important part of young children's life in the family concerns involvement in play, being present at all kinds of household routines in the sense of legitimate yet peripheral participation (Lave, 1988), helping the parents, becoming familiar with instances of craft, observing adults' problem solving, and eventually exploring particular domains of knowledge and skill themselves (Rogoff, 1990).

From this angle most of family life—not exclusively specific literacy-related events in a narrow sense, if there are any at all—can be seen as microsystems to learn informally and to prepare for school, by being present or actively participating under guidance. Although it is clear at the onset that not all possible learning experiences provided by young children's homes are equally relevant for school learning and prepare young children equally well for the demands of the formal curriculum, it is the intention of the present chapter to broaden the perspective on the kinds of preparation for literacy that children's homes potentially can provide.

EARLY LITERACY EDUCATIONAL PROGRAMS

Home literacy programs are typically carried out in target populations with often very different traditions regarding the use of written language than the mainstream middle class. Often, families are involved who are living in circumstances that are not conducive to home literacy. Even in industrialized countries with an accessible and extensive compulsory education system, large sections of the adult population can be considered to be functionally or semi-illiterate, both because of their low reading and writing profiency and because of the marginal role of literacy in daily life (Leseman, 1994). Part of this functional illiteracy among adults is attributable to recent immigration from poor developing countries. Many immigrants from countries (or regions within these countries) with a low schooling level, forming young families presently, came to the new country with underdeveloped reading and writing skills.

There are also adults in indigenous populations who can be characterized in a way as semi-illiterate. Although it is clear from nationwide assessment studies that full illiteracy (not being able to read and write simple texts at all) among indigenous populations is rare (Doets, 1992; Kirsch & Jungebluth, 1987; Leseman, 1994), putting literacy skills in practice—for instance, reading books for pleasure or writing to communicate with a distant audience—is not at the heart of daily (family) life, to say the least. The kind of *cultural* illiteracy intended here is rather strongly associated with low educational level and low literacy demands in the daily work (Leseman, 1994). Cultural practices in the wider community also influence an individual's literacy (Heath, 1983).

Here is a dilemma. Children growing up in these immigrant and lower class communities are at risk for educational failure and, for that reason, they often are the primary target groups of early educational interventions and home literacy programs. However, if we assume that the success of these interventions depends on building on the motivation and skill of the parents to work with their children, and on the enduring integration of the program content into family life, a narrow focus on promoting home literacy seems inappropriate.

These issues inspired a research project that we conducted during recent years in the Netherlands, concerning the relation of home literacy in a more narrow sense (e.g., joint storybook reading) with other everyday situations of informal education, such as conversational talk, joint play, and practical problem solving in household routines. Literacy situations in a narrow sense and the situations intended here probably have much in common, such as the use of language to establish, explain, coordinate, and evaluate complex activities. Common to all is also the social-emotional bond between parent and child, with similar implications for the development of particular social-emotional dispositions that may facilitate school learning. Questions arise as to the relative contributions of the different forms of informal education at home in preparing children for formal literacy education at school. How important is home literacy in a narrow sense? Are there perhaps other routes of preparation for literacy learning at school?

The second issue concerns the contextuality of home literacy and informal education. The home environment, seen as a social microsystem for young children to acquire all kinds of skills that are relevant for school learning and literacy acquisition in particular, cannot be separated from the surrounding social and cultural contexts constituted by parents' education, work, social networks, and cultural practices. For instance, low literacy levels among parents determine strongly opportunities for literacy-related interactions at home. Parents' literacy use at home depends on their educational background, present jobs, and cultural practices within their social networks (Heath, 1983; Leseman, 1994). Changing one or more facets of the home microsystem as part of an early intervention program risks being ineffective unless important context factors support the intervention. How supportive is the surrounding sociocultural context of families with children at risk of educational failure to home literacy and home educational processes in general?

THE DUTCH HOME AND SCHOOL LITERACY STUDY

In the remainder of this chapter we report and discuss findings from our Home and School Literacy Study that are pertinent to the issues raised here. In the study, the effects of several facets of informal education in the home environment, including literacy, on children's language development and on reading and math learning in school were assessed, controlling for previous developmental differences. The facets of home informal education were also related to the family's sociocultural context.

Sample

The study involved a cohort of 127 children of 4–7 years of age. The sample was socioeconomically and ethnic-culturally varied, consisting of four subsamples. The first subsample involved indigenous Dutch middle-class families. The second consisted of Dutch lower class families. The children of the latter families were, according to the national Educational Priority Policy, eligible for extra educational support measures. The other two subsamples were composed of immigrant families from Surinam and Turkey.

Surinam is a former Dutch colony in the Caribbean. There were roughly equal numbers of Creoles, having African roots, and Hindustani, having Asian roots, in the subsample. The Surinamese migrated to the Netherlands for better educational and economic opportunities, and also for political reasons after Surinam became an independent state.

The majority of the Turks in the Netherlands originated from poor regions of eastern Turkey, with traditional agricultural economies, low schooling, and high rates of illiteracy. Most of the Turkish parents in the present sample came to the Netherlands between their 6th and 18th birthdays, joining their fathers, who were hired for unskilled labor.

Most children in the Surinamese and all in the Turkish subsample were also eligible for support within the frame of the Educational Priority Policy.

The children attended 28 inner-city elementary schools, and the families were recruited via the schools. In the Netherlands, elementary school begins at the age of 4 years. The first 2 years encompass kindergarten. Formal instruction in reading, writing, and mathematics usually does not start before the third year, that is to say, first grade.

Procedures

Each family was visited three times by a female researcher of the same ethnic origin. During these visits, the primary caregiver of the child was interviewed, being always the mother in the present sample. In addition, video recordings were made of a book-reading and joint-play interaction.

For the book-reading interaction, a newly released picture book was brought along by the researcher. The book was of the genre of realistic narratives, with many pictures and with young children as protagonists. On the second and third occasion of measurement, new books, but in the same genre, were used. Turkish versions of the books were available. Parents were asked to read the book to the child in the way they were used to or, anyway, in the way they felt was appropriate.

For the play interaction, a categorization game was introduced that required the child to sort pictures, three at a time, according to their superordinate (e.g., fruits, tools). On the second and third occasion, the game was slightly changed to be more challenging. The parents were instructed to assist the child whenever they felt this to be appropriate.

The first visit of a family was scheduled around the time the child entered primary school. On the first measurement occasion, the children were aged on average 4.3 years. Home visits were repeated when the children were averagely about 5 and about 6 years of age.

At the beginning of kindergarten, tests were administered at school (see de Jong & van der Leij, 1997). At the end of Grade 1, one year after the last home visit, when the children were 7, children's vocabulary and achievements in reading and math were assessed, again at school.

Measurements

The measurements taken by means of interviews and observations at home concerned socioeconomic, cultural, and educational process characteristics involving literacy and play.

Socioeconomic Status. The socioeconomic status of the target child's family was computed as the mean of both parents' educational levels.

Symbolic Job Content. The symbolic (e.g., accounting and computer-related) and literate content of the parents' jobs was assessed with a questionnaire based on the work of Kohn and Schooler (1983). The mean score of both job content measures was computed to serve as indicator of the specific literacy input from the work context.

Parents' Literacy. Parents' literacy activities were measured using a list of different kinds of literacy use, for instance, reading literary novels, detective stories, newspaper front-page articles, feature articles, TV schedules, and so on. Parents were asked to indicate how frequently they were involved in the activity mentioned.

Home Language. Language use at home was considered a cultural characteristic also. Parents were asked to indicate which language was used in normally occurring situations such as mealtime conversations, family visits, and intimate personal conversations with the child. The questions were posed on all occasions, but because correlations between the measurements were very high, a single home language variable was computed as the mean of the three measurements.

Child-Rearing Beliefs. A translated version of Schaefer and Edgerton's (1985) Parental Modernity Scale was used to assess parents' ideas on a number of child-rearing issues, concerning, for instance, appropriate behavior (obedience, respect for authority), acceptable disciplining strategies, and the role of parents in child development. Confirmatory factor analysis indicated a one-dimensional structure that was similar to the original *modern-traditional* dimension found by Schaefer and Edgerton.

Opportunity for Literacy Interactions. In the interview, parents were asked how often a number of literacy-related activities normally occurred. Literacy activities were, for example, parents reading books or newspapers in the child's vicinity, reading storybooks to the child at bedtime or in the daytime, parents reading "environmental print" (e.g., advertising magazines) in the child's presence, and acknowledging spontaneous prereading (i.e., "as if" reading) and prewriting by the child.

Opportunity for Joint Play and Practical Problem Solving. In the same way parents were asked to rate the occurrence of play activities and everyday practical problem-solving activities. Play activities mentioned were playing with dolls and toy cars, completing a jigsaw puzzle, playing with construction materials, memory and thinking games, and painting and drawing. Situations of child and parent together being involved in practical problem solving mentioned were, for instance, sewing, cooking, and shopping, with the child participating.

Social-Emotional Quality of Book Reading and Game Playing. Social-emotional quality was assessed by observations of parent–child interactions during joint book reading and playing the categorization task. Rating scales developed by Erickson, Sroufe, and Egeland (1985) were used to evaluate the mother's behavior toward the child in both situations. The ratings on the scales were highly intercorrelated and, therefore, combined to one score referring to the degree in which mothers supported an emotionally positive experience during reading and playing, respectively.

Instruction Quality of Book Reading. To evaluate instruction level, a coding scheme was developed based on the distancing theory developed by Sigel and colleagues (Pellegrini, Galda, Jones, & Perlmutter, 1995; Sigel, Stinson, & Flaugherty, 1991; for further details see also Leseman & de Jong, 1998). Several categories of utterances by the mother were distinghuished, including nonverbal pointing to pictures. In order to construct an instruction quality index, a category denoted as *high distancing* was defined, comprising explanatory, evaluative, narrative-extending, and topical extending utterances. Instruction quality was defined as the proportion of higher distancing utterances out of all coded utterances.

Instruction Quality of the Categorization Task. To score the quality of the mother's instruction to the child regarding the categorization game, a coding scheme was developed that distinguished between task instruction at the start of the session (mother explaining the purpose and semantic–taxonomic principles of the task in advance), instructions and extensions during the game. Categorization on the basis of a semantic dimension or set of properties ("paradigmatic" categorization) was considered to be more distancing than perception-based and thematic (or "syntagmatic") categorization (Markman, 1989; for further details see also Leseman, 1994, 1997). Instruction quality was a combined measure of the score for the advance task instruction, and the proportions of semantic–taxonomic instruction and higher distancing extensions.

Cognitive Abilities. Vocabulary and nonverbal intelligence were tested a few months after the children entered school. At the end of Grade 1, receptive vocabulary was assessed once more. The vocabulary test had the same format as the Peabody Picture Vocabulary Test (PPVT); that is, the child has to choose from four alternatives the picture that best matches a given word. To measure nonverbal spatial intelligence, a block-design test was used that was part of a norm-referenced intelligence test for young children.

School Achievement at Age 7. By the end of first grade, when the children were aging about 7 years, norm-referenced tests were administered to assess reading achievement (decoding and reading comprehension) and math achievement. The tests were all widely used in the Netherlands (for more details on the tests, see de Jong & van der Leij, 1997). All tests were in Dutch.

RESULTS

The results are reported in three parts. The first part presents the stability over time of the home educational processes and the intercorrelations between the several facets of these processes. In the second part, descriptive

statistics are presented concerning the sociocultural context and characteristics of the informal educational processes in the four groups. The third
part reports the results of the correlational and multiple regression analyses that were performed.

Stability of Informal Education at Home

The home informal education processes were measured three times and
concerned the facets of opportunity, instruction quality, and social-emotional quality with regard to literacy and play interactions. The mean cross-
lag correlations obtained for each facet on the three occasions were .66 for
literacy opportunity, .52 for play opportunity, .53 for book-reading instruction quality, .46 for play instruction quality, .51 for book-reading social-
emotional quality, and .48 for play social-emotional quality. These correlations indicated a fairly stable home environment over time. To reduce the
number of variables in subsequent analyses, the measures for every facet
were combined into single indexes representing the mean of the scores obtained on the three measurement occasions.

The intercorrelations between the literacy and play facets are presented
in Table 4.1. There was a very strong correlation between the two social-
emotional quality measures. Strong correlations were also found between
opportunity for literacy and opportunity for play. There were moderate correlations between the instruction quality and social-emotional quality measures of book reading and play. Not displayed in Table 4.1 are the intercorrelations found between opportunity, instruction, and support within
each of the two situations. Instruction and support correlated at .62 ($p <$
.001) and .73 ($p < .000$) for book reading and play, respectively. The intercorrelations between the opportunity facets on the one hand and the instruction and social-emotional quality facets on the other hand were
smaller overall, between as well as within situations.

TABLE 4.1
Intercorrelations of Informal Home Education Facets
Between Two Situations (Literacy and Play)

	Correlation With Play		
Literacy	*Opportunity for Play*	*Instruction Quality of Play*	*Emotional Quality of Play*
Opportunity for literacy	.65**	.41**	.32**
Instruction quality of reading	.07	.50**	.51**
Emotional quality of reading	.18*	.66**	.74**

*$p < .10$. **$p < .01$.

The pattern of intercorrelations was interpreted as indicating sufficient distinctness of the opportunity, instruction, and social-emotional quality facets, and partial distinctness of the two interaction situations that were studied, the exception being social-emotional quality of mothers' behavior, which appeared to be a cross-situationally stable characteristic.

Differences Between the Four Groups

Table 4.2 lists the means and standard deviations of the social-cultural context characteristics of the family, the home education processes, the children's vocabulary and nonverbal intelligence at age 4 years, and their school achievement measures at age 7 years (end of first grade).

The family's socioeconomic status was based on both parents' level of formal schooling. This characteristic showed the expected differences between the four groups, rising to more than $1\frac{1}{2}$ standard deviations between the Dutch middle-class families and the Turkish families.

Related to the socioeconomic status was the symbolic job content measure. The kinds of jobs held by Dutch middle-class parents outranked the jobs of the other groups in the degree of literate and symbolic information-

TABLE 4.2
Means and Standard Deviations of Sociocultural Background Characteristics and
the Facets of Informal Home Education, With Amount of Predicted Variance η^2
Based on One-Way Analysis of Variance (ANOVA)

		Social Class and Ethnic Minority				
Family Characteristics	Max	Dutch Middle Class	Dutch Lower Class	Turkish Minority	Surinamese Minority	η^2
SES[a]		.61 (.80)	−.23 (.53)	−.61 (.92)	.12 (.76)	.26*
Symbolic job content	4	1.95 (.51)	1.29 (.62)	1.04 (.58)	1.48 (.63)	.29*
Parents' literacy	3	2.04 (.37)	1.90 (.35)	1.33 (.27)	1.76 (.27)	.39*
Home language	1	0.98 (.06)	0.99 (.02)	0.11 (.15)	0.87 (.18)	.91*
Child-rearing beliefs	5	2.95 (.31)	2.82 (.31)	1.66 (.31)	2.38 (.42)	.68*
Opportunity for literacy	7	3.77 (.66)	3.50 (.73)	2.62 (.73)	3.39 (.73)	.24*
Opportunity for play	7	3.80 (.80)	3.89 (.70)	3.41 (.60)	3.44 (.76)	.08*
Instruction quality of reading	10	3.84 (1.9)	3.57 (1.7)	1.50 (1.0)	2.02 (1.6)	.27*
Instruction quality of play	10	5.34 (1.5)	4.42 (1.5)	2.81 (1.4)	3.71 (1.9)	.25*
Emotional quality of reading	7	5.85 (.61)	5.66 (.44)	4.53 (1.0)	4.99 (1.0)	.30*
Emotional quality of play	7	5.94 (.61)	5.57 (.81)	4.57 (.82)	4.70 (.99)	.34*

Note. Max. is maximum score. For the Dutch middle-class children, $n = 35$; for the Dutch lower class children, $n = 41$; for the Surinamese children, $n = 27$; and for the Turkish children, $n = 24$.
[a]Z-scores. [b]Raw number, absolute value.
*$p < .01$.

processing demands. The jobs of the Turkish parents had the least symbolic content (the mean score is close to the minimum of 1).

The cultural characteristics of the family covered parents' literacy activities at home, the predominant home language, and parents' child-rearing beliefs. Literacy use at home for various purposes (information, recreation) differed clearly between the four groups. The highest level was found in the homes of the higher educated; the lowest level, as was expected, in the Turkish families.

Differences between the groups were especially strong regarding home language and parental beliefs. In these cases, Turkish and Surinamese parents as a group deviated remarkably from Dutch parents. In the Turkish homes, with only few exceptions, Turkish was the predominant language for conversation. In part of the Surinamese homes, Surinamese Creole or Surinamese Hindustan was used in some of the presented situations.

Considering child-rearing beliefs, Surinamese and Turkish were far more "traditional" than the Dutch parents, far more in favor of an authoritarian child-rearing style with great emphasis on traditional values like obedience, neatness, and respect for authorities, and more often used physical discipline techniques.

We also found important differences regarding the home environment as a system of informal learning processes, indicating that families prepare children differently for school learning. With respect to the opportunity facet, differences were large regarding literacy, but small and statistically not significant regarding play. Literacy opportunities in the Turkish and, to a lesser degree, Surinamese homes were relatively scarce. Between Dutch middle-class and Dutch working-class homes, differences in literacy opportunities were negligible.

On closer scrutiny, it appeared that of the list of presented literacy events, particularly those concerned with reading books either alone (with the child present) or to the child, and writing letters and postcards made the biggest difference between the groups, whereas interaction with environmental print and use of written language for instrumental purposes (e.g., writing a shopping list) did not significantly differ between the groups.

Regarding opportunities for play, the most pronounced differences concerned joint play with dolls, toys, and construction materials. According to the reports, this happened least in the Turkish homes and most in the Dutch working-class homes. However, with respect to other items, the score pattern was almost the reverse. Mother and child drawing and painting occurred relatively often in Turkish and Dutch working-class homes, and least often in Dutch middle-class families. The fact that Dutch middle-class mothers reported being less engaged in joint play activities with their children may be partly due to the fact that they spent more time working (Leseman, 1999).

Both measures of instruction quality regarding book reading and the categorization task, respectively, showed rather large differences between the groups. As to the share of higher level instruction in both joint book reading and the categorization game, the Turkish mothers occupied the lowest and the Dutch middle-class mothers the highest position. The most pronounced differences in joint book reading concerned the comparatively high proportion of procedural negotiation in the Turkish families, which was indicative of difficult interaction between mother and child in the group, of repeating word by word read sentences in both the Turkish and Surinamese groups (cf. Tabors & De Temple, 1996), and of narrative extensions and evaluations that were characteristic for joint book reading in the Dutch middle-class families.

Concerning play, the most pronounced difference between the four groups concerned the quality of the advance task instruction, which was highest (i.e., best matching the semantic–taxonomic structure of the task) in Dutch middle-class families and lowest in Turkish families. Furthermore, differences were found, although less pronounced, regarding the use of irrelevant instructions (comparatively high in Turkish and Surinamese families), thematic instructions (high in Dutch lower class families), semantic–taxonomic instructions and formal definitions (high in Dutch middle-class families), and mere labeling of the pictures (high in Turkish families).

The groups also differed very strongly on the social-emotional quality facet of the book reading interaction and joint categorization game. In both situations, the highest quality scores were obtained by the Dutch middle-class parents, with Dutch working-class parents about a half standard deviation lower, the Surinamese about 1, and the Turks even about $1\frac{1}{2}$ standard deviations below the mean of the Dutch middle-class families.

Developmental and school achievement measures also showed large differences between the four groups, with differences being largest with respect to Dutch vocabulary and smallest with respect to nonverbal intelligence and math, putting the Turkish children in the least favorable position in the verbal domain.

INFORMAL HOME EDUCATION AND SCHOOL ACHIEVEMENT

The correlations presented in Table 4.3 between background characteristics and home informal education measures showed that family background explained most of the differences in the six facets of home education. Ethnicity, indicated by two dummy variables representing whether the child is Surinamese, Turkish, or (implicitly) Dutch, and the socioeconomic and cultural background characteristics correlated strongly with the liter-

TABLE 4.3
Pearson Correlations of Family Background Characteristics, Including Ethnicity, With Facets of Informal Home Education

Predictors	Home Informal Education Facets					
	Opportunity for Literacy	Opportunity for Play	Instruction Quality of Reading	Instruction Quality of Play	Emotional Quality of Reading	Emotional Quality of Play
Surinamese	.01	-.12	-.25**	-.15*	-.18*	-.29**
Turkish	-.45**	-.16*	-.37**	-.39**	-.44**	-.34**
SES	.37**	.09	.35**	.46**	.49**	.43**
Symbolic job content	.40**	.14	.45**	.46**	.55**	.46**
Parents' literacy	.55**	.18**	.43**	.36**	.33**	.32**
Home language	.46**	.20**	.44**	.43**	.53**	.43**
Modern child-rearing beliefs	.47**	.20**	.43**	.51**	.51**	.50**

*p < .05. **p < .01.

acy opportunity measure, and with the instruction and social-emotional quality measures of literacy and play, respectively. The correlations with the opportunity for play, however, were much smaller (and neither showed strong differences between the four groups).

The home educational process measures were as such not influenced by the predominant home language. For instance, the observed mother–child interactions took place in the family's own language and were coded independently of the specific language code used. Therefore, the rather strong correlations of home language with all facets of the home informal education system were at least partly attributable to confounding with more general effects of being Turkish or Surinamese.

Table 4.4 presents the correlations found between the home informal education facets and the developmental and school achievement measures. In general, correlations were modest at best. The correlations with Dutch vocabulary were the strongest, which may be partly caused by confounding with the effects of the family's home language. Regarding reading achievement, both expected and unexpected patterns of associations were found. Opportunity for literacy, instruction quality of book reading, and social-emotional quality of book reading correlated statistically significantly but weakly with technical reading (word decoding), even less strongly with reading comprehension, and zero with math achievement.

In contrast, the instruction quality and social-emotional quality of play correlated more strongly overall with both language and nonverbal intelligence developmental level at age 4 years, and with technical reading, reading comprehension, and math at age 7 years, suggesting a nonspecific effect of these process characteristics in addition to specific effects of home literacy in a more narrow sense. However, the degree of opportunities for play and problem-solving interactions at home did not seem to matter very much.

To test whether home educational processes, as indicated by the six facets, in this sample really mattered for vocabulary acquisition, and for reading and math achievement in school at age 7 years, a series of multiple regression analyses was performed, controlling for previous cognitive development (vocabulary and nonverbal intelligence at age 4 years) and predominant home language. After including these variables as the first block of predictors in the regression equations, each home education facet was subsequently entered *separately* as the second predictor block to determine whether additional variance was predicted by this single facet.

The results are presented in Table 4.5. Home education facets did not predict statistically significant additional amounts of variance, R^2, in reading comprehension and math when controlling for early verbal and nonverbal cognitive development and home language, with the exception of a small effect of play instruction quality on math achievement. A statistically

TABLE 4.4

Pearson Correlations of the Informal Home Education Facets With Developmental Measures at Age 4 Years and School Achievement Measures at Age 7 Years

Predictors: Informal Education Facets	Cognitive-Verbal Development and School Achievement					
	Age 4 Vocabulary	Age 4 Nonverbal Intelligence	Age 7 Vocabulary	Age 7 Word Decoding	Age 7 Reading Comprehension	Age 7 Math
Opportunity for literacy	.42†	.20*	.30†	.35†	.29†	.06
Opportunity for play	.13	.05	.06	.19*	.04	-.02
Instruction quality of reading	.28†	.06	.43†	.24**	.04	.07
Instruction quality of play	.37†	.29†	.40†	.44†	.24†	.28†
Emotional quality of reading	.39†	.09	.47†	.24**	.10	.11
Emotional quality of play	.31†	.21**	.39†	.29†	.16	.22*

$*p < .10.$ $**p < .05.$ $†p < .01.$

TABLE 4.5
Additional Amounts of Variance Predicted, R^2, Controlling for Age 4 Years
Vocabulary, Age 4 Years Nonverbal Intelligence, and Home Language

| | | School Achievement Age 7 | | |
Predictors	Vocabulary Age 7	Word Decoding	Reading Comprehension	Mathematics
Opportunity for literacy	0.7	3.5**	0.8	0.0
Opportunity for play	0.2	1.7*	0.0	0.1
Instruction quality of reading	3.1**	2.4*	0.7	0.7
Instruction quality of play	0.6	6.7†	0.0	2.3*
Emotional quality of reading	1.9**	1.2	0.6	1.1
Emotional quality of play	1.5*	1.9*	0.1	1.7
All facets	4.4*	9.2*	1.1	2.5

$*p < .10.$ $**p < .05.$ $†p < .01.$

significant additional amount of variance, however, was predicted in age 7
vocabulary by the observed instruction quality of book reading, and by the
social-emotional quality of book-reading and play interactions (maximum
3.1% of the total amount of variance). The largest additional amounts of
variance that were predicted by home education processes (opportunity
for literacy, instruction quality of book reading, and instruction quality of
play) concerned children's technical reading (word decoding) achievement
(maximum 6.7%).

Entering all home facets simultaneously in the regression equation while
controlling for cognitive development at age 4 years and for home language
yielded statistically significant additional amounts of predicted variance of
9.2% in technical reading and 4.4% in vocabulary at age 7 years.

CONCLUSIONS AND DISCUSSION

In the introduction to this chapter we expressed doubts about the importance of home literacy in a more narrow sense for school achievement, including vocabulary development and literacy acquisition. These doubts
were based on two grounds. First, substantial empirical evidence of causal
effects of home literacy is lacking, because virtually all relevant studies
were correlational in nature, and thus inconclusive as to the cause–effect issue. Second, there is evidence from various sources that the development
of component skills of literacy not only profits from home literacy in a narrow sense, but can probably also be promoted by quite different informal
educational practices at home.

As to the first issue, the results of the current study were reassuring in
our opinion. The research set out to examine the presupposition that home

education facets really mattered for language development and early literacy acquisition. Applying multiple regression analysis in order to control for early vocabulary, nonverbal intelligence, and predominant home language, and to determine whether statistically significant additional variance in the outcome measure was predicted, can be seen as a conservative test of this hypothesis. This notwithstanding, the results confirmed the alleged role of home literacy, although the effects were small and limited to vocabulary and word decoding.

The fact that no effects were found for reading comprehension is probably attributable to the early stage of literacy acquisition of the present sample of children, who were tested at the end of first grade, after less than one year of reading instruction. Also, the kind of test used may not have been adequate to assess comprehension skill.

The fact that effects on math achievements were also negligible overall was not very surprising. Math achievement as measured in this study concerned knowledge of arithmetic facts (e.g., "one plus one makes two," "six minus two makes four"), that is, highly specific declarative knowledge, instead of more general procedural knowledge such as thinking and problem-solving skills. This specific factual knowledge is probably for the most part learned in school. As far as it is learned at home, this may happen incidentally (too incidentally to be detectable by the procedures of this study) or, contrarily, in deliberate instruction situations of a more formal character (e.g., parents and children working through arithmetic work sheets) instead of the more informal "play" and "literacy" situations studied here.

As to the second issue, the results of the current study supported the hypothesis of multiple routes to literacy. Besides home literacy in a narrow sense, such as joint book reading, other situations of everyday family life may also enter into the preparation of young children for school. In this study, only one additional type of situation was included, namely, goal-oriented play (e.g., problem solving) in a predominantly verbal-semantic domain. The results indicated that there were both specific (home literacy) and nonspecific (home play, or home play and home literacy) effects on literacy acquisition in school. The findings were in accordance with results from other studies like, for instance, the Home-School Language and Literacy study of Snow and Dickinson (Snow, 1991, 1999). Further support was found in a study involving Dutch and minority families with 3-year-old children, revealing effects of the quality of mothers' instruction in a situation of practical problem solving (e.g., blocks construction task) on language development (Leseman & Sijsling, 1996).

Furthermore, the bivariate correlations of the instruction and social-emotional quality measures of play interactions with word decoding and reading comprehension were stronger than the correlations of any of the home literacy facets. This further suggested that nonspecific effects may be more important overall.

Home literacy and informal home education in general were multifaceted processes that could be described by degree of exposure, particular instruction content, and particular affective experience. On the basis of the correlational and multiple regression analyses, it can be concluded that all facets may be important in enhancing language development and literacy achievement in school (cf. Bus & van IJzendoorn, 1995).

In the present study, the total amount of additionally predicted variance, controlling for early verbal and nonverbal cognitive development and home language, by all six facets together was always substantially larger than the amount of variance predicted by each of the facets separately (for similar results, see also Leseman & de Jong, 1998). Therefore, in designing educational programs that include home literacy, it is advisable to adopt a multifaceted approach and to focus on the opportunity as well as quality dimensions of home literacy and related educational processes (cf. Arnold & Whitehurst, 1994).

Home literacy and informal education at home in general were rather strongly related to the family's sociocultural context, as was indicated in the current study by the correlations found between home education processes and a number of socioeconomic and cultural background factors. The strong links between opportunity, instruction quality, and social-emotional quality of informal home education, on the one hand, and the parents' educational history, job content, literacy practice, and child-rearing beliefs, on the other hand, raise the question of whether a narrow focus on promoting literacy interactions with children is sufficient to bring about lasting effects. Attention should be paid to supporting changes in the wider sociocultural context of home literacy interactions as well. For example, combinations with adult literacy programs, adult basic education, and family support programs may be necessary to maintain effects in the long term (Darling & Paull, 1994; Delgado-Gaitan, 1995).

Another finding of the present study should be considered. The home informal education system, measured on three occasions separated by about one year, appeared to be a rather stable system. Between the first measurement occasion, at age 4 years, and the last, at age 6 years (in the home study), the differences between the families in educational processes did not change very much. The consequences may be twofold.

First, assuming that the home educational system was already operative in roughly the same way before age 4 years, affecting children's cognitive scores in interaction with genetic factors, a large part of the variance in development related to (that is to say, assumed to be caused by) the system was already accounted for in the age 4 years cognitive measures, therefore, technically speaking, leaving little additional variance to be explained. Although it is by no means certain that the system indeed affected cognitive development mainly in the period before age 4 years and only in a small degree thereafter, the present design and statistical analysis are not conclusive on this matter.

Second, it can be argued that there was almost no differential development between ages 4 to 7 years because of the stability of the home educational system. That is to say, almost all individual developmental curves were steadily rising (on different levels and with different slopes between individuals, to be sure, but) with little changes over time within the individual slopes that could have been caused by corresponding changes in the home environment. Nevertheless, the home educational system may still have been contributing importantly to the increasing mean level of the individual child's knowledge and skill by providing constant "nurture" to the developmental process—for instance, a vocabulary item to be learned, exciting literacy events to be experienced, models of problem-solving behavior to be followed, or emotional support, to be able to cope better with the demands of the school.

Correlational longitudinal studies are perhaps not very well suited to detect home education effects on steady developmental processes or to disentangle previous and actual effects when the system under consideration appears to be fairly stable over time. Seen from this angle, the small effects of home educational processes found in this study do count. However, quasi-experimental intervention studies, changing the home system fundamentally in one group while leaving it unaffected in an equivalent group, are needed for more conclusive results on the issue.

In conclusion, there are probably more routes of preparation for schooling than home literacy in a narrow sense. A narrow focus on home literacy, therefore, is perhaps not the best strategy to obtain more sizeable effects of early education programs. Extrapolating the present findings and related research results referred to in the introduction of this chapter, it seems likely that enhancing opportunity for and quality of play and problem-solving interactions, and of conversations, oral storytelling, and so forth, may contribute to preparing young children for acquiring literacy and learning other school subjects (e.g., math) as well.

It may be advisable to focus even more intensively on other preparatory routes to school literacy in the case of families and communities with low literacy levels, providing a sociocultural context that is not conducive to literacy. Other domains of educational activities, some of them perhaps better matched with the strengths of the parents than book reading, and activities aiming at the wider sociocultural context—in particular the parents themselves and their knowledge, skill, and attitudes—should be included as well. Finally, well-designed intervention studies, as recommended here, are needed to resolve the pending issue of effects of home socialization practices on literacy acquisition and school success.

REFERENCES

Arnold, D. S., & Whitehurst, G. J. (1994). Accelerating language development through picture book reading: A summary of dialogic reading and its effects. In D. K. Dickinson (Ed.), *Bridges to literacy: Children, families, and schools* (pp. 103–128). Cambridge, MA: Blackwell.

Beals, D. E., & Tabors, P. O. (1993, March 25). *Arboretum, Bureaucratic, and Carbohydrates: Preschoolers' exposure to rare vocabulary at home.* Paper presented at the Biennial Meeting of the Society for Research in Child Development. New Orleans, LA.

Beals, D. E., De Temple, J. M., & Dickinson, D. K. (1994). Talking and listening that support early literacy development of children from low-income families. In D. K. Dickinson (Ed.), *Bridges to literacy* (pp. 19–40). Cambridge, MA: Blackwell.

Bus, A. G., & van IJzendoorn, M. H. (1995). Mothers' reading to their 3-year-olds: The role of mother-child attachment security in becoming literate. *Reading Research Quarterly, 30*(4), 998–1015.

Bus, A. G., van IJzendoorn, M. H., & Pellegrini, A. D. (1995). Joint book reading makes for success in learning to read. A meta-analysis on intergenerational transmission of literacy. *Review of Educational Research, 65,* 1–21.

Darling, S., & Paull, S. (1994). Implications for family literacy programs. In D. K. Dickinson (Ed.), *Bridges to literacy* (pp. 273–284). Cambridge, MA: Blackwell.

de Jong, P. F., Leseman, P. P. M., & van der Leij, A. (1997). Affective quality of mother-child interaction as a predictor of children's school achievement: Evidence for a situation specific relationship. In W. Koops, J. B. Hoeksma, & D. C. van den Boom (Eds.), *Early mother-child interaction and attachment: Traditional and nontraditional approaches* (pp. 313–314). Amsterdam: Elsevier North Holland.

de Jong, P. F., & van der Leij, A. (1997). *Schoolcareers from 4–7: The relationships between cognitive development and the acquisition of reading and arithmetics.* Amsterdam: Department of Psychology and Pedagogics of the Free University.

Delgado-Gaitan, C. (1995). *Protean literacy. Extending the discourse on empowerment.* London: Falmer Press.

de Ruiter, C., & van IJzendoorn, M. H. (1993). Attachment and cognition: A review of literature. *International Journal of Educational Research, 19,* 5–20.

Dickinson, D. K., & Snow, C. E. (1987). Interrelationships among prereading and oral language skills in kindergartners from two social classes. *Early Childhood Research Quarterly, 2,* 1–25.

Doets, C. (1992). Functionele ongeletterdheid onder volwassen Nederlanders [Functional illiteracy among adults in the Netherlands]. *Pedagogische Studiën, 69*(5), 388–399.

Erickson, M. F., Sroufe, L. A., & Egeland, B. (1985). The relationship between quality of attachment and behavior problems in pre-school in a high-risk sample. In I. Bretherton & E. Waters (Eds.), *Growing points of attachment theory and research. Monographs of the Society for Research in Child Development, 50,* 147–166.

Goswami, U., & Bryant, P. (1990). *Phonological skills and learning to read.* Hillsdale, NJ: Lawrence Erlbaum Associates.

Heath, S. B. (1983). *Ways with words.* Cambridge: Cambridge University Press.

Hoff-Ginsberg, E. (1991). Mother-child conversation in different social classes and communicative settings. *Child Development, 62*(6), 782–796.

Kirsch, I. S., & Jungebluth, A. (1987). *Literacy: Profiles of America's young adults. National Assessment of Educational Progress.* Washington, DC: Educational Testing Service.

Kohn, M. L., & Schooler, C. (1983). *Work and personality: An inquiry into the impact of social stratification.* Norwood, NJ: Ablex.

Lave, J. (1988). *Cognition in practice.* New York: Cambridge University Press.

Leseman, P. (1994). Socio-cultural determinants of literacy development. In L. Verhoeven (Ed.), *Functional literacy: theoretical issues and educational implications* (pp. 163–184). Philadelphia: John Benjamins.

Leseman, P. P. M. (1997). *School careers from 4–7: Informal home education in Dutch, Surinamese, and Turkish families. Technical report.* Amsterdam: SCO Kohnstamm Institute.

Leseman, P. P. M. (1999). Home and school literacy in a multicultural society. In L. Eldering & P. P. M. Leseman (Eds.), *Effective early education: Cross-cultural perspectives* (pp. 163–190). New York: Falmer Press.

Leseman, P. P. M., & de Jong, P. F. (1998). Home literacy: Opportunity, instruction, cooperation, and social-emotional quality predicting early reading achievement. *Reading Research Quarterly, 33*(3), 294–318.

Leseman, P. P. M., & Sijsling, F. F. (1996). Cooperation and instruction in practical problem-solving: Differences in interaction styles of mother–child dyads as related to socioeconomic background and cognitive development. *Learning and Instruction, 6*(4), 307–323.

Leseman, P. P. M., & van den Boom, D. C. (1999). Effects of quantity and quality of home proximal processes on Dutch, Surinamese-Dutch, and Turkish-Dutch preschoolers' cognitive development. *Infant and Child Development, 8,* 19–38.

Markman, E. M. (1989). *Categorization and naming in children.* Cambridge, MA: MIT Press.

McGillicuddy-DeLisi, A. V., & Sigel, I. E. (1991). Family environments and children's representational thinking. In S. B. Silvern & B. A. Hutson (Eds.), *Advances in reading/language research* (vol. 5, pp. 63–90). Greenwich, CT: JAI.

Pellegrini, A. D., Galda, L., Jones, I., & Perlmutter, J. (1995). Joint reading between mothers and their Head Start children: Vocabulary development in two text formats. *Discourse Processes, 19,* 441–463.

Pontecorvo, C. (1994). Emergent literacy and education. In L. Verhoeven (Ed.), *Functional literacy: Theoretical issues and educational implications* (pp. 333–348). Philadelphia: John Benjamins.

Rogoff, B. (1990). *Apprenticeship in thinking. Cognitive development in social context.* New York: Oxford University Press.

Scarborough, H. S., & Dobrich, W. (1994). On the efficacy of reading to preschoolers. *Developmental Review, 14,* 245–302.

Scarr, S. (1997). Behavior-genetic and socialization theories of intelligence: Truce and reconciliation. In R. J. Sternberg & E. Grigorenko (Eds.), *Intelligence, heredity, and environment* (pp. 3–41). Cambridge: Cambridge University Press.

Schaefer, E. S., & Edgerton, M. (1985). Parent and child correlates of parental modernity. In I. E. Sigel (Ed.), *Parental belief systems: The psychological consequences for children* (pp. 287–318). Hillsdale, NJ: Lawrence Erlbaum Associates.

Sigel, I. E., Stinson, E. T., & Flaugherty, J. (1991). Socialization of representational competence in the family: The distancing paradigm. In L. Okagaki & R. J. Sternberg (Eds.), *Directors of development. Influences on the development of children's thinking* (pp. 121–144). Hillsdale, NJ: Lawrence Erlbaum Associates.

Snow, C. E. (1991). The theoretical basis for relationships between language and literacy development. *Journal of Research in Childhood Education, 6,* 1, 5–10.

Snow, C. E. (1993). Linguistic development as related to literacy. In L. Eldering & P. Leseman (Eds.), *Early intervention and culture* (pp. 133–147). Paris: UNESCO.

Snow, C. E. (1999). Facilitating language development promotes literacy learning. In L. Eldering & P. P. M. Leseman (Eds.), *Effective early education: Cross-cultural perspectives* (pp. 141–161). New York: Falmer Press.

Tabors, P. O., & De Temple, J. M. (1996, July 15). *"But ain't no nasty word": Mothers' use of recitation style in picture book reading.* Paper presented at the VIIth International Congress for the Study of Child Language, Istanbul, Turkey.

van Dijk, T. A., & Kintsch, W. (1983). *Strategies of discourse comprehension.* Orlando, FL: Academic Press.

Wells, G. (1985). *Language development in the pre-school years.* Cambridge: Cambridge University Press.

5

Television's Impact on Children's Leisure-Time Reading and Reading Skills

Tom H. A. van der Voort
University of Leiden

There is widespread concern about our reading culture today. In essays and lectures, in newspapers and journals, in policy papers and scholarly papers, the fear has been expressed that children are reading less and less or, put differently, that leisure-time reading is on the decline. A second concern is that children's reading skills are declining or, at least, leave much to be desired. In this chapter I examine whether television is to blame. Is television, in fact, contributing to the decline in reading? And does television harm the development of children's reading skills?

The first part of this chapter is devoted to the effect of television on children's reading behavior. Three questions are considered. The first is whether reading really is on the decline, a question that is answered in the affirmative. The second is whether television is in any way responsible for this decline in reading, and, again, I answer affirmatively. Finally, I ask the question of whether it really is an undesirable change when children turn to television for their leisure-time recreation, and watch television programs instead of reading books. Once again, I take the affirmative view.

The second part of this chapter is devoted to the question of whether television helps or harms the development of children's reading skills. A distinction is made between the effects of television on children's reading comprehension and television's impact on children's decoding skills. Although the evidence is not unequivocal, I argue that television is likely to have a small negative effect on children's reading comprehension. However, in small countries like the Netherlands, where foreign films are subtitled, watching television may also have a beneficial effect on children's reading performance. Specifically, there is evidence that watching subtitled foreign programs can further the development of children's decoding skills, that is, their ability to convert printed characters into words.

Most of the research into television's influence on children's leisure-time reading and reading performance has been done in non-European countries, especially in the United States. Although I refer to evidence obtained from international research, special attention is paid to Dutch research that has been carried out in this area.

TELEVISION AND LEISURE-TIME READING

The Decline of Reading

Is reading really on the decline? In the Dutch case, different opinions are expressed on this issue, depending on the indicator that is taken into consideration. Publishers in the Netherlands have little doubt that people are reading less and less because, between 1970 and 1990, they have been faced with falling book sales (van Ours, 1990). Dutch librarians, on the other hand, seem to have reason for optimism, because, over the same time period, they have witnessed an increase in membership and the number of books borrowed (van Ours, 1990). The percentages of regular readers, infrequent readers, and nonreaders in the general population also seem to give little reason for pessimism, as surveys indicate that these percentages have remained fairly stable during the last few decades (Schoonderwoerd & Knulst, 1982).

However, there is only one method that provides an unambiguous means of measuring changes over time in reading habits, namely, time-use diaries in which respondents report the time spent on all their leisure activities, reading included (van der Voort & Beentjes, 1992). Diary measures of reading are considerably more valid than figures for book sales or library borrowing, because these figures do not indicate whether the material that is bought or borrowed is actually read. A measure such as the percentage of regular readers also has to be accepted with reservation, as the percentage of regular readers can remain the same while the average number of books they read declines. Moreover, in responding to survey questions, people are likely to present themselves in a better light than is actually the case. This social desirability effect does not occur in time-use diaries in which children report the time spent on all their leisure activities, including reading, because the respondent remains ignorant of any special interest the researcher may have in reading activity.

An indication of changes in reading time since 1955 is given in a recently published study by Knulst and Kraaykamp (1996). In this study, results of Dutch time-use studies that were carried out in 1975, 1980, 1985, and 1990 were adjusted to be comparable with time-use data that were collected in 1955 and 1962 by the Dutch Central Bureau of Statistics (CBS, 1957, 1965). As shown in Fig. 5.1, the percentage of leisure time spent reading by Dutch 12- to 17-year-olds has been considerably reduced in the period between 1955 and 1990. In 1955, Dutch girls spent 20% of their free time on reading. Thirty-five years later, in 1990, they spent less than 10% of their free time on reading. The decline in reading was greater for boys. In 1955, boys spent more time reading than girls did. From 1962, however, boys read less than girls did, and the percentage of time spent reading fell back from about 22% in 1955 to only 6% in 1990.

Note that the decline in reading time was particularly sharp in the period between 1955 and 1962. In 1955, only 1 or 2% of Dutch households owned a television set, a percentage that had risen to 50% in 1962. This strong rise in television ownership leads one to suspect that the advent of television could have been responsible for the sharp decline in reading found in this time period. And as I show, television indeed was to blame. Also note that reading time showed a marked decline between 1980 and 1985, a period in which a strong expansion occurred in the amount of television broadcasting available to Dutch viewers, and in this time period broadcasting during

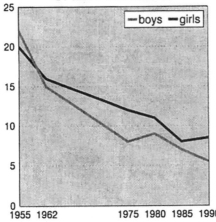

FIG. 5.1. Changes in the percentage of leisure time spent reading by Dutch 12- to 17-year-olds between 1955 and 1990. From W. Knulst and G. Kraaykamp (1996). *Leesgewoonten* [Reading habits]. Rijswijk/Den Haag: Sociaal en Cultureel Planbureau/SCP, the Netherlands.

afternoon hours was introduced. This expansion of broadcasting time also occurred at the cost of the amount of time spent reading.

Research on Television's Effects on Reading Time

Studies Conducted During the Introductory Stage of Television. Studies of the influence of television on children's leisure-time reading can be divided into three categories: (a) studies conducted during the introductory stage of television; (b) television-restriction and television-deprivation studies; and (c) correlational studies.

The quasi-experimental studies conducted during the introductory stage of television compared either the reading behavior of children with or without a television set at home or children's reading behavior before and after the introduction of television in the home. Two classic studies of the effect of the introduction of television on children's reading—a British study conducted by Himmelweit, Oppenheim, and Vince (1958), and an American study carried out by Schramm, Lyle, and Parker (1961)—suggested that the appearance of television caused a decline in the amount of time spent reading comic books, but left the time spent reading books unaffected. However, several studies that were conducted in non-English-speaking countries did find a television-induced decrease in book reading (e.g., Furu, 1962; Werner, 1971).

In studies that did not distinguish between books and comics (e.g., Murray & Kippax, 1978; Mutz, Roberts, & van Vuuren, 1993), television's introduction was associated with reductions in children's total reading time. A Dutch study (CBS, 1957, 1965) analyzed the amount of time the Dutch population spent reading in 1955, when only 1 or 2% of the households had a television set in the home, and the amount of time spent reading in 1962, when television ownership had risen to 50%. In 1955, when nearly no one owned a television set, reading was very common in the Netherlands, and the amount of time spent on leisure-time reading was about the same in all strata of society. Both younger and older people, and both people with little education and the more highly educated, spent about 20% of their leisure-time reading (CBS, 1957). In 1962, reading was at the same level—that is, for people who were not in the possession of a television set (CBS, 1965). However, among people who had a television set in the home, reading time was reduced almost by half, a finding that suggests that the advent of television was responsible for the observed decline of reading time.

The studies conducted during the introductory stage of television involved children (and adults) whose reading habits had already been established at the time of television's arrival (Beentjes & van der Voort, 1989; Signorielli, 1991). Therefore, it is questionable whether the findings from these studies may be generalized to generations of children who have grown up with television. McLuhan (1964) predicted that television would primarily reduce reading among generations who were brought up with television and among people with little education. As phrased by Knulst and Kalmijn (1988), who tested McLuhan's predictions, television will first affect reading among these two groups because they have not adequately learned to enjoy reading. People who have grown up with television may not learn to enjoy the pleasures of reading because, from an early age, they have had a simpler and more attractive source of amusement to fall back on (*socialization hypothesis*). People with little education may lack the capacity to derive enjoyment from reading (*competence hypothesis*).

Knulst and Kalmijn (1988) tested these two hypotheses by analyzing Dutch time-use data collected in 1980 and 1985. As a result of a marked expansion in the amount of television broadcasting available to Dutch viewers, television viewing time increased considerably in this 5-year period, which was coupled with a fall in the amount spent reading. Knulst and Kalmijn decided that this decrease in reading time was attributable to the increase in viewing time if two conditions had been met: (a) Subgroups within the total sample that showed the greatest increase in viewing time should also show the greatest decrease in reading time; and (b) the greatest decrease in reading time should occur during the times of the day in which the greatest increase in viewing occurred. This is precisely what the researchers found to be the case. The introduction of broadcasting during afternoon hours in particular appeared to occur at the cost of reading. In addition, McLuhan's (1964) predictions proved to hold true. The reductive effect of television on reading appeared to operate most strongly among the generations of people born after 1950. Among these "television generations," reading declined regardless of their educational attainment level, confirming the socialization hypothesis. Among the older Dutch population born before 1950, the reductive effect on reading was limited to the less educated, as the competence hypothesis predicted.

TV-Restriction and TV-Deprivation Studies. During the 1980s, TV-restriction and TV-deprivation studies also showed that television viewing has the effect of reducing reading. In two studies, parents reduced the amount of television their children watched by half (Gadberry, 1980; Wolfe, Mendes, & Factor, 1984). Both of the studies showed that the experimental restriction of viewing time was associated with a considerable increase in the amount of time spent reading.

Increased reading also has been found among people who were unable to watch television because their television set had been broken or stolen (Winick, 1988) and among people deprived of television viewing due to a national broadcast strike (Windahl, Höjerback, & Hedinsson, 1986).

In a Belgian TV-deprivation experiment (de Meyer, Hendriks, & Fauconnier, 1987), 20 families were deprived of their television sets during a period

BOOK READING TIME

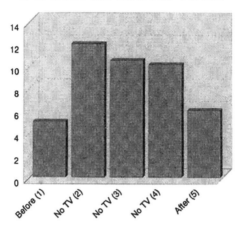

FIG. 5.2. Amount of leisure time (quarters per week) spent reading books be-fore, during, and after the three TV-deprivation weeks. Adapted from G. de Meyer, A. Hendriks, and G. de Fauconnier (1987). Een ontwenningskuur tegen televisieverslaving [Breaking TV addiction: An experimental panel study of television's impact upon everyday life]. *Vrijetijd en Samenleving, 5*(1), 51–73.

of 3 weeks, which reduced their viewing time to about nil. One week before the intervention began, children's leisure-time use was measured by means of time-use diaries. This measurement procedure was repeated during each of the three TV-deprivation weeks as well as during the week following the intervention. As shown in Fig. 5.2, the temporary abolition of television re-sulted in a strong increase in the time spent on reading books. In the 3 weeks during which the Belgian families had to make do without a televi-sion set in the home, reading time was doubled. However, when the televi-sion set returned in the home, reading time dropped back to about its origi-nal level.

Correlational Research. Most of the correlational research that has been done in this area was cross-sectional: that is, the correlation between children's amount of television viewing and reading was established using same-time data. The majority of cross-sectional correlational studies have reported a nonsignificant relation between television viewing and reading (Beentjes & van der Voort, 1989). Many have drawn the conclusion from these "null findings" that television does not impede reading (e.g., Schoonderwoerd & Knulst, 1982). This seems a hasty conclusion, however, because the cross-sectional correlational studies were subject to a number of methodological limitations (Beentjes & van der Voort, 1989; van der

Voort, 1991). First, the reliability and validity of the measures of viewing and reading were often questionable. Second, the studies only explored the relation between viewing and total reading time, without determining whether the relation differed for the time invested in different kind of reading material such as books, comics, magazines, and newspapers. Third, the studies only looked for linear relations. As shown by studies in a related field, namely, studies of television's relation to reading achievement, in cases where no linear relation is found, there may very well be a curvilinear relation (Beentjes & van der Voort, 1988; Neuman, 1988). Finally, the correlational studies failed to explore whether the television-reading relation was sensitive to background characteristics of the subjects.

Of course, the main problem with cross-sectional correlational research is that it does not support conclusions about causality, a problem that can be partially solved by using a panel design. To date, only three panel studies have explored the longitudinal influence of television viewing on children's reading behavior: one U.S. study (Morgan, 1980; Morgan & Gross, 1982), one study that was carried out in South Africa (Mutz et al., 1993), and a Dutch study (Koolstra & van der Voort, 1996). In each of these three studies, children were surveyed multiple times, at 1-year intervals. In the American study, students originally in Grades 6 to 9 were surveyed three times. A positive longitudinal correlation was found between viewing time in the first year and reading time in the third year, suggesting that television viewing may stimulate reading. In the South African study, children originally in Grade 5 estimated the time spent watching and reading eight times. Only one significant longitudinal relation was found between television viewing and reading, a positive relationship in the interval between the last 2 measurement years. On the basis of these findings, Mutz and colleagues concluded that the time spent reading was unaffected by television viewing.

However, the design of the American and the South African panel study suffered from methodological limitations that were similar to the limitations that van der Voort (1991) pointed out in relation to the cross-sectional studies. Among other things, the validity of the measures the two studies used to assess the amount of time spent television viewing and reading was less than optimal. Both television exposure and time spent reading were assessed with one-item, child-reported, direct time estimates, which have been shown to be less valid than diary and multi-item measures of television viewing and reading (van der Voort & Vooijs, 1990; Vooijs, van der Voort, & Beentjes, 1987). In addition, these two panel studies examined only the relationship between television viewing and children's total reading time, without making a distinction between different types of reading material. If this distinction is ignored, negative effects of television viewing on reading one type of material could be obscured by nonexistent or positive effects of television viewing on reading another type.

In the Dutch panel study (Koolstra & van der Voort, 1996), children who were in Grades 2 and 4 at the outset of the study were surveyed three times, at 1-year intervals. This study was designed not only to investigate whether television has a reductive effect on children's reading behavior, but also to test a number of hypotheses regarding the mechanisms underlying television's effects on children's reading. A distinction was made between the amount of time children spent reading books and comic books. Unlike the American and South African panel studies, the Dutch panel study did provide support for theories positing that television viewing exerts a reductive effect on children's leisure-time reading, and in particular on the frequency with which children read books. Although television's effect on comic-book reading was found to be negligible, children's book reading was affected. A significant negative longitudinal effect of television on book reading was found, both in the interval between year 1 and year 2, and in the interval between year 2 and year 3. Two causal mechanisms were found to be responsible for television's reductive effect on book reading. The first process by which television was found to interfere with children's book reading was by affecting children's attitude toward book reading. The study showed that television had an adverse influence on children's reading attitude, which in turn resulted in a reduction of children's willingness to read at home (see Fig. 5.3). The second process by which television viewing proved to interfere with children's book reading was by affecting children's

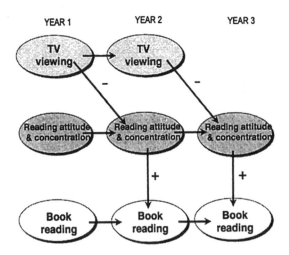

FIG. 5.3. Explanatory model for the reductive effect of television viewing on book reading. Adapted from C. M. Koolstra. (1993). *Television and children's reading: A three-year panel study* [unpublished doctoral dissertation]. Leiden: Center for Child and Media Studies, Leiden University.

ability to concentrate on reading. Television viewing appeared to lead to a decrease in children's ability to concentrate on reading, which in turn led to a decrease in book reading (see Fig. 5.3).

According to Koolstra and van der Voort (1996), one reason why a reduction effect of television was not observed in the previous panel studies (Morgan & Gross, 1982; Mutz et al., 1993) may be that the children participating in these studies were older than those involved in the Dutch study. Because at the outset of the two previous panel studies children were 11 to 12 years old, they probably already had established reading habits, which may reduce the likelihood of finding effects of television on reading. The 8- to 10-year-olds participating in the Dutch study, on the other hand, had just begun to develop reading habits, with the result that their reading habits were still susceptible to television's influence. A second reason why the previous panel studies did not find a reductive effect on reading may be that these studies did not make a distinction between time spent reading books and time devoted to other reading materials. As discussed previously, grouping different types of reading material into one measure may reduce the likelihood that reductive effects of television will be found. The findings from the Dutch study may serve to illustrate this point. If the estimates of reading books and comic books had been combined in this study, a significant reductive effect on reading might not have been detected, because television's effect on comic books reading was negligible.

Conclusion. In sum, there is evidence that the rise of television is at least partially responsible for the decline in reading that has been going on for a number of decades in the Netherlands. As predicted by McLuhan (1964), the decrease in reading is greatest among the television generations. Growing up with television means that at a very young age, before reading skills are acquired, television viewing becomes an established part of behavior, giving television a great advantage over the book. The book is also at a disadvantage among older people with little education who, compared to the higher educated, take less pleasure in books and therefore more readily exchange reading time for viewing time.

The Dutch panel study (Koolstra & van der Voort, 1996) suggested that one of the explanations for television's reductive effect on reading is that the medium may damage children's attitudes toward books. The authors referred to this explanation as the *reading-depreciation hypothesis*. They argued that the medium preferences children acquire at home may be responsible for the negative effect of television on reading attitude. As a result of years of pleasant experiences with television, children might come to regard the medium as an easy and attractive source of entertainment that provides more and more direct satisfaction than books, with the result that children's willingness to read books at home is reduced.

According to the Dutch panel study, a second causal mechanism that may be responsible for the reductive effect of television on book reading is that the medium may reduce children's ability to concentrate on reading (*concentration-deterioration hypothesis*), making children less able to read for extended periods of time. Television's reductive effect on children's ability to concentrate is usually ascribed to the fast pace and rapidly changing scenes in television programs, which leave little time for reflection on the information conveyed (e.g., Greenfield, 1984). In addition, television can serve as a model for a nonreflective, impulsive style of thought. In quiz shows and talk shows, the guests are not expected to give a question a second thought, but are assumed to produce an answer without delay.

However, television need not diminish children's reading in all cases. There is little doubt that, as a rule, the sale and borrowing from libraries of books discussed or directly recommended in television programs rises after their broadcast. A similar beneficial effect may result from the broadcasting of so-called TV tie-ins, that is, films and television series of which a book version exists. To date, however, it has only been shown that TV tie-ins, book review programs, and reading promotion programs can boost the reading of specific books (Beentjes & van der Voort, 1989). It does not necessarily follow, however, that television induces children to read more, for it is quite possible that the reading gain so attained is offset by a diminished interest in books that television did not bring to the child's attention. At any rate, the available evidence indicates that in the aggregate, television does not add to children's reading but has the effect of reducing it.

The Merits of Viewing and Reading

The next question is whether it is undesirable when children watch television films instead of reading a book. Cultural relativists argue that it is not; for them, reading and watching television permit mutual substitution. I dispute this position, but not because I consider television a less valuable medium than the book. Television and the printed word each have specific merits and limitations, and there is little evidence that the one is better than the other. I do think, however, that children's cognitive development is better served by a balanced "media mix," a pattern of media use that accommodates both television viewing and reading. When television takes the place of reading, one can only enjoy the fruits of one medium, whereas a more balanced mix provides opportunities to profit from the specific merits of each of the media used.

In the 1980s, a number of experimental comparisons of the distinctive strengths of television and books were made in the United States (for a review, see Beentjes & Walma van der Molen, 1997). These studies compared the processing of television stories watched by children and printed stories read to children (so-called "TV-audio research"). Researchers in the Center for Child and Media Studies at Leiden University investigated whether the medium-specific effects found in the TV-audio comparisons also occur for televised stories and printed stories that are read by children themselves (Beentjes & van der Voort, 1991a, 1991b; Walma van der Molen & van der Voort, 1997, 1998). These studies give support to McLuhan's notion that the medium is the message—that is, that the media create effects that have nothing to do with the specific message that is transmitted.

Both the American and the Dutch studies indicated that the visual support provided by the addition of moving images to the story results in better (long-term) retention of the story. The studies by Walma van der Molen and van der Voort (1997, 1998) suggest, however, that children's recall benefits not just from any form of television presentation, but especially from the extra memory codes offered by a television presentation that uses redundant pictures to complete the verbal message.

From a cognitive perspective, the merits of television lie in particular in the possibilities it offers for creating clear visual images, even when words are inadequate. The merit of books, on the other hand, lies in their positive effects on children's ability for oral and written expression. When retelling the story, children who have been confronted with a verbal story use more expressive language and refer in a clearer and more specific manner to both story characters (Beagles-Roos & Gat, 1983; Greenfield & Beagles-Roos, 1988) and other story elements, such as story locations (Beentjes & van der Voort, 1991a, 1991b). Children who have seen a televised story refer more vaguely to story characters and other story elements, perhaps because they still see these elements in their mind's eye and do not realize that the listener does not (Greenfield, 1984). A second reason why children who have seen a television story are less able to express themselves may be that when watching the story the television images divert their attention away from the verbal narrative.

In most of the media comparison experiments, the narratives in film and book were kept the same for the sake of comparison. By contrast, the nonexperimental films that are broadcast by television offer a very incomplete language model. The "text" is limited to dialogue, and visual images convey the rest of the story information. By comparison, the book offers a complete language model, conveying time, location, and actions as well as dialogue in words. Hence, when children are requested to retell the story, viewers are faced with a considerably more difficult task than readers are. For readers, it is easy to find the right words because they can use the verbal story as a model. The viewers, on the other hand, have a hard nut to crack because they have to put the television images into words. That may be the reason why a study of children's essays showed a clear relationship between writing style and television viewing time. The essays by heavy viewers were less well written, contained fewer words per sentence, and described more external and superficial elements than the essays of light viewers (Watkins, Cojuc, Mills, Kaitek, & Tan, 1981).

An additional advantage of the printed narrative is that children's creative imagination is stimulated. A number of media comparison experiments showed that printed stories are more likely to evoke novel, creative responses than television stories are (see Valkenburg & van der Voort, 1994, for a review). When making up endings and doing drawings of a televised story, children frequently use ideas that were already included in the story, whereas a printed story evokes story endings and drawings containing more novel outside-story elements. According to the *visualization hypothesis* (Valkenburg & van der Voort, 1994), television is less likely to stimulate children's creative imagination because the ready-made television images leave the viewer little room to create his or her own images. Children who have seen a television story may have difficulties dissociating themselves from the television images during creative thinking, and therefore may be less able to come up with novel ideas than children who have been exposed to a printed story.

TELEVISION AND READING SKILLS

Research on Television's Effects on Reading Skills

Studies Conducted During the Introductory Stage of Television. Concern about the effects of television viewing on the development of children's reading skills has led to a substantial body of research investigating whether television inhibits this process. There is some evidence from studies of the introduction of television that the medium may have a negative influence on the development of children's reading skills. Although two early studies showed no relationship between television's introduction and teacher-assigned reading grades (Greenstein, 1954; Himmelweit et al., 1958), later studies in which children's reading performance was assessed with more objective measures—standardized reading achievement tests—suggested that the arrival of television did hinder the development of children's reading performance (Corteen & Williams, 1986; Hornik, 1978).

Hornik (1978) examined the effects of television access, in particular the effects of recent acquisition of a television set, on the reading growth of junior high school students in El Salvador. Some of the families acquired a television set during the 2-year period studied, whereas others did not. Hornik found that the acquisition of a television set was associated with slowed development of reading skills. A Canadian study (Corteen & Williams, 1986) compared the development of reading skills of children from three towns,

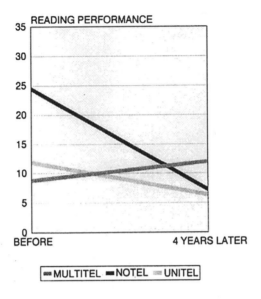

FIG. 5.4. Reading fluency scores for second grade boys in Notel, Unitel, and Multitel, both before and 4 years after Notel gained access to television. Adapted from R. S. Corteen and T. M. Williams. (1986). *The impact of television: A natural experiment in three communities.* New York: Academic Press.

one without television (Notel), one with only one television channel (Unitel), and one with multiple channels (Multitel). Although not all the findings were consistent with a negative effect of television, there were indications that the arrival of television in Notel hindered the development of children's reading skills (see Fig. 5.4). For example, before television had arrived in Notel, second-grade boys scored higher on a reading fluency test than boys in the other two towns who had grown up with television. After 4 years of television, however, the Notel children had lost their lead, and their reading scores were similar to those of children who had grown up with television.

Experimental Studies. To my knowledge, researchers have not conducted experiments that examined how the development of children's reading skills is affected by a temporary reduction in the amount of television watched by children. It is quite understandable that researchers have decided not to conduct television-restriction experiments. Theories that argue that television interferes with the development of children's reading skills do not posit an instantaneous effect, but rather predict a cumulative effect of years of viewing. Hence, to find an effect on reading skills, the television-restriction experiment should be continued for rather a long period, and it is unlikely that cooperation for such long-term deprivation of television can be obtained (Beentjes & van der Voort, 1988).

However, there is experimental evidence that television may interfere with performance on reading tasks that are carried out in combination with television viewing. The experiments in question investigated the *qualitative displacement hypothesis*, which argues that television may inhibit the child's growth in reading skills by displacing reading in a qualitative sense, which may occur when children use television as a background to reading tasks. In home study conditions, doing homework, including reading assignments, is often combined with television viewing (Beentjes, Koolstra, & van der Voort, 1996). As Armstrong and Greenberg (1990) suggested, children who habitually combine leisure reading and doing reading assignments with watching television are likely to be getting less benefit from these activities, which might impair the child's growth in reading skills.

Over the past several years, Armstrong and colleagues conducted a number of experiments examining how the use of television as a secondary activity affects students' concurrent performance on intellectual tasks (Armstrong, 1993, 1995; Armstrong, Boiarsky, & Mares, 1991; Armstrong & Greenberg, 1990). These experiments demonstrated that the use of background television may interfere with performance on difficult cognitive tasks, including reading tasks, which demand a lot of attention, probably because the combination of complex tasks with television exceeds human attentional capacity limits. The experiments have shown that background television may have adverse short-time effects on reading performance, but do not reveal whether combining reading with television viewing hinders the child's growth in reading skills in the long term. To my knowledge, no research has addressed this question. Armstrong and Greenberg (1990) suggested that for children who habitually combine intellectual tasks with television, the resultant distraction effects could easily translate into substantial cumulative effects on reading achievement.

Cross-Sectional Correlational Research. Most of the studies of the impact of television on children's reading skills documented only cross-sectional relations between television viewing and reading achievement. Numerous cross-sectional correlational studies have reported negative relationships between the amount of television children watch and reading achievement (Comstock & Paik, 1991). In a limited number of studies that involved elementary school children and children in the early grades of secondary school, the relationship between amount of viewing and reading skills was found to be curvilinear, with achievement rising with 1 or 2 hours of television viewing per day and then falling continuously as viewing increased (e.g., Neuman, 1988). However, the curvilinear pattern appeared to disappear with age; older adolescents tended to show monotonic linear negative associations (Beentjes & van der Voort, 1988; Comstock & Paik,

1991). At all stages of middle childhood and adolescence, however, those who watch a great deal of television tended to perform worse on reading achievement tests.

Some of the cross-sectional studies suggested that besides heavy viewers, two other subgroups of children are most vulnerable to an inhibitory effect of television on reading performance: socially advantaged children (e.g., Fetler, 1984) and intelligent children (Morgan & Gross, 1982). According to Fetler (1984), children highest in socioeconomic status and mental ability are most vulnerable to the inhibitory effects of television because they usually grow up in families that offer an intellectually and experientially rich environment. For these children in particular, television may displace activities that are cognitively more stimulating than television viewing.

A limited number of cross-sectional studies have suggested that the effect of television on children's reading performance is sensitive to the types of programs children watch. Negative relationships have been found for time spent watching light entertainment programs (e.g, Neuman, 1981), whereas a positive relationship has been reported for informational programs (Potter, 1987). A possible explanation for this pattern of findings is that children who frequently watch informational programs are more information oriented in their use of television than are children who often watch entertainment programs (Comstock & Paik, 1991). As a consequence, children who frequently watch informational programs may learn more from television, which may help them comprehend texts, especially those related to topics earlier seen on television.

The frequently reported inverse associations between amount of viewing and reading achievement do not necessarily imply that television actually impedes children's growth of reading skills. One test of the plausibility that television contributes causally is whether the inverse associations survive when controls are imposed for third variables. In most cases, the television–reading achievement relationship was unaffected by the use of socioeconomic status and gender as a control variable (Beentjes & van der Voort, 1988). On the other hand, when IQ was controlled, the overall association was often found to be reduced or even eliminated. However, with IQ controlled, a number of studies have found negative associations for specific subgroups of children (e.g., heavy viewers, and high-IQ children) or for specific types of television programs, in particular various types of light entertainment programs (Beentjes & van der Voort, 1988).

Panel Studies.   During the past decade, four longitudinal investigations have examined the relationship between amount of viewing and later reading achievement: two studies that were conducted in the United States (Gaddy, 1986; Ritchie, Price, & Roberts, 1987), one South African study (Gortmaker, Salter, Walker, & Dietz, 1990), and, more recently, a Dutch study (Koolstra, van der Voort, & van der Kamp, 1997). All four studies reported clear negative associations between television and reading achievement in the same-time data. When the data were examined longitudinally, however, the two American studies and the South African study did not report evidence that television viewing leads to lower reading achievement over time. However, as Morgan (1993) noted, the results of these three studies fail to demonstrate convincingly that television viewing has no effect on reading achievement. Problems and limitations with each of these three studies may have invalidated their conclusions. Perhaps the most serious limitation was that the instruments used to measure television exposure were less than optimal. All three of the panel studies used concise viewing measures, usually a single-indicator direct time estimate reported by children or their parents. Because reading performance is a relatively stable characteristic that changes little over time (Ritchie et al., 1987), the use of an insufficiently sensitive measure of television viewing may have been responsible for the absence of significant longitudinal effects of television viewing on the development of reading performance, especially because effects of television viewing on reading performance are generally assumed to be modest (e.g., Morgan, 1993).

The Dutch panel study (Koolstra et al., 1997), however, did find evidence of a negative longitudinal contribution of television to children's reading ability. In this study, children initially in Grades 2 and 4 were surveyed three times, at 1-year intervals. The study differed in five respects from the previous panel studies:

1. Although the previous panel studies focused on children's reading comprehension, the Dutch study also examined the longitudinal influence on children's decoding skills.
2. In addition to the influence of children's total amount of television on reading comprehension, the study examined whether children's reading comprehension is dependent on types of programs watched.
3. The study investigated whether television's longitudinal influence on reading comprehension is different for subgroups of children formed in terms of viewing time, socioeconomic status, and intelligence.
4. The study examined the validity of four types of hypotheses that provided alternative explanations for an inhibitory effect of television on children's reading comprehension.
5. The study examined whether watching subtitled foreign television programs may further the development of children's reading comprehension and decoding skills.

Results indicated that television had a small but significant negative longitudinal influence on children's reading comprehension, both from year 1 to year 2, and from year 2 to year 3. Television's negative effect on reading

comprehension was confined to entertainment programs, whereas a positive but statistically nonsignificant effect was found for watching informational programs. The longitudinal effects of television on reading comprehension were about equal in subgroups varying in SES and IQ, which
implied that television's inhibitory effect persisted after controlling for
these background variables.

Koolstra et al. (1997) concluded that television's inhibitory effect on
reading comprehension resulted partly from a television-induced reduction
in children's leisure-time reading (see Fig. 5.5). The study showed that over
time, television viewing resulted in a reduction of book reading (which is indicated by the negative longitudinal path between TV viewing in year 1 and
book reading in year 2, and that between TV viewing in year 2 and book
reading in year 3). In turn, this TV-induced reduction in book reading led to
a decrease in children's reading comprehension (which is indicated by the
positive same-time paths from book reading to reading comprehension
within year 2 and year 3). However, the hypothesis that television inhibits
children's growth in reading comprehension was only partially supported
because the effect of book reading and reading comprehension was not significant within year 3. As shown in Fig. 5.5, children's book reading was influenced not only by television viewing (and earlier reading habits), but
also by children's level of reading comprehension. Over time, children with
high scores on the reading comprehension test tended to read more books.

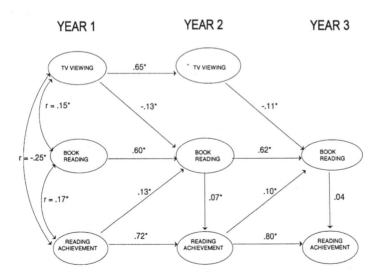

FIG. 5.5. Longitudinal test of the quantitative displacement hypothesis.
Adapted from C. M. Koolstra. (1993). *Television and children's reading: A three-
year panel study* [unpublished doctoral dissertation]. Leiden: Center for Child
and Media Studies, Leiden University.

A second causal mechanism that was found to underlie television's inhibitory effect on reading comprehension was a television-induced reduction in children's interest in reading. Over time, television had a negative longitudinal effect on children's attitude toward book reading, which, in turn, led to a decrease in book reading.

Finally, the Dutch study suggested that watching subtitled foreign television programs had a beneficial effect on children's reading ability. However, the facilitative effect of television viewing on children's reading ability was confined to children's decoding skills, and did not extend to reading comprehension.

Conclusion.   In sum, most of the cross-sectional correlational studies suggested that there is a negative association between television viewing and reading ability. For some subgroups of children the inverse relationship between the amount of viewing and reading ability was barely observable or even clearly absent. However, the most common finding was that as children's amount of television viewing increased, they tended to perform worse on reading achievement tests, an inverse relationship that usually survived when controls were imposed for possible third variables. Research designed to identify causal relationships—(quasi-)experimental research and longitudinal panel studies—did not always find a causal negative influence of television, but the most well-designed studies suggested that television does inhibit the growth of children's skills, in particular the development of reading comprehension.

The observed inhibitory effects of television on the development of children's reading skills are not very strong. For example, the negative longitudinal relations found in the Koolstra et al. (1997) panel study did not exceed a value of −.09. As Koolstra et al. noted, however, the effects found in their study could have been small only because both the predictor variable (television viewing) and the variable to be predicted (reading comprehension) showed high stability over time. Moreover, both the age range and the time period studied were limited. Because of these methodological limitations, the strength of television's effect on reading comprehension may have been underestimated. However, there is reason to believe that television's "real" inhibitory effect, irrespective of how it is assessed, cannot be but small. Because reading comprehension is for the most part taught and practiced at school, out-of-school media behavior can have only a minor influence on the development of children's reading skills.

There is evidence that three types of causal mechanisms may underlie an inhibitory effect of television on the growth of children's reading skills. First, television may exert a negative influence on children's reading performance through a quantitative displacement of other leisure-time activities. The *quantitative displacement hypothesis* argues that television inhibits the growth of children's reading skills by displacing time children would otherwise spend on leisure reading and other out-of-school activities that are thought to further reading skills. To date, there is only some evidence that television may slow reading growth by taking time that otherwise would have been spent on reading. However, television may inhibit the growth of reading skills not only via direct displacement of leisure reading, but also in a more indirect way, namely, by displacement of activities that are likely to further the child's general cognitive development. For example, there is evidence to suggest that television viewing may reduce the time spent on homework (Dorr, 1986). However, I know of no research that investigated whether a television-induced reduction in time spent on doing homework impairs the development of reading skills.

The second process by which television may hinder children's growth in reading skills is by displacing reading and homework in a qualitative sense, which may occur when these activities are carried out in combination with television viewing. The *qualitative displacement hypothesis* is supported by experimental research that showed that background television may interfere with the performance on difficult cognitive tasks, including reading tasks, which demand ample attention, probably because the combination of complex tasks with television viewing exceeds human attention capacity.

Finally, there is some evidence that lends support to the *reading-depreciation hypothesis* (Koolstra et al., 1997), which argues that television hinders children's acquisition of reading skills by damaging their attitude toward reading. A less favorable attitude toward reading may impede the growth of reading skills because children who have little interest in reading may tend to read books in a sloppy way, without attempting to understand each part of the text—for instance, by skipping words that are difficult to understand or by refraining from rereading passages that are only partly understood (Koolstra et al., 1997). An alternative explanation is that children who derive little pleasure from reading choose to read easy books that provide little practice in comprehending difficult texts (Neuman, 1991).

Note that all of these three explanations mentioned for an inhibitory effect of television on the development of children's reading comprehension are based on an underlying model of reading that assumes that practice is crucial to reading proficiency. According to the quantitative displacement hypothesis, a television-induced reduction in reading practice at home is fully responsible for television's inhibitory effect on children's growth in reading skills. The qualitative displacement hypothesis argues that children derive less profit from reading practice because it is combined with watching television. The reading-depreciation hypothesis also assumes that reading practice is crucial to reading proficience, because the television-induced impairment of children's attitude toward reading is supposed to result in less practice in comprehending difficult texts.

Although television viewing usually has been found to inhibit rather than facilitate the growth of children's reading skills, there are a number of exceptions to this rule. As shown by evaluation studies of programs like *Sesame Street* and *The Electric Company*, educational television programs can improve the reading skills of kindergartners and children in the early grades of the elementary school (Bryant, Alexander, & Brown, 1983). In addition, there is evidence that television programs may contribute to young viewers' vocabulary acquisition (Rice, Huston, Truglio, & Wright, 1990; Rice & Woodsmall, 1988). Neuman and Koskinen (1992) showed that watching captioned educational programs can promote students' acquisition of science vocabulary. Theoretically speaking, television may offer an intellectually and experientially rich environment to all children, because the multitude of channels from which children can choose provide a variety of informational and educational programs, including reading promotion programs and educational programs designed to improve young children's reading skills. In actual practice, however, most children prefer to watch light entertainment fare, a program genre that has been shown to impair the development of children's reading skills.

However, the multitude of entertainment programs children see on television can also be beneficial to the child's reading growth. In small countries like the Netherlands, Belgium, and the Scandinavian countries, children are exposed to a particularly large amount of on-screen texts, because almost all foreign-language television movies and series are subtitled, and thus television may provide ample opportunity for additional practice of reading skills. However, frequent reading has been found to further only children's decoding skills but not reading comprehension. It is easy to understand why the beneficial effect of watching subtitled foreign-language programs was confined to children's decoding skills. Subtitles are only short transcriptions of the dialogues in television programs and therefore provide no practice in comprehending normal coherent texts. However, reading subtitles that quickly vanish from the screen does provide an opportunity to practice decoding skills, and to improve both accuracy and speed of word recognition.

IMPLICATIONS FOR READING PROMOTION

The findings from research on television's influence on children's reading suggest four recommendations concerning how and when children's reading can be promoted (Koolstra & van der Voort, 1996). One way to stimulate children's reading might simply be to restrict the amount of time they spend watching television. This recommendation is inspired by findings from television-restriction and television-deprivation experiments in which parents were requested to reduce the amount of television watched by children by 50% or to nil. The finding that a temporary reduction of viewing time was associated with considerable increase in the amount of time spent reading suggests that children's willingness to read could increase significantly if parents remembered that television sets have an "off" as well as an "on" switch.

A reduction of the amount of television watched by children might also be beneficial to the development of children's reading skills. As mentioned previously, in some of the cross-sectional studies a small amount of television viewing was found to be associated with higher reading achievement scores among younger children (elementary schoolchildren and children in the early grades of secondary school) but not among older children, suggesting that a small amount of viewing could further the development of younger children's reading skills. The fact that a positive television-reading achievement was found only for younger children who watched a small amount of television may be explained from Gaddy's (1986) theory of diminishing challenge. According to this theory, television becomes less and less mentally challenging as children grow more mature. Gaddy speculates that as older students are scarcely cognitively stimulated by television, they can put their time to better use. For younger children, on the other hand, a selection of the programs watched can be cognitively stimulating, which would explain why for younger children a small amount of viewing might further the development of reading skills.

A second way in which parents might encourage children's reading is by helping them make more selective use of television. Although the available research evidence suggests that in the aggregate, children's reading decreases as a result of exposure to television, there are also indications that watching specific types of television programs may serve to promote the reading of specific books. Television can promote children's book reading by broadcasting movies or series of which a book version exists and through book review programs in which children learn about new publications. A more selective use of television could also have a beneficial effect on the development of children's reading skills. The panel study by Koolstra et al. (1997) showed that watching informational programs was related positively to the development of children's reading skills. In addition, there are indications that educational television programs that are specifically designed to improve children's reading skills (e.g., *Sesame Street* and *The Electric Company*) can improve the reading skills of kindergartners and children in the early grades of elementary school.

A third recommendation is that measures designed to promote children's reading should be focused on young children and their parents. Growing up with television means that at a very young age, before children start to talk, let alone read, television viewing becomes an established part of behavior, giving television a great advantage over the book, a lead that is hard to catch up when children are at the age where they are ready to read. Because from an early age children have had a more simple and more attractive source of amusement to fall back on, they may not learn to enjoy the pleasures of reading. Hence, it seems advisable to focus measures designed to promote reading on young children, the more so because recreational reading has been shown to be an activity for which fairly stable individual differences have emerged at the age of 8 years (Koolstra & van der Voort, 1996).

Finally, the finding that television may reduce children's book reading and inhibit the development of reading skills by damaging children's attitudes toward reading suggests that measures should be focused on promoting children's enjoyment of reading. In particular, as many experts on reading have suggested, schools should put less emphasis on reading to acquire information and leave more room for reading for fun.

REFERENCES

Armstrong, G. B. (1993). Cognitive interference from background television: Structural effects on verbal and spatial processing. *Communication Studies, 44,* 56–70.

Armstrong, G. B. (1995, May). *Experimental studies of the cognitive effects of the use of television as background to intellectual activities.* Paper presented to the International Communication Association at its 45th Annual Conference, Albuquerque, NM.

Armstrong, G. B., Boiarsky, G. A., & Mares, M. (1991). Background television and reading performance. *Communication Monographs, 58,* 235–253.

Armstrong, G. B., & Greenberg, B. S. (1990). Background television as an inhibitor of cognitive processing. *Human Communication Research, 16,* 355–386.

Beagles-Roos, J., & Gat, I. (1983). Specific impact of radio and television on children's story comprehension. *Journal of Educational Psychology, 75,* 128–137.

Beentjes, J. W. J., Koolstra, C. M., & van der Voort, T. H. A. (1996). Combining background media with doing homework: Incidence of background media use and perceived effects. *Communication Education, 45,* 59–72.

Beentjes, J. W. J., & van der Voort, T. H. A. (1988). Television's impact on children's reading skills: A review of research. *Reading Research Quarterly, 23,* 389–413.

Beentjes, J. W. J., & van der Voort, T. H. A. (1989). Television and young people's reading behaviour: A review of research. *European Journal of Communication, 4,* 51–77.

Beentjes, J. W. J., & van der Voort, T. H. A. (1991a). Children's written accounts of televised and printed stories. *Educational Technology Research and Development, 39*(3), 15–26.

Beentjes, J. W. J., & van der Voort, T. H. A. (1991b). Recall and language usage in retellings of televised and printed stories. *Poetics, Journal of Empirical Research on Literature, the Media and the Arts, 20,* 91–104.

Beentjes, J. W. J., & Walma van der Molen, J. H. (1997). The impact of television, radio, and print on children's recall and creative imagination: A review of media comparison research. *Trends in Communication, 2,* 31–47.

Bryant, J., Alexander, A. E., & Brown, D. (1983). Learning from educational television programs. In M. J. A. Howe (Ed.), *Learning from television, psychological and educational research* (pp. 1–30). London: Academic Press.

CBS. (1957). *Vrije-tijdsbesteding in Nederland: Avond- en weekendbesteding, winter 1955/'56* [Leisure time use in the Netherlands: Time use in the evening and on weekends, winter 1955/'56]. Zeist, the Netherlands: De Haan.

CBS. (1965). *Vrije-tijdsbesteding in Nederland: Avond- en weekendbesteding, herfst 1962* [Leisure time use in the Netherlands: Time use in the evening and on weekends, autumn 1962]. Zeist, the Netherlands: De Haan.

Comstock, G. A., & Paik, H. (1991). *Television and the American child.* San Diego, CA: Academic Press.

Corteen, R. S., & Williams, T. M. (1986). Television and reading skills. In T. M. Williams (Ed.), *The impact of television: A natural experiment in three communities* (pp. 39–86). New York: Academic Press.

de Meyer, G., Hendriks, A., & Fauconnier, G. (1987). Een ontwenningskuur tegen televisieverslaving: Een experimenteel panelonderzoek naar de impact van de televisie op het alledaagse leven [Breaking TV addiction: An experimental panel study of television's impact upon everyday life]. *Vrijetijd en Samenleving, 5,* 51–73.

Dorr, A. (1986). *Television and children: A special medium for a special audience.* Beverly Hills, CA: Sage.

Fetler, M. (1984). Television viewing and school achievement. *Journal of Communication, 34*(2), 104–118.

Furu, T. (1962). *Television and children's life: A before–after study.* Tokyo: Japan Broadcasting Corporation.

Gadberry, S. (1980). Effects of restricting first graders' TV viewing on leisure time use, IQ change, and cognitive style. *Journal of Applied Developmental Psychology, 1,* 45–57.

Gaddy, G. D. (1986). Television's impact on high school achievement. *Public Opinion Quarterly, 50,* 340–359.

Gortmaker, S. L., Salter, C. A., Walker, D. K., & Dietz, W. H. (1990). The impact of television viewing on mental aptitude and achievement: A longitudinal study. *Public Opinion Quarterly, 54,* 594–604.

Greenfield, P. M. (1984). *Mind and media: The effects of television, video games, and computers.* Cambridge, MA: Harvard University Press.

Greenfield, P. M., & Beagles-Roos, J. (1988). Radio vs. television: Their cognitive impact on children of different socioeconomic and ethnic groups. *Journal of Communication, 38*(2), 71–92.

Greenstein, J. (1954). Effects of television on elementary school grades. *Journal of Educational Research, 48,* 161–176.

Himmelweit, H. T., Oppenheim, A. N., & Vince, P. (1958). *Television and the child.* London: Oxford University Press.

Hornik, R. (1978). Television access and the slowing of cognitive growth. *American Educational Research Journal, 15,* 1–15.

Knulst, W. P., & Kalmijn, M. (1988). *Van woord naar beeld? Onderzoek naar de verschuivingen in tijdsbestedingen aan media in de periode 1975–1985* [From word to image? Research into shifts in time spent with media in the period 1975–1985]. Rijswijk, the Netherlands: Sociaal en Cultureel Planbureau.

Knulst, W. P., & Kraaykamp, G. (1996). *Leesgewoonten: Een halve eeuw onderzoek naar het lezen en zijn belagers* [Reading habits: Half a century of research on reading and its enemies]. Rijswijk, the Netherlands: Sociaal en Cultureel Planbureau.

Koolstra, C. M., & van der Voort, T. H. A. (1996). Longitudinal effects of television on children's leisure-time reading: A test of three explanatory models. *Human Communication Research, 23,* 4–35.

Koolstra, C. M., van der Voort, T. H. A., & van der Kamp, L. J. T. (1997). Television's impact on children's reading comprehension and decoding skills: A three-year panel study. *Reading Research Quarterly, 32,* 128–151.

McLuhan, M. (1964). *Understanding media: The extensions of man.* New York: Signet.

Morgan, M. (1980). Television and reading: Does more equal better? *Journal of Communication, 30*(1), 159–165.

Morgan, M. (1993). Television and school performance. *Adolescent Medicine: State of the Art Reviews, 4,* 607–622.

Morgan, M., & Gross, L. (1982). Television and educational achievement. In D. Pearl, L. Bouthilet, & J. Lazar (Eds.), *Television and behavior: Ten years of scientific progress and implications for the eighties: Vol. 2. Technical reviews* (pp. 78–90). Rockville, MD: National Institute of Mental Health.

Murray, J. P., & Kippax, S. (1978). Children's social behavior in three towns with differing television experience. *Journal of Communication, 28*(1), 19–29.

Mutz, D. C., Roberts, D. F., & van Vuuren, D. P. (1993). Reconsidering the displacement hypothesis: Television's influence on children's time use. *Communication Research, 20,* 51–75.

Neuman, S. B. (1981). *The effects of television on reading behavior.* Willimantic, CT: Eastern Connecticut State College. (ERIC Document Reproduction Service No. ED 205 941)

Neuman, S. B. (1988). The displacement effect: Assessing the relation between television viewing and reading performance. *Reading Research Quarterly, 23,* 414–440.

Neuman, S. B. (1991). *Literacy in the television age: The myth of the TV effect.* Norwood, NJ: Ablex.

Neuman, S. B., & Koskinen, P. (1992). Captioned television as comprehensible input: Effects of incidental word learning from context for language minority students. *Reading Research Quarterly, 27,* 95–106.

Potter, W. J. (1987). Does television viewing hinder academic achievement among adolescents? *Human Communication Research, 14,* 27–46.

Rice, M. L., Huston, A. C., Truglio, R., & Wright, J. (1990). Words from "Sesame Street": Learning vocabulary while viewing. *Developmental Psychology, 26,* 421–428.

Rice, M. L., & Woodsmall, L. (1988). Lessons from television: Children's word learning when viewing. *Child Development, 59,* 420–29.

Ritchie, D., Price, V., & Roberts, D. F. (1987). Television, reading and reading achievement: A reappraisal. *Communication Research, 14,* 292–315.

Schoonderwoerd, L. P. H., & Knulst, W. P. (1982). *Mediagebruik bij verruiming van het aanbod* [Media use when offering is extended]. 's-Gravenhage, the Netherlands: Staatsuitgeverij.

Schramm, W., Lyle, J., & Parker, E. B. (1961). *Television in the lives of our children.* Stanford, CA: Stanford University Press.

Signorielli, N. (1991). *Sourcebook on children and television.* New York: Greenwood.

Valkenburg, P. M., & van der Voort, T. H. A. (1994). Influence of TV on daydreaming and creative imagination: A review of research. *Psychological Bulletin, 116,* 316–339.

van der Voort, T. H. A. (1991). Television and the decline of reading. *Poetics, Journal of Empirical Research on Literature, the Media and the Arts, 20,* 73–89.

van der Voort, T. H. A., & Beentjes, J. W. J. (1992). De bruikbaarheid van indicatoren voor het vaststellen van historische trends in het lezen [The validity of indicators for assessing historical trends in reading]. *Massacommunicatie, 20,* 226–234.

van der Voort, T. H. A., & Vooijs, M. W. (1990). Validity of children's direct estimates of time spent television viewing. *Journal of Broadcasting & Electronic Media, 34,* 93–99.

van Ours, J. (1990). De Nederlandse boekenmarkt tussen stabiliteit en verandering [Dutch book trade between stability and change]. *Massacommunicatie, 18,* 22–35.

Vooijs, M. W., van der Voort, T. H. A., & Beentjes, J. W. J. (1987). De geschiktheid van verschillende typen vragen om de kijktijd en leestijd van kinderen te meten: Een validatieonderzoek [Validity of self-report measures of children's television viewing and reading time]. *Massacommunicatie, 15,* 65–80.

Walma van der Molen, J. H., & van der Voort, T. H. A. (1997). Children's recall of television and print news: A media comparison study. *Journal of Educational Psychology, 89,* 82–91.

Walma van der Molen, J. H., & van der Voort, T. H. A. (1998). Children's recall of the news: TV news stories compared to three print versions. *Educational Technology Research and Development, 46*, 39–52.

Watkins, B., Cojuc, J. R., Mills, S., Kaitek, K., & Tan, Z. (1981). *Children's use of TV and real life story structure and content as a a function of age, and prime-time television viewing* (First Annual Report to the Spencer Foundation). Ann Arbor, MI: Children's Media Project, University of Michigan.

Werner, A. (1971). Children and television in Norway. *Gazette, 16*, 133–151.

Windahl, S., Höjerback, I., & Hedinsson, E. (1986). Adolescents without television: A study in media deprivation. *Journal of Broadcasting and Electronic Media, 30*, 47–63.

Winick, C. (1988). The functions of television: Life without the big box. In S. Oskamp (Ed.), *Television as a social issue* (pp. 217–237). Beverly Hills, CA: Sage.

Wolfe, D., Mendes, M., & Factor, D. (1984). A parent-administered program to reduce children's television viewing. *Journal of Applied Behavior Analysis, 17*, 267–272.

PREVENTION AND INSTRUCTION PROGRAMS THAT PROMOTE LITERACY ENGAGEMENT

6

Prevention of Reading Difficulties

Ludo Verhoeven
Nijmegen University

Over the years there has been continuous evidence of literacy problems. Because of increasing societal demands, the literacy standards in industrialized societies have become higher. Although the breadth of distribution of literacy has been greatly enlarged during the past century, literacy has become more and more urgent for individuals. Rapid social and technological changes have sharply increased the literacy demands on the citizen during the past decades. Meanwhile, economic crises have resulted in increased demands on literacy levels (Mikulecki, 1990; Verhoeven, 1993). Even with compulsory primary education, many people do not reach a level of competence in literacy sufficient to cope with everyday demands. Literacy problems appear to occur among various groups in society, both indigenous and nonindigenous, urban and rural. Substantial differences in literacy performance have been found as a function of children's socioeconomic status and ethnicity. Literacy seems to be associated with unequal structures and poverty within societies throughout the world (e.g., Barton & Hamilton, 1990; Dave, Ouane, & Perera, 1988; Elley, chap. 11, this volume; Tanguiane, 1990). It turns out that there are large differences in the knowledge of, and the desire for, literacy among children entering school. In many cases, there is a mismatch between the linguistic abilities children bring to the classroom and the language and literacy curriculum at school.

Schools have not been very successful in helping slow readers catch up with their peers. The question is, how can education be restructured in such a way that children at risk become better readers and do not have to face years of failure? Poor children with insufficient access to high-quality literacy instruction must be given access to appropriate early literacy interventions. Such interventions would prevent these children from falling behind their peers and would accelerate their process of literacy development (Pikulski, 1992; Wasik & Slavin, 1993). There is reason to believe that social interaction can be seen as the motor of children's language and literacy development. The responsivity of parents and teachers turns out to play an important role in helping children gain insight into the functions and structure of both oral and written language. Scaffolding can be seen as a major conversational strategy. In the present chapter, the role of scaffolding in early language and literacy education for children at risk is further explored. Vygotsky's work on the mediation of human thought is taken as a starting point. With respect to a Vygotskian approach to development, it is claimed that cultural tools, such as language and literacy, are optimally learned in social interaction with others, and that in guided participation with skilled partners the child's repertoire can be gradually expanded.

In this chapter an attempt is made to provide evidence for this claim. I start out with a short introduction on scaffolded literacy instruction for children at risk. In addition, two empirical studies on the role of scaffolded instruction in early literacy education are discussed. Children with early successes in literacy are known to be more highly motivated. It is hypothesized that children's early literacy development can be enhanced by offering them challenging, motivating instruction programs. In the first study, I examined to what extent a transactional kindergarten curriculum based on storybook reading as a routinized activity had a beneficial effect on the language and literacy development of low socioeconomic status (SES) children. The role of small-group instruction in this program was also explored. In the second study, the effect of a literature-based one-to-one tutoring program for children with reading difficulties was examined.

SCAFFOLDED LITERACY INSTRUCTION

The study of how young children growing up in a print-oriented environment succeed in understanding the functional and structural configurations of reading and writing has been a lively area of research over the past several years (see Sulzby & Teale, 1991). Many researchers focusing on emergent literacy have attempted to show how children are making sense of the way literacy works in their culture. Detailed analyses of literacy environments highlight the importance of early encounters with print in the home (see Bus, chap. 2, this volume; Leseman & de Jong, chap. 4, this volume). Research has shown the crucial influence of the home and family on the development of language and literacy in children. Yet, although a considerable body of research has been conducted on the relevant precursors of literacy processes in middle-class populations of children, the study of early literacy acquisition in more disadvantaged settings has received only scant attention. Wells (1981, 1985, 1990) showed that a match between linguistic experience in children's home environments and the linguistic demands in the classroom is essential for academic progress. He found that the degree of experience with literate practices in the home had a positive influence on the understanding of the functions and mechanisms of literacy. Teale (1980) found four home factors to be crucial for children's early literacy development: the range of printed materials in the home (i.e., written language input), the accessibility of writing materials, the frequency of shared reading, and the responsivity of parents. Furthermore, Snow and Ninio (1986) showed that success in early literacy acquisition is related both to the values attached to literacy in the home and to the steps that parents take to explain this value to their children. In a longitudinal study by Snow, Barnes, Chandler, Goodman, and Hemphill (1991) on the literacy development of children from lower socioeconomic backgrounds, it was shown that different home factors predict various literacy skills. The most powerful predictors of children's literacy development were the literacy environment of the home, the mother's education, and the mother's expectations for the child.

With respect to schooling, an important general conclusion of the research has been that the attainment of literacy can be stimulated by offering children an environment where valid understandings about literacy can continue to emerge. In a supportive school environment, children have the opportunity to enhance the positive literacy experiences they have had prior to school. During the past decades there has been a marked shift in perspectives on language pedagogy (cf. Verhoeven, 1996). Traditionally, the focus was on direct teaching predetermined by a strict program that was controlled by the teacher. Within this transmission model of teaching, learning is seen as going from from simple to complex knowledge and from smaller to larger skills. In principle, the child is viewed as a grammarian and a lexicographer who has to extend his or her linguistic repertoire. Furthermore, there is a strong focus on the correctness of the learners' responses. The reproduction of predetermined responses is viewed as evidence of learning, whereas risk taking is discouraged. In recent years, the focus has moved toward children's competence and as creators of meaning within social contexts (see DeTemple & Snow, chap. 3, this volume). Within this transactional perspective, the emphasis is on learning how to ask the teacher for help, or how to engage in peer interaction. The ability to apply new knowledge and the ability to use strategies in a variety of contexts are seen as evidence of learning. Risk taking on the part of the child is viewed as an essential part of learning.

The transactional model of schooling is primarily based on Vygotsky's theory of learning through social interaction. In this theory of learning, it is assumed that individuals acquire knowledge and skills by participating in activities with more experienced members of the culture. For learning to be effective, the child's intellectual growth must be contingent on mastering language as a social means of thought. The basic premise of activity theory is that development takes place on the social level within the historical–cultural context. In a dialogue with an adult, the child has the opportunity to internalize the mental processes that occur on the social level. By means of social interaction, mental processes move from interpsychological functioning to intrapsychological functioning. According to Vygotsky (1934/ 1987), higher mental functions have a social origin. From his perspective, language can be defined as a sign system that can be used for symbolic activities, permitting intellectual accomplishments. Intellectual development demands the conscious realization of mental processes on the part of the child. The task of the adult can be seen as maximizing the growth of the intrapsychological functioning of the child. Vygotsky introduced the concept of a *zone of proximal development* as the distance between the actual developmental level of problem solving and the potential developmental level under the guidance of an adult.

With reference to a Vygotskian approach to development, the basic assumption is that the child learns in an individualized, active manner while being influenced by one or more environmental agents. By means of contingent social interaction, a system of reciprocal interaction is initiated to engage students in zones of proximal development. In order to support children's motivations toward literacy, it is important to focus on meaningful experiences, and to stimulate both critical thinking in reading and creative expression in writing. Although in many publications a language experience approach to literacy acquisition is promoted, it is generally accepted that a naturalistic model that relies exclusively on exposure and immersion does not always suffice for the complex task of learning to read and write (Cazden, 1992). Accumulated research evidence indicates that especially at-risk children need sequentially structured activities that are mediated either by a teacher or by skilled peers in order to acquire automaticity in (de)coding and appropriate strategies for reading and writing (Adams, 1989). Children in disadvantaged settings need more time to practice and experience relevant transactions than normal children (see Serpell, chap. 12, this volume). In order to compensate for greater difficulty in learning from experience, a more intensive set of experiences is required. Through experience with literacy tasks in guided participation with skilled partners, the child's repertoire of relevant strategies can be gradually expanded.

In the context of education, scaffolding can be seen as a major conversational strategy on the part of the teacher. Scaffolding relates to a conversational strategy in which the teacher and child build on and extend each other's statements and contributions. Through scaffolding, the teacher is able to motivate the child to work on a task, to define the number of task steps related to the child's abilities, to diagnose discrepancies between the child's production and the ideal solution, and to control for frustration and risk in finding task solutions. Teachers may scaffold children's comprehension by introducing unfamiliar words before storytelling, so that their attention to the story line can be maintained. Tharp and Gallimore (1988) elaborated the metaphor of scaffolding toward a theory of teaching as assisted performance. According to this theory, the child's performance can be assisted by the following means: modeling, contingency management, feedback, instruction, questioning, and cognitive structuring. Modeling refers to the imitation of the tutor's behavior by the child. Contingency management involves the use of rewards, such as praise and encouragement. By means of feedback, the teacher is able to correct the child's performance. Instruction helps the child to regulate his or her own learning. By means of questioning, the child can be invited to perform mental operations with the assistence of the teacher. Cognitive structuring implies the provision of a structure for acting out a given task. In Vygotskian terms, these six ways of assisting child performance constitute teaching within children's zone of proximal development.

LITERACY INTERVENTIONS FOR CHILDREN AT RISK

Scaffolded Literacy Instruction in Kindergarten

In a recent study (Van Kuijk & Verhoeven, 1996) the effects of a literacy intervention program for kindergarten children in the Netherlands were examined. In traditional Dutch kindergartens the focus is, aside from play and arts and crafts, on the transmission of oral language skills with only minimal attention to literacy. The experimental program can be characterized as a transactional approach to literacy instruction with a strong emphasis on natural language-stimulating activities, such as storybook reading, coconstruction of stories, and language games. In an open curriculum, the primary teacher strategy is a semantically contingent response—for example, relating the content of adult speech to the immediately preceding child speech. The child is given the initiative to start a topic and is given help to express ideas by means of repetitions, expansions, responses to questions, and confirmations of child assertions on the part of the teacher. Teachers working with this program received a collection of materials and followed an inservice training focused on scaffolding strategies, as mentioned be-

128   VERHOEVEN

fore. In this program, an optional small-group intervention was built in. In the small-group program, metalinguistic games were played by a trained teacher assistant with the aim of guiding the children to discover meaning and structural characteristics of language, including the phonological structure of language. The aim of the present study was, first of all, to determine the effects of the transactional approach of literacy instruction over the first and second year of kindergarten. In addition, the impact of the small-group intervention was investigated in the second year only.

A total of 141 4-year-old children participated in the study: 56 children were enrolled in the transactional program, 41 children in the combined transactional-small group program, and 44 children in a traditional kindergarten program as a control group. All children were from a low socioeconomic background. Children's ethnicity and cognitive capacity were kept constant over the three groups. At the beginning and at the end of their first year and at the end of their second year of kindergarten, a battery of tasks was administered, measuring narrative skills, word and phonological awareness skills, and early literacy skills: narrative skills (n = 20), book orientation (n = 24), rhyme (n = 10), word objectivation (n = 10), word segmentation (n = 10), phonemic segmentation (n = 20), syllabic synthesis (n = 20), phonemic synthesis (word blending, n = 20), reading conventions (n = 20), and knowledge of graphemes (n = 34). In the narrative task, children were asked to describe two series of events on the basis of pictures. The coherence of retellings were measured by counting the number of relevant idea units and inferences produced by the child (16 items). The book orientation task was based on Clay (1985). In this task, the children were asked about literacy conventions in a specifically designed booklet. In the rhyme task, the children were auditorily presented with a stimulus along with four pictures. They were then asked to select from the pictures the right rhyme word. In the word objectivation task children were asked questions about the relative length of word pairs, such as *cat–caterpillar*. In the syllabic synthesis task, children were asked to blend sequentially, auditorily presented syllables to a word. The phonemic segmentation task and the phonemic synthesis task consisted of two different series of 10 monosyllabic words. In the reading conventions task, children were asked to answer questions about the position of letters in words, and words in sentences. In the letter recognition task, children were asked to name individual letters of the Dutch alphabet, presented in a random order. All measures showed internal consistency: Cronbach's alpha proved higher than .86.

The effects of the two types of interventions were tested following a pretest–posttest design. In the study, we first examined to what extent a transactional approach based on storybook reading as a routinized activity had a beneficial effect on children's language and literacy development in comparison with a control group of children. We found that in all skills tested the children in the experimental classes did better than in the con-

TABLE 6.1
Effects for the Transactional Literacy Intervention

| | Transactional Group | | | | Control Group | | | | |
| | Pretest | | Posttest | | Pretest | | Posttest | | |
Test	Mean	SD	Mean	SD	Mean	SD	Mean	SD	p
Narrative skills	4.55	3.22	9.72	2.68	6.48	3.27	9.91	2.04	<.001
Rhyme	2.35	2.29	8.04	2.51	3.23	2.81	8.34	2.62	n.s.
Word objectivation	4.16	2.13	6.71	2.16	5.45	1.64	7.03	2.53	<.05
Word segmentation	2.89	2.45	6.37	2.31	3.21	3.03	4.97	2.15	<.01
Syllabic synthesis	11.41	6.96	16.86	5.58	13.04	6.11	16.37	5.42	<.05
Phonemic synthesis	2.21	2.59	7.31	5.17	1.96	2.15	6.48	5.37	n.s.
Phonemic segmentation	.43	1.14	2.72	4.39	.40	1.16	5.06	5.13	n.s.
Book orientation	4.87	3.26	12.63	3.96	4.74	2.80	12.47	3.43	n.s.
Reading conventions	5.98	4.06	13.45	4.07	5.42	5.00	13.56	5.20	n.s.
Letter knowledge	.53	1.08	5.52	6.65	.94	1.98	5.19	6.51	n.s.

trol classes. For narrative skills, word objectivation, word segmentation, and syllabic synthesis, the differences were significant (see Table 6.1).

In addition, the effect of a small-group transactional literacy intervention on children's language and literacy development was examined by contrasting the results of the children in the whole-class transactional approach with those of the children in the small-group transactional intervention. On three measures the children in the small-group approach did significantly better than the children in the whole-class approach. Table 6.2 shows that for syllabic synthesis, phonemic synthesis, and reading conventions, there is a significant time × program interaction.

TABLE 6.2
Effects for the Small-Group Transactional Literacy Intervention

| | Small-Group Intervention | | | | Whole-Class Intervention | | | | |
| | Pretest | | Posttest | | Pretest | | Posttest | | |
Test	Mean	SD	Mean	SD	Mean	SD	Mean	SD	p
Narrative skills	5.41	3.54	9.21	2.38	5.64	2.75	9.72	2.74	n.s.
Rhyme	4.35	3.36	8.11	2.68	3.15	2.52	7.98	2.49	n.s.
Word objectivation	5.86	2.54	7.71	2.14	5.23	1.96	6.79	2.19	n.s.
Word segmentation	3.64	2.16	5.16	2.03	4.75	2.30	6.35	2.31	n.s.
Syllabic synthesis	12.56	7.53	18.60	2.38	14.24	7.73	16.72	5.21	<.05
Phonemic synthesis	3.27	3.77	7.91	5.85	2.73	3.98	4.02	4.92	<.001
Phonemic. segmentation	.96	1.85	3.83	4.85	.95	2.99	2.67	4.45	n.s.
Book orientation	7.34	4.14	13.78	3.31	6.99	3.57	12.47	3.91	n.s.
Reading conventions	8.45	5.52	13.97	5.32	8.29	4.49	13.55	4.11	<.05
Letter knowledge	1.14	2.34	5.10	6.21	2.47	4.50	5.56	6.77	n.s.

From this study it can be concluded that the transactional approach had a positive effect on narrative skills, and on metalinguistic skills at the word level. The small-group literacy intervention yielded an additional positive effect on phonological awareness skills: syllabic and phonemic synthesis, and reading conventions.

Early Reading Intervention

In a second study (Verhoeven & van de Ven, 1997), we examined the effectiveness of an intervention procedure based on Success for All (Slavin, Madden, Karweit, Dolan, & Wasik, 1992) and Reading Recovery (Clay, 1991). Success for All is a schoolwide improvement program providing early literacy intervention through individual tutoring in the early grades. It has proved to be effective, especially in disadvantaged urban schools. Reading Recovery is a one-to-one tutoring program for low-achieving first graders that has had widespread effects in New Zealand (Clay, 1993), the United States (Pinell, Lyons, DeFord, Bryk, & Seltzer, 1994; Allen & Mason, 1989), and England (Wright, 1992).

After 6 weeks of a structured program of beginning reading instruction in the first grades of 54 different schools, 108 children with reading problems were selected. A randomly selected group of 52 of these children, assessed at risk as far as their reading progress is concerned, were brought into an intervention program for half an hour a day during a 6-week period. In the program the child worked together with a specially trained teacher who provided opportunities for ongoing conversation while the child was engaged in authentic reading and writing tasks. The basic notion of this program was to help at-risk children to learn at an accelerated pace, so that they could catch up with their peers and profit more from regular classroom instruction. The lesson framework for each session, based on Clay (1991, 1993), included the following steps:

1. Book selection and book orientation.
2. Reading and rereading of easy texts.
3. Analysis of child reading through the use of running record techniques.
4. Letter identification.
5. Writing a message or a story the child has composed.
6. Reading new and challenging texts with teacher support in preparation for regular classroom instruction.

The following pre - and posttests were administered: Letter Recognition ($n = 34$), Letter Production ($n = 34$), Phonemic Synthesis ($n = 20$) and Phonemic Segmentation ($n = 20$), Word Decoding Speed, and Text Reading. The

TABLE 6.3

Pre- and Posttest Scores of the Experimental and Control Group
on Tests for Word Decoding, Recognition and Production
of Letters, and Synthesis and Segmentation of Phonemes

| | Experimental Group | | | | Control Group | | | | |
| | Pretest | | Posttest | | Pretest | | Posttest | | |
Test	Mean	SD	Mean	SD	Mean	SD	Mean	SD	p
Letter Recognition	13.93	5.53	32.04	2.77	15.30	5.93	31.61	2.95	<.01
Letter Production	9.29	4.36	29.32	4.72	10.57	5.42	29.27	4.92	n.s.
Phonemic Synthesis	7.11	4.61	16.24	5.59	7.56	3.98	15.89	3.86	n.s.
Phonemic Segmentation	5.24	3.49	14.45	4.75	5.40	3.40	13.41	4.86	<.05
Book Orientation	14.41	3.04	18.83	2.59	14.70	3.28	18.06	2.99	n.s.
Word Decoding Speed	11.67	5.70	16.26	7.88	13.42	6.28	14.15	7.88	<.01
Text Reading	18.78	7.71	71.86	10.89	20.20	7.89	70.26	10.57	<.05

word decoding task required children to read isolated words for 1 minute. The results for the experimental group of children who followed the program and the the control group of children who did not are given in Table 6.3. It can be seen that substantial gains in scores were evidenced. For word decoding, text reading, letter recognition, and phonemic segmentation there was a significant time × program interaction, indicating that the children in the experimental group made better progress on these measures than their peers in the control group. Thus, it can be concluded that the program is effective in accelerating the initial reading skills of high-risk first graders.

CONCLUSIONS AND DISCUSSION

The empirical studies being reported on give evidence for a positive effect of the transactional approach to early literacy instruction on children's literacy development. As such, it is shown that a responsive pattern of social interaction helps children overcome the transition from the use of oral language in real contexts to the use of decontextualized content in written texts.

The first study examined to what extent a kindergarten curriculum based on storybook reading as a routinized activity had a beneficial effect on children's language and literacy development. We found that in all skills tested the children in the experimental classes did better than in the control classes. For narrative skills, word objectivation, word segmentation, and syllabic synthesis the differences were significant. If the option of small-group interaction is built into the transactional program, an additional effect is evidenced on both syllabic and phonemic synthesis, and on reading conventions. It seems evident that the more supportive the context, the more the child will gain positive experiences.

The second study was based on Marie Clay's ideas about reading recovery. Thirty first graders with early literacy problems were selected to participate in daily individual teaching sessions over 1 month. In these sessions, activities involved book selection, book orientation, story reading, story retelling, story writing, strategy training, and preparation for group teaching. The children significantly improved their skills on word decoding, text reading, letter recognition, and phonemic segmentation.

For both studies under consideration, it can be concluded that social interaction is the key to children's progress. The provision of opportunities for ongoing conversation while the child is engaged in authentic reading and writing tasks turns out to be an effective device in early language and literacy instruction. These findings can be explained in terms of a Vygotskian interpretation of learning and instruction. By collaborating in shared literacy tasks, the child is enabled to employ relevant skills with the assistance of an adult and to internalize these skills as well.

Studies of literacy education including those reported here should yield guidelines for teacher training. Early intervention programs focusing on authentic reading and written experiences make it clear that many children can be prevented from falling behind their peers in literacy skills. Low-achieving children not only need more time to engage in learning to read and write, but they also need supplemental high-quality instruction to accelerate their literacy development. Teachers should provide children with authentic reading and writing tasks in small-group settings, instead of repetitive practice of isolated skills.

In the context of teacher training programs, the social context of language should be emphasized, taking into account sociocultural aspects of development and the concerns of different communities and individuals. Schools should cultivate a climate that motivates children to explore the meaning of human experience through the language of literature. Literature has the power of enhancing the intrinsic motivation of students to read because of its appeal to their natural curiosity and aesthetic involvement. Such intrinsic motivations help children to activate their conceptual knowledge as well as their cognitive strategies. The instructional implication of this notion is that cognitive aspects of language and literacy should be taught by integrating literature into the curriculum. By using literature in the classroom, meaningful encounters with the most effective sources of human expression can be devised (see Cox & Zarrillo, 1993; Langer, chap. 9, this volume). It provides an in-depth study of universal values and needs, and it captures students' interests and challenges them to explore new avenues of meaning. A literature-based program offers a good opportunity to attune the curriculum to the linguistic and cultural diversity in the school by allowing children to respond to literature in ways that are consistent with their gender, social class, and ethnicity.

Given the different cultural backgrounds, distinct learning styles, and varying affective responses to language instruction, a crucial focus in teacher training should be the creation of a classroom atmosphere in which there are equal opportunities for all learners (see Gaffney & Anderson, 1991). As such, teachers must learn to be flexible in the instructional grouping of students. They must become able to decide for which tasks whole-group interactions versus small groupings are suited. They must also learn to be sensitive to the preferences of students to work alone, or with partners. In general, variety and diversity in grouping students should be reinforced in order to counteract the negative potential of grouping based on ability, gender, race, or achievement. Teachers must also practice strategies such as scaffolding and supporting an apprenticeship. Through these methods of interaction they learn to help children perform independently on increasingly complex operations. However, for students to be eager to accept challenges and risks in classroom interactions, it is important that teachers learn to create a basis of trust and mutual respect between teacher and student, as well as among students themselves.

REFERENCES

Adams, M. J. (1989). *Beginning to read: Learning and thinking about print.* Cambridge, MA: MIT Press.

Allen, V. G., & Mason, J. M. (1989). *Risk makers, risk takers, risk breakers: Reducing the risks for young literacy learners.* Portsmouth, NH: Heinemann.

Barton, D., & Hamilton, M. E. (1990). *Researching literacy in industrialised countries: Trends and prospects* (UIE Rep. No. 2). Hamburg: UNESCO Institute for Education.

Cazden, C. (1992). *Whole language plus: Essays on literacy in the United States and New Zealand.* New York: Teacher College Press

Clay, M. M. (1985). *The early detection of reading difficulties.* Portsmouth, NH: Heinemann.

Clay, M. M. (1991). *Becoming literate: The construction of inner control.* Portsmouth, NH: Heinemann.

Clay, M. (1993). *Reading Recovery. A guidebook for teachers in training.* Auckland: Heineman.

Cox, C., & Zarrillo, J. (1993). *Teaching reading with children's literature.* New York: MacMillan.

Dave, R., Ouane, A., & Perera, D. A. (1988). *Learning strategies for post-literacy and continuing education: A cross-national perspective.* Hamburg: UNESCO Institute of Education.

Gaffney, J. S., & Anderson, R. C. (1991). *Two-tiered scaffolding: Congruent processes of teaching and learning* (Tech. Rep. No. 523). Champaign, IL: Center for the Study or Reading.

Mikulecky, L. (1990). Literacy for what purpose? In R. L. Venezky, D. A. Wagner, & B. S. Ciliberti (Eds.), *Toward defining literacy* (pp. 24–34). Newark, DE: International Reading Association.

Pikulski, J. J. (1994). Preventing reading failure: A review of five effective programs. *Reading Teacher, 48,* 1.

Pinnell, G. S., Lyons, C. A., DeFord, D. E., Bryk, A. S., & Seltzer, M. (1994). Comparing models for the literacy education of high-risk first graders. *Reading Research Quarterly, 29*(1), 9–39.

Slavin, R. E., Madden, N. L., Karweit, N., Dolan, L., & Wasik, B. A. (1992). Research directions; Success for All: Ending reading failure from the beginning. *Language Arts, 68,* 404–409.

Snow, C. E. (1983). Literacy and language: Relationships during the preschool years. *Harvard Educational Review, 53,* 165–189.

Snow, C. E., & Ninio, A. (1986). The contracts of literacy: What children learn from learning to read books. In W. H. Teale & E. Sulzby (Eds.), *Emergent literacy: Writing and reading* (pp. 116–137). Norwood, NJ: Ablex.

Snow, C. E., Barnes, W., Chandler, J., Goodman, I., & Hemphill, L. (1991). *Unfulfilled expectations: Home and school influences on literacy.* Boston: Harvard University Press.

Sulzby, E., & Teale, W. H. (1991). Emergent literacy. In R. Barr & D. Pearson (Eds.), *Handbook of reading research* (pp. 727–757). New York: Longman.

Tanguiane, S. (1990). *World literacy: Issues and trends.* Geneva: IBE.

Teale, W. H. (1980). *Early reading: An annotated bibliography.* Newark, DE: International Reading Association.

Tharp, R., & Gallimore, R. (1988). *Rousing minds to life: Teaching, learning and schooling in social context.* New York: Cambridge University Press.

van Kuijk, J., & Verhoeven, L. (1996). Stimulering van geletterdheid bij kleuters. *Tijdschrift voor Onderwijsresearch 21*(1), 33–53.

Verhoeven, L. (1993). Demographics of literacy. In H. Günther & O. Ludwig (Eds.), *Writing and its use* (pp. 767–778). Berlin: Mouton/DeGruyter.

Verhoeven, L. (1996). Language in education. In F. Coulmas (Ed.), *Handbook of sociolinguistics* (pp. 389–404). London: Basil Blackwell.

Verhoeven, L., & van de Ven, H. (1997). Vroegtijdige interventie van leesproblemen met nadruk op metacognitie en leesmotivatie. *Tijdschrift voor Orthopedagogiek 36,* 118–130.

Vygotzky, L. S. (1987). *Thought and language.* Cambridge: Cambridge University Press. [Original work published 1934].

Wasik, B., & Slavin, R. (1993). Preventing early reading failure with one-to-one tutoring: A review of five programs. *Reading Research Quarterly, 28*(2), 179–200.

Wells, G. (1981). *Learning through interaction.* Cambridge: Cambridge University Press.

Wells, G. (1985). *Language development in the preschool years.* Cambridge: Cambridge University Press.

Wells, G. (1990). Talk about text: Where literacy is learned and taught. *Curriculum Inquiry, 20*(4), 369–405.

Wright, A. (1992). Evaluation of the first British Reading Recovery programme. *British Educational Research Journal, 18,* 351–368.

7

Development of Reading Attitudes

Michael C. McKenna
Georgia Southern University

Reading educators, so often divided on matters of methodology, are undeniably unified on the need to foster in their students positive attitudes toward reading. Perhaps this unanimity arises from the fact that attitude remains a concept about which relatively little is understood. It has an everyday meaning, to be sure, and it is on the basis of this meaning that educators ground their endorsement, but as a psychological construct, attitude has a history that is murky and a bit perplexing. My own belief is that attitude is nonetheless a concept vital to any effort to systematically foster engaged readers. The purpose of this chapter is to offer an overview of current theories of attitude formation, to present a summary of research into reading attitudes, and to suggest what these theories tell us about effective instructional practice and related educational policies.

THE NATURE OF ATTITUDES

Problems of Definition and Measurement

The study of attitudes has thrived during most of the 20th century. The subjective nature of the concept led naturally to a variety of definitions, compelling psychologists to come to grips with the range of conceptualizations each time they addressed the topic. As Rokeach (1968) observed, "A favorite way to proceed in defining an attitude is to first present a dozen or two definitions from the literature and then, after commenting on their common elements, present one's own with the hope that it is a distillation of the essence of these other definitions" (p. 111). Such a practice has, of course, only contributed to the proliferation of definitions. Eiser (1994) pointed out that some theorists have consequently come to view attitude as "an umbrella term for a variety of processes that ought strictly to be distinguished" (p. 1). Examples of notable definitions do, however, give the impression that there is more communality than disparity across them and that a good working consensus exists as to the fundamental nature of attitudes:

- *A mental and neural state of readiness, organized through experience, exerting a directive or dynamic influence upon the individual's response to all objects and situations with which it is related* (Allport, 1935, p. 810, original emphasis).
- Primarily a way of being "set" toward or against certain things (Murphy, Murphy, & Newcomb, 1937, p. 889).
- A relatively stable affective response to an object (Rosenberg, 1956, p. 367).
- A relatively enduring organization of beliefs around an object or situation predisposing one to respond in some preferential manner (Rokeach, 1968, p. 112).
- *A learned predisposition to respond in a consistently favorable or unfavorable manner with respect to a given object* (Fishbein & Ajzen, 1975, p. 6, original emphasis).

To these we might add a reading-specific definition proposed by Alexander and Filler (1976) and clearly reflective of the general definitions:

- A system of feelings related to reading which causes the learner to approach or avoid a reading situation (p. 1).

From these definitions we can conclude that attitudes are often viewed as affective in nature (but that they have cognitive components as well), that they are precursors of behavior (although they may not always be translated into behavior), and that they are acquired on the basis of experience. We can also infer that attitudes are seen to vary along a continuum from positive to negative, a notion used in the measurement of attitudes since the pioneering work of Thurstone (1928) and frequently applied to the measurement of reading attitudes (e.g., Estes, 1971; McKenna & Kear, 1990). But measurement is hampered by the complexity of attitude structures. It is now customary to think of attitudinal hierarchies, in which the objects of attitudes range from general to specific (Rajecki, 1990). This scheme provides a vertical dimension to attitude structures. One may, for example, harbor a positive general attitude toward reading, a less positive attitude toward science fiction, and a distinctly negative attitude toward a particular science fiction writer. Reading attitudes also exist in relation to the attitudes we have toward potentially competing activities. These relationships can be thought of as horizontal. A decision to read will always be the product of one's attitude toward reading but also of one's attitude toward alternative actions. In addition, the decision will be made on the basis of contingencies, such as the availability of books and the ability to read them.

These complications make it problematic to judge attitudes on the basis of student behavior alone. We might propose a simple experiment to test the extent to which an individual's reading attitude is positive. Imagine that a child has been left alone in a room and asked to wait there. In the room are only a comfortable chair, a book, and a handheld, portable video game. Surely this arrangement would test the relative attitudes the child harbors toward these two kinds of diversions. But the difficulty inherent in this design is that it presupposes a single, unified attitude toward reading and another single, unified attitude toward video games. It is likely that the child's response might depend on *which* book and on *which* video game had been made available by the experimenter. Even the child with an extraordinarily negative attitude toward reading in general might under certain circumstances turn first to the book. Consider, for example, a situation in which the book was a manual telling how to play the video game. But let us suppose that the book and game are not linked in a way that begs the question. Assume instead that what the child finds is a book of science fiction short stories by the same author and an action-packed martial arts video game. Although the child possesses general attitudes toward reading and toward video games, these attitudes are at the top of hierarchies comprising more specfic attitudes. The latter will be more instrumental in leading first to intentions and finally to a choice of actions. Figure 7.1 depicts how the two hierarchies might interact as the child is confronted with the experimental situation.

All this is not to say that the measurement of attitudes is impossible or even unduly problematic. However, the complexities associated with the construct require a degree of care and caution in the interpretation of attitude data, a situation that is really no different from that of achievement data.

The Role of Beliefs in Attitude Change

Contemporary attitude theories acknowledge the central role played by an individual's belief structures. Whether we incorporate beliefs into the formal definition of attitude, as Rokeach did (described earlier), or describe them as factors related to attitude, as other theorists have done (e.g., Ajzen,

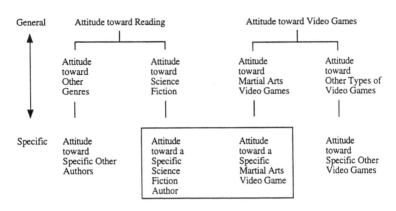

FIG. 7.1. Partial representation of a reading attitude hierarchy in relation to a second hierarchy. Boxed portion represents the attitudes of critical importance to the scenario described.

1989; Ajzen & Fishbein, 1980; Fishbein & Ajzen, 1975; Liska, 1984), seems of little real importance. What is critical is the need to understand how beliefs originate and how they can be targeted as a means of changing children's attitudes.

One view of beliefs is that they have a cognitive origin—that is, that they result from the reasoned consideration of our experiences. Fishbein and Ajzen (1975) categorized such beliefs as descriptive, inferential, and informational. Descriptive beliefs are those that derive from personal observation and experience (e.g., "This book is interesting"). Inferential beliefs entail logical conclusions reached on the basis of existing beliefs ("Because this book is interesting, others may be"). Informational beliefs come from outside sources regarded by the individual as significant ("My friends say books can be interesting").

A useful realization (by no means new) about the origin of beliefs is that they are not always based on reasoned consideration of available facts. In the 17th century, Pascal (1658/1954) attributed beliefs to two sources: the understanding and the will. The latter source leads to beliefs that may be attractive in some respects but that will not bear scrutiny. Broudon (1990/1994) extended this notion by describing three models of belief formation, only the first of which is based on reasoned evaluation of objective evidence. The other two have a more subjective origin. Of these, one describes the formation of beliefs on the basis of passion or emotion, and the other on the basis of cultural traditions of thought and judgment, such as the belief of primitive cultures in magic. Beliefs that originate through these two models may lead the individual to produce "reasons" in defense of them, but such reasoning is frequently incomplete and illusory and is more akin to rationalization and self-deception than to discursive, logical thought. When beliefs have an emotional as opposed to a logical origin, attempts to alter them by introducing the individual to new facts and arguments frequently fail. To tell a child who has experienced difficulties learning to read and who consequently harbors a negative attitude that reading can be fun and useful is generally futile.

In addition to the origins of beliefs, useful types of beliefs have been proposed. Fishbein and Ajzen described two principal kinds: those concerning the object itself (in our case, reading) and those of a normative nature (such as how one's friends view reading). This distinction was especially useful in my own adaptation of their general model of attitude formation to the specific case of reading (McKenna, 1994). My model identifies three principal factors in the acquisition of attitudes toward reading: (a) the direct impact of episodes of reading, (b) beliefs about the outcomes of reading, and (c) beliefs about cultural norms concerning reading (conditioned by one's desire to conform to those norms). The causal relationship between beliefs and attitudes led Fishbein and Ajzen to view the process of introducing new beliefs and challenging old ones as an important avenue for shaping attitudes in any context. This same prospect is true for reading. If we are to be successful in changing children's attitudes toward reading, we must target the factors that affect those attitudes.

The McKenna model of reading attitude acquisition, depicted schematically in Fig. 7.2, predicts that attitudes are shaped over an extended period through the influence of these three sources. Their effect is ongoing and cumulative. Examining each source in detail provides a richer notion of how the model works.

Direct Effect of Reading. Each incidence of reading is predicted to have a small but real effect on attitudes. This effect may be to reinforce existing attitudes or to alter them by providing something other than what the reader would have expected. Moreover, the reading episode affects attitudes at more than one level of the hierarchy. If one reads a book by a relatively unfamiliar author and is pleasantly surprised, one's attitude toward reading that author's works is positively altered, whereas further up the hierarchy, one's attitude toward reading in general may be altered only slightly.

Beliefs About the Outcomes of Reading. Each episode of reading not only has a small direct effect on attitudes but also contributes to the individual's belief structure. These modified beliefs then have their own, less direct impact on attitudes. A child slowly comes to anticipate what reading will be like: whether it will be frustrating or pleasurable, informative or tedious. Two dimensions of the child's expectations are especially relevant. One is the expectation of success versus failure; the other is the expectation

Model of Reading Attitude Acquisition

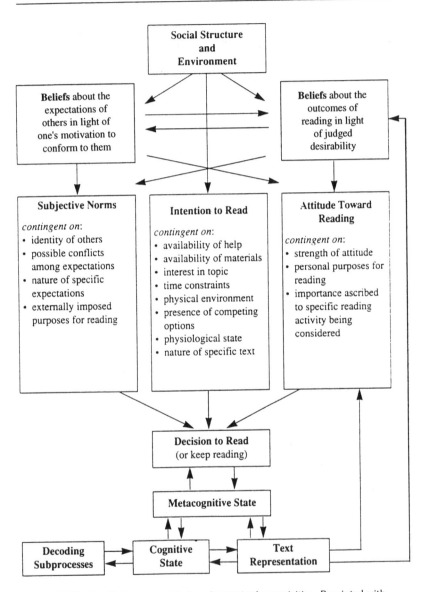

FIG. 7.2. The McKenna model of reading attitude acquisition. Reprinted with permission of the International Reading Association.

of pleasure versus boredom. These dimensions have clear implications for teachers:

- Attempt to ensure early success and to provide adequate support for reading so that students quickly come to believe that they *can* read if they wish.
- Expose students to a range of genres, topics, styles, and authors so that student beliefs about reading will reflect the true range of possibilities, a range that is likely to include materials they find relevant and enjoyable.

Beliefs About Subjective Norms. The cultural setting leads to an individual's beliefs about how reading is valued by significant others. This cultural valuing is a subjective norm and implies a standard of behavior for members of a particular culture. The impact of norms begins as parental influence even before a child enters school. Interaction with parents during this critical developmental period may or may not entail positive interactions with print (see Bus, chap. 2, this volume). As children grow older, the scope of cultural influence broadens to include members of the social environment beyond the family. Members may reinforce normative beliefs in one another through a process that Festinger (1950, 1954) called *social comparison*. He described the need to validate one's beliefs about conditions that are social (and therefore abstract and invisible) as opposed to physical (and therefore concrete and visible). Validation consists of expressing beliefs to other group members so that the beliefs become mutually confirming:

> Where the dependence on physical reality is low, the dependence upon social reality is correspondingly high. An opinion, a belief, an attitude is "correct," "valid," and "proper" to the extent that it is anchored in a group of people with similar beliefs, opinions, and attitudes. (Festinger, 1950, p. 272)

If a peer group views reading as boring and as a waste of time, this view may be expressed orally from time to time in classroom settings when reading is required or suggested. The degree to which such expressions influence an individual's attitude is determined by how strongly the individual identifies with the group, especially when concurrent membership in more than one group (e.g., classroom, family, ethnic group, and gender) complicates the issue of identity. Research confirming a tendency of groups to reject those who deviate from consensus views is consistent (see Levine, 1980), although few studies have involved natural settings. Of course, individuals vary in their tendency to conform to such norms, but where reading is negatively valued by people from whom a student seeks approval, the student is unlikely to develop positive reading attitudes. As Cohen (1964) indicated, "Those who place a high value on their membership in a group are most vulnerable to threats of social punishment from the group, inasmuch as they have the strongest motives to maintain friendly relationships with fellow members and the strongest desire to secure the prestige and privileges associated with their status as members" (p. 41). Combatting the effects of negative social influences can be daunting. To make a start, teachers should attempt to do the following:

- Take stock of social norms present in student populations.
- Seek ways to challenge the belief that significant group members negatively value reading.

A recent example involves an interesting attempt to pose such a challenge. In America, an antischooling norm among some minority groups can lead, quite predictably, to negative reading attitudes. One attempt to combat the influence of this cultural pressure is to display posters of minority athletes engaged in reading (see Fig. 7.3). Later in the chapter, I revisit this issue in the context of effective instructional approaches.

It is important to realize that beliefs about the outcomes of reading and about subjective norms are related in complex ways and that each set of beliefs changes as the child matures. Beliefs about the outcomes of reading—whether those outcomes are likely to be pleasurable, useful, frustrating, or boring—are formed, in part, in relation to children's beliefs about the outcomes of competing activities. As they grow older and more leisure options are open to them, the prospect of reading will be weighed against available alternatives, each of which is associated with an attitude. Consequently, students who become capable readers may not have strong positive attitudes toward reading if they expect more satisfying results from other pastimes. Nonetheless, beliefs about the outcomes of reading must relate in part to the ability to read. The necessity of this relationship is to a certain extent self-evident, but growth in ability is linked in turn, normatively, to one's perception of the value of reading within a particular social context. If its perceived value is low, the development of reading ability will be constrained and beliefs about the outcomes of reading (namely, that the result is frustration) will tend to confirm one's normative belief that reading has little value to begin with. This mutually confirming process of normative and predictive beliefs suggests the true complexity of the situation.

An important theory of belief change involves the notion of inconsistency. When evidence that is at odds with an individual's preexisting beliefs is introduced, a state of cognitive dissonance (Festinger, 1957) is created that may cause the inconsistency to be resolved. This is not an inevitable result, however, especially when beliefs have an emotional origin. The individual may rationalize the inconsistency, an example of "self-persuasion"

FIG. 7.3. Poster designed to appeal to social norms by depicting a minority athlete reading. Reprinted with permission of the American Library Association.

(Broudon, 1990/1994), and thus avoid the unpleasant but logical necessity of altering the earlier beliefs. Posner, Strike, Hewson, and Gertzog (1982) identified four sequential conditions for inconsistent new experiences to alter the belief system meaningfully.

1. The student must recognize the new experience as anomalous.

   "I dislike reading but I must admit this book is good."

2. The student must believe there is a need to reconcile the disparate beliefs.

   "Perhaps I need to reevaluate how I feel about reading."

3. The student must wish to reduce the inconsistencies among beliefs.

"If I dislike reading, I need to explain to myself how certain books can be enjoyable."

4. The student must realize that the two beliefs cannot be assimilated.

"I cannot dislike reading and at the same time like this book."

These insights from the general study of belief acquisition have importance for the improvement of reading attitudes by suggesting intervention strategies based on active processing of students' beliefs and their rational foundations (see Pajares, 1992).

FINDINGS OF READING ATTITUDE RESEARCH

Numerous investigations have examined various questions associated with reading attitude acquisition. Although some inconsistencies persist, the general picture is now fairly clear. The following generalizations have been largely supported.

General Trends

Reading Attitudes Tend to Worsen Over Time. Evidence concerning the development of reading attitudes over time, although somewhat inconsistent, largely supports a steady downward trend. Attitude theory predicts that as children mature and as more and more leisure options compete with reading, positive attitudes toward reading will on average worsen. This trend may well apply even to many skillful readers because their beliefs that reading can be pleasurable are likely to compete with beliefs that other activities may be even more pleasurable. Findings supporting this prediction have been reported by Anderson, Tollefson, and Gilbert (1985), Kush and Watkins (1996), McKenna, Kear, and Ellsworth (1995), and Martin (1984). For readers experiencing problems, the prediction of worsening attitudes is more emphatic, and again supportive evidence is available (Ishikawa, 1985; McKenna, Kear, & Ellsworth, 1995; Ross & Fletcher, 1989; Shapiro, 1980).

A few studies have not shown gradual declines, however. Wallbrown, Levine, and Engin (1981) reported no significant differences between the fifth and sixth graders they studied (children of approximately 10–12 years of age). Parker and Paradis (1986) reported no significant differences in attitude among Grades 1–3 (children from 6 to 8 years of age, on average) and higher scores for fifth than for fourth graders. Historically, a "peaking" of reading attitude was often discussed (e.g., see Witty & Kopel, 1939), although theory leads to the prediction that attitudes will on average begin to decline almost from the onset of instruction. In studies that do not report a gradual worsening of attitudes, a general decline may be masked in small, possibly idiosyncratic samples.

The fact that general declines have been documented in cultures as diverse as Japan (Ishikawa, 1985) and Brazil (Rea, Romine, McKenna, & Griffin, 1997) suggests that the worsening of children's reading attitudes is a widespread phenomenon. This is not to say that it is characteristic of all readers or all subcultures, of course, but its prevalence is now well documented.

Reading Attitudes Worsen More Rapidly for Poor Readers. An impressive body of evidence relates reading attitude to ability (Askov & Fishback, 1973; Lipsky, 1983; Martin, 1984; Ransbury, 1973; Richards & Bear, 1986; Swanson, 1982; Walberg & Tsai, 1985; Wallbrown, Brown, & Engin, 1978; Wallbrown, Vance, & Prichard, 1979). These studies, although documenting a relationship between ability and attitude at various ages, cast little light on the cumulative effect of reading difficulty over time. McKenna, Kear, and Ellsworth (1995), however, in an American study designed to track the phenomenon across the elementary grades, reported a significant interaction between grade level and ability. The older the students, the wider is the difference in reading attitudes between good and poor readers. This is a gulf that might be bridged by effective instructional intervention in the early grades.

The overall negative trend in reading attitude can only be explained in part by the increasing impact of poor reading ability in the upper grades. Although the sharply worsening attitudes of poor readers contribute substantially to the downward trend across the total population of students, the attitudes of good readers decline over the same span of years, although not nearly as precipitously.

Girls Tend to Possess More Positive Reading Attitudes Than Boys. Attitude theory suggests that normative beliefs (those concerned with the expectations of significant others) play a formative role in the development of attitudes. If a child's cultural environment encourages, models, and reinforces reading, positive attitudes should result. Gender-specific beliefs concerning what others expect about reading may explain consistent findings that girls tend to possess more positive attitudes than boys (Anderson, Tollefson, & Gilbert, 1985; Askov & Fishback, 1973; Kush & Watkins, 1996; Ross & Fletcher, 1989; Shapiro, 1980; Smith, 1990; Stevenson & Newman, 1986; Wallbrown, Levine, & Engin, 1981). In their large-scale study, McKenna, Kear, and Ellsworth (1995) also found a consistent gender effect as early as Grade 1, an effect that appeared to grow more pronounced among older children. Because girls tend to outperform boys on measures of reading proficiency (e.g., Mullis, Campbell, & Farstrup, 1993), they controlled for ability in a reanalysis and achieved the same results. This finding suggests that the gender effect in reading attitudes cannot be explained on the basis of superior reading ability on the part of girls but is probably attributable to cultural expectations. Precisely how these expectations function is unclear, but a replication among Brazilian children (Rea, Romine, McKenna, & Griffin, 1997) yielded a similar result, indicating that such expectations are not unique to a single culture.

Ethnic Group Membership Is Not, In Itself, Strongly Related to Reading Attitudes. Membership in an ethnic group might be expected to impose subjective norms about reading, but only to the extent that the group was cohesive and uniform. Somewhat surprisingly, few studies have examined this prospect. Saracho and Dayton (1991) reported that among a large sample of preschool children African Americans tended to possess more negative attitudes than Whites or Mexican Americans. Because this study involved children who had not yet begun to learn to read, the cumulative effects of reading difficulty cannot account for the difference. On the other hand, McKenna, Kear, and Ellsworth (1995) categorized students as African American, Hispanic, or White and found no attitudinal differences by ethnicity. This lack of any meaningful effects of ethnic group membership may indicate that cultural norms regarding reading are similar across the three American subcultures studied. It may also mean that mere membership in an ethnic group may involve too broad a categorization for meaningful social norms to affect beliefs. Membership in smaller social units, such as families, classrooms, clubs, gangs, cliques, and friendships, may well exert stronger normative influences. In the case of African Americans, these results appear to reflect Heath's contention that there is "no single black experience" (1994, p. 209). Other factors, such as age, proficiency, and gender, do a far better job of predicting an individual's attitude toward reading.

Effects of Techniques and Materials

A growing number of studies have demonstrated positive attitudinal effects attributable to specific techniques. The following list is illustrative rather than exhaustive:

- Avoiding denegrating reading group placement (Wallbrown, Brown, & Engin, 1978).
- Using high-quality literature (Morrow, 1983).
- Using questions to activate prior knowledge (Jagacinski & Nicholls, 1987).

- Reading aloud to students (Herrold, Stanchfield, & Serabian, 1989).
- Stressing links between literature and the lives of students (Guzzetti, 1990).
- Training children in metacognitive thinking (Payne & Manning, 1992).
- Arranging for students to participate in literature discussion groups (Leal, 1993).
- Arranging for children to correspond with college students about reading (Bromley, Winters, & Schlimmer, 1994).

Recent studies of whether the use of basal readers negatively influences reading attitudes, a lingering issue in the United States and much of the British Commonwealth, have reported no observable effects of basals on attitudes (McKenna, Stratton, Grindler, & Jenkins, 1995; McKenna, Kear, & Ellsworth, 1995). The fact that for the samples in these studies reading attitude becomes steadily more negative irrespective of whether basals were in use suggests that these trends are not easily curbed. Use or nonuse of basals is clearly a gross categorization that allows a range of methodologies on either side. The fact that numerous techniques (as just listed) have been shown to cause improved attitudes is hopeful and suggests that how materials are used is a crucial variable under the control of teachers.

THEORY-BASED INSTRUCTIONAL APPROACHES

What specific approaches can be recommended to teachers on the basis of attitude theory? In a previous article (McKenna, 1994), I identified a number of implications, but for the most part these constituted guidelines rather than specific instructional techniques. They included (a) assessing students' beliefs about reading, (b) working to instill positive beliefs, (c) creating an environment that promotes reading, (d) planning a varied program, (e) ensuring early success, (f) striving to show students the relevance of reading, (g) providing positive adult models, (h) providing positive student models, (i) seeking parent involvement, (j) reading aloud to students, (k) facilitating learning through text, and (l) recommending books on the basis of student opinion.

In the previous section, techniques validated in at least one study were listed, and this is a powerful endorsement although their generality to a range of contexts remains speculative. In this section, I examine additional approaches to improving student attitudes toward reading. My concern is less with specific approaches than with *kinds* of approaches—avenues to a range of possible applications. My goal is to describe how these kinds of approaches emanate from attitude theory, and I argue that that is the reason why specific applications of each kind have achieved a good measure of empirical support.

Incentive Programs

American experiences with incentive programs leave no doubt that the quantity of reading in which children engage can be increased, often dramatically. But do greater amounts of reading lead to more positive attitudes toward reading? The attitude model I have proposed suggests that the answer to this question depends on three more fundamental questions.

1. Has the increased amount of reading assisted the child in achieving fluency? If the practice involved in extensive reading helps bring the child to the point of automatic word recognition and fluency (and with these to the development of an adequate reading rate and the ability to apply mental resources to comprehension rather than decoding), then we can expect the child's beliefs about the outcomes of reading to change. No longer will they include an expectation of inevitable frustration and laboriousness. When extensive reading leads to fluency, the child will increasingly come to see reading as an activity that can be undertaken with success. There is currently evidence that incentive programs can lead to enhanced ability (McQuillan, 1997), although the conditions under which this result will occur are not fully understood. The expectation of success on the part of students, however, is necessary but not sufficient to produce the positive attitudes we desire as educators.

2. Has the increased amount of reading exposed the child to written materials that the child finds important and interesting? Children typically understand that reading can result in the acquisition of knowledge. But the additional expectation that reading will, or at least can, result in entertainment or edification may or may not be the result of incentive programs. Much depends on the individual choices students make in what they read, choices that are sometimes, unfortunately, guided as much by the length or difficulty of a book as by its content. When a child and a book "connect," so that an extraordinary personal significance is attached by the child to the reading experience, then the belief structures regarding the child's expectations about reading and books will change positively. When the child's choices are not guided by teachers attempting to bring about such connections, reading may never be more than an extended series of relatively tedious and largely superficial encounters with print. This outcome is an inherent danger in any incentive program in which quantity is the overriding goal.

3. Are the incentives likely to prevent the child from reexamining beliefs about reading? Festinger (1957) argued that when a behavior is forced, through either rewards or the threat of punishment, cognitive dissonance is reduced or eliminated so that the individual will be likely to disregard results that are inconsistent with preexisting beliefs. The tendency to disregard such an inconsistency is directly proportional to the amount of the reward.

That is, the greater the incentive, the less likely a child may be to reevaluate beliefs about reading even after experiencing positive reading episodes caused by the incentive. If this aspect of cognitive dissonance theory applies to reading incentive programs, it argues for nominal rewards or rewards that consist of books. Cognitive dissonance theory likewise argues against required participation in incentive programs, because a free choice appears to facilitate the process of creating and resolving dissonance.

To these three questions, stemming from attitude theory, must be added a fourth, originating in the theory of motivation: What effects are incentives likely to have on the child who is already a habitual reader? Some psychologists warn that where intrinsic motivation exists, incentives can actually reduce this motivation once they are removed (e.g., see Kohn, 1993). In other words, an avid reader, suddenly given material incentives to read, might, once the rewards are no longer available, actually choose to read less than before the incentives were applied. I know of no study testing this hypothesis with respect to reading. A recent meta-analysis based on investigations in contexts other than reading, however, has suggested that this fear is groundless—that incentives do not in fact curtail intrinsic motivation (Cameron & Pierce, 1994). An exception appeared to be cases in which incentives were applied for merely engaging in a behavior so that level of performance was ignored. These conclusions suggest that an incentive program in which children are rewarded for the number of books they read with verified comprehension is not likely to impair the tendency of habitual readers to continue reading after the incentive program ends. They further suggest that rewarding children for merely participating in an unmonitored program of self-selected reading, such as sustained silent reading, might have a later inhibiting effect on such children.

There are three caveats to note with regard to the conclusions of Cameron and Pierce, however. First, the studies they examined did not involve reading incentive programs, and the extent to which their conclusions are applicable to such programs is unknown. Second, their methodology and results have been questioned (Kohn, 1996; Lepper, Keavney, & Drake, 1996; Ryan & Deci, 1996; but see Cameron & Pierce, 1996). Third, there is an important distinction between attitude and motivation. The latter is customarily investigated, as it was in most of the studies included in the meta-analysis, by observing the effects of incentives on behaviors. Attitudes, however, may or may not be translated into behaviors. The model of Fishbein and Ajzen that I have adapted to reading (Ajzen, 1989; Ajzen & Fishbein, 1980; Fishbein & Ajzen, 1975; Liska, 1984; McKenna, 1994) maintains that attitudes first influence *intentions*, which are in turn subject to *contingencies*, which will often prevent a decision to read under a particular set of circumstances.

Tentative Conclusions About Reading Incentive Programs. What conclusions are justified about reading incentive programs? To begin with, they typically increase the amount of reading undertaken. With skillful guidance, these new experiences with reading might alter belief structures of children who are not intrinsically motivated to read. Two cautions must be considered, however. First, incentives and required participation in incentive programs may prevent cognitive dissonance from forming and therefore inhibit active reconsideration of prior beliefs that are at odds with positive reading experiences. This possibility argues for minimal incentives, for incentives consisting of books, and against required participation in incentive programs. Second, the effects of incentive programs on preexisting positive attitudes toward reading are not clearly understood. However, the related evidence must be interpreted as encouraging as long as the incentives are applied to the complete reading of books at an acceptable level of comprehension.

Peer Interactions

Creating situations in which students encounter other members of the same age and similar cultural background can be effective in challenging negative normative beliefs about reading. Situations of this kind have the potential to backfire, of course, by affording an opportunity for negative beliefs to be communicated and reinforced. Research suggests, however, that prudent approaches to peer interactions lead to improved attitudes toward reading (e.g., Leal, 1993).

There are doubtless many ways of providing for this sort of interaction, but literature response groups, also called literature circles and literature study groups, are an excellent example. These are student discussion groups in which risk-free interchanges about mutually read books are invited. Their popularity and success have recently occasioned entire books on how to implement them (e.g., Gambrell & Almasi, 1996; Roser & Martinez, 1995), and their rationale is persuasive. It is essentially as follows. Literature response groups represent one way of modeling the sort of behavior that teachers should seek to foster in children if they are to participate in a literate culture. Although reading can be done on a cloistered, solitary basis, it is an inherently social act because it involves at least two individuals: reader and writer. In the case of published works, multiple readers afford the opportunity of introducing a second social dimension, among readers of the same work. Certainly current constructivist views about the nature of comprehension and about learning to read suggest that discussion among readers is a desirable activity, not only for its contributions to a literate culture but for its potential to broaden children's critical perspectives on what reading is and should be (e.g., Eeds & Wells, 1989; Leal, 1993). There are, however, additional and equally compelling arguments that originate in attitude theory and that have been generally ignored in the discussions of this technique. Attitude theory predicts that participation in literature response groups will inevitably challenge beliefs harbored by some children that reading comprehension is a unitary end, based on a single text meaning. More important perhaps is the prediction that such participation may also expose children to peers whose positive attitudes may affect the perception of social norms. ("If my friend Juan, who is Latino, likes to read, maybe reading is good for other Latinos, like me.")

Cross-Age Interactions

Beliefs about social norms can also be challenged by arranging for children to interact with older individuals. The poster depicted in Fig. 7.3 is aimed at this goal, although it does not provide for interaction. The broad range of validated techniques that do entail interaction suggests a rich source of new theory-based approaches. The following examples give some idea of the possibilities. Hudley (1992) described a program in which successful minority women shared some of their favorite reading materials with African American and Hispanic high school girls during lunch. Bromley, Winters, and Schlimmer (1994) created a system by which young children and college students exchanged written comments about reading. Leland and Fitzpatrick (1993/1994) described a cross-age tutoring program that led to improved attitudes on the part of sixth graders (children typically 11 or 12 years of age). As Leland and Fitzpatrick acknowledged, cross-age tutoring can simultaneously challenge two types of beliefs that underlie negative reading attitudes. One type is the belief that proficiency is poor. ("I see that my skills are good enough to help this child. I am now a teacher.") The other type is the belief that one's peers place a low value on reading. ("My friends have always hated reading, but now we argue about which children's books are best to use in our tutoring.")

Bibliotherapy

Bibliotherapy represents a unique method of attempting to make a highly personal connection between a child and a particular book. Defined by Bromley (1992) as "the practice of using books to promote mental health, solve personal problems, and become aware of societal concerns" (p. 59), bibliotherapy has acquired an unfortunate clinical connotation. Due in part to its origin in the field of psychiatry, it is often viewed as a technique useful principally with the emotionally disabled individual and therefore requiring special expertise to apply.

My colleagues and I have taken a broader view, one that extends to classroom teachers and to emotionally stable children encountering a variety of problems (Grindler, Stratton, & McKenna, 1997). We have witnessed remarkable changes in students' perspectives on reading, even on the part of beginning readers, following bibliotherapeutic instructional units. In one particularly dramatic case, a kindergarten teacher suspected that one of her students had been sexually abused at home, although the child declined to discuss the matter. The teacher created a bibliotherapy unit involving both fiction and nonfiction picture books. These she read aloud to the entire class to avoid singling out the target child. (With respect to the other students, she justified such a unit on the basis of its proactive effects on these children's awareness.) Following the unit, the abused child sought out the teacher without prompting and revealed the situation so that legal action could be taken (Grindler, Stratton, McKenna, & Smith, 1995). Although most classroom applications of bibliotherapy are not likely to be as striking—or, arguably, as controversial—the resulting intimate connection between book and child will be likely to do more than help the child cope with the problem situation at hand. It also contributes to the child's beliefs about the possible outcomes of reading and, consequently, builds a more positive general attitude toward books and reading.

Electronic Text

The phrase "attitude toward reading" is generally taken to refer to printed sources. The increasing prevalence of digitized text, however, a prevalence that has led some to forecast a "posttypographic age" (see Reinking, chap. 10, this volume), has profound implications for the development of reading attitudes. If the digital transformation of text resulted in only trivial changes to what we read, we could expect the affective impact of medium to be minimal. In fact, however, digitized text entails important features not shared with its print counterpart:

1. It is literally interactive.
2. It can accommodate textual supports (electronic scaffolds) for poor or developing readers.
3. It invites and often requires nonlinear strategies.
4. It incorporates multimedia components.
5. It is fluid rather than fixed and immutable (see McKenna, 1998; Reinking, 1994).

Moreover, the exciting potential of these features, together with the increasing affordability of technology in developed nations, has already tempted authors to explore and create new genres.

What effect will these transformations be likely to have on children's attitudes in an era when the very nature of literacy is being fundamentally altered? Our work at the National Reading Research Center (McKenna & Watkins, 1995), conducted on the foundation of similar investigations undertaken in the Netherlands (Reitsma, 1988), indicates that even beginning readers can experience early success when exposed to electronic text equipped with digitized pronunciations available to children on demand. A majority of the children with whom we have worked cited this built-in support as the reason they preferred electronic trade books to their printed versions. It is plausible that a combination of early positive experiences with electronic text and the variety of new formats made possible by digital media will positively alter the beliefs of coming generations of children concerning the nature and outcomes of reading.

FUTURE DIRECTIONS

Victor Nell (1988) offered now-classic speculations on "ludic" readers, those who approach reading as a form of play and for whom reading is a lifelong source of joy. Notably, Nell could find only one characteristic that such readers appeared to share: proficiency. All were excellent readers. Certainly this is a prerequisite for lifelong engagement, and it frequently constitutes the primary focus of our efforts in classrooms. Indeed, it is tempting to settle for the development of reading ability, irrespective of attitude, as an acceptable outcome of schooling. Thus, it may be self-consolatory to say to our colleagues, "These students may not choose to read, but at least we have fostered within them the ability to read successfully when they find it necessary."

But this condition of being able to read but electing not to do so, a condition that has been termed *aliteracy*, represents only a fallback target of instruction in the philosophy of every teacher of my acquaintance. As educators, we must acknowledge that reading does have an instrumental utility, in the workplace and in a range of other contexts, but we also aver that optimal participation in a literate culture requires frequent, active engagement in reading as a valued social activity and as an intellectual agency that Neisser (1967) aptly called "externally guided thinking." This, to me, is the proper ideal of engagement, a quality that exists in addition to, and on the basis of, ability and that gives attitude formation its importance for teachers. It is a lofty goal, to be sure—one that can only be attained through the skillful application of appropriate techniques.

Using Theory to Generate Methods

How, then, do educators identify instructional techniques with the potential to improve student attitudes toward reading? One method is to examine the research literature for the emergence of approaches with validating evidence. The fact that research has in fact validated the positive attitudinal effects of specific techniques, such as those discussed in this chapter, is encouraging. But such techniques are often the products of educators' instinctive hunches about what may work. There is nothing wrong with reliance on instinct, of course, except that it is a commodity that has never been uniformly distributed among educators. I believe there are better tools for the creation of effective methods.

My suggestion is that attitude theory be used to generate possible methods of fostering more positive attitudes. Knowledge of the possible causal links between an activity or practice and improved reading attitudes has its real potential in helping us conceive new ideas and evaluate them prior to implementation. Theory suggests that instructional techniques might cause improved attitudes by virtually any of the three channels available:

1. A direct effect due to the positive nature of the experience afforded by the technique.
2. An indirect effect on the beliefs a student harbors about the outcomes of reading (e.g., the technique might induce the student to believe that reading will be less frustrating).
3. An indirect effect on a student's beliefs about how influential others view reading (e.g., a collaborative technique might afford one student the opportunity to hear another's positive comments about reading).

Techniques that (a) incidentally cause students to reconsider negative beliefs or (b) lead to a more direct examination of their beliefs (e.g., Posner et al., 1982) would follow from theory. In this chapter, I have attempted to summarize the abundant evidence on belief formation that might be useful in creating such techniques and to inspect a few techniques that conform to that literature. Clearly, the range of currently available techniques provides only a hint of those that theory implies and that resourceful educators can create.

Conducting Large-Scale Assessments of Reading Attitudes

The goal of creating and implementing effective new strategies can be assisted through giving attitude its place in the constellation of characteristics currently measured in national and international assessments. Some progress has been made in this respect, such as America's National Assessment of Educational Progress (NAEP) surveys of students' reading habits. But attitude measures have not been incorporated, to my knowledge, in the literacy assessments conducted by any nation. Although the need to monitor reading proficiency is undebatably the foremost reason for conducting state-sponsored large-scale literacy assessments, there are compelling reasons for adding an attitudinal component. Such a component would enable attitudinal trends to be charted over time. It would also invite correlational studies involving data captured through other components of the assessment (reading proficiency, habits, etc.). The secondary analysis of attitude data in this way might very well lead to useful insights into the development and characteristics of reading attitudes. Further, an attitude component in state-sponsored assessments would faciltate international comparisons useful in gaining cross-cultural perspectives on attitude development. Finally, well-publicized, large-scale assessments would be likely to raise the awareness of educators and the public with respect to the importance of attitudes toward reading. Such an awareness is a necessary precursor to action.

REFERENCES

Ajzen, I. (1989). Attitude structure and behavior. In A. R. Pratkanis, S. J. Brecker, & A. G. Greenwald (Eds.), *Attitude structure and function* (pp. 241–274). Hillsdale, NJ: Lawrence Erlbaum Associates.

Ajzen, I., & Fishbein, M. (1980). *Understanding attitudes and predicting social behavior.* New York: Prentice Hall.

Alexander, J. E., & Filler, R. C. (1976). *Attitudes and reading.* Newark, DE: International Reading Association.

Allport, G. (1935). Attitudes. In C. Murchison (Ed.), *A handbook of social psychology* (pp. 798–844). Worcester, MA: Clark University Press.

Anderson, M. A., Tollefson, N. A., & Gilbert, E. C. (1985). Giftedness and reading: A cross-sectional view of differences in reading attitudes and behaviors. *Gifted Child Quarterly, 29,* 186–189.

Askov, E., & Fishback, T. (1973). An investigation of primary pupils' attitudes toward reading. *Journal of Experimental Education, 41,* 1–7.

Bromley, K. D. (1992). *Language arts: Exploring connections* (2nd ed.). Needham Heights, MA: Allyn and Bacon.

Bromley, K. D., Winters, D., & Schlimmer, K. (1994). Book buddies: Creating enthusiasm for literacy learning. *Reading Teacher, 47,* 392–400.

Broudon, R. (1994). *The art of self-persuasion: The social explanation of false beliefs* (M. Slater, Trans.). Cambridge, UK: Polity Press. (Original work published 1990)

Cameron, J., & Pierce, W. D. (1994). Reinforcement, reward, and intrinsic motivation: A meta-analysis. *Review of Educational Research, 64,* 363–423.

Cameron, J., & Pierce, W. D. (1996). The debate about rewards and intrinsic motivation: Protests and accusations do not alter the results. *Review of Educational Research, 66,* 39–51.

Cohen, A. R. (1964). *Attitude change and social influence.* New York: Basic Books.

Eeds, M., & Wells, D. (1989). Grand conversations: An exploration of meaning construction in literature study groups. *Research in the Teaching of English, 23*(1), 4–29.

Eiser, J. R. (1994). *Attitudes, chaos, and the connectionist mind.* Oxford, UK: Blackwell.

Estes, T. H. (1971). A scale to measure attitudes toward reading. *Journal of Reading, 15,* 135–138.

Festinger, L. (1950). Informal social communication. *Psychological Review, 57,* 271–282.

Festinger, L. (1954). A theory of social comparison processes. *Human Relations, 7,* 117–140.

Festinger, L. (1957). *A theory of cognitive dissonance.* Palo Alto, CA: Stanford University Press.

Fishbein, M., & Ajzen, I. (1975). *Belief, attitude, intention, and behavior: An introduction to theory and research.* Reading, MA: Addison-Wesley.

Gambrell, L. B., & Almasi, J. F. (1996). *Lively discussions! Fostering engaged reading.* Newark, DE: International Reading Association.

Grindler, M. C., Stratton, B. D., & McKenna, M. C. (1997). *The right book, the right time: Helping children cope.* Needham Heights, MA: Allyn and Bacon.

Grindler, M. C., Stratton, B. D., McKenna, M. C., & Smith, P. (1995). Bookmatching in the classroom: How action research reached the lives of children through books. *Action in Teacher Education, 16*(4), 50–58.

Guzzetti, B. J. (1990). Enhancing comprehension through trade books in high school English classes. *Journal of Reading, 33*, 411–413.

Heath, S. B. (1994). The children of Trackton's children: Spoken and written language in social change. In R. B. Ruddell, M. R. Ruddell, & H. Singer (Eds.), *Theoretical models and processes of reading* (pp. 208–230). Newark, DE: International Reading Association.

Herrold, W. G., Jr., Stanchfield, J., & Serabian, A. J. (1989). Comparison of the effect of a middle school, literature-based listening program on male and female attitudes toward reading. *Educational Research Quarterly, 13*(4), 43–46.

Hudley, C. A. (1992). Using role models to improve the reading attitude of ethnic minority high school girls. *Journal of Reading, 36*, 182–188.

Ishikawa, K. (1985). Developmental study of school children's attitudes toward reading. *Science of Reading, 29*, 89–98.

Jagacinski, C., & Nicholls, J. (1987). Confidence and affect in task involvement and ego involvement: The impact of social comparison information. *Journal of Educational Psychology, 79*, 107–114.

Kohn, A. (1993). *Punished by rewards.* Boston: Houghton Mifflin.

Kohn, A. (1996). By all available means: Cameron and Pierce's defense of extrinsic motivators. *Review of Educational Research, 66*, 1–4.

Kush, J. C., & Watkins, M. W. (1996). Long-term stability of children's attitudes toward reading. *Journal of Educational Research, 89*, 315–319.

Leal, D. J. (1993). The power of literary peer group discussions: How children collaboratively negotiate meaning. *Reading Teacher, 47*, 114–120.

Leland, C., & Fitzpatrick, R. (1993/1994). Cross-age interaction builds enthusiasm for reading and writing. *Reading Teacher, 47*, 292–301.

Lepper, M. R., Keavney, M., & Drake, M. (1996). Intrinsic motivation and extrinsic rewards: A commentary on Cameron and Pierce's meta-analysis. *Review of Educational Research, 66*, 5–32.

Levine, J. M. (1980). Reaction to opinion deviance in small groups. In P. B. Paulus (Ed.), *Psychology of group influence* (pp. 375–429). Hillsdale, NJ: Lawrence Erlbaum Associates.

Lipsky, J. A. (1983). A picture-story technique to uncover covert attitudes associated with reading failure. *Reading Psychology, 4*, 151–155.

Liska, A. E. (1984). A critical examination of the causal structure of the Fishbein/Ajzen attitude-behavior model. *Social Psychology Quarterly, 47*, 61–74.

Martin, C. E. (1984). Why some gifted children do not like to read. *Roeper Review, 7*, 72–75.

McKenna, M. C. (1994). Toward a model of reading attitude acquisition. In E. H. Cramer & M. Castle (Eds.), *Fostering the life-long love of reading: The affective domain in reading education* (pp. 18–40). Newark, DE: International Reading Association.

McKenna, M. C. (1998). Electronic texts and the transformation of beginning reading. In D. Reinking, M. C. McKenna, L. D. Labbo, & R. Kieffer (Eds.), *Handbook of literacy and technology: Transformations in a post-typographic world* (pp. 45–59). Hillsdale, NJ: Lawrence Erlbaum Associates.

McKenna, M. C., & Kear, D. J. (1990). Measuring attitude toward reading: A new tool for teachers. *Reading Teacher, 43*, 626–639.

McKenna, M. C., Kear, D. J., & Ellsworth, R. A. (1995). Children's attitudes toward reading: A national survey. *Reading Research Quarterly, 30*, 934–956.

McKenna, M. C., Stratton, B. D., Grindler, M. C., & Jenkins, S. (1995). Differential effects of whole language and traditional instruction on reading attitudes. *Journal of Reading Behavior, 27*, 19–44.

McKenna, M. C., & Watkins, J. H. (1995, November). *Effects of computer-mediated books on the development of beginning readers.* Paper presented at the meeting of the National Reading Conference, New Orleans, LA.

McQuillan, J. (1997). The effects of incentives on reading. *Reading Research and Instruction, 36*, 111–125.

Morrow, L. M. (1983). Home and school correlates of early interest in literature. *Journal of Educational Research, 76*, 221–230.

Mullis, I. V. S., Campbell, J. R., & Farstrup, A. E. (1993). *NAEP 1992: Reading report card for the nation and the states.* Washington, DC: U.S. Department of Education.

Murphy, G., Murphy, L., & Newcomb, T. (1937). *Experimental and social psychology.* New York: Harper and Row.

Neisser, U. (1967). *Cognitive psychology.* New York: Appleton-Century-Crofts.

Nell, V. (1988). *Lost in a book: The psychology of reading for pleasure.* New Haven, CT: Yale University Press.

Pajares, M. F. (1992). Teachers' beliefs and educational research: Cleaning up a messy construct. *Review of Educational Research, 62*, 307–332.

Parker, A., & Paradis, E. (1986). Attitude development toward reading in grades one through six. *Journal of Educational Research, 79*, 313–315.

Pascal, B. (1954). De l'esprit géométrique. In *Oeuvres complètes* (pp. 575–604). Paris: Gallimard. (Original work published 1658)

Payne, B. D., & Manning, B. H. (1992). Basal reader instruction: Effects of comprehension monitoring training on reading comprehension, strategy use and attitude. *Reading Research and Instruction, 32*(1), 29–38.

Posner, G. J., Strike K. A., Hewson, P. W., & Gertzog, W. A. (1982). Accommodation of a scientific conception: Toward a theory of conceptual change. *Science Education, 66*, 211–227.

Rajecki, D. W. (1990). *Attitudes* (2nd ed.). Sunderland, MA: Sinauer Associates, Inc.

Ransbury, M. (1973). An assessment of reading attitudes. *Journal of Reading, 17*, 25–28.

Rea, D., Romine, B. C., McKenna, M. C., & Griffin, B. (1997, March). *A cross-cultural analysis of reading attitude development.* Paper presented at the meeting of the American Educational Research Association, Chicago.

Reinking, D. (1994). *Electronic literacy* (Perspectives in Reading Research No. 4). Athens, GA, and College Park, MD: National Reading Research Center.

Reitsma, P. (1988). Reading practice for beginners: Effects of guided reading, reading-while-listening, and independent reading with computer-based speech feedback. *Reading Research Quarterly, 23*, 219–235.

Richards, H. C., & Bear, G. G. (1986, April). *Attitudes toward school subjects of academically unpredictable elementary school children.* Paper presented at the meeting of the American Educational Research Association, San Francisco.

Rokeach, M. (1968). *Beliefs, attitudes, and values: A theory of organization and change.* San Francisco: Jossey-Bass.

Rosenberg, M. (1956). Cognitive structure and attitudinal affect. *Journal of Abnormal Social Psychology, 53*, 367–372.

Roser, N. L., & Martinez, M. G. (1995). *Book Talk and beyond: Children and teachers respond to literature.* Newark, DE: International Reading Association.

Ross, E. P., & Fletcher, R. K. (1989). Responses to children's literature by environment, grade level, and sex. *Reading Instruction Journal, 32*(2), 22–28.

Ryan, R. M., & Deci, E. L. (1996). When paradigms clash: Comments on Cameron and Pierce's claim that rewards do not undermine intrinsic motivation. *Review of Educational Research, 66*, 33–38.

Saracho, O. N., & Dayton, C. M. (1991). Age-related changes in reading attitudes of young children: A cross-cultural study. *Journal of Research in Reading, 14*, 33–45.

Shapiro, J. E. (1980). Primary children's attitudes toward reading in male and female teachers' classrooms: An exploratory study. *Journal of Reading Behavior, 12*, 255–257.

Smith, M. C. (1990). A longitudinal investigation of reading attitude development from childhood to adulthood. *Journal of Educational Research, 83*, 215–219.

Stevenson, H. W., & Newman, R. S. (1986). Long-term prediction of achievement and attitudes in mathematics and reading. *Child Development, 57*, 646–657.

Swanson, B. B. (1982). The relationship between attitude toward reading and reading achievement. *Educational and Psychological Measurement, 42*, 1303–1304.

Thurstone, L. L. (1928). Attitudes can be measured. *American Journal of Sociology, 33*, 529–554.

Walberg, H. J., & Tsai, S. L. (1985). Correlates of reading achievement and attitude: A national assessment study. *Journal of Educational Research, 78*, 159–167.

Wallbrown, F. H., Brown, D. H., & Engin, A. W. (1978). A factor analysis of reading attitudes along with measures of reading achievement and scholastic aptitude. *Psychology in the Schools, 15*, 160–165.

Wallbrown, F. H., Levine, M. A., & Engin, A. W. (1981). *Sex differences in reading attitudes. Reading Improvement, 18*, 226–234.

Wallbrown, F. H., Vance, H. H., & Prichard, K. K. (1979). Discriminating between attitudes expressed by normal and disabled readers. *Psychology in the Schools, 16*, 472–477.

Witty, P., & Kopel, D. (1939). *Reading and its educative process.* Boston: Ginn.

8

Promoting Reading Motivation

John T. Guthrie
University of Maryland

Kaeli T. Knowles
National Research Council

In pursuing the theme of this volume, creating a world of engaged readers, we think it is crucial to consider reading motivation. The phrase *engaged reading* refers to the fusion of cognitive strategies, conceptual knowledge, and motivational goals during reading (for an explication see Guthrie & Anderson, 1999). Central to reading engagement are many aspects of motivation that relate to reading. In this chapter, we first distinguish among intrinsic motivation, extrinsic motivation, interest, and attitude. We then discuss how these aspects of motivation are important contributors to the cognitive and conceptual processes that are vital to reading comprehension. Having argued that reading motivation is indispensable to reading engagement, we present several dimensions of the instructional and school contexts that facilitate reading motivation. We have formulated these dimensions into principles for promoting reading motivation. They consist of the following: (a) conceptual themes, (b) real-world interactions, (c) support for self-direction, (d) using interesting texts, (e) cognitive strategy instruction, (f) social collaboration, and (g) supporting students' self-expression (see also Guthrie, Cox, Anderson, Harris, Mazonni, & Rach, 1998). Each principle is described briefly. In addition, cautions or pitfalls that should accompany the implementation of each principle are discussed.

PERSPECTIVES ON READING MOTIVATION

Intrinsic Versus Extrinsic Motivation

Many investigators adopt a goal-oriented perspective on motivation. In this view, motivations are goals or reasons for behavior. In a goal-oriented perspective, motivation can be regarded as the individual's reason for engaging in reading. Motivations for reading can be classified as either intrinsic or extrinsic. Intrinsic motivations refer to the desire to be engaged in a task for its own sake rather than for a reward (Wigfield & Guthrie, 1997). Extrinsic motivation refers to external rewards as goals for reading. Newman (1990) showed that students display intrinsic motivation through a preference for academic challenge, showing curiosity and interest in their school work, and by striving for independent mastery. Pintrich and De Groot (1990) reported that seventh graders having higher levels of intrinsic motivation were more likely to say they use cognitive strategies and to be more self-regulating than students low in intrinsic motivation. Based on their findings, the researchers stated that "students who were more likely to learn the material (not just get good grades) and believe that their school work was interesting and important were cognitively engaged in trying to learn and comprehend the material" (Pintrich & DeGroot, 1990, p. 37).

The construct of intrinsic motivation has recently been examined by researchers in terms of trait-like individual differences in intrinsic motivation (Harter, 1981; Nicholls, Cheung, Lauer, & Patashnick, 1989; Schiefele, 1996). Several enduring intrinsic motivational orientations have been defined and include: (a) preference for hard or challenging tasks, (b) learning that is driven by curiosity or interest, and (c) striving for competence and mastery (Wigfield, Eccles, & Rodriguez, 1998). Empirical research has also shown that high levels of intrinsic motivation can facilitate positive emotional experiences (Matsumoto & Sanders, 1988), self-esteem (Ryan & Deci, 2000), and mastery-oriented coping with failure and high academic achievement (Benware & Deci, 1984). These traits contrast with those shown by students possessing high levels of extrinsic motivation who do activities for instrumental or other reasons, such as receiving an award, not because of their interest or curiosity in learning (Wigfield et al., 1998).

Intrinsic and extrinsic motivations can be related to task-oriented and performance-oriented goals. Ames and Archer (1988) showed that students who possess a mastery goal will assign importance to the development of new skills, the process of learning, and—depending on their effort—the attainment of mastery. In contrast, students who possess a performance goal that reflects their valuing of ability will focus on outperforming others or on achieving success with little effort. Ames and Archer showed that when students perceive an emphasis on mastery goals, in an educational setting, they used more learning strategies, preferred tasks that offered challenge, and had a more positive attitude toward their class.

Interest

Researchers have recently begun to differentiate between personal and situational interest (Alexander, Kulikowich, & Jetton, 1994; Renninger, Hidi, & Krapp, 1992; Schiefele, 1992). Personal interest is an enduring attraction to a topic that exists prior to reading a particular text (Schiefele, 1992). In contrast, situational interest is a short-lived emotional state, educed within a particular context (Renninger et al., 1992). Many researchers have shown a positive relationship between personal interest and reading comprehension. Schiefele (1992) noted that "this phenomenon is relatively independent of age of students, type of text (narrative vs. expository), the modes of the text presentation (written vs. oral) and kind of comprehension test (free and cued recall, 'cloze' procedure, multiple choice and open-ended questions)" (p. 153).

In addition, Schraw, Bruning, and Svoboda (1995) found that the higher a reader's perceived situational interest in the text, the more text information he or she recalled. In examining the relationship between six sources of perceived situational interest and recall, Schraw et al. found that ease of comprehension, cohesion, vividness, and emotiveness were significantly related to text recall. In conjunction, personal and situational interest increase reading achievement.

Attitude

One's attitude toward an object or a subject can be conceptualized as a sense of "liking" or a continuum with positive and negative extremes. Alexander and Filler (1976) offered a reading-specific definition, suggesting that reading attitude is "a system of feelings related to reading which causes the learner to approach or avoid a reading situation" (p. 1). Two dimensions of reading attitude have been documented, attitude toward recreational reading, and attitude toward academic or school-related learning (McKenna & Kerr, 1990). This sense of "liking" is distinct from motivations as goals for reading. Attitudes are not objectives that guide behavior and are fulfilled. Attitudes do not reflect a belief that prompts behavior as motivations do. Attitudes are affective responses that accompany a behavior of reading initiated by a motivational state.

Change Over Time

McKenna, Kear, and Ellsworth (1995) found that attitude toward reading decreased as children progressed through elementary school. In a national survey of 18,000 students, McKenna et al. documented that recreational and academic reading attitudes, on average, began at a relatively positive point in first grade, grew increasingly negative as students passed from first to sixth grade, and ended in relatively difference by sixth grade. The increasingly negative attitude was clearly related to ability. Low achievers and modest achievers declined most, but high-achieving students did not decline.

A negative trend was also found in students' reading behavior. We documented a significant decrease in amount and breadth of reading from fourth to fifth grade. Younger students read about 22 minutes per day, whereas older students read about 12 minutes per day. Younger students read more widely and frequently than older students. Wigfield and Guthrie (1997) also found a negative trend in students' reading motivation. Self-efficacy declined significantly and social motivation for reading decreased from Grade 4 to Grade 5. Changes in motivations of curiosity, involvement, and social interchange are consistent with the decline in amount of reading. As motivation declines, without promotional activities, children are less likely to read.

MOTIVATIONAL VARIABLES: LINKS TO COGNITIVE READING PROCESSES

Several myths surround the potential contribution of motivation to the science and practice of reading. Many researchers think that motivation cannot be measured. Motivation is regarded as illusive and so dependent on self-report that its objectivity is doubted. Even if it can be measured, motivation is often regarded as a weak variable, unlikely to predict the hard cognitive stuff of reading. Some think motivation is a consequence of cognitive competence in reading rather than a cause or antecedent. To many cognitive scientists, motivation is boring. If it is not boring, motivation is considered someone else's domain. We suggest that at least some of these myths should be questioned.

Many authors concur that reading achievement is predicted by cognitive variables. We suggest that motivational variables also make significant contributions to our ability to account for reading achievement. We can specify a simple model of reading in which paragraph comprehension is a dependent variable representing achievement, summarizing is the independent cognitive variable, and intrinsic motivation is the independent motivational variable. We have substantial evidence that the cognitive activity of summarizing increases paragraph comprehension (Dole, Duffy, Roehler, & Pearson, 1991). In addition, intrinsically motivated students who enjoy learning new things or "getting lost" in a narration show higher comprehension. Meece and Holt (1993) showed that students possessing a high intrinsic motivation (e.g., they said, "I want to learn as much as possible from this text") reported more frequently using comprehension strategies (e.g., "I asked myself questions as I went along") and showed higher comprehension of paragraphs of science content than other students. Very little data are available to show that both the cognitive and the motivational variables predict paragraph comprehension when they are controlled for each other. However, we have ample evidence that each of them separately contributes to the prediction of paragraph comprehension.

The basic model can be presented with interest as the motivational variable. Schiefele (1996) documented the independent contribution of interest to paragraph comprehension. Interested students were those who reported that they were stimulated, engaged, and not bored when they were reading a text on prehistoric people or television. Interest accounted for 16% of the variance in comprehending texts on prehistoric people when prior knowledge of the topic and verbal ability (e.g., SAT scores) were controlled.

The basic model can be further represented with self-efficacy as the motivational variable. Self-efficacy is the belief that "I can do it" regarding a reading task. Schunk and Rice (1991) showed with fourth- and fifth-grade students that if children were taught a strategy for finding the main idea in a paragraph and were provided feedback on the use of their strategy, they improved their strategy use and their comprehension of new texts. In addition, children increased their self-efficacy for reading in comparison to control groups who were not provided this self-efficacy treatment. Increases in self-efficacy were associated with increases in paragraph comprehension and strategy use under true experimental conditions. These studies illustrate that three different motivational variables (intrinsic motivation, text-based interest, and self-efficacy) have been shown to account for variance in reading achievement measured as paragraph comprehension.

Another factor that predicts paragraph comprehension is amount of reading. In one illustration of this pattern, Echols, West, Stanovich, and Zehr (1996) measured amount of reading of fourth- and sixth-grade children with indicators of print exposure that consisted of the Title Recognition Test (TRT) and the Author Recognition Test (ART). The TRT measure of print exposure accounted for 8% and the ART measure accounted for 5% of the variance in reading comprehension when vocabulary, chronological age, and TV viewing were controlled. In that same study, amount of reading also contributed significantly to vocabulary, general information, and spelling after other cognitive variables were controlled. This predictive power of print exposure is now a widely replicated effect showing substantial correlations from age 3 years (Senechal, Thomas, & Monker, 1995) through adulthood (West, Stanovich, & Mitchell, 1993).

Allan Wigfield, along with others at the National Reading Research Center, asked, "What might predict amount of reading?" The answer, of course, was motivation. He expected that three aspects of motivation might predict amount of reading. He divided motivation into three general constructs including intrinsic motivation for reading (which consists of curiosity, involvement, and challenge), self-efficacy (which refers to self-perceived competence in reading tasks), and social motivation (which refers to fulfilling classroom responsibilities or sharing books with others). In one study, Wigfield and Guthrie (1995) found that intrinsic motivations for reading accounted for 15% of the variance in amount of reading even after accounting for the prior measures of amount of reading and prior levels of intrinsic motivation. In this study, Wigfield and Guthrie (1997) used data from 2 years of diaries recorded by children and confirmed by their parents. They also used a self-report questionnaire of breadth of reading. The data showed that motivation significantly predicted the growth of amount of reading from Grade 4 to Grade 5.

The initial framework of achievement, cognition, and motivation can be represented for beginning readers. The dependent variable becomes word recognition and, for this discussion, letter-sound knowledge and self-efficacy become the cognitive and motivational variables, respectively. There is abundant evidence that letter-sound knowledge predicts word recognition (Ehri, 1994). There is also growing evidence that self-efficacy predicts word recognition. For example, Gaa (1973) conducted an experiment in which first and second graders were trained to set cognitive goals for particular reading skills. Compared with students who were not provided this training, these trained students increased in word recognition and appropriateness of goal setting, which is central to self-regulated learning and self-efficacy. To complement these findings, Matheny and Edwards (1974) showed that teachers who provided support for self-efficacy by scaffolding students' responsibility for learning reading skills had higher proportions of high-achieving students than other teachers. More extensive reports of these findings can be found in Stipek (1996) in the *Handbook of Educational Psychology* and Schunk and Zimmermann (1997) in *Reading Engagement: Motivating Readers Through Integrated Instruction.*

A decade earlier, Stanovich (1986), in discussing the "Matthew Effect in Reading Achievement," said, "perhaps just as importantly as the cognitive consequences of reading failure are the motivational side effects . . . the motivational spinoffs of reading failure can lead to increasingly global performance deficits" (p. 389). At that time, Stanovich relied on the Butkowsky and Willows (1980) finding that low-achieving readers in fifth grade were characterized by learned helplessness. Butkowsky and Willows showed that poor readers attributed failure to low ability, and they attributed success to luck or outside factors. By fifth grade, low achievers had low self-efficacy and a sense of helplessness. It is known that the decline of intrinsic motivation (Wigfield & Guthrie, 1997) and attitude toward reading (McKenna et al., 1995) begins in Grade 1 and proceeds through Grade 5. By middle school, a substantial proportion of students have lost most of their intrinsic motivation and have become extrinsically oriented to learning in school. What we do not understand well are the dynamics of this process in the early stages of reading development.

We have attempted to illustrate that motivational variables enhance our prediction of reading achievement. However, cognitive psychologists of reading might be skeptical. They might hold that motivational variables are at best additive. They may suggest that motivation is like a main effect in an analysis of the variance. It adds to the predictability of reading outcomes but does not change the overall cognitive pattern. If motivation does not alter the relationships among cognitive variables, then it might be argued that the motivation variables do not change the nature of the cognitive theory under discussion. However, we do not know that the motivational variables are only additive.

Motivation may also interact with the cognitive system, influencing some cognitive constructs but not others. For example, intrinsic motivation appears to interact with the cognitive system to predict word identification. Graham and Golan (1991) gave some students task-oriented learning goals designed to increase their intrinsic motivation. They gave other students ego-oriented learning goals designed to increase extrinsic motivation. The intrinsically motivated students surpassed the extrinsically motivated group in category naming tasks that required taxonomic analysis and memory. However, students having intrinsic motivations achieved the same as students with extrinsic motivations on identification of rhyme. The category naming task required deeper processing, more long-term memory, and was probably less automated than the rhyming tasks for these fifth and sixth graders. Graham and Golan concluded that a task orientation in reading influenced performance on the memory-demanding tasks, but not the rhyming tasks. In other words, a given motivational construct may predict one type of cognitive task but not another type of cognitive task. It appears that intrinsic motivations for reading are likely to influence some but not all cognitive variables in reading.

In conclusion, we submit that motivational variables do currently contribute to the prediction of some reading phenomena for children at some ages. Motivational variables are already part of our scientific understanding of reading comprehension because the variables of intrinsic motivation, self-efficacy, and interest have been documented to predict paragraph comprehension. These motivational effects, however, have not been as fully examined for cognitive processes that undergird word recognition and other basic processes. In closing, because motivational variables hold substantial promise for clarifying and augmenting our cognitive accounts of reading and learning to read, it appears that a full science of reading cannot afford to omit motivation.

PRINCIPLES FOR PROMOTING READING MOTIVATION

Up to this point of the chapter, we have described what we mean by motivation for reading. Although many constructs are referring to motivation, we discuss principles to support intrinsic motivation for reading, which includes curiosity, involvement, challenge, and social dispositions for reading. Our principles for promoting reading motivation have been derived from two sources. The first source is the empirical literature on contexts that support reading motivation. This literature has been more extensively reviewed in articles by Guthrie and Alao (1997) in *Educational Psychologist* and Guthrie, Cox, Anderson, Harris, Mazonni, and Rach (1998) *in Educational Psychology Review*. A sampling of the empirical literature represented in those two articles is provided here for illustrative purposes.

Our second source of evidence is a series of videotapes of classrooms in which motivation was a high priority in the instructional context. For 3 years, in association with the National Reading Research Center, we collaboratively designed and implemented classroom instruction in which the goal of teaching was reading engagement. Our aim, in the classroom, was to enable students to use strategies for their reading and learning and to motivate them to want to read frequently and widely, as described more extensively in another source (Guthrie, Van Meter, Hancock, Anderson, & Alao, 1998). We interviewed teachers as they viewed videotapes of their instruction and developed principles of the instructional contexts that promote reading motivation.

In combination with each principle, we present potential threats or hazards in the implementation of this principle in reading programs. We believe that these contextual principles are sufficiently powerful that they can undermine motivation as well as promote motivation. Therefore, we not only portray the principles but also identify some conditions that influence whether they are likely to be optimally effective.

Conceptual Theme

Instruction is organized around broad interdisciplinary themes in which the skills, strategies, and contents of language, science, and history are integrated.

Conceptual themes are productive starting points for designing instruction because they invite teachers and students to form learning goals. Understanding the theme is an overarching goal around which a variety of skills, strategies, and content can be organized (Lipson, Valencia, Wixson, & Peters, 1993). From a motivational perspective, conceptually thematic classrooms support a mastery orientation (Anderman & Young, 1994). In this context, teachers can focus on student learning and progress toward the conceptual goal, rather than emphasizing ability-based practices that tend to undermine motivation for reading (Pintrich & Schrauben, 1992). Conceptual goals for reading have been shown to increase interest, enjoyment, and the willingness to process text more deeply than performance goals or ego-oriented objectives (Benware & Deci, 1984).

One limitation of using a conceptual theme that emphasizes a mastery orientation may be the entering motivations of the students. In one school-based study with 10- and 11-year-old children, Lehtinen, Vauras, Salonen, Olkinuora, and Kinnunen (1995) reported that students who possessed a task orientation before entering a mastery-oriented environment increased their motivations for reading and learning. However, students who entered the classroom with performance orientations were less productive in the environment and were socially dependent on the teacher for extensive help. Performance-oriented students in the mastery-based context needed extended guidance in making choices and focusing on personal progress.

At least three potential hazards surround the use of conceptual themes for motivating reading. First, a conceptual theme explores a topic in depth. To be productive, this topic must be academically significant, such as adaptation or the solar system. Many critics complain about academically trivial themes, appearing frequently in classrooms, that do not warrant in-depth study. Because the content is explored in depth, traditional criteria for coverage of a multitude of topics must be suspended. The trend in science education in the United States is to promote in-depth understanding of a few expansive concepts, such as cycles and patterns in life science. A conceptual theme needs to be abstract, expansive, and generative enough to spawn multiple subtopics. This enables the theme to embrace the particular interest of different students and to be informed by a range of books.

The role of a teacher in thematic instruction shifts from the traditional. In many traditional classrooms, the teacher is a transmitter of information and possessor of knowledge. To be successful in supporting an instructional theme, the teacher must become a facilitator, enabling students to pursue particular aspects of a conceptual theme of interest to them. The teacher supports the process of inquiry, rather than presenting or delivering the knowledge and content.

Real-World Interactions

Students interact with tangible objects, events, and experiences related to a conceptual theme by observing, manipulating, and recording.

Real-world interactions, such as collecting "crickets" or viewing the metamorphosis of a butterfly, serve multiple functions in a conceptually thematic instructional unit. First, these experiences are exciting for an extremely large majority of students. This arousal represents a situational interest (Schraw et al., 1995) that we believe develops into long-term motivation for reading. If the energy aroused by situated phenomena is directed to supportive interesting texts, students will read them naturally. Real-world experiences usually evoke a sense of awe and wonder. Ross (1988) reviewed experiments showing that "hands-on" treatments in classrooms enhance the quality and number of questions the students asked. These questions ranged from issues related to structural features to probing inquiries about causes and explanations. In a study related to this principle of real-world interaction, Bruning, Schweiger, and Nietfeld (1996) reported that young students who were given the opportunity to observe the Madagascar giant hissing cockroach were motivated to read widely about this creature and remembered their texts better than other students who did not have this observational opportunity. These real-world interactions provide a personal meaningfulness (Stipek, 1996) and a sense of ownership (Au & Asam, 1996) for the books chosen from these interactions with real-world situations.

One hazard of using real-world interactions as a context for promoting reading motivation is related to time and scheduling. If too much time is devoted to the real-world interaction in the form of field trips, specimen collection, and recording phenomena, time may be subtracted from productive reading activities. We find that a relatively few minutes of observing tangible objects and events can launch literacy activities that will last one or two weeks. Although the interactions are exciting and students prefer them for long amounts of time, the motivational benefit is gained in a short period. In a short time students will be excited and aroused. They will pose a rich array of questions. If books can be provided to help answer these questions, students' motivations for reading will be promoted.

To be motivating for students, real-world interactions should be conceptual rather than procedural. Students should be encouraged to see and hear but should also be encouraged to explain. Unfortunately, some teachers overproceduralize real-world observation. They give students a long number of steps for observing and recording. These steps may interfere with rather than facilitate conceptual interaction with the phenomenon. Although students need some guidance, the danger is that the guidance will become more prominent than the phenomenon of original interest. Finally, the experience of real-world interactions should be iterative. Students should visit and revisit the phenomenon, beginning at the outset of instruction and recurring as their interests dictate and their need for reinvigoration may suggest.

Self-Direction

Teachers enable students to assume responsibility for reading by helping them to select a topic, text, tasks, and multimedia for reading about the conceptual theme.

The principle of self-direction is grounded in self-determination theory (Deci, 1992). Deci, Swartz, Sheinman, and Ryan (1981) suggested that teachers who enable students to make choices about their learning, participate in instructional decisions, and personally identify with the goals of the classroom are likely to create classroom environments in which students are intrinsically motivated to learn the content and participate actively in classroom activities. Grolnick and Ryan (1987) said that autonomy support specifically for reading increased motivation and comprehension. In their study, a group of students who read social studies text to answer their own questions showed higher interest and comprehension than students who were instructed to memorize the content or read without any directions. Not only does teacher support for student autonomy increase motivation for reading, but students' active involvement in learning increases the autonomy support they receive from teachers. In other words, autonomy support from the teacher and students engagement in reading are reciprocal (Skinner & Belmont, 1993). Among primary children, self-direction is also effective. Working with first-grade children, Turner (1995) showed that providing a small degree of freedom of choice was intrinsically motivating. Likewise, Gaa (1979) found that helping young children in Grades 1 and 2 set their own goals for reading increased their disposition to work independently.

The principle of self-direction must be implemented with care and deliberation. If students are provided too little self-direction, they are confined, bored, and unimaginative. On the other side of the coin, if students are provided too much self-direction, they may feel lost and aimless. An excessive number of choices (e.g., context of total freedom) may be dispiriting rather than motivating. If students do not possess the knowledge on which to make good book selections, opportunity for choice will not be effective. If students do not have strategies to find books of interest to them in a given situation, they will be more frustrated than motivated by opportunities for choosing.

Multiple selections of books must be available for successful implementation of the self-direction principle. If students are encouraged to choose, they must experience reward by having attractive books and texts available. A range of genres including informational stories, reference books, and so on is useful in a self-directed situation. It is not always possible to predict the types of interests students will bring to a choice or the types of interests they may discover when they are given the opportunity to choose. Consequently, promoting reading motivation requires the adroit implementation of this powerful principle of self-direction.

Interesting Texts

Teachers provide a variety of books (e.g., exposition, references, literary texts, folk tales, poetry, and electronic database) in a wide range of difficulty.

Researchers have found that students will rate a book to be "interesting" if it is familiar and easy to comprehend (Schraw et al., 1995). Interesting texts, furthermore, contain vivid details and attractive illustrations. These features attract students to spend more time and read a larger number of words within these books (McLoyd, 1979). When children are provided an opportunity to read books that are interesting according to these criteria, their achievement and motivation for reading are increased jointly (Morrow, 1996). When a diversity of interesting texts is provided and student choice and self-direction are encouraged, ownership of literacy begins to develop (Au & Asam, 1996). If one interesting text is located and devoured with relish by a student, the student will want another similar book. However, if a second highly related book is not available, the student may find other books to be comparably dull, and the student may become demotivated in this situation.

Coupled with the need of an abundant supply is a need for some connection. Even if books are located under the umbrella of a conceptual theme, teachers need to point to connections among them that may not be obvious to students. For example, informational books about birds may reveal their feeding and nesting habitats, whereas poetry may reveal the aesthetics of catching insects or a safe nest. The connections among these, however, may make the texts interesting. According to Hartman and Allison (1996), intertextuality or the linkages across texts are intriguing and motivating.

Cognitive Strategies

Teachers provide a variety of supports for strategic reading including modeling, explaining, coaching, peer discussions, practice, and student reflection.

Collins-Block (1992) reported that teaching strategies of planning, predicting, and inferring increased self-perceived competence (Harter, 1982) for reading. Students who received strategy instruction felt empowered in their application strategies to new reading situations. Likewise, Payne and Manning (1992) showed that students who gained strategies for understanding the narrative structure of stories discovered stories to be more interesting than students who did not enjoy their strategy learning. Other investigators have linked strategy learning to self-efficacy for reading. For example, Schunk and Swartz (1993) showed that training in reading comprehension strategies increased students' self-confidence for using those skills in new situations. Students who possessed effective strategies are likely to have an increased sense of self-efficacy and to approach new books with a confidence that other students do not possess. Enabling students to read fluently is also empowering. Blum et al. (1995) found that when students (especially second language learners) were able to increase their oral reading fluency, their attitude toward reading increased. In other words, fluency development and intrinsic motivation for reading are reciprocally related in beginning readers.

Several hazards surround strategy training. The first is the relevance of the strategies. If students do not need a cognitive strategy to fulfill their own goals for reading or learning, the strategy will not be well learned. Extensive strategy instruction, in the absence of any significant need to know the strategy, will be counterproductive rather than motivating. The second hazard is that strategies may not be easily transferred. Teachers need to help students bridge the strategy to new situations. Otherwise the strategy, even if it is learned well in one content with one type of book, may not be used in another content with another type of book. Finally, strategies such as finding books in the library, finding favorite authors, and identifying specific topics within books must be learned to a high level of fluency. In the absence of fluency, the strategies are effortful and not rewarding. The sense of empowerment and self-perceived competence that strategy learning can bestow depends on an original purpose for learning the strategy, a bridge to a range of useful settings for applying the strategy, and comfort in using the strategy based on successful and useful work.

Social Collaboration

Students work together in a variety of social structures, including individual work, partnerships, small teams, and whole-class activities as they learn the content in reading strategies relevant to the conceptual theme.

The social milieu in which students read is likely to influence their motivation. Guthrie, Schafer, Wang, and Afflerbach (1995) showed that when students are encouraged by the teacher to shared books with friends, talk about their writing, and discuss reactions to their reading, they are more likely to read widely and frequently. In that study, the teachers' influence on students' amount and breadth of reading was mediated by the social structure. In other words, if teachers created an environment for sharing books and discussing writing, students were likely to choose to read more widely and frequently on their own. However, if teachers emphasized individual work and solitary reading, students were less likely to seek out their own books to read for enjoyment voluntarily. Turner (1995) also reported that for young children, a socially interactive milieu for book reading increased intrinsic motivation for the tasks for initially learning to read. Finally, the independent reading and writing centers provided by Morrow (1996) contained not only interesting books and ample time for reading them but a socially supportive opportunity for relaxed conversation with peers. This blend of interesting texts and conversational context has been seen to increase reading motivations.

Several hazards of collaboration for reading motivation do exist. One threat to the principle of social collaboration is low group cohesion. If the social group has not acquired the disposition to listen, exchange, and value the thoughts of all participants, the group is unlikely to motivate reading activity. Almasi (1995) reported that it may require many weeks of interaction before a group of 9-year-olds becomes cohesive enough to talk, discuss, and understand stories at a new level. In her work on fostering communities of learners, Brown (1997) worked with fifth-grade students over a 12-week conceptually thematic unit. The cohesiveness of groups is deliberately cultivated by the teacher, enabling them to battle out ideas about environmental science and become personally invested in their reading and thinking. Although she has not measured student motivation quantitatively, reports of the classrooms make it seem that students have acquired a mastery orientation and an intrinsic motivation for reading. Another threat to the social collaborative principle is a loss of cognitive challenge. If social groups are not conceptual, they may not continue to motivate extended reading. If the conversational interchange is off-task, nonconceptual, or cliquish, it may decrease rather than increase the motivation of the members for extended reading and thinking.

Self-Expression

Students are supported in articulating their understanding of the books and texts in ways that are personally and culturally relevant to them and their audiences.

If students are able to have ideas their about books heard and appreciated by other students, they feel that they are legitimated and valued (Oldfather & McLaughlin, 1993). By inviting a wide range of reactions and allowing students freedom in discussing texts, teachers encourage students to believe that their voices are "honored" in the classroom (Oldfather & Dahl, 1994). The principle of self-expression is embodied in Blumenfeld et al.'s (1991) emphasis on developing an artifact in project-based teaching. By teachers encouraging students to build models or illustrate science concepts in their own forms, students are motivated to read widely and think creatively.

Some real limitations of the self-expression principle are as follows. First, the principle is not well established in traditionally empirical research. The principle has been induced from case studies (e.g., described by Oldfather and her colleagues) and it has been induced from videotapes of Concept-Oriented Reading Instruction (Guthrie, McGough, Bennett, & Rice, 1996). It has not been tested with traditional hypothetical deductive research. Therefore, the principle itself is not as well established as others in this set of principles. One potential limit to its application is that students will become too extreme in their subjectivism. Although the self-expressive principle encourages students to believe in their own ability to construct meaning and knowledge from books, in its extreme form the students may believe that the text does not constrain their thinking and that any ideas are acceptable. Helping the reader to realize that there is a *text* in the reader–text interaction that we call reading comprehension is an important aspect of implementing the self-expression principle.

CONCLUDING COMMENT

In our view, promoting reading motivation depends on all these principles operating in concert. Although each principle has been shown to increase motivation in experimental, correlational, or case-based research, an isolated principle is unlikely to be effective. For example, self-direction cannot be applied without texts to which students can direct themselves. Self-direction relies on strategies for finding books, reading them, and self-regulating the comprehension process. Consequently, these principles are woven in a tapestry that we call *coherence*. The context for promoting reading motivation consists of a pattern of these principles. It is not a single variable but a network of variables that is likely to spark and sustain the long-term motivation required for students to become full members in the world of engaged readers.

REFERENCES

Alexander, P. A., & Filler, R. C. (1976). *Attitudes and reading.* Newark, DE: International Reading Association.

Alexander, P. A., Kulikowich, J. M., & Jetton, T. L. (1994). The role of subject-matter knowledge and interest in the processing of linear and nonlinear texts. *Review of Educational Research, 64,* 201–252.

Almasi, J. F. (1995). The nature of fourth graders' sociocognitive conflicts in peer-led and teacher-led discussion of literature. *Reading Research Quarterly, 30,* 314–351.

Ames, C., & Archer, J. (1988). Achievement goals in the classroom: Students' learning strategies and motivational processes. *Journal of Educational Psychology, 80,* 260–267.

Anderman, E. M., & Young, A. J. (1994). Motivation and strategy use in science: Individual differences and classroom effects. *Journal of Research in Science Teaching, 31,* 811–831.

Au, K. H., & Asam, C. L. (1996). Improving the literacy achievement of low-income students of diverse backgrounds. In M. F. Graves, P. van den Broek, & B. M. Taylor (Eds.), *The first R: Every child's right to read* (pp. 199–223). New York: Teachers College Press.

Benware, C. A., & Deci, E. L. (1984). Quality of learning with an active versus passive motivational set. *American Educational Research Journal, 21,* 775–765.

Blum, I. H., Koskinen, P. S., Tennant, N., Parker, E. M., Straub, J., & Curry, C. (1995). *Using audiotaped books to extend classroom literacy instruction into the home of second language learners* (Research Report No. 39). Athens, GA: National Reading Research Center, Universities of Georgia and Maryland.

Blumenfeld, P. C., Soloway, E., Marx, R. W., Krajcik, J. S., Guzdial, M., & Palincsar, A. (1991). Motivating project-based learning: Sustaining the doing, supporting the learning. *Edcational Psychologist, 26*, 369–398.

Brown, A. L. (1997). Transforming schools into communities of thinking and learning about serious matters. *American Psychologist, 52*, 399–413.

Bruning, R., Schweiger, B., & Nietfeld, J. (1996). *The role of observation in reading recall and interest: A preliminary study* (National Reading Research Center Progress Report). Athens, GA: National Reading Research Center, Universities of Georgia and Maryland.

Butkowsky, S., & Willows, D. (1980). Cognitive-motivational characteristics of children varying in reading ability: Evidence for learned helplessness in poor readers. *Journal of Educational Psychology, 72*, 408–422.

Collins-Block, C. (1992). Strategy instruction in a literature-based reading program. *Elementary School Journal, 94*, 139–151.

Deci, E. L. (1992). The relation of interest to the motivation of behavior: A self-determination theory perspective. In A. Renninger, S. Hidi, & A. Krapp (Eds.), *The role of interest in learning and development* (pp. 43–70). Hillsdale, NJ: Lawrence Erlbaum Associates.

Deci, E. L., Swartz, A. J., Sheinman, L., Ryan, R. M. (1981). Motivation and education: The self-determination perspective. *Educational Psychologist, 26*, 325–346.

Dole, J. A., Duffy, G. G., Roehler, L. R., & Pearson, P. D. (1991). Moving from the old to the new: Research on reading comprehension instruction. *Review of Educational Research, 61*, 239–264.

Echols, L. D., West, R. F., Stanovich, K. E., & Zehr, K. S. (1996). Using children's literacy activities to predict growth in verbal cognitive skills: A longitudinal investigation. *Journal of Educational Psychology, 88*(2), 296–304.

Ehri, L. C. (1994). Development of the ability to read words: Update. In R. B. Ruddell, M. R. Ruddell, & H. Singer (Eds.), *Theoretical models and processes of reading* (pp. 323–358). Newark, DE: International Reading Association.

Gaa, J. P. (1973). Effects of individual goal-setting conferences on achievement, attitudes, and goal-setting behavior. *Journal of Experimental Education, 42*, 22–28.

Gaa, J. P. (1979). The effects of individual goal-setting conferences on academic achievement and modification of locus of control orientation. *Psychology in the Schools, 16*, 591–597.

Graham, S., & Golan, S. (1991). Motivational influences on cognition: Task involvement, ego involvement, and depth of information processing. *Journal of Educational Psychology, 83*, 187–194.

Grolnick, W. S., & Ryan, R. M. (1987). Autonomy in children's learning: An experimental and individual difference investigation. *Journal of Personality and Social Psychology, 52*, 890–898.

Guthrie, J. T., & Alao, S. (1997). Designing contexts to increase motivations for reading. *Educational Psychologist, 32*, 95–107.

Guthrie, J. T., & Anderson, E. (1999). Engagement in reading: Processes of motivated, strategic, knowledgeable, social readers. In J. T. Guthrie & D. E. Alvermann (Eds.), *Engaged reading: Processes, practices and policy implications* (pp. 17–45). New York: Teachers College Press.

Guthrie, J. T., Cox, K., Anderson, E., Harris, K., Mazonni, S., & Rach, L. (1998). Principles of integrated instruction for engagement in reading. *Educational Psychology Review, 10*(2), 177–199.

Guthrie, J. T., McGough, K., Bennett, L., & Rice, M. E. (1996). Concept-Oriented Reading Instruction: An integrated curriculum to develop motivations and strategies for reading. In L. Baker, P. Afflerbach, & D. Reinking (Eds.), *Developing engaged readers in school and home communities* (pp. 165–190). Mahwah, NJ: Lawrence Erlbaum Associates.

Guthrie, J. T., Schafer, W. D., Wang, Y. Y., & Afflerbach, P. (1995). Relationships of instruction of reading: An exploration of a social, cognitive, and instructional connections. *Reading Research Quarterly, 30*(1), 8–25.

Guthrie, J. T., Van Meter, P., Hancock, G. R., McCann, A., Anderson, E., & Alao, S. (1998). Does Concept-Oriented Reading Instruction increase strategy-use and conceptual learning from text? *Journal of Educational Psychology, 90*(2), 261–278.

Harter, S. (1981). A new self-report scale of intrinsic versus extrinsic orientation in the classroom: Motivational and informational components. *Developmental Psychology, 17,* 300–312.

Harter, S. (1982). The perceived competence scale for children. *Child Development, 53,* 87–97.

Hartman, D. K., & Allison, J. (1996). Promoting inquiry-oriented discussions using multiple texts. In L. Gambrell & J. Almasi, (Eds.) *Lively discussions!* (pp. 106–133). Newark, DE: International Reading Association.

Lehtinen, E., Vauras, M., Salonen, P., Olkinuora, E., & Kinnunen R. (1995). Long-term development of learning activity: Motivational, cognitive, and social interaction. *Educational Psychologist, 30,* 21–35.

Lipson, M. Y., Valencia, S. W., Wixson, K. K., & Peters, C. W. (1993). Integration and thematic teaching: Integration to improve teaching and learning. *Language Arts, 70,* 252–271.

Matheny, K., & Edwards, C. (1974). Academic improvement through an experimental classroom management system. *Journal of School Psychology,* 222–232.

Matsumoto, D., & Sanders, M. (1988). Emotional experiences during engagement in intrinsically and extrinsically motivated tasks. *Motivation and Emotion, 12,* 353–369.

McKenna, M. C., & Kerr, D. J. (1990). Measuring attitude toward reading: A new tool for teachers. *The Reading Teacher, 43,* 626–639.

McKenna, M. C., Kear, D. J., & Ellsworth, R. A. (1995). Children's attitudes toward reading: A national survey. *Reading Research Quarterly, 30,* 934–956.

McLoyd, V. (1979). The effects on extrinsic rewards of differential value on high and low intrinsic interest. *Child Development, 50,* 1010–1019.

Meece, J. L., & Holt, K. (1993). A pattern analysis of students' achievement goals. *Journal of Educational Psychology, 85,* 582–590.

Morrow, L. M. (1996). *Motivating reading writing in diverse classrooms: Social and physical contexts in a literature-based program* (NCTE Research Report No. 28). Urbana, IL: National Council of Teachers of English.

Newman, R. S. (1990). Children's help-seeking in the classroom: The role of motivational factors and attitudes. *Journal of Educational Psychology, 82,* 71–80.

Nicholls, J. G., Cheung, P., Lauer, J., & Patashnick, M. (1989). Individual differences in academic motivation: Perceived ability, goals, beliefs, and values. *Learning and Individual Differences, 1,* 63–84.

Oldfather, P., & Dahl, K. (1994). Toward a social constructivist reconceptualization of intrinsic motivation for literacy learning. *Journal of Reading Behavior, 26,* 139–158.

Oldfather, P., & McLaughlin, J. (1993). Gaining and losing voice: A longitudinal study of students' continuing impulse to learn across elementary and middle school contexts. *Research in Middle Level Education, 11,* 1–25.

Payne, B. D., & Manning, B. H. (1992). Basal reader instruction: Effects of comprehension monitoring training on reading comprehension, strategy use and attitude. *Reading Research and Instruction, 32,* 29–38.

Pintrich, P. R., & De Groot, E. V. (1990). Motivational and self-regulated learning components of classroom academic performance. *Journal of Educational Psychology, 82,* 33–40.

Pintrich, P. R., & Schrauben, B. (1992). Students' motivational beliefs and their cognitive engagement in classroom academic tasks. In D. H. Schunk & J. L. Meece (Eds.), *Student perceptions in the classroom* (pp. 149–184). Hillsdale, NJ: Lawrence Erlbaum Associates.

Renninger, K. A., Hidi, S., & Krapp, A. (1992). *The role of interest in learning an development.* Hillsdale, NJ: Lawrence Erlbaum Associates.

Ross, J. A. (1988). Controlling variables: A meta-anlaysis of training studies. *Review of Educational Research, 58,* 405–437.

Ryan, R. M., & Deci, E. L. (2000). Intrinsic and extrinsic motivations: Classic definitions and new directions. *Contemporary Educational Psychology, 25,* 54–67.

Schiefele, U. (1992). Topic interest and levels of text comprehension. In K. A. Renninger, S. Hidi, & A. Krapp (Eds.), *The role of interest and development* (pp. 151–212). Hillsdale, NJ: Lawrence Erlbaum Associates.

Schiefele, U. (1996). Topic interest, text representation, and quality of experience. *Contemporary Educational Psychology, 21,* 3–18.

Schraw, G., Bruning, R., & Svoboda, C. (1995). Source of situational interest. *Journal of Reading Behavior, 27*(1), 1–17.

Schunk, D. H., & Rice, J. M. (1991). Learning goals and progress feedback during reading comprehension instruction. *Journal of Reading Behavior, 23,* 351–364.

Schunk, D. H., & Swartz, C. W. (1993). Goals and progress feedback: Effects on self-efficacy and writing achievement. *Contemporary Educational Psychology, 18,* 337–354.

Schunk, D. H., & Zimmerman, B. J. (1997). Developing self-efficacious readers and writers: The role of social and self-regulatory processes. In J. T. Guthrie & A. Wigfield (Eds.), *Reading engagement: Motivating readers through integrated instruction* (pp. 34–50). Newark, DE: International Reading Association.

Senechal, M., Thomas, E. H., & Monker, J. A. (1995). Individual differences in 4-year-old children acquisition of vocabulary during storybook reading. *Journal of Educational Psychology, 87,* 218–229.

Skinner, E. A., & Belmont, M. J. (1993). Motivation in the classroom: Reciprocal effects of teacher behavior and student engagement across the school year. *Journal of Educational Psychology, 85,* 571–581.

Stanovich, K. E. (1986). Matthew effects in reading: Some consequences of individual differences in the acquisition of literacy. *Reading Research Quarterly, 24,* 360–406.

Stipek, D. (1996). Motivation and instruction. In D. C. Berliner & R. C. Calfee (Eds.), *Handbook of educational psychology* (pp. 85–113). New York: Simon & Schuster Macmillan.

Turner, J. C. (1995). The influence of classroom contexts on young children's motivation for literacy. *Reading Research Quarterly, 30,* 410–441.

West, R. F., Stanovich, K. E., & Mitchell, H. R. (1993). Reading in the real world and its correlates. *Reading Research Quarterly, 28,* 34–51.

Wigfield, A., Eccles, J. S., & Rodriguez, D. (1998). The development of children's motivation in school contexts. *Review of Research In Education, 23,* 73–118.

Wigfield, A., & Guthrie, J. T. (1995). *Dimensions of children's motivations for reading: An initial study* (Reading Research Report #34). Athens, GA: National Reading Research Center.

Wigfield, A., & Guthrie, J. T. (1997). Relations of children's motivation for reading to the amount and breadth of their reading. *Journal of Educational Psychology, 89,* 420–432.

9

Literature as an Environment for Engaged Readers

Judith A. Langer

State University of New York–Albany

Literature can play a central role in students' intellectual, social, and personal development. In this chapter, I describe ways in which literary imagination provokes us to explore options, solve problems, and understand others—to engage in social activity with literary, imagined, and real situations. As such, it calls us to rethink the contribution literature can make to intelligent and humane thinking as well as the need to nurture students' literary experiences in the development of thoughtful literacy, not only in literature course work, but across the curriculum. Since 1987, through my work funded by the U.S. Department of Education, Office of Educational Research and Improvement, I have been working toward a reader-based theory for the teaching of literature. My goal has been to understand what it means to make sense of literature from a reader's point of view, ways in which it can support a community of engaged and highly literate readers, and what that means for refocusing instructional goals and practice. (See Langer, 1995, for the most complete discussion of this work, some of which I call on in this chapter.) In the first part of this chapter, I describe what I have learned from my studies about the web of sense-making underlying literary understanding. I then discuss how it can support the conception of literacy as a social activity, and thereby affect our notions of literate engagement, generativity, and instruction.

Through literature, students learn to explore possibilities and consider options for themselves and the world. They imagine others, try on selves they might become, and examine difference from many angles of vision. All literature, the stories and expositions we read as well as those we tell, provides us with a way to imagine human potential and what else might be. It has a drawing-in quality that invites readers, writers, speakers, and listeners into the experiences being depicted, to participate in the events and ideas. It is here we come face to face with a life (or a part of a life), a human existence. In real life we cannot parcel out certain conditions and put others aside, nor can we do this when we try to understand literature. History counts, as do desire and conflict; varied perspectives come into play. We need to deal with the many forces that create a living reality, including the connectedness of the parts, the gaps, the shifts in perspective and time, as well as the multiple vantage points from which each situation can be viewed and the many participating voices. When engaging in a literary experience, we not only examine things from many perspectives, but also become aware that there are many possibilities, and no final resolutions. There is always another possible interpretation yet to come.

Literature invites the reader or listener into the piece, to consider the ideas or events from an insider's perspective. Literary structure is fraught with gaps that pull the reader into the moment, yet it offers opportunities to fill in untold portions and fill out details and elaborations. I call these insider perspectives a *literary orientation*. In this orientation, people explore "horizons of possibilities" (Langer, 1990, 1995), raising questions for the moment and rethinking the shape of what is yet to come. Here, people create scenarios, take multiple perspectives, seek motives and relationships—they search for the "real" story. They examine language, make connections, analyze perspectives, and consider possible interpretations. And they use their imaginations with generative creativity, to solve the problems and puzzles they seek to untangle. They engage in highly literate activity. Literary thought is a critical component of the well-formed mind. It offers a productive route to understanding (see, e.g., Britton, 1970; Bruner, 1986; S. Langer, 1942; Lauter, 1990; Ricoeur, 1980). It is important that we not lose sight of what these notions can contribute to our conceptions of literacy development as a social activity.

EXPLORING HORIZONS OF POSSIBILITIES

I have found it helpful to think of the literary orientation as "exploring horizons of possibilities," because from this orientation people explore emotions, relationships, motives, and reactions, calling on all we know about what it is to be human in order to make sense. The literary experience and the exploration it engenders are essentially social. Here, we consider feelings, intentions, and implications in our quest for the "hidden" story we must uncover. We place ourselves into the events, activities, or thoughts and try to make our way by exploring social meanings. Often we create scenarios as a way to situate ourselves and imagine others. A literary orientation is essentially one of exploration, where uncertainty and openness, filling in and filling out, are a normal part of the thinking, and new understandings provoke still other possibilities.

For example, once we read and think we understand that Romeo and Juliet really love each other, we may begin to question how their parents would really feel about their relationship if they took the time to understand its depth, and this begins to reshape our understanding of the entire play. And then as we read on, we might begin to question whether Romeo and Juliet are bigger-than-life tragic figures, with their destiny somehow controlled by forces beyond even their parents' control—more so when we try to make sense of Juliet's decision to die. How, we might ponder, could someone have prevented this from occurring? As we read, we often take many perspectives, exploring possible points of view of other characters (such as the parents and townspeople, even the society at large), of other eras (whether such a thing could happen now), and of other texts (how different is it really, from *West Side Story*?). We also embark on different kinds of interpretations, doing, say, a feminist, Marxist, or mythic reading, or we might look at the piece through the lens of cultural criticism. Throughout the reading (and even after we have closed the book), our ideas constantly shift and swell. Possibilities arise; other interpretations come to mind that shift not only our understanding of that particular portion of the text, but often its implications for the piece as a whole, thereby expanding the complexity of our understandings and providing yet another possible "take" on the whole. Political, cultural, and ideological realities invade the meanings we create and provide layers of opportunity to read with or against the text (Fetterly, 1978), to take a variety of perspectives and positions. This is why many readings of the same text and many viewings of the same play are in part always new, inviting us to relive known experiences while at the same time feeding our openness to previously unexplored possibilities. Most recently, I saw a new ballet performance of *Romeo and Juliet* and was delighted to witness the very somber lovers meeting their death as knowing martyrs, sending their message of societal doom to the townspeople blind to the ills within their stratified world. In literature, there are no absolute endings, only the potential for other possibilities.

In a literary experience, reading proceeds at two levels at the same time: As we read, we use our sense of the piece as a whole in order to explore possibilities that can clarify ideas and expand our understandings for the moment, but as each possibility brings new ideas to mind it also affects our broad sense of the piece, providing a possible way to rethink the whole. There is an ever-emerging "horizon of possibilities" (Langer, 1995) that enriches the reader's understanding. Readers always try to go beyond the information, exploring possibilities about the characters, settings, situations, or actions and the ways in which they might interrelate. In doing so, through social interaction with the piece and its potential they leave themselves open to the alternative interpretations, changing points of view, complex characterizations, and unresolved questions that underlie the open-endedness inherent in the interpretation of literature. It is this openness that invites the imagination and becomes a way to look beyond things as they are, in search of potentially enriching perspectives (for related ideas, see Benton, 1992; Egan & Nadaner, 1988; Greene, 1995). And this can become one essential part of how students learn to reason, understand, and find themselves in relation to their worlds.

POSSIBILITIES AND PROBLEMS

A literary orientation involves a great deal of highly literate thinking but is different from the kinds of thinking students are generally expected to engage in for their other academic course work, although my studies show it can bring important new perspectives to, say, science or history studies, to augment students' understandings in interesting ways (see Langer, 1995a, 1995b). Further, there is a growing body of evidence from a number of fields that the processes involved are useful at work, helping doctors (Elstein, Shulman, & Sprafka, 1978), lawyers (Putnam, 1978), and computer repairers (Orr, 1987) think through difficult problems and develop possible solutions.

Nevertheless, we have ample evidence that despite many literature-based and response-based "movements" in the United States, literature is still too often shaped by a text-based set of beliefs and behaviors that guide instructional goals, interactions, and assessments. In the United States, the traditional approach called for close readings of texts, with particular emphasis on the narrator, the point of view, and the "correct" interpretation. Among other things, this view has often led to the assumption in planning instruction that contemplating, analyzing, and theorizing about a piece come only after students know the facts, what happened to whom. Thus, traditional lessons generally begin with a "quick check," a plot summary and a beginning-to-end retracing to be sure the facts are known. In short, they rely on hierarchical notions of complexity, on text-based notions of comprehension, and on the teacher or field as knowledge holders. A number of theories provide alternatives (e.g., Bleich, 1978; Britton, 1970; Iser, 1974; Langer, 1995; Rosenblatt, 1938/1983; Scholes, 1985; Tompkins, 1980). My perspective on literacy as a social activity, and on its contribution to notions of engagement, follows.

THE CLASSROOM AS A LITERATURE COMMUNITY

A Sociocognitive Perspective

I come to my work with what I call a sociocognitive view of learning (Langer, 1987), which posits that as students learn literacy, the ways in which they approach, become engaged with, and think about the material is affected by the social experiences in their lives in general, and their classroom in particular (e.g., Bakhtin, 1981; New London Group, 1996; Rogoff, 1994; Vygotsky, 1987; Wells & Chang-Wells, 1992). Helping students gain new or different literacy practices, in this case ways of becoming engaged with literature, involves not merely a connection to their lives, but a shift in the focus and social interactions within the classroom itself, in the beliefs about what counts as knowing, the nature of the values and conversations, and the kinds of support that is offered.

Envisionments as Thoughts-in-Motion

I use the word *envisionment* (Langer, 1985, 1987a, 1987b, 1995; Langer, Bartolome, & Lucas, 1990) to refer to the world of understanding a person has about a text or topic at any point in time. Envisionments are text worlds in the mind, and they differ from individual to individual due to personal and cultural experiences, relationships to the present experience, what a person knows and feels, and what one is after. They are meanings-in-motion, the dynamic set of ideas an images a person has in mind that are subject to change as the text progresses, as ideas are discussed, or with time, thought, and experience. The notion of comprehension as the act of envisionment building provides us with a way to conceptualize the possibilities of engagement through redefining literacy as social activity, where readers have opportunities to interact with the text and each other in ways that invite the generation of ideas and elaboration of texts.

CLASSROOM OF ENGAGED AND GENERATIVE READERS

For an example of a classroom using social interactive processes as a mechanism for enhancing engagement as well as skill, let us look at portions of one literature discussion in Barbara Furst's seventh-grade class of primarily 12-year-olds. Ms. Furst is one of more than 50 teachers with whom we had been collaborating to learn more about ways in which classrooms could become social environments that actively create and support engaged readers. Within this environment, we see the students thoughtfully involved in developing, supporting, analyzing, and enriching their own interpretations.

(See Roberts & Langer, 1991, for the detailed analysis of this lesson.) It is a heterogeneously grouped class in which students' academic achievement ranges from 3 years above to 3 years below grade level, as measured by standardized tests. Here, Ms. Furst invites social interaction; she invites her students to collaborate in their efforts to reach their own understandings using exploration as a way to gain ideas. We can see how the students share impressions and explore alternatives, and Ms. Furst offers scaffolding in ways to think about their ideas and communicate them to their classmates in a manner that is truly interactive, moves the conversation along, and enriches their growing interpretations. She creates what I call an *envisionment-building community* (Langer, 1995), where students are invited to, and actually do, become engaged with and share literature as the opening of possibilities. The underlying culture of the class calls for and expects the active and thoughtful participation and engagement of the students and provides them with help to learn to do so (Langer, 1991; Roberts & Langer, 1991). I chose this lesson because it is a good example of one in which the entire classroom has become a social environment that supports engagement as well as generative thinking. The students' ideas are valued, they interact with and gain ideas from each other, and they explore horizons of possibilities rather than try to figure out what the teacher is after.

The students are reading an adolescent novel, *The Girl Who Owned a City*, by O. T. Nelson (1975). Similar in theme to *Lord of the Flies*, it is about a city ruled by children after everyone over the age of 12 mysteriously dies. Lisa is the girl who becomes leader, and the story involves the situations and problems she faces. When the lesson took place, the students had been keeping literature journals and had discussed their in-process thoughts and questions in small readers' groups as well as in whole-class discussions, and had just completed the book. This lesson was intended as a time for the full class to reflect on their responses to the whole story, particularly their envisionments, the ideas and questions they had when they finished reading.

The discussion is initiated by Ms. Furst, who invites the students to share what is on their minds. She has done this many times, and the students know she truly wants them to reengage with the piece and discuss their ideas. She recognizes Marissa, who begins by raising the issue of whether or not the ending is "too perfect." Because the students already know that the social norm in this classroom is to engage in discussion about the piece and each others' ideas, other students join in.

Teacher: Okay, do we have something that we want to talk about today? All right, Marissa.

Marissa: I didn't like the ending. I thought it was like too perfect. Like she gets the city back and everything's just peachy dandy. I thought something else would happen. It just didn't feel right.

Teacher: Charlene?

Charlene: When you said peachy dandy, it's not peachy dandy, there are *tons* of problems that she's got to face. I mean she's got the problem, what if the gang comes back?

Marissa: Well, Tom Logan's a wimp!

Charlene: Well, you've got to think about it, because when they were going around doing all this other stuff, they heard mention of this other gang called the Chicago Gang I think it was, and what if that gang comes? I mean, they're very, they've got a lot of problems. It's not perfect, nothing is perfect by all means.

Teacher: Conrad?

Conrad: I agree with Charlene, that it's not really perfect, it is kind of a happy ending, because there are, there's other problems, like, they still have the food problem and all the gangs and stuff, they're kind of used to it, but it still, and it's gonna take a long time to get over this, to get over that problem.

Teacher: Gep?

Gep: It is a too happy, perfect, it's like they have problems, but they don't have that many problems, like the Chicago Gang doesn't really have that high of a chance of coming.

Teacher: You don't believe that's gonna happen?

Gep: No. Because, even if they do, they have a lot of defense. And I think it wouldn't be like that the Chicago Gang would just take them over. They'd still have a defense and stuff. And the food problem, they'd probably overcome after a little while, because they'd get more people thinking than just like Lisa and that group.

Teacher: I'm gonna use the word vulnerable. You don't think they're vulnerable to the Chicago Gang? You think they'll have enough to overcome that?

Gep: Yeah . . .

Teacher: Sheila.

Sheila: I didn't like the ending either. Because it just seemed like towards the ending, I mean at the beginning of the book, Lisa wasn't the only person who, with ideas. But towards the ending, the kids seemed to be like really dumb. And they were just we need Lisa, we can't survive without her. And I just, this is like another topic, sort of, but it goes into this, it seems like that isn't very realistic at all. I mean, I don't see how one person can be smart and have all these ideas, and the rest of them be like, frogs.

Teacher: So you're very unhappy with the idea that there's just one person who seems to be able to pick up this leadership and go, that's not, to use that word, realistic. Which is another word we've been wanting to talk about . . . O.K., let's go here with Betsy. Betsy?

Betsy: I sort of agree with Sheila, because the end is like, *unreal*, okay?

Teacher: Is that, do you agree? Does anybody have a different feeling about
the ending? Gerrick?

In this opening segment of the discussion, we can see that the students
are totally engaged with the text and each others' responses to it. They are
an envisionment-building community, comfortable sharing their ideas,
thinking about them, and discussing them. Here they are voicing their
thoughts and explaining why they came to mind. We can see by their interactive turns that they are really listening to one another, challenging each
other, and offering possible alternatives. From Marissa's initial comment
about the ending being too perfect, they embark on an exploration of other
possible interpretations of the ending. As the discussion continues, the students provide evidence for their assertions, and also step out as more distant critics to evaluate the ending. Yet they leave themselves open to explore new possibilities, as when Charlene asks, "What about the other
gangs?"

Thus, the students spend the first 10 minutes in a rather free-flowing and
idea-generating conversation, discussing their responses to the end of the
story and using these comments as a way back into the story, where they
consider the interactions, intentions, and feelings of the characters. The
teacher helps the students focus on their thoughts and on ways to communicate them. Sometimes she helps them think about their ideas in more
complex ways, as when she asks Kent and Betsy to explain or provide evidence for their interpretations. And, as we see by her last comment, Ms.
Furst continues to invite the students to remain engaged, asking them to
search for yet other possibilities.

In the next section, the students explore whether Lisa has changed.
Here, they use their knowledge of human emotions, motives, fears, and decisions to explore possible aspects of Lisa's character as a way to gain insight into whether or how she might have changed, and why. They even
imagine themselves in Lisa's situation, and return to the text for evidence.
They are engrossed in their text-worlds and building their envisionments
(Langer, 1990, 1995), using all they know about Lisa, the other characters,
the plot, themselves, and life, to live through and explore possibilities.
Once again, we view the class as a community of readers who are actively
engaged in highly literate discussion with and about the text.

Gerrick: I don't know if Kent has any truth to what he said about, like she's,
sort of like, brain dead, I think he said that means sarcastic, but,
maybe something *did* happen, maybe she has a difficult time in the
book, I don't know, like maybe she thinks a little differently ever
since she got shot she says, "Wait a minute, I made a mistake, now, I
hadn't been thinking of discipline, maybe I should change the way I
think, so I won't *make* another mistake."

Teacher: So you think Lisa changed, and maybe she changed because she was shot?

Gerrick: Yeah . . .

Candy: I want to disagree with Gerrick. You can't wake up one morning and say I'm gonna change the way I think. I don't think you can wake up and say, I want to change the way I think, and just have a whole different personality then.

Teacher: So you don't think she changed?

Candy: No.

Teacher: Charlene.

Charlene: Well, I'm disagreeing with you, just because, because like I agree with you that you can't just wake up one morning and say I'm gonna change. But I think when she got shot she realizes that she was doing something wrong, and she's gotta *start* to change it. And it could be like over that period of time when she had to lay on the couch forever and ever, that could have been going like subconsciously in her mind. Saying, that, "Well, I made a mistake, what if I make another mistake?" That could be like at the ending when she's saying why do they want me? What if I make another mistake? What if I get us all killed? That could be like why she's so scared at the end to go out and talk to all these people. She might be afraid she's get them *all* killed.

Conrad: But that's like a part of life.

Charlene: Yes. But I think, I mean, aren't you afraid, like if you were in this position, wouldn't you be afraid that you had all these people's lives right in your hands? Wouldn't you be afraid?

Conrad: Yeah, but, you don't really have to be afraid of making mistakes and stuff, because it's always a part of life, and it's gonna happen, even if you try to make it *not* to, it's only gonna happen.

Charlene: I think the bullet wound, it wasn't an overnight thing that happened to her, knocking some sense into her, but I think it did sort of change her. Because you could tell just by the way she thinks. Because I think before that she hadn't gotten shot, she would have been very glad to go out and see those people and talk to them, and tell them all about her great idea. And I think,

Conrad: (Interrupting) Yes. I agree . . .

Gerrick: It says right here, (Reads) "Then Jill told Lisa about what had happened that day. 'Well,' Lisa said, 'sometimes one mistake is all it takes. I suppose, in a way, if I could make a stupid error like that, I deserved to lose the city. You've got to be smart to earn good things. And even that's not enough. You've got to be smart to keep them, too . . .' After a long pause, she said, 'I guess I'll just have to *earn* it all back. I'll figure something out.' " She had *never* had to figure something else out. The ideas just pop in her head. Like she'll tell Todd a good-night story, and then all of a sudden ideas start

Teacher: popping in her head, just like popcorn, and now all of a sudden she doesn't *have* an idea, and she wants an idea. So I think she *has* changed.

Teacher: You think she has changed because now she has to work harder to do it?

Gerrick: Yeah.

Teacher: All right, Betsy?

Betsy: Well first, I sort of agree with Gerrick. Because I see what Lisa's saying, okay? She said she has to earn it all back, but do you think she said that just because she beat Tom Logan just with words, and not really *want it* all back? When I read that, I thought that she had a sense that she didn't *earn* the city back, that it was too easy for her ... So I had a feeling that she wasn't, she only talked about earning things, and I had the feeling she didn't, she felt she didn't earn the city by just talking to Tom Logan and him leaving.

Teacher: Is that why she's having some questions at the end? . . .

Betsy: Yeah, but I want to ask people if they think she really *owns* the city now, or whether she really ... (several students talking at once)

As the discussion continues, the students agree, disagree, and raise questions for the others to consider. It is a connected and communicative discussion. They draw links to what others have said, sometimes build on each others' comments, and at other times let things go. And they show that they value each others' opinions, as Betsy did when she asked what the others thought about whether Lisa "really owns the city now." This give and take helps students modify their positions, as Conrad does in his interactions with Charlene. Throughout this portion of the discussion, the issues the students consider are at the heart of Lisa's characterization, and create very different possible interpretations of the story as a whole.

At the end of class time, after 40 minutes of discussion, Ms. Furst tells the students that she must stop them. She ends the class by summarizing the major issues they have addressed, and indicates that they will have the next day to consider these and any other issues anyone may want to bring up about the story. In so doing, she conveys to the students that she expects questions to arise and their envisionments to continue to change, that this (as opposed to closure) is normal, expected.

Teacher: I have to do something. I have to stop you. (Moans and groans.) Tomorrow we still have, we still have a question about realism. Kent brought it back again. We have a question about changing. We still haven't finished that. And if there's anything anyone else wants to say about the ending of the story. Because, we've talked about the ending, we've talked about change, and we've only touched on Jimmy's issue of realism. Thank you.

I have used this classroom example to illustrate how the process of literate engagement and understanding can develop through social interaction, and how the teacher's role is critical in how this is accomplished. By her behaviors and her words, Ms. Furst creates a community in which student thinking is valued. She has orchestrated the discussion so that each student's understanding is viewed as legitimate (although open to change) and where everyone's comments can affect others', where there is no privileged right answer, and thus where several possible (and eventually well-defended) interpretations can live side by side, offering different credible "takes" on the story.

Notice that the students did not move toward consensus, either a collaboratively agreed on or an externally sanctioned interpretation, but instead used the group as a discourse community, a think tank with whom to explore their own concerns and issues, weaving in and out of topics to get ideas, raise others, and in so doing to generate ideas as they work through their own understandings. It is a good example of an instructional environment where the social fabric supports student engagement as well as highly literate thinking, helping students to question, evaluate, and reach their own interpretations. Neither the students nor the teacher functioned earlier in the year as they did in this lesson. By this point in the year (it was spring), the teacher had changed from standing in front of the room to sitting in a large circle with her students, and from imposing her own agenda on discussions and insisting on only text-based support to encouraging them to build and refine their own developing understandings, drawing on their own experiences and other reading experiences in the process (Close, 1990, 1992). Across the year, the students had also evolved from restrained talkers to interactive discussants, from responding to teacher questions to generating their own questions and pursuing their own possibilities, firmly developing their own ideas yet open to others.

It is important to remember that this is a class of diverse students. First, they differed in background, interests, and experiences. Because multiple interpretations were considered desirable ways to stimulate each other's thinking and bring rich alternatives to mind (the way "good" readers extend their interpretations of literature), the students assumed they would benefit from each others' comments, even ideas they did not accept as their own. In addition, the students had not been able to read the book with equal ease, yet they had all read the book and engaged with the ideas as best they could, and were able to participate as their understandings permitted and to build on them. They did not need to be given easier work or different literature; instead, they were in a thoughtful and interactive social environment where their understandings (as everyone else's) could grow during the reading-in-process small-group discussion meetings as well as during this discussion. They were in a learning community where, from a sociocognitive perspective, they learned to engage in the community's culture, to act as literary thinkers, to maintain their own identities, to respect those of others, and to learn literature, to learn through literature, and to learn about literature. They were also helped to learn ways to participate in those highly literate activities.

INSTRUCTIONAL PRINCIPLES FOR AN ENGAGED CLASSROOM

Ms. Furst was one of many teachers who had been collaborating with us; the teachers wished to learn ways to help their students engage in more thoughtful literature experiences, and we wished to learn more about the nature of literary thinking in such classrooms, and ways to develop classroom cultures that organically embody these. From our analyses of the many classrooms we observed on an almost daily basis over 8 years, I have been able to identify several pedagogical principles that permeate the social fabric of the engaged communities I have been describing. They follow.

Students Are Treated as Lifelong Envisionment Builders

At an essential level, student engagement is a given. There is an overriding belief by teachers and students alike that everyone has spent their entire lifetimes building envisionments in their efforts to make sense of themselves and their worlds, and that students can use this knowledge effectively to become engaged, as they create their own envisionments and explore possibilities during their experiences with literature. In doing so, they can also extend their knowledge of both literature and life. Thus, it is assumed that each and every student is both a thinker and a resource in the classroom. All students are invited to share their ideas, converse with others, and further develop their understandings. They use the knowledge they came to school with to make sense, they observe and interact with others, and they seek assistance when they need it in their efforts to explore their understandings and elaborate on them. From this perspective, the teacher's role is to listen carefully to the ideas the students are contemplating and help them find ways to work them through.

As we saw in Ms. Furst's class, students are treated as thinking individuals who have ownership for their own ideas and exist in a community of cothinkers. Instead of leading them to thoughts that are not their own, the teacher provides support for students in ways to participate and ways to think, giving them the space to pursue their own ideas, to use what they know. She sometimes "ups the ante," helping them think about the issues at hand in more complex ways (Langer, 1991), and to inquire beyond. In this way, they become more adept thinkers who can learn from as well as tolerate ideas that are not their own, and develop arguments in response to those with which they disagree, including received and widely sanctioned interpretations or critical reviews from the field at large (e.g., Graff & Phelan, 1995).

QUESTIONS ARE TREATED AS PART OF THE LITERARY EXPERIENCE

Both students and teachers assume that the reading of literature necessarily raises questions. The questions that come to mind are the outgrowth of normal engagement with literature; they are part and parcel of what people experience when they step into a text world and try to make sense of it. Thus, sense-making in literature is treated as both essentially inquisitive and open-ended. It is assumed that reading, thinking about, and discussing literature involve the raising of questions as a way to come to understand, and that there are likely always going to be more questions that will come to mind. Envisionments are filled with questions, and these form one source of inquiry. But the hunches, as well as more fully formed ideas and predictions that are also contained in people's envisionments, are also turned into questions, as readers are curious to fill in more of the story. They raise questions that help them imagine situations, events, emotions, and connections they are never told about. It is these sorts of questions that draw the reader more deeply into the text and propel him or her to explore horizons of possibilities. They lead to explorations of relationships, motives, and reactions, as well as intentions and implications. They mobilize readers to use their imaginations, fill in the inevitable gaps, explore options, and develop fuller understandings.

When teachers view questions as a central way in which literary understandings develop, instruction becomes a process by which they help students both raise them and explore possible answers and alternatives. They ask their students to jot down questions they had when they were reading and to come up with questions that will be interesting to discuss in class. They teach their students to become good questioners and to use their questions as a way to explore possibilities and deepen their understandings. Ms. Furst did this throughout her students' reading of the book. She began with an ongoing assignment for the students to bring good questions to class for their groups to discuss, and continued by recognizing questions as points of sanctioned inquiry during the discussion we have just read. Note, too, that she ends the lesson by inviting still more questions for discussion tomorrow.

Class Meetings Are a Time to Develop Understandings

Because it is assumed that understandings and interpretations develop over time, through engagement with the ideas during discussion and writing as well as reading, the very purpose of class lessons becomes an opportunity to help students explore and further develop their understandings. Both teachers and students take it for granted that the thoughts they have about a piece of literature as they enter the classroom door will change before they leave, and that class meetings are an interesting and useful time to explore and move beyond earlier ideas. A good learner is considered one who explores possibilities and actively seeks ideas and hints of things they have not yet considered. It is this openness to ideas that makes class time productive. A good lesson is judged as one that has provoked students to explore new ideas and propelled them toward more considered and complex interpretations.

In these classes, discussion begins with the students' ideas, as when Ms. Furst opened with, "Okay, do we have something we want to talk about today?" It places students' current impressions at the center of concern, even as they are expected to be changing. The group or class explores these ideas as provisional possibilities, leading them into a wider range of explorations. Thus, class meetings become a time when students as individuals and the group as a collective participate in reworking their understandings, raising questions, exploring possibilities, and entering the text more deeply as individuals within a group, as each is building an array of possible interpretations from his or her perspective.

In traditional classes, meetings are often a time for the teacher and students to review the understandings the students came to class with, using the omissions and inaccuracies as a basis for "filling in," instead of as an experience in which the students can reflect on their understandings, gain others, reason with and about them, and elaborate on them.

Multiple Perspectives Are Used to Enrich Interpretations

In engaged and interactive classes, multiple perspectives are of great importance. Here everyone, teachers and students alike, assumes that each individual has a complex of social identities as well as personal interests, knowledge, and concerns, and that a person's understandings are necessarily affected by the many groups and subgroups with whom she or he associates. Therefore, it is also taken for granted that individuals will likely attribute different meanings to the works being read, and to rob them of these differences would be to render them invisible. It would make them less rather than more able to construct their own envisionments and interpretations, and to stimulate the thoughts of others. Therefore, it becomes both interesting and intellectually provocative and empowering for students not only to share and explore their own points of departure, but also to assume the perspective of different characters within the text, other texts, the world, or history, and also to approach the story from the vantage point of other eras, cultures, and political realities as well as their own.

As in Ms. Furst's class, hearing others' perspectives serves as a way to help students confront their own ideas more reflectively, a way to consider ideas they did not initially think of, a way to develop interpretations based on more than one view, and a way to gain sensitivity toward perspectives that are not their own. Students come to understand that a story can be interpreted in different ways based on the perspective taken, and that taking a number of perspectives helps them to build and inspect their own understandings. It also helps them see that holding several perspectives makes one's understanding of a story more interesting and more complex. They also gain ways to make sense of themselves and the world.

CONCLUSIONS AND DISCUSSION

The literary classrooms I have described support a variety of literacy practices, both formal and informal, both direct and implicit. They involve reading, rereading, and referring to reading; writing of all sorts; and speaking with, about, and in response to language and text as well as content. They treat students' experiences outside of school not merely as givens, but as assets, to be mined for the knowledge they bring and can lead to. In part, we can see parallels between my notions of a sociocognitive perspective on literacy and students' engagement in literature through social activity and Barton's discussion (chap. 1, this volume) of everyday literacies. With a focus on literacy in the community, he described the multiple and overlapping significance literacy activities can play in peoples' lives based on the context, motivation, or cultural resources they bring to it. I, in turn consider these critical to the kinds of inclinations and meanings students bring to their classes and texts. As discussed in my last section, classrooms of engaged readers treat students as lifelong envisionment builders well supplied with an array of sense-making abilities. Such classrooms provide students with opportunities not only to use but also to build on the wide range of print and nonprint literacy they experience in their lives. More importantly, my studies suggest that literacy practices in the classroom need to become imbued with social significance for the students involved in much the way it does in the community practices Barton described.

We can also see connections in this volume to the chapters by Bus (chap. 2) and by De Temple and Snow (chap. 3) and Leseman and de Jong (chap. 4), who describe the highly interactive book reading practices shared by mothers and their young children. On the one hand, we can see these studies as reminding us of the major contribution such experiences make to children's literacy development both at home and at school. We can also see them as highlighting the importance of redefining literacy as a social activity in ways that can make a significant contribution to instruction throughout the school years. My example of Ms. Furst's class and the principles I have described provide a connecting link, highlighting the ways in which social interaction can become a mechanism for enhancing students' engagement with literacy.

In literary communities of the sort I have been describing, students use their interactions with others to engage literature from their own perspectives and to hear other voices, and to situate themselves in their worlds. They consider alternatives for understanding the issues they are currently probing, as Ms. Furst's students did when discussing whether or not Lisa had changed, but these considerations inevitably shade and shape possible interpretations of the entire piece. Such changes help students see from various angles of vision, providing them with increasing sensitivity to the complexities in life as well as in literature. From this comes their growing ability to understand the options people seem to have before them, as well as the ability to find new ones.

Through interactions with each other, students learn to develop their own capabilities as thinkers and participants in the complex social relations inside the class as well as outside. As they learn to listen to and confront one another, students enter into a multivocal dialogue in the sense Bakhtin (1981) described. They use the echoes of their many voices to consider other ways of interpreting and viewing their individual selves and others, reading against as well as through the text. The participants, and thus the community, are open to difference, awareness, empathy, and change. In this environment, students learn to treat literature in ways that enrich their personal as well as intellectual development, their understandings of social differences as well as connectedness. Inherent in the act of literary understanding is the promise of becoming sensitive to the many-sidedness of human sensibility, of opening possibilities. It creates vision.

As we explore new horizons of possibility, we can at least begin to imagine the stories and perspectives of others. This kind of thinking helps us to become not only more engaged and more literate thinkers, but also more humane.

ACKNOWLEDGMENTS

The work I discuss here is the outgrowth of a series of studies I have been engaged in since 1987, funded by the U.S. Department of Education, Office of Educational Research and Improvement, grants G0088720278, R117G10015, and R117E00051 to the National Research Center on English Learning and Achievement. However, the opinions expressed herein do not necessarily reflect the views of OERI/ED, and no official endorsement should be inferred. My writing of this chapter was supported by the Benton Foundation, as an endowed scholar-in-residence at the University of Chicago.

REFERENCES

Bakhtin, M. (1981). *The dialogic imagination*. (C. Emerson & M. Helquist, Trans.) Austin: University of Texas Press.

Benton, S. (1992). *Secondary worlds: Literature teaching and the visual arts*. Buckingham, England: Open University Press.

Bleich, D. (1978). *Subjective criticism*. Baltimore, MD: Johns Hopkins University Press.

Britton, J. (1970). *Language and learning*. London: Penguin Press.

Bruner, J. (1986). *Actual minds, possible worlds*. Cambridge, MA: Harvard University Press.

Close, E. E. (1990). How did we get here: Seventh-graders sharing literature. *Language Arts, 67*, 813–823.

Close, E. E. (1992). Literature discussion: A classroom environment for thinking and sharing. *English Journal, 81*, 65–71.

Egan, K., & Nadaner, D. (Eds.). (1988). *Imagination and education*. New York: Teachers College Press.

Elstein, A., Shulman, L., & Sprafka, S. (1978). *Medical problem-solving: The analysis of clinical reasoning*. Cambridge, MA: Harvard University Press.

Fetterly, J. (1978). *The resisting reader: A feminist approach to American fiction*. Bloomington: Indiana University Press.

Graff, G., & Phelan, J. (1995). *Adventures of Huckleberry Finn: A case study in critical controversy*. New York: St. Martin's Press.

Greene, M. (1995). Art and imagination: Reclaiming the sense of possiblity. *Phi Delta Kappan, 76*(5), 378–382.

Iser, W. (1974). *The implied reader*. Baltimore, MD: Johns Hopkins University Press.

Langer, J. A. (1985). Levels of questioning: An alternative view. *Reading Research Quarterly, 20*(5), 586–602.

Langer, J. A. (1987a). A sociocognitive perspective on literacy. In J. Langer (Ed.), *Language, literacy, and culture: Issues of society and schooling* (pp. 1–20). Norwood, NJ: Ablex.

Langer, J. A. (1987b). The construction of meaning and the assessment of comprehension. In R. Freedle & R. Duran (Eds.), *Cognitive and linguistic analysis of test performance* (pp. 225–244). Norwood, NJ: Ablex.

Langer, J. A. (1990). The process of understanding: Reading for literary and informative purposes. *Research in the Teaching of English, 24*(3), 229–260.

Langer, J. A. (1991). *Literary understanding and literature instruction* (Report Series 2.11). Albany, NY: Center for the Learning and Teaching of Literature.

Langer, J. A. (1995). *Envisioning literature: Literary understanding and literature instruction*. New York: Teachers College Press.

Langer, J. A., Bartolome, L., & Vasquez, O. (1990). Meaning construction in school literacy tasks: A study of bilingual students. *American Educational Research Journal, 27*(3), 427–471.

Langer, S. (1942). *Philosophy in a new key*. Cambridge, MA: Harvard University Press.

Lauter, P. (1990). The literatures of America: A comparative discipline. In A. L. B. Ruoff & J. W. Ward, Jr. (Eds.), *Redefining American literary history* (pp. 9–34). New York: Modern Language Association.

Nelson, O. T. (1975). *The girl who owned a city*. New York: Dell.

New London Group. (1996). A pedagogy of multiliteracies: Designing social futures. *Harvard Education Review, 66*(1), 60–92.

Orr, J. (1987, June). Narratives at work: Storytelling as a cooperative diagnostic activity. *Field Service Manager: The Journal of the Association of Field Service Managers International*, pp. 47–60.

Putnam, H. (1978). *Meaning and the moral sciences*. London: Routledge and Kegan Paul.

Ricoeur, P. (1980). *On narrative time*. Ithaca, NY: Cornell University Press.

Roberts, D., & Langer, J. (1991). *Supporting the process of literary understanding: Analysis of a classroom discussion* (Rep. Ser. 2.15). Albany, NY: National Research Center on Literature Teaching and Learning.

Rogoff, B. (1994). Developing understanding of the ideas of communties of learners. *Mind, Culture and Activity, 1*(4), 209–229.

Rosenblatt, L. M. (1983). *The reader, the text, the poem*. Cambridge, MA: Harvard University Press. (Original work published 1938).

Scholes, R. (1989). *Textual power: Literary theory and the teaching of English*. New Haven, CT: Yale University Press.

Tompkins, J. (1980). *Reader-response criticism: From formalism to post-structuralism*. Baltimore, MD: Johns Hopkins University Press.

Vygotsky, L. S. (1987). *Problems of general psychology: Vol. I* (R. W. Rieber & A. S. Carton, Eds.; N. Minnick, Trans.). New York: Plenum.

Wells, G., & Chang-Wells, G. L. (1992). *Constructing knowledge together*. Portsmouth, NH: Heinemann.

10

Multimedia and Engaged Reading in a Digital World

David Reinking
University of Georgia

Anyone who has spent more than a few minutes "surfing the 'net" has an intuitive awareness of how different it feels to encounter textual information in a digital as opposed to a typographic environment. The inert features of the printed page that make reading essentially a solitary psycholinguistic process and only incidentally a visual one, as Goodman argued many years ago, are transformed on the computer screen to make reading more dynamic, more interactive, more essentially visual, and even auditory. In comparison, the experience of reading printed materials, especially books, as Richard Lanham (1993) has argued, is static, silent, introspective, and typically serious (see also Olson, 1994; Ong, 1982). These characteristics of conventional reading derived from printed materials have come to be culturally valued (see Birkerts, 1994, for a romantic expression of these values), and they have been reinforced, if not determined, by the material concreteness of conventional printed materials and the relative expense and difficulty in producing them.

Web pages and other electronic texts, on the other hand, regardless of their topic, purpose, or audience, seem mundane if they only simulate the staid features of printed texts. They more naturally invite authors and readers to exploit a variety of visual and auditory effects that on the computer screen compete equally with the alphabetic code for space and attention (Bolter, 1991; Lanham, 1993). The experience of reading in digital environments, therefore, is typically more sensuous, interactive, and playful, in part because electronic texts make available an array of audiovisual effects that can be integrated flexibly in interesting and creative ways. Animated graphics, sound effects, synthesized and digital speech, and full-motion video can be combined with the written prose and static graphics to which the technology of print has traditionally been limited.

This capability to juxtapose flexibly so many audiovisual representations in a single, seamless display is why the term *multimedia* has been associated with electronic texts. Thus, one dimension of contemplating how electronic texts may shape or promote literacy in comparison to conventional texts is to analyze them as multimedia documents. Specifically, given the focus of this book, it might be asked whether the fact that electronic texts can be multimedia documents has any bearing on promoting engagement in reading. The rapidly expanding presence of digital texts in increasingly diverse areas of daily life including schooling makes this a timely and potentially consequential issue.

In this chapter I examine electronic texts specifically as multimedia artifacts and how as such they might relate to engaged reading. I do so in the context of a larger discussion among some literacy researchers who are struggling to define what a text is and what literacy is in an increasingly post-typographic world (Cognition and Technology Group at Vanderbilt University, 1991; Flood & Lapp, 1995; Reinking, 1995; Reinking, McKenna, Labbo, & Kieffer, 1998). That ongoing discussion includes the development of theoretical perspectives that capture the uniqueness of digital texts across several dimensions, ultimately aimed at improving their quality, their effectiveness in promoting learning, and their contribution to enhancing literacy education.

To address electronic texts as multimedia artifacts I begin by considering historically what is meant by the term *multimedia* as it has been used in the conventional discourse of education and more currently as a theoretical construct. Then I propose several assertions derived from current theoretical views of how printed and electronic texts differ. These assertions argue that electronic texts as multimedia documents may be inherently more engaging to more readers than are conventional printed texts. In a subsequent section I illustrate these assertions and the potential of exploiting the multimedia capabilities of electronic text by describing a research project in which my colleagues and I involved teachers and students in creating multimedia book reviews as an alternative to the conventional book report.

MULTIMEDIA OR MEDIUM?

The term *multimedia* means literally "many media," but that definition begs an important question: What exactly is a medium or, more precisely, how can one medium be distinguished from another? As in most areas of inquiry, to move from intuitive to theoretical answers, precise definitions are needed. For example, considering digital texts as "multimedia" artifacts at all may be misleading or at least theoretically shallow. Conceptualizing digital texts as multimedia artifacts might for the sake of analysis be more productively viewed as a configuration of symbol systems defining a single medium. So one issue that must be addressed theoretically is whether digital texts might be considered multimedia or a single medium with diffuse symbol systems. That distinction has theoretical implications and perhaps practical ones as well. In this section, therefore, I discuss the antecedents of considering multimedia and engaged reading, first by considering multimedia historically in relation to research and then in relation to a more recent and elaborated theory of instructional media and reading digital texts.

A Historical Perspective

In everyday speech, *media* usually refers to a means of mass communication, for example, *the news media,* or to forms of artistic expression such as watercolors or marble. To educators, media have been viewed more as individual technologies that might be used for instruction. In considering educational media, educators and educational researchers have been interested in global and often atheoretical issues such as how much students learn when they are alternatively presented content in various media such as a film, a slide presentation, an audio recording, or a book. Books are clearly a technology, but their unexamined centrality in education, and indeed in Western culture, is reflected by that fact that they are rarely seen as such (Reinking, 1997). In fact, educational media and the technologies that define them are often judged solely on how they compare with a book in producing comprehension and learning. Consequently, among literacy educators in particular, questions about media are often naively seen as an issue of books versus technology.

Indeed, the early research investigating electronic texts was guided first by the assumption that electronic texts represented little more than a change in the technology of how texts were presented. Such studies, which I have categorized as convergent studies (Reinking, 1992; Reinking & Bridwell-Bowles, 1991), compared reading with and without a computer under conditions that typically varied only to the extent that otherwise identical texts were displayed on a computer screen or on printed pages. Findings typically provided little, if any, support for reading on a computer screen over printed pages. For example, on the computer screen reading speed was slower (Gould & Grischkowsky, 1983; Hansen, Doring, & Whitlock, 1978; Kruk & Muter, 1984; Muter, Latremouille, Treurniet, & Beam, 1982), performance on multiple-choice tests presented on the computer was poorer (Heppner, Anderson, Farstrup, & Weiderman, 1985), and comprehension was no different when comparing the alternative displays (Fish & Feldman, 1987; Gambrell, Bradley, & McLaughlin, 1987). These "horse-race" comparisons, which were often atheoretical (i.e., there was no basis for predicting or interpreting differences), have been criticized frequently in the literature (Reinking & Bridwell-Bowles, 1991).

Gradually, however, researchers came to realize that such superficial uses of the technology to vary only the visual display of text were less important than how electronic texts might differ conceptually from printed texts; researchers began to conduct what I have characterized as *divergent studies* (Reinking, 1992; Reinking & Bridwell-Bowles, 1991). That is, they began to investigate how the technological capabilities afforded by electronic texts might diverge from printed texts beyond simply differences in their visual display. Some examples include providing various types of assistance during reading (e.g., Blohm, 1982, 1987; Reinking, 1988; Reinking & Rickman, 1990; Reinking & Schreiner, 1985), providing adaptive guidance and feedback (e.g., MacGregor, 1988a, 1988b), exploring the effects of nonlinear reading of hypertexts (e.g., Spiro, Feltovitch, Jacobson, & Coulson, 1992), presenting textual information electronically under conditions aimed at affecting readers' strategies (e.g., Reinking, Pickle, & Tao, 1996; Salomon, Globerson, & Guterman, 1989; Tobias, 1987, 1988), providing students with immediate access to multiple documents describing conflicting perspectives (Stahl, Hynd, Britton, McNish, & Bosquet, 1996), and, most relevant to the current topic, using auditory and visual effects made possible by the computer (e.g., Hegarty, Carpenter, & Just, 1991; Reitsma, 1988; Sherwood, Kinzer, Hasselbring, & Bransford, 1987). More often than not, divergent studies have produced results suggesting that, at least under certain conditions, digital texts do have some advantages over printed texts in increasing comprehension and learning and in influencing reading strategies.

More recently, I would argue, educators and researchers are moving to an even more liberal and less biased view of digital texts that goes beyond thinking of them simply as unproven alternatives to conventional print. Put another way, digital texts are moving closer to the mainstream of reading and writing. For example, early studies compared students writing with pencil and paper and with word processors (e.g., Collier, 1983; Daiute, 1986). Such studies are no longer considered relevant because no study, regardless of the strength of its findings, would convince anyone that word processing should be abandoned. Likewise, few would consider abandoning the World Wide Web as a source of textual information, regardless of how many studies might show it to be in some way inferior to printed materials. Researchers today are, correctly I think, much more interested in investigating how digital texts might be presented and used more effectively than in comparing them to printed materials—what Wright (1987) calls intra- rather than intermedia comparisons.

To summarize what I think are relevant points for making the assertions that follow in a subsequent section:

1. Media in education have been viewed primarily in terms of technologies.
2. Books and other conventional printed materials are technologies even though they have not been viewed as such.
3. Digital texts have been shown to have some advantages over printed texts when viewed in terms of their conceptual as opposed to more superficial visual differences.
4. It is short-sighted and unproductive to evaluate the potential of digital texts only in terms of how they compare to conventional printed texts.

A Theoretical View of Media

Although important to my assertions, these points still beg the question of what a medium is and how one medium can be distinguished from another. To address that issue, I have drawn in my own work on the theoretical perspective of Gavriel Salomon as presented most thoroughly in his seminal book entitled *Interaction of Media, Cognition, and Learning* (1979). He argued that popular intuitive conceptions of media will lead to no more than superficial understandings of media and their potential consequence for cognition and learning. He proposed instead that a medium should be defined and analyzed in relation to four attributes: contents, situations of use, technologies, and symbol systems. A particular medium, then, can be defined in terms of its unique configuration of attributes in these four areas. For example, the symbol systems of television and film (or, more aptly, cinema) are similar but their technologies, situations of use, and contents typically vary. It is a relatively stable configuration of attributes within these four categories that defines a medium, separating it from other media.

According to Salomon (1979), "media are our cultural apparatus for selecting, gathering, storing, and conveying knowledge in representational forms, [and] representation, as distinguished from raw experience, is always coded within a symbol system" (p. 3). Thus, to Salomon, of the four classes of media attributes, the symbol systems and the technologies that make them available are the most critical factors in affecting or effecting cognition and learning. The unique symbols systems afforded by particular technologies require specific cognitive skills to extract information from them and consequently determine what cognitive skills become well practiced. Furthermore, symbol systems and the technologies that make them possible vary in the degree to which they can supplant needed skills for those who lack them.

Situations and contents, although important to separating media, are only correlated with a particular medium. For example, cinematography has typically been associated with viewing certain genres of drama (contents) in a theater where people go for entertainment (the situational context). One can go to a movie theater to view a documentary (e.g., movies shown in a museum), but such situations are atypical of the medium of film, whereas they are more typical of television and video.

Applying Salomon's Theoretical Framework to Multimedia and Reading

I believe Salomon's theoretical framework is useful in considering the topic of multimedia and reading. First, his framework allows digital texts to be considered theoretically a distinctly new medium of communication, not just a new technology for extending an old one. In other words, digital texts are not just printed texts that happen to be displayed on a computer screen. More directly relevant to the present discussion, neither is it appropriate, given Salomon's theoretical position, to conceptualize digital texts as simply a combination of existing media, as is perhaps implied by the term *multimedia*. Instead, digital texts might better be conceived as a unique configuration of symbol systems, technologies, contents, and situations of use.

Even a superficial analysis of digital texts along these four dimensions reveals some clearly identifiable differences between printed and digital texts, which is the first step in establishing that they can be considered separate media. As I pointed out in the beginning of this chapter, digital texts make available a wider range of symbol systems than do printed texts. Indeed, that is why they are often described with the term *multimedia*. Likewise, in considering the category of technology, the computer obviously provides a range of options and contingencies quite unlike print. Although the content of printed and digital texts is theoretically unlimited, the content of digital texts is often much more open-ended, less often divided into discrete units, and increasingly more accessible (e.g., the World Wide Web). Situations of use are currently different too (e.g., the common observation of bibliophiles who remind us that computers are not conducive to reading in bed or on the beach) but are likely to change as the technology becomes more portable and convenient to use.

According to Salomon, even more important in defending the argument that printed and digital texts are different media is finding evidence that they can uniquely affect and effect cognitive processes. The empirical evidence in that regard is fairly well established, perhaps not surprisingly so given the major differences between printed and digital texts in terms of symbol systems and technologies. For example, in his own work (Salomon et al., 1989), Salomon showed how the computer can act as a "reading partner" to improve comprehension among low-ability readers. Likewise, Spiro, Coulson, Feltovich, and Anderson (1988) showed that hypertexts can effect positive changes in learning content in what they call ill-structured domains such as conducting medical diagnoses. Hegarty et al. (1991) were able to show how digital texts can through animation supplant the cognitive skills unavailable to participants with low mechanical ability in learning the operation of a machine. In our own work, my colleagues and I (Reinking, Pickle, & Tao, 1996) have extended Tobias's (1987, 1988) work studying how mandatory review after incorrect responses to questions affects study strategies and learning of digital texts. These and similar studies indicate at least short-term cognitive effects, what Salomon called effects *with* media, and raises the possibility of long-term effects, what Salomon called effects *of* media (1979; see also Salomon, Perkins, & Globerson, 1991).

The point I wish to make through this analysis is that it may be appropriate to associate the term *multimedia* with digital texts in considering topics such as engaged reading. However, it may be inappropriate or misleading to do so if by using the term, we mean only that digital texts are essentially printed texts supplemented by some other media such as film or music. On the other hand, the term may be appropriate and useful if we see it as emphasizing that digital texts are a unique medium, separate from printed texts mainly because, unlike printed texts, they entail a wide variety of symbol systems. The latter perspective opens up the possibility of considering the extent to which digital texts might be engaging in ways not available in printed forms. Although our biases toward print may seek to make that comparison a threatening competition, it need not be so any more than an analysis of the advantages and limitations and the consequent potential uses of any media.

HOW MIGHT DIGITAL TEXTS PROMOTE ENGAGED READING?

The concept of engaged reading has strong intuitive appeal, capturing many of the ultimate goals of educators interested in promoting literacy beyond rudimentary decoding ability. However, engaged reading is not an easy concept to define precisely. It may not be too much of an exaggeration to say that trying to define engaged reading precisely is akin to the frustrated response of a U.S. Supreme Court Justice when he was pressed for a definition of pornography. He said something to the effect of, "I don't know what it is, but I know it when I see it." Likewise, most teachers could easily identify students whom they would categorize as engaged readers and others who are not, even if they could not define the term precisely. And it is perhaps worth noting that the differences between students who might be described as engaged readers may be as noteworthy as their similarities. Suggesting that engaged reading may not be precisely defined may be somewhat unfair to researchers who have tried to define it more precisely, including myself (e.g., Alvermann & Guthrie, 1993; Baker, Afflerbach, & Reinking, 1996). However, these definitions often contain other rather broad, amorphous, and question-begging concepts such as strategic reading, critical reading, motivated reading, reading for enjoyment, and so forth.

Although it may be unsatisfactory from a theoretical perspective, it may not be critical to press for a precise definition of engaged reading. Rather, it may be more important to focus on achieving rather than defining a goal that has strong intuitive appeal. Likewise, it may sometimes be difficult to assert precisely what conditions may promote engaged reading, but in this area there is more pedagogical theory or tradition that can be drawn on for guidance, although some of that tradition too may be founded on more intuitive ideas than most of us would like to admit. All this is to say that in making the assertions that follow about conditions that may promote engaged reading and how digital texts may uniquely further those conditions, I do not devote much space to defending the claims that certain conditions promote engagement in reading. Instead, I focus on arguments concerning how digital texts are unique in helping to create the conditions that are agreed to promote reading engagement.

Active Orientation to Texts

Readers will be more engaged when they read under conditions that create an active rather than a passive orientation to texts. For more than 20 years, we have been aware that successful reading requires a reader who is cognitively active in processing information presented in a text. For example, when reading a text, readers must activate their existing knowledge, connect it to the content of the text, monitor their own understanding, and employ appropriate strategies if they are having difficulty. Indeed, such activity would undoubtedly be part of any definition of engaged reading. Theoretical orientations highlighting the importance of active reading describe reading as an interaction or transaction between a text and a reader. However, this interaction is figurative, not literal, because it is entirely one-sided. That is, because texts are static and inert, the entire burden of activity is on the side of the reader. If a reader cannot be or chooses not to be active or engaged, a printed text can do nothing to promote the active orientation that is necessary to successful reading.

Gradually, however, we are coming to understand that digital texts and the symbol systems they entail can create a reading experience that is literally interactive (see Leu & Reinking, 1996). That is, unlike printed texts, digital texts, through the computer programs that present them contingently to a reader, can respond in a variety of different ways to promote active reading. Digital texts can present text in such a way as to guarantee that a reader must be active, and they can be modified automatically or at the request of a reader. A single digital text, which need not be the same for all readers, can take on some of the burden of helping the reader to become appropriately engaged.

There are many other ways of conceptualizing this assertion and a wide range of examples of how digital texts can require or encourage an active orientation to reading. For example, Landow (1992) pointed out that digital texts, particularly hypertexts, which do not have the single linear and hierarchical structure characteristic of printed texts, blur the distinction between a reader and a writer. Readers can be passive but writers cannot, as Roland Barthes (1970/1974) pointed out by making the distinction between what he calls "readerly" and "writerly" texts. Hypertexts in particular and digital texts in general instantiate this view implicitly and explicitly. For example, readers of hypertext implicitly become writers when they must choose their own paths through linked textual nodes. Readers can, on the other hand, explicitly assume the role of author because the margins of digital texts, figuratively speaking, are infinitely large. That is, unlike the literal margins of the printed page, which typically provide little room for reader input, digital texts are not limited by margins because they can easily be enlarged, revised, enhanced, and extended. This possibility is greatly facilitated by flexible cut-and-paste functions that are becoming standard across many different applications and textual displays. Some hypertexts even are explicitly designed to invite the reader to become an author. One such hypertext is *Marble Springs* (Larson, 1993), which used written poems, maps, and other simple graphical representations to portray characters and events in an imaginary pioneer town in the 1800s. However, readers were provided with tools to extend the town's "story" by adding their own characters and poems, which might include a variety of audio and visual effects.

As this example suggests, the availability of various symbol systems for creating digital texts might enhance further the active orientation to reading that digital texts naturally promote. Readers of digital texts are often presented with the opportunity to select from among and to juxtapose a variety of symbolic representations in the process of reading. Not only must readers sometimes select from among various media that are available, but they must make a more explicit choice about when it would be most appropriate to do so.

Relatively little is known about how the more active orientation to reading that digital texts seem to create may affect the reading and learning of a particular text, let alone what the effects of reading such texts over an extended time might be. However, there are some findings that suggest directions for further research. For example, Spiro et al. (1988) showed that hypertexts can effect positive changes in learning content in what they call ill-structured domains such as conducting medical diagnoses. Medical students reading hypertexts, when compared to those reading conventional printed texts, did less well in recalling factual information but were more able to apply the information in conducting a diagnosis, presumably because they had to more actively construct connections among the nodes of information and because their complex interrelationships could be shown through the hypertext. These and other studies (e.g., Reinking et al., 1996; Tobias, 1987, 1988) demonstrated that digital texts have the capability to engage readers more actively in processing textual information. Thus, there is some evidence that digital texts can enhance readers engagement with texts in learning expository content, at least in the short term.

Easy Rather Than Difficult Reading

Readers will be more engaged when reading is easy rather than difficult. Considering the relative difficulty of texts is firmly embedded in theoretical and pedagogical understandings of reading. For example, the rationale for the development of readability formulas is that establishing a relative estimate of textual difficulty is useful for instructional purposes. Indeed, a principle of reading pedagogy is that teachers should be conscious of how difficult texts are, particularly whether they are at a frustration, independent, or instructional level. That is, teachers should avoid situations in which texts are so difficult that students may become frustrated in trying to read them. Texts classified at the independent level are considered to be easy enough that students require no assistance to read them, whereas texts at an instructional level are considered appropriately challenging to extend students abilities with appropriate support from a teacher or other more competent reader. Put in terms of engagement, it is customarily considered unlikely that students will become motivated to read, that is, engaged in reading, texts that are too easy or too difficult. A similar rationale is the basis for Stanovich's (1986) explication of the Matthew effects to explain why poor readers fall further and further behind good readers. Taken from the biblical passage in the book of Matthew stating that the rich get richer and the poor get poorer, Matthew effects highlight the fact that poor readers must more often than good readers contend with difficult texts, which discourages poor readers from engaging in reading, which reduces their motivation to read, which in turn provides less opportunity to obtain the benefits of reading. Better readers, on the other hand, experience fewer frustrating texts, receive intrinsic or extrinsic rewards for their success, and are therefore likely to read more. Pedagogically and theoretically, therefore, the more often readers encounter texts that are too difficult, the less likely, overall, they might be expected to be engaged readers and the more likely they are to acquire a general aversion to reading.

Thus, it is important to note that digital texts undermine current understandings of textual difficulty. That is, what makes printed texts difficult or easy is determined directly by their available symbol systems and technologies. Because digital texts entail a much different set of symbol systems and technologies, they are not necessarily bound by the same concepts of difficulty. For example, there is an extensive research literature devoted to investigating how difficulty can be moderated in printed texts while increasing engagement. Advance organizers, inserted questions, and concept maps are a few examples. Although some of these have proven marginally effective, these efforts pale in comparison to the range of assistance that might be included in digital texts to assist a particular reader independently reading a particular text.

For example, there have been many studies investigating the effects of providing various forms of assistance to readers while reading digital texts (e.g., Blohm, 1982, 1987; MacGregor, 1988a, 1988b; Reinking, 1988; Reinking & Rickman, 1990; Reinking & Schreiner, 1985). An early example of contingent displays using only the computer's capability to sample and analyze input is a study by L'Allier (1980), who used a computer to simplify, as needed, the structure, content, vocabulary, and so forth of written prose based on a complex algorithm that took into account factors such as reading rate and response times to inserted questions. Poor high school readers reading the adaptive digital texts performed as well on a postexperimental comprehension measure as good readers. It is not difficult to imagine other more technologically sophisticated input that might be used to monitor readers' difficulty toward modifying texts. For example, new technologies make the tracking of readers' eye movements increasingly less obtrusive, as does the recording of galvanic skin response and other physiological factors associated with measuring anxiety. These too might be used to determine when readers are having difficulty and to implement automatically some appropriate adaptations of a text.

Digital texts can also be less difficult than printed texts because they make available a wider range of symbol systems that can provide assistance to individual readers. For example, Olson (Olson & Wise, 1987), Reitsma (1988), and more recently my colleague Michael McKenna (1998) have studied respectively the effects of providing beginning readers synthesized and digitized pronunciations of unfamiliar words in texts displayed on the computer screen. Although they have been more interested in how such assistance effects decoding and sight-word learning, their work illustrates how digital texts can make texts easier by reducing unknown words to only those not in a readers' listening vocabulary. Further, if the word's meaning is unknown, for example, *jovial*, a computer could also provide a video illustrating a context in which someone exhibited this emotion.

Digital texts might also be less difficult and more engaging because they entail a variety of symbol systems. For example, Pavio (1986) has proposed the "dual encoding" hypothesis to suggest that learning is enhanced when information is encoded through both a linguistic channel and a visual channel as opposed to one or the other.

How can the relative difficulty of texts be established and compared when such assistance is available? Or is textual difficulty and entirely outmoded concept in digital texts? How far above their independent level (i.e., as established with printed texts) may readers choose to read when such assistance is available? Is it more beneficial under some conditions for the computer as opposed to the individual reader to select the amount or type of assistance? Do readers need guidance and practice in making such choices? These and similar questions related to textual difficulty become relevant when engaged reading is considered in relation to digital texts.

Fulfilling a Broad Range of Needs

Readers will be more engaged when reading fulfills a broad range of psychological and social needs. Theorists and researchers have recognized that reading is an activity that meets specific psychological and social needs that in turn affects the degree to which individuals become engaged in reading. Indeed, the psychological and social dimensions of literacy that affect engagement may be inseparable (see De Temple & Snow, chap. 3, and Bus, chap. 2, this volume). For example, Nell (1988) analyzed the psychological gratifications associated with readers who seek the pleasurable sensation of being "lost in a book." Other researchers have investigated the relation between television viewing and reading in terms of meeting differing social and psychological needs. Some (e.g., Neuman, 1991) argue that television and reading meet different psychological and social needs and are thus not competitive activities, whereas others see a more competitive relation (see van der Voort, chap. 5, this volume). Historically, engagement in reading and writing has been affected by sociocultural factors (Kauffer & Carley, 1993; Olson, 1994). For example, prior to the modern era, reading was much more of a social activity involving oral reading, as opposed to the predominantly silent solitary experience it is today.

Electronic texts, because they entail a wider variety of symbol systems and an expanded range of opportunities for highly participatory social interaction (see Garner & Gillingham, 1998; Rheingold, 1993), may meet a wider variety of social and psychological needs, both directly and indirectly. An indirect effect may be achieved by creating a more attractive and functional environment for reading. For example, as I pointed out in the two previous sections, electronic texts are literally interactive, which allows texts to assist more passive and perhaps less skilled readers. Thus, reading might be inherently more appealing to those who are typically inactive during reading. Likewise, removing some of the barriers to decoding and comprehension, which is made possible by electronic texts, may increase the appeal of reading.

Certainly the greater accessibility of electronic texts, at least in theory, plays a role in allowing them to be more appealing. If one has to trek to the library to explore a topic of immediate interest followed by a tedious manual search to find an appropriate source, one is less likely to engage in that activity, especially when success in finding the title of a good book is often followed by the discovery that the book has been checked out. It takes considerable psychological and sometimes physical perseverance to pursue topics of interest under such conditions.

E-mail is an increasingly popular activity that is an example of how electronic texts can more directly meet psychological and social needs. The immediacy of e-mail, which is sometimes exchanged in real time, and its informality make it akin to oral conversations, replacing to some degree the need for activities such as talking on the telephone or composing a formal letter. It can extend offline discussions and interactions, and it encourages collaborative writing and reading through the easy exchange of textual information. The work of Garner and Gillingham (1996, 1998) documented the extent to which e-mail and internet connections can meet students' need to consider the narratives of their own lives and the lives of others who may be from entirely different cultural groups and geographical regions. Likewise, electronic texts expand the options for engaging readers in narrative (Murray, 1997), which is central to students' intellectual, social, and personal development (Langer, chap. 9, this volume). For example, Internet activities such as MUDs and MOOs allow students to adopt an imaginary persona in interacting with others in imaginative worlds or adventures. Likewise, students can grow plants remotely over the Internet, and they can interact with astronauts orbiting the earth. In short, electronic texts provide a wide array of need-fulfilling leisure activities not possible in printed materials, and they are thus more likely to increase engagement in reading.

Reading as a Creative and Playful Activity

Readers will be more engaged when reading is conceived as a less serious and more creative and playful activity. This assertion is to some extent an extension of the previous one stating that electronic texts fulfill a broad range of social and psychological needs. Certainly, engaged reading is promoted through creative and sometimes playful involvement with texts; just as certainly, educators have exposed students to such texts in printed form to engage them in reading. However, such an approach may often be viewed as a ploy to capture readers' interest or extend their abilities so that they might become engaged in reading a more serious, culturally valued literature. Electronic texts, on the other hand, in some sense because they allow for easy manipulation of various symbol systems, tend to invite less serious, more creative and playful stances toward reading and writing that are perhaps more naturally engaging.

Several writers have argued that the ascension of electronic media and their less introspective and serious intents have broad cultural implications. For example, Richard Lanham (1993) argued that printed texts are typically more philosophical, while electronic texts are typically more rhetorical. That is, the meaning of printed texts is communicated in a manner that is primarily nonvisual, introspective, and based on the assumption of a contract of "perceptual self denial." As he stated more poetically, "The ideal decorum for prose style [in print] has always been . . . unselfconscious transparency; like the typography that enshrined it, it should be a crystal goblet to set off the wine of thought it contained" (p. 74). In short, printed texts are serious and reflective, encouraging a reader to focus on an author's intent using the essentially nonvisual, and relatively limited, symbol systems available on the printed page.

Some printed texts are purposefully designed to shed this serious intent through whimsical visual presentations (e.g., *Wired* magazine), but such texts are constrained by the limited symbol systems and modes of presentation available on the printed page. They are noteworthy because they are seeking to transcend the limitations of printed texts. Electronic texts, because they are presented by computers enabling a wide variety of audio and visual effects, represent a medium that more naturally invites readers to look at the textual presentation rather than through it. Meaning in electronic texts is represented less discursively, depending more on nonnotational symbol systems (Salomon, 1979), which in turn encourage personal involvement and interpretation. Moreover, electronic texts strip away the authority and autonomy of the author because they are easily manipulated and modified by the reader. In such an environment, texts project an aura that is simultaneously less serious and less permanent, which also invites a more creative and playful stance.

Lanham (1993) offered a poignant illustration of how such a stance might manifest itself if Milton's *Paradise Lost* were made available to students on a computer:

> Wouldn't [they] begin to play games with it? A weapon in [their] hands after 2,500 years of pompous pedantry about the Great Books. Hey man, how about some music with this stuff? Let's voice this rascal and see what happens. Add

some graphics and graffiti! Print it out in [different fonts] San Francisco for Lucifer and Gothic for God. (p. 7)

This example too points to the cultural implications that may affect the degree to which people become engaged in reading texts. For example, as Purves (1990) argued in his chapter "Becoming a Scribe and Other Unnatural Acts," we live in a "scribal society" in which being literate entails an awareness of literacy that extends far beyond the mechanics of reading and writing. Yet schools tend to treat reading and writing simplistically as if it existed in a cultural vacuum. To promote engaged reading, teachers must portray the richness of literate behaviors. Electronic texts, because they invite playful experimentation, may play a role in heightening teachers' and students' awareness of the cultural complexities of literacy, which is perhaps more engaging. Similarly, electronic texts may change the nature of literacy changing our expectations in a way that makes literacy less intimidating for many teachers and students. Tuman (1992) went so far as to suggest that

> [teachers] must confront the possibility that the sustained, detailed crafting of written language is too difficult a task, too removed from normal, informal, sporadic uses of oral language, to be the normative impulse driving a truly democratic language arts curriculum . . . [because in doing so] we doom many students to be labeled as failures. (p. 124)

This view is at least indirectly supported by the increasing calls for expanding definitions of literacy to include visual literacy (Flood & Lapp, 1995) or representational literacy (Cognition and Technology Group at Vanderbilt University, 1994). In short, it may be easier to promote engaged reading and writing when we adopt definitions of literacy that are less serious, and thus less confining. The more informal, sometimes conversational modes of expression that are characteristic of electronic texts, coupled with the availability of easily used tools for blending various symbol systems, may make reading and writing inherently more engaging, more interesting, and less intimidating. Likewise, highly refined skills necessary for a relatively small proportion of students to excel as readers and writers may no longer set them apart and may even put them at some disadvantage because different skills are needed to excel in the creation of electronic texts.

An excellent example of how the less serious, playful aspects of electronic texts could begin to shape an expanded and more enlightened view of literacy among young children is the work of my colleague Linda Labbo (1996). In a 2-year research project she studied how a computer could become an informal literacy tool in a kindergarten classroom. She used the metaphor *playland* to describe how children in this project used some drawing and writing applications for their imaginary creations on the computer screen. For children the computer screen became a "playground," a "stage," and a "canvas." Each of these functions reflects a natural form of expression not constrained by the children's relatively limited literacy development but that nonetheless contributes to their development of conventional forms of reading and writing.

AN EXAMPLE OF USING MULTIMEDIA IN CLASSROOMS TO PROMOTE ENGAGED READING

In this section I provide an overview of a 2-year research project my colleagues and I conducted to investigate if a computer-based activity designed to exploit the multimedia dimensions of electronic texts might effect increases in middle-grade students' independent reading (see Reinking & Watkins, 1996, for a more detailed description). Specifically, we studied the effects of involving students in creating multimedia reviews of books they read independently. The multimedia book reviews were introduced to teachers and to students as an alternative to the conventional book report. During the 2 years of the project we worked with teachers and students in three schools and in nine classrooms, where we systematically gathered quantitative and qualitative data concerning students' interest in reading inside and outside of school, the amount and type of their reading, teachers' and students' reaction to the activities, unanticipated developments, and so forth. The framework for the investigation was a formative experiment, as described by Newman (1990). In a formative experiment, researchers set a pedagogical goal, introduce an intervention designed to move students toward that goal, determine what factors enhance or inhibit the interventions success in accomplishing the goal, and continually modify the intervention on the basis of knowing those factors. Our pedagogical goal was to increase the amount and diversity of students' independent reading.

Overview of the Intervention and Data Collection

To enable students to create multimedia book reviews on the computer, we first introduced them and their teachers to Hypercard, a widely used Macintosh application that permits users considerable flexibility in creating interlinked texts that can include prose, graphical displays, and audio. We taught teachers and students the basics of Hypercard, including how to enter texts, how to include graphical displays (created by using the drawing tools or by cutting and pasting clip art) and audio effects into Hypercard documents, and how to create "buttons" that linked the screens or "cards" in a Hypercard program or "stack." During the first year of the project, the researchers and graduate assistants from the university taught students how to use Hypercard and how to create multimedia book reviews, although students' teachers assisted while learning along with the students. During the second year, teachers took charge of teaching students how to use Hypercard and how to create multimedia book reviews. After students became familiar with Hypercard, they collaborated to develop a standard template with specific categories of information related to books they read. A standard template was necessary because the ultimate goal of the project was to construct a searchable database of books students had read, so that other students, teachers, and parents could search the database to find books to read, to see what a particular student was reading, and so forth. Nonetheless, each template contained a button labeled "More About This Book," which was linked to unique cards created by individual students who could add various information as prose, pictures imported from clip-art files or drawn using drawing tools, sound effects, and so forth. Although not searchable from the database, this option allowed each student to go beyond the standard template.

Figure 10.1 shows the three linked cards that comprise the book review template that was developed with input from teachers and students. Each student used this template as a starting point for creating their multimedia book reviews. The card shown in Fig. 10.1(a) serves as a menu showing as

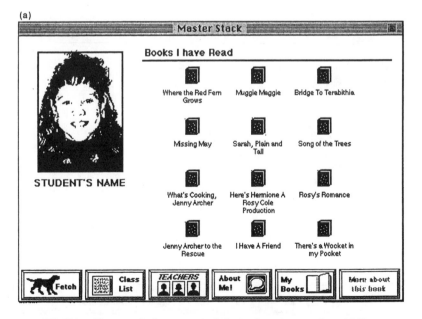

FIG. 10.1a. Three cards that comprised the book review template. (a) Template card 1: Main menu screen showing the books a student has read and reviewed.

(b)

Master Stack copy 1

Title: Bridge To Terabithia

Author: Katherine Paterson
Category: Fiction, friendship, death
Reviewer: STUDENT'S NAME   **Audio:** ◀))

Summary:

Jess had always wanted to be the fastest runner in his grade. So he could run all summer trying to get fast He would have been if it hadn't been for Leslie Burke. Later in the story Jess and Leslie become best friends. They have their own secert place called Terabithia. They gather every day Jess is King Leslie is Queen until one terible day when Leslie gets killed to find

Review:

I liked this book even though it was sad. You'd better be prepared to cry if you read this book because it is so sad. I don't know what I'd do if my best friend died. I liked the secret place they had to get away to. Last summer my friends and me had a secret hiding place too. I guess that's why I liked this book so much!

| Fetch | Class List | TEACHERS | About Me! | My Books | More about this book |

FIG. 10.1b. (b) Template card 2: Review screen completed by students for each book reviewed.

(c)

Master Stack copy 1

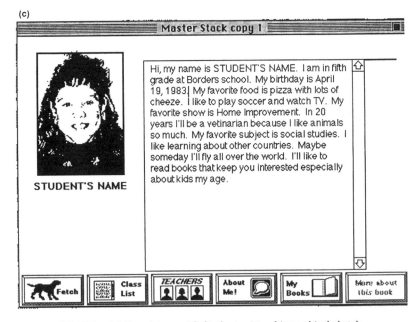

STUDENT'S NAME

Hi, my name is STUDENT'S NAME. I am in fifth grade at Borders school. My birthday is April 19, 1983] My favorite food is pizza with lots of cheeze. I like to play soccer and watch TV. My favorite show is Home Improvement. In 20 years I'll be a vetinarian because I like animals so much. My favorite subject is social studies. I like learning about other countries. Maybe someday I'll fly all over the world. I'll like to read books that keep you interested especially about kids my age.

| Fetch | Class List | TEACHERS | About Me! | My Books | More about this book |

FIG. 10.1c. (c) Template card 3: Student-written biographical sketch.

icons the books a student has read and reviewed. Clicking on one of the book icons revealed a second card in the template card [Fig. 10.1(b)], where students provided information about the book and their reaction to it. Clicking on the "About Me" button revealed a third card in the template [Fig. 10.1(c)], providing a brief biographical sketch that students wrote about themselves. The card displayed in Fig. 10.2 shows the search screen from which the database of all students' reviews could be searched across the various categories of information in the templates. Anyone exploring the book reviews could also begin by clicking on a picture of a teacher to see a list of the students in that teacher's class and could then select a student to go to the menu template shown in Fig. 10.1(a).

Throughout the project, we collected qualitative data that included semistructured interviews with teachers, students, and parents; observations in the classroom and school, which were recorded as field notes or as tape recordings that were later transcribed; teacher logs in which teachers recorded their observations about the project; and focus-group discussions with teachers and students. Quantitative measures were employed before the intervention was introduced to establish baseline data and again at the end of the school year to determine if there were statistical differences among the experimental classrooms and two comparison classrooms using the Accelerated Reader, a program aimed at increasing students' reading by providing computer-based tests to determine if a student could receive

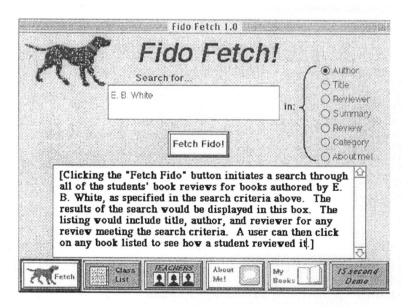

FIG. 10.2. "Fido Fetch" screen used to direct the search of the database containing all students' reviews.

credit for reading a book. Unlike the multimedia book review project, which was the focus of our study, the Accelerated Reader program is based on extrinsic motivation because students are typically provided with some reward for achieving certain point totals, as was the case in the comparison classrooms in our study. To investigate the effects of the project over the course of a school year, quantitative measures included the Teacher Orientation to Reading Instruction (TORP; see DeFord, 1985) to determine if teachers changed their orientation to teaching reading; the Elementary Reading Attitude Survey (ERAS, see McKenna & Kear, 1990) to determine if students' attitudes toward reading changed in school and out of school; and two researcher-developed, Lickert-scale surveys, one for students and one for their parents, to determine any changes in students' attitudes, behaviors, and preferences regarding reading in and outside of school.

Summary of Findings

Both the quantitative and qualitative data indicated that involvement in creating multimedia book reviews increased the amount of students' independent reading across the schools and classrooms, but there was considerable variation in its effectiveness with particular students in particular classrooms. The analysis of the quantitative data revealed statistically significant effects in favor of several classrooms involved in using multimedia book reviews when compared to the classrooms using the Accelerated Reader program. However, more insightful were the qualitative data that informed us about the factors that seemed to be important in accounting for the intervention's success or lack of success in achieving the pedagogical goal in particular classrooms and with particular students. The ongoing collection of qualitative data and our attempts to modify the intervention to address relevant factors revealed the complex mechanisms that influence the intervention's effects.

For example, we discovered that the challenge of working with Hypercard changed the social dynamics of the classrooms. Interactions among students increased when they were working with Hypercard in the computer lab. The teacher was no longer the focal point of class activities. Likewise, many students seemed to acquire a different persona in the computer lab. Some low-achieving students who were often marginalized in other academic activities became class experts in using Hypercard because of their ability to create interesting effects on the computer screen. In that role, they were often consulted by their higher achieving classmates. We observed some low-achieving students in this role develop more positive attitudes toward reading, which in turn led to increased reading.

However, our formative approach also revealed that under some circumstances the compilation of the book reviews into a database discouraged low-achieving students from participating in the activity. For example, in one classroom with a relatively high percentage of students reading below grade level, the low-achieving students resisted creating book reviews, even though working on the computer seemed to be enjoyable to them. In analyzing this situation, we discovered that low-achieving students did not want to enter books into the database because they could only enter books below grade level, which made their limited reading ability public. We discussed this situation with the classroom teacher, who proposed a simple and effective solution. She announced the next day that because the database would be used by children in lower grades, that she hoped some of the class would review easier books for younger children who would be using the database to find books to read. This strategy worked. Shortly thereafter we found that one low-achieving reader in the class began to enter many book reviews. Because this student was seen as a leader among the low-achieving students, his involvement seemed to sanction the activity for other students, who quickly followed suit.

The challenge of using Hypercard to create multimedia book reviews also subtly mediated increases in the amount and diversity of students' independent reading. That is, students became aware of various books in the process of learning about Hypercard or in helping each other create reviews. For example, in working with a small group of students to explain how audio could be included in a Hypercard program, I asked a student to get a book he was currently reading to use an example. When he returned with the book and as we proceeded with a demonstration, another student in the group asked him if it was a good book. In a subsequent visit to the school a few days later, I saw the book on the second student's desk. She responded affirmatively when I asked her if she was reading it. Thus, her selection of this book seemed to be directly mediated by her involvement in learning how to use the technology.

Overall, we found that students' engagement with literacy activities inside and outside the school increased while they participated in using the computer to create multimedia book reviews. We also saw evidence that at least some of the assertions discussed previously in this chapter were operating. For example, students were involved in creating and later searching for book reviews much more interactively than when they were involved in writing a conventional book report that was submitted to a teacher and typically not shared with their peers. Although there were no purposeful attempts to make the reading of the text itself easier, the multimedia book review activity created an environment in which students across a wide range of achievement levels could succeed. That success and the more social aspects of creating multimedia book reviews suggest that this activity met a broader range of psychological and social needs than would reading a book and submitting a written book review. Likewise, the atmosphere during the multimedia book review activity was decidedly less formal and more playful than in other academic activities during the school day. Teachers generally were more tolerant of unstructured time and interactions among students. The content of the multimedia book reviews themselves was more whimsical and humorous. One memorable example was when students used their Hypercard skills to create a special Valentine's Day stack for their teacher. The valentine presented a story that contained some good-natured teasing of the unmarried teacher's boyfriend. Thus, among the findings of this research project, it is possible to see evidence of how the multimedia dimension of electronic texts might promote engaged reading.

CONCLUSIONS AND DISCUSSION

The tack that might be taken in examining the topic of multimedia and engaged reading is likely to vary depending on one's conception of and investment in literacy. For some, literacy emanates exclusively from print. They are heavily invested in books—culturally, educationally, and for some, professionally or materially. To them, electronic reading and writing, which make multimedia an issue, are interlopers in an almost sacred domain. A lifetime of positive experiences associated with reading books for pleasure and edification powerfully sustains this orientation to some degree in virtually every adult today who might be described as an engaged reader.

However, to those who unabashedly and unapologetically believe that the digital world is a threat to the longstanding and inherently superior typographic one, my conclusions will be unpalatable. For in this chapter I have argued that multimedia—more technically speaking, the multiple symbol systems available to the new medium of electronic texts—creates a reading experience that is inherently more engaging than printed materials. Electronic texts that exploit multimedia inherently foster engagement because they naturally promote an active orientation to reading, are easier to read for more readers, fulfill a broad range of social and psychological needs, and more naturally make reading a creative, playful, and less serious activity.

Underlying my argument is a theoretical framework suggesting that electronic texts, identified in no small measure by their capabilities to subsume many symbol systems, represent an entirely new medium for reading and writing. Using Salomon's (1979) theory of media, I have argued that the multimedia capabilities of electronic texts are more expansive than printed texts in each of the four areas defining any medium: symbol systems, technologies, contents, and contexts.

Thus, electronic texts, I would argue, should be seen as no less divergent from printed texts than printed texts were from the handwritten documents that preceded them. Just as the printing press had profound effects on engagement in reading in an earlier era, electronic texts represent a similar promise today. However, it is unlikely that we will begin to capitalize on the potential of electronic texts to promote engagement in reading until we accept electronic texts on their own unique terms, without seeing them as some variation, if not aberration, of print, particularly books. We might do well to guard against the shortsightedness that led an official in the 16th century to argue for the status quo by asking the following rhetorical questions about the new printed book:

> Could a portable, private instrument like the new book take the place of a book made by hand and memorized as one made it? Could a book which could be read quickly and even silently take the place of a book read slowly aloud? Could students trained by such printed books measure up to the skilled orators and disputants produced by manuscript means?

Taking a similar view toward multimedia and engaged reading in an increasingly digital world may be more than shortsighted or riskier than simply looking foolish to future generations. It may actually undermine the goals even the most ardent bibliophile wishes to promote. That is, there are many reasons to believe that the engaging aspects of electronic texts are already enhancing the goals of conventional literacy based on print. For example, electronic forms of reading and writing have been shown to support the emergent literacy of beginning readers in ways that allow them to move naturally between electronic and printed forms of expression (Labbo, 1996). Multimedia encyclopedias pique interest in topics that are often pursued in conventional printed books. One of the most popular commercial Web sites is for a company that allows users to search for and order books. These examples suggest that more research is needed to explore not only how electronic texts can exploit multimedia to promote engaged reading but also how electronic and printed texts can be mutually supportive in achieving the over arching goal of engaged reading.

Avoiding the potential of digital texts to promote engaged reading also risks the possibility that we will inadequately prepare our children for the future digital world. Today, educators are faced with the formidable challenge of helping children become literate for a digital world that cannot be clearly seen from our current vantage point. Perhaps even more difficult for today's educators is to inculcate in children a literacy that they themselves have not fully acquired. In any event, it is inconceivable that engaged reading in the future will not entail electronic texts. A significant part of addressing that reality is inevitably to think seriously about the role of multimedia in promoting engaged reading in an increasingly digital world.

REFERENCES

Alvermann, D. E., & Guthrie, J. (1993). The national reading research center. In A. Sweet & J. I. Anderson (Eds.), *Reading Research in the year 2000* (pp. 129–150). Hillsdale, NJ: Lawrence Erlbaum Associates.

Baker, L., Afflerbach, P., & Reinking, D. (Eds.). (1996). Developing engaged readers in *school and home communities.* Mahwah, NJ: Lawrence Erlbaum Associates.

Barthes, R. (1974). *S/Z* (R. Miller, Trans). New York: Hill & Wang. (Original work published 1970)

Birkerts, S. (1994). *The Gutenberg elegies: The fate of reading in an electronic age.* Boston: Faber & Faber.

Blohm, P. J. (1982). Computer-aided glossing and facilitated learning in prose recall. In J. A. Niles & L. A. Harris (Eds.), *New inquiries in reading research and instruction* (pp. 24–28). Thirty-First Yearbook of the National Reading Conference. Rochester, NY: National Reading Conference.

Blohm, P. J. (1987). Effect on [sic] lookup aids on mature readers' recall of technical text. *Reading Research and Instruction, 26,* 77–88.

Bolter, J. D. (1991). *Writing space: The computer, hypertext, and the history of writing.* Hillsdale, NJ: Lawrence Erlbaum Associates. [Also available as hypertext computer program]

Cognition and Technology Group at Vanderbilt University. (1994). Multimedia environments for developing literacy in at-risk students. In B. Means (Ed.), *Technology and education reform: The reality behind the promise* (pp. 23–56). San Francisco, CA: Jossey-Bass.

Collier, R. M. (1983). The word processor and revision strategies. *College Composition and Communication, 34,* 149–155.

Daiute, C. (1986). Physical and cognitive factors in revising: Insights from studies with computers. *Research in the Teaching of English, 20,* 141–159.

DeFord, D. E. (1985). Validating the construct of theoretical orientation in reading instruction. *Reading Research Quarterly, 20,* 351–367.

Fish, M. C., & Feldman, S. C. (1987). A comparison of reading comprehension using print and microcomputer presentation. *Journal of Computer-Based Instruction, 14,* 57–61.

Flood, J., & Lapp, D. (1995). Broadening the lens: Toward an expanded conceptualization of literacy. In K. A. Hinchman, D. J. Leu, & C. K. Kinzer (Eds.), *Perspectives on literacy research and practice: The 44th Yearbook of the National Reading Conference* (pp. 1–16). Chicago: National Reading Conference.

Gambrell, L. B., Bradley, V. N., & McLaughlin, E. M. (1987). Young children's comprehension and recall of computer screen displayed text. *Journal of Research in Reading, 10,* 156–163.

Garner, R., & Gillingham, M. G. (1996). *Conversations across time, space, and culture: Internet communication in six classroom.* Hillsdale, NJ: Lawrence Erlbaum Associates.

Garner, R., & Gillingham, M. G. (1998). The internet in the classroom: Is it the end of transmission-oriented pedagogy? In D. Reinking, M. C. McKenna, L. D. Labbo, & R. Kieffer (Eds.), *Handbook of literacy and technology: Technological transformations in a post-typographic world* (pp. 221–233) Mahwah, NJ: Lawrence Erlbaum Associates.

Gould, J. D., & Gischkowsky, N. (1983). Doing the same work with paper and cathode ray tube displays (CRT). *Human Factors, 24,* 329–338.

Hansen, W. J., Doring, R. R., & Whitlock, L. R. (1978). Why an examination was slower on-line than on paper. *International Journal of Man-Machine Studies, 10,* 507–519.

Hegarty, M., Carpenter, P. A., & Just, M. A. (1991). Diagrams in the comprehension of scientific texts. In R. Barr, M. L. Kamil, P. Mosenthal, & P. D. Pearson (Eds.), *Handbook of reading research* (Vol. 2, pp. 641–668). New York: Longman.

Heppner, F. H., Anderson, J. G. T., Farstrup, A. E., & Weidermann, N. H. (1985). Reading performance on a standardized test is better from print than from computer display. *Journal of Reading, 28,* 321–325.

Kaufer, D. S., & Carley, K. M. (1993). *Communication at a distance: The influence of print on sociocultural organization and change.* Hillsdale, NJ: Lawrence Erlbaum Associates.

Kruk, R. S., & Muter, P. (1984). Reading continuous text on video screens. *Human Factors, 26,* 339–345.

L'Allier, J. J. (1980). *An evaluation study of a computer-based lesson that adjusts reading level by monitoring on task reader characteristics.* Unpublished doctoral dissertation, University of Minnesota, Minneapolis, MN.

Labbo, L. D. (1996). A semiotic analysis of young children's symbol making in a classroom computer center. *Reading Research Quarterly, 31*(4), 356–385.

Landow, G. (1992). *Hypertext: The convergence of contemporary critical theory and technology.* Baltimore, MD: Johns Hopkins University Press.

Lanham, R. A. (1993). *The electronic word: Democracy, technology, and the arts.* Chicago: University of Chicago Press.

Larson, D. (1993). *Marble Springs* [Computer software]. Cambridge, MA: Eastgate Systems.

Leu, D. J., & Reinking, D. (1996). Bringing insights from reading research to research on electronic learning environments. In H. V. Oostendorp & S. D. Mul (Eds.), *Cognitive aspects of electronic text processing* (pp. 43–75). Norwood, NJ: Ablex.

MacGregor, S. K. (1988a). Instructional design for computer-mediated text systems: Effects of motivation, learner control, and collaboration on reading performance. *Journal of Experimental Education, 56,* 142–147.

MacGregor, S. K. (1988b). Use of self-questioning with a computer-mediated text system and measures of reading performance. *Journal of Reading Behavior, 20,* 131–148.

McKenna, M. C. (1998). Electronic texts and the transformation of beginning reading. In D. Reinking, M. C. McKenna, L. D. Labbo, & R. Kieffer (Eds.), *Handbook of literacy and technology: Technological transformations in a post-typographic world* (pp. 45–59) Mahwah, NJ: Lawrence Erlbaum Associates.

McKenna, M. C., & Kear, D. J. (1990). Measuring attitude toward reading: A new tool for teachers. *Reading Teacher, 43,* 626–639.

Murray, J. H. (1997). *Hamlet on the holodeck: The future of narrative in cyberspace.* New York: Free Press.

Muter, P., Latremouille, S., Treurniet, W., & Beam, P. (1982). Extended reading of continuous text on television screens. *Human Factors, 24,* 501–508.

Nell, V. (1988). The psychology of reading for pleasure: Needs and gratifications. *Reading Research Quarterly, 23,* 6–50.

Neuman, S. B. (1991). *Literacy in the television age: The myth of the TV effect.* Norwood, NJ: Ablex.

Newman, D. (1990). Opportunities for research on the organizational impact of school computers. *Educational Researcher, 19,* 8–13.

Olson, D. R. (1994). *The world on paper: The conceptual and cognitive implications of writing and reading.* New York: Cambridge Press.

Olson, R. K., & Wise, B. W. (1987). Computer speech in reading instruction. In D. Reinking (Ed.), *Reading and computers: Issues for theory and practice* (pp. 156–177). New York: Teachers College Press.

Ong, W. (1982). *Orality and literacy: The technologizing of the word.* New York: Methuen.

Pavio, A. (1986). *Mental representation: A dual encoding approach.* New York: Oxford University Press.

Purves, A. C. (1990). *The scribal society.* New York: Longman.

Reinking, D. (1988). Computer-mediated text and comprehension differences: The role of reading time, reader preference, and estimation of learning. *Reading Research Quarterly, 23,* 484–498.

Reinking, D. (1992). Differences between electronic and printed texts: An agenda for research. *Journal of Educational Multimedia and Hypermedia, 1*(1), 11–24.

Reinking, D. (1994). *Electronic literacy* (Perspective in Reading Research No. 4). Athens, GA: National Reading Research Center, University of Georgia, University of Maryland.

Reinking, D. (1995). Reading and writing with computers: Literacy research in a post-typographic world. In K. A. Hinchman, D. J. Leu, & C. K. Kinzer (Eds.), *Perspectives on literacy research and practice: The 44th Yearbook of the National Reading Conference* (pp. 17–33).

Reinking, D. (1997). Me and my hypertext:) A multiple digression analysis of technology and literacy. *Reading Teacher, 50,* 626–643.

Reinking, D. (1998). Synthesizing technological transformations of literacy in a post-typographic world. In D. Reinking, M. C. McKenna, L. D. Labbo, & R. Kieffer (Eds.), *Handbook of literacy and technology: Technological transformations in a post-typographic world* (pp. xi–xxx). Mahwah, NJ: Lawrence Erlbaum Associates.

Reinking, D., & Bridwell-Bowles, L. (1991). Computers in reading and writing research. In P. D. Pearson (Ed.), *Handbook of reading research* (Vol. II, pp. 310–340). New York: Longman.

Reinking, D., McKenna, M. C., Labbo, L. D., & Kieffer, R. D. (Eds). (1998). *Handbook of literacy and technology: Transformations in a post-typographic world.* Mahwah, NJ: Lawrence Erlbaum Associates.

Reinking, D., Pickle, M. & Tao, L. (1996). *The effects of inserted questions and mandatory review in computer-mediated texts* (Reading Research Report #50). Athens, GA: National Reading Research Center.

Reinking, D., & Rickman, S. S. (1990). The effects of computer-mediated texts on the vocabulary learning and comprehension of intermediate-grade readers. *Journal of Reading Behavior, 22,* 395–411.

Reinking, D., & Schreiner, R. (1985). The effects of computer-mediated text on measures of reading comprehension and reading behavior. *Reading Research Quarterly, 20,* 536–552.

Reinking, D., & Watkins, J. (1966). A formative experiment investigating the use of multimedia book reviews to increase elementary students' independent reading. *Reading Research Quarterly, 35,* 384-419.

Reitsma, P. (1988). Reading practice for beginners: Effects of guided reading, reading-while-listening, and independent reading with computer-based speech feedback. *Reading Research Quarterly, 23,* 219–235.

Rheingold, H. (1993). *The virtual community: Homesteading on the electronic frontier.* Reading, MA: Addison-Wesley.

Salomon, G. (1979). *Interaction of media, cognition, and learning.* San Francisco: Jossey-Bass.

Salomon, G., Globerson, T., & Guterman, E. (1989). The computer as a zone of proximal development: Internalizing reading-related metacognitions from a reading partner. *Journal of Educational Psychology, 81,* 620–627.

Salomon, G., Perkins, D. N., & Globerson, T. (1991). Partners in cognition: Extending human intelligence with intelligent technologies. *Eductional Researcher, 20*(3), 2–9.

Sherwood, R. D., Kinzer, C. K., Hasselbring, S., & Bransford, J. D. (1987). Macro-contexts for learning: Initial findings and issues. *Applied Cognitive Psychology, 1,* 93–108.

Spiro, R. J., Coulson, R. L., Feltovich, P. J., & Anderson, D. K. (1988). *Cognitive flexibility theory: Advanced knowledge acquisition in ill-structured domains* (Tech. Rep. No. 441). Urbana-Champaign: University of Illinois, Center for the Study of Reading.

Spiro, R. J., Feltovich, P. J., Jacobson, M. J., & Coulson, R. L. (1992). Cognitive flexibility, constructivism, and hypertext: Random access instruction for advanced knowledge acquisition in ill-structured domains. In T. M. Duffy & D. H. Jonassen (Eds.), *Constructivism and the technology of instruction: A conversation* (pp. 57–75). Hillsdale, NJ: Lawrence Erlbaum Associates.

Stahl, S. A, Hynd, C. R., Britton, B. K., McNish, M. M., & Bosquet, D. (1996). What happens when students read multiple source documents in history? *Reading Research Quarterly, 4,* 430–456.

Stanovich, K. E. (1986). Matthew effects in reading: Some consequences of individual differences in the acquisition of literacy. *Reading Research Quarterly, 21,* 360–407.

Tobias, S. (1987). Mandatory text review and interaction with student characteristics. *Journal of Educational Psychology, 79,* 154–161.

Tobias, S. (1988). Teaching strategic text review by computer and interaction with student characteristics. *Computers in Human Behavior, 4,* 299–310.

Tuman, M. C. (Ed.). (1992). *Literacy online: The promise (and peril) of reading and writing with computers.* Pittsburgh, PA: University of Pittsburgh Press.

Wright, P. (1987). Reading and writing for electronic journals. In B. K. Britton & S. M. Glynn (Eds.), *Executive control processes in reading* (pp. 23–55). Hillsdale, NJ: Lawrence Erlbaum Associates.

POLICY PERSPECTIVES
ON PROMOTING
LITERACY ENGAGEMENT

11

Literacy in the Present World: Realities and Possibilities

Warwick B. Elley
University of Canterbury

This chapter outlines, in very broad terms, what was known about the state of the world's literacy at the end of the 20th century. To do this, two large data sets are reviewed. First, there are the statistics on adult literacy published annually by UNESCO. These figures are subject to severe limitations, which are explained below. However, I believe that they are sufficiently accurate to identify many of the main trends and priority needs for policy formation.

Second, I describe the major findings of a recent cross-national survey of school achievement in literacy, conducted by the International Association for the Evaluation of Educational Achievement (IEA). These surveys also have their limitations, but they complement and confirm some of the trends observed in the adult figures, and, as one of the organizers, I do happen to be very familiar with the strengths and weaknesses of this data set. The IEA findings are called on also to identify factors that appear to differ between nations and that correlate well with levels of achievement in literacy. Such findings can only be suggestive, but many of them do fit well with my other sources of evidence about fruitful ways to improve literacy in developing countries.

Finally, I outline a series of little-known studies that some of us in the southern hemisphere have been conducting, in an effort to improve literacy levels where they are unacceptably low. It is my view that, collectively, these studies have lessons that, suitably applied, could make a real impact in creating a world of engaged readers.

UNESCO STATISTICS ON ADULT LITERACY AROUND THE WORLD

There are currently almost 4 billion adults (over 15 years old) on the planet, and some 77% of them (3 billion) are classified as literate, by UNESCO statistics (see Table 11.1). The good news is that this figure of 77% is a healthy improvement on the past rates of 62% in 1970 and 70% in 1980. However, the reverse side of this coin is that the absolute number of people classified as illiterate has changed very little as the world population continues to expand. Officially, the number classified as illiterate has been close to 900 million (plus or minus 2%) for some time. In these terms, the fond ideal of abolishing illiteracy by the end of the century was clearly impractical.

One interpretation of these figures is that one adult in every four on the planet is unable to read or write, with all that this implies for dependence on others, for lack of autonomy, for unrealized potential, and for restricted contribution to nationhood. We cannot be content with such a scenario.

Literacy by Region

Some 98% of those classified as illiterate live in developing countries—where most of the population growth will occur in the future. Particular weak spots are southern Asia, sub-Saharan Africa, and the Arab States (see Table 11.1). More specifically, about three-quarters of the world's illiterate adults live in nine countries: India, China, Pakistan, Bangladesh, Nigeria, Indonesia, Ethiopia, Egypt, and Brazil. India and China have over half. However, there are many other smaller countries with low levels of literacy. For instance, one UNESCO report lists 28 countries in Africa with over 90% female illiteracy; Asia has 17 such countries. In contrast, the figures for Europe, America, and Oceania are much healthier, with over 90% literacy overall. Regional differences are striking and, so far, resistant to systematic reduction.

Literacy by Gender

Approximately two-thirds of those who cannot read are women, the mothers of the next generation. A breakdown by gender in each region, for 1995, shows that the gender gap is largest in southern Asia (26.3%), and the Arab States (24%), followed by sub-Saharan Africa (19.3%). In contrast, the barriers to literacy acquisition amongst females have been largely overcome in Europe, America, and Oceania. Here the gender gap is negligible. Indeed the irony is that females tend to read more, and more competently, in these regions (discussed later).

TABLE 11.1
Estimated Adult Literacy Rates (%) by Sex and by Region, 1980–2010

	Both Sexes					Male					Female				
	1980	1990	1995	2000	2010	1980	1990	1995	2000	2010	1980	1990	1995	2000	2010
World	69.5	75.3	77.4	79.4	83.1	77.2	81.9	83.6	85.2	87.9	61.9	68.7	71.2	73.6	78.3
Developing countries	58.0	67.2	70.4	73.4	78.9	68.9	76.3	78.9	81.2	85.0	46.8	57.8	61.7	65.5	72.5
Sub-Saharan Africa	40.2	51.3	56.8	62.0	71.4	51.8	61.8	66.6	70.9	78.4	29.2	41.1	47.3	53.3	64.6
Arab states	40.8	51.7	56.6	61.5	70.0	55.0	64.5	68.4	72.2	78.6	26.2	38.1	44.2	50.1	61.0
Latin America/Caribbean	79.7	84.9	86.6	88.2	90.9	82.1	86.4	87.7	89.0	91.2	77.5	83.5	85.5	87.4	90.6
Eastern Asia/Oceania	69.3	80.3	83.6	86.8	92.1	80.4	88.2	90.6	92.8	96.0	58.0	72.2	76.3	80.5	88.0
Southern Asia	39.1	46.6	50.2	53.7	60.6	52.8	59.8	62.9	66.0	71.5	24.5	32.6	36.6	40.7	49.1
Least developed countries	35.5	44.8	48.8	52.7	60.6	48.3	55.9	59.5	62.9	69.5	24.9	33.7	38.1	42.4	51.7
Developed Countries	96.6	98.2	98.7	98.9	99.3	98.0	98.7	98.9	99.1	99.4	95.4	97.7	98.4	98.6	99.3
Classification by continents															
Africa	30.8	52.8	56.2	61.3	70.5	52.0	61.9	66.5	70.7	76.0	28.1	39.9	46.0	52.0	53.2
America	88.4	90.9	91.7	92.6	94.1	89.8	91.8	92.4	93.1	94.3	87.1	90.1	91.1	92.1	94.0
Asia	60.7	69.4	72.3	75.0	79.9	71.8	78.6	80.9	82.9	86.3	49.3	59.9	83.4	58.8	73.3
Europe	95.9	97.9	98.5	98.8	99.3	97.8	98.6	98.8	99.0	99.4	94.2	97.3	98.2	98.6	99.2
Oceania	92.1	94.1	94.8	96.4	96.5	94.0	96.5	96.1	96.6	97.4	90.2	92.6	93.5	94.2	95.6

Note. From *Compendium of Statistics on Illiteracy*, 1995, copyright UNESCO. Reprinted with permission of UNESCO.

The relative disadvantage of females in the Third World should be considered alongside the close correlation found between mother's education level and health statistics for their children. More schooling for the mother is associated with later marriage, smaller families, better nutrition, lower infant mortality, and higher status and influence in the community (see Greaney, 1996). After reviewing such evidence, Summers (1994) concluded that enrolling girls in school could be the single most effective antipoverty policy in the Third World.

Literacy by Age

One potentially encouraging sign in the UNESCO statistics is found in the relationship between literacy and age. As Table 11.2 shows, literacy rates in developing countries are considerably higher in the younger age groups than in those over 44 years. Clearly, the impact of greater efforts to expand schooling in recent years is seen in these figures. However, they should be read in conjunction with other statistics, which show that increased quantity of enrollments has been accompanied by a decrease in expenditure per pupil and, by all accounts, in quality (see Greaney, 1996). The recent IALS survey of adult literacy in seven countries (OECD & Statistics, Canada, 1995) confirms these age differentials. Ironically, in nearly every country, the older generation still criticizes the literacy levels of the younger.

CROSS-NATIONAL SURVEYS OF READING AT THE SCHOOL LEVEL

UNESCO figures are only rough and ready indicators. They assume that people are either literate or not—a black–white distinction, based largely on years of schooling. They ignore levels of quality in reading, and writing. For instance, many school graduates are functionally illiterate because they

TABLE 11.2
Illiteracy Rates in Developing Countries by Region and Age Group

Age Group (years)	Sub-Saharan Africa	Arab States	Latin American, Caribbean	East Asia	South Asia
15–19	35.9	27.7	6.2	6.3	37.7
20–24	40.3	32.9	7.6	8.5	42.3
25–44	55.5	48.5	12.7	16.8	53.1
44+	82.0	76.3	27.5	51.8	71.1

Note. UNESCO figures, quoted by Greaney (1996). From *Compendium of Statistics on Illiteracy,* 1995, copyright UNESCO. Reproduced with permission of UNESCO.

cannot read well enough to cope with their daily vocational or community reading requirements. Others with limited schooling may learn to read adequately at home, or on the job. How can we assess levels of reading more accurately, and compare such levels around the world? The IEA surveys attempt to do this at the school level.

IEA is a loose confederation of more than 50 nations, with headquarters in the Netherlands. Since 1979, IEA has been conducting cross-national surveys of achievement in representative samples of pupils of comparable age in participating countries. Each nation's representatives meet annually to plan and review their educational surveys. Two large surveys of reading ability have been conducted, one in 1971 in 15 nations (Thorndike, 1973) and the other in 1990–1991 in 32 school systems (Elley, 1992, 1994; Lundberg & Linnakyla, 1993; Postlethwaite & Ross 1992; Wagemaker 1996). In both surveys, reading researchers from each country met regularly to agree on aims, hypotheses, suitable tasks, and methods of presentation, translation, trialing, analysis, and reporting. The process is clumsy, expensive, and often frustrating, but it is essentially democratic, and it has produced findings that are helpful to those who participate, and to international organizations such as the World Bank and Organization for Economic Cooperation and Development (OECD). Findings show the relative levels of reading ability at two or more age levels in each country and help policymakers identify factors that appear to need closer attention at home. IEA studies can also reveal, on closer analysis, how well students can read specific tasks at different age levels, and which variables do and do not correlate well with reading performance levels and levels of interest in reading, across nations.

The findings of any IEA study should, of course, be viewed with some caution. There are inevitably some minor differences in the average age of the students in each system. For instance, in the 1991 survey, such differences meant that we underestimated slightly the mean reading levels of 14-year-olds in Canada (British Columbia), Italy, Hungary, Spain, and Belgium, by up to 5% (Elley, 1992). There were some problems in the representativeness of the samples in the case of the United States, Portugal, France, and some of the developing countries. However, the survey was well conducted in most countries, and the results for each age level correlated highly with each other across nations, and with the pilot test surveys on judgement samples. In addition, they correlated moderately well with UNESCO indices of adult literacy, with life expectancy, and with newspaper circulation figures. These and the findings that showed high correlations between difficulty levels of tasks, across countries, are all positive indicators of validity (see Elley, 1992). A difficult reading task in Singapore proved to be a difficult task in the Netherlands, Botswana, New Zealand, and every other country. The elaborate screening procedures adopted to minimize cultural and translation bias in test items did pay off.

Main IEA Findings

What did the massive survey of 210,000 pupils in 32 countries in 1991 reveal about students' reading around the world? First of all, the enormous gap between rich and poor countries in reading levels was confirmed. By and large, countries with low economic indicators (mostly in Africa and Asia) show low reading achievement levels, as measured by the IEA tests. These tests included a broad selection of questions in narrative reading, expository reading, and interpretation of documents, tables, and maps. Figure 11.1 shows the means on the total reading scores for the 14-year-old samples in each country. Most countries with high means—Finland, France, Sweden, the United States, Iceland, and Switzerland—have high indices on gross na-

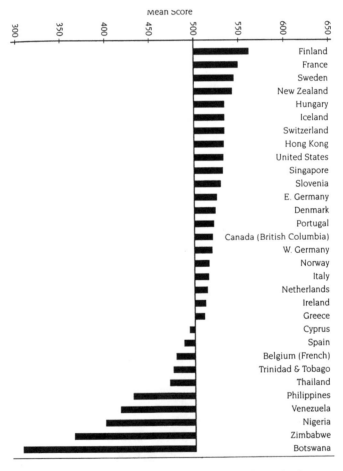

FIG. 11.1. 1990–1991 IEA reading literacy: Population B, total achievement scores.

tional product (GNP) per capita (over US$16,000) and on expenditure on education per pupil. By contrast, those at the right-hand end of the scale had low economic indices of US$1,000 or less on GNP, with correspondingly little to spend per pupil.

Of course, the causal link between wealth and achievement is contentious. Does better literacy contribute to greater national wealth, or does greater wealth allow more money to be spent on schools? There must be some truth in both positions. It is relevant to note that there are a number of oil-rich nations, with high GNP per capita, not in our survey, which show only low adult literacy figures on UNESCO scales. In contrast, we should note the examples of Hungary, New Zealand, and Singapore, whose students scored very highly on the IEA tests (and on UNESCO figures) but whose economic indicators are only moderate. These three cases lend some support to the belief that it is possible to achieve high literacy levels with only modest inputs of funds. At the time of the survey, the high-scoring nations of Finland, France, and Sweden all spent more than US$2,900 per student on education; in contrast, high-scoring New Zealand spent only $1,261, Singapore $1,252, and Hungary only $768.

In one respect, the IEA findings contrasted clearly with UNESCO statistics. In virtually every country, girls report more reading of books than boys and in most cases their test scores are better than boys (Wagemaker, 1996). The main exceptions to this trend were found (at age 14 years only) in the developing countries of Zimbabwe and Nigeria (and the differences were negligible in Portugal, Singapore, and France). Such findings can be reconciled with the UNESCO figures, of course, as the gender gap in those figures, favoring males, is found only in developing countries.

The reader may be assisted to interpret the size of the gap between developed and developing countries with some more specific findings.

- Finland, the highest scoring nation on almost every kind of task, at each age level, averaged approximately 80% overall at the 14-year level. In contrast, the Botswana mean was only 27% on the same tasks. The vast majority of students in Finland, France, Sweden, and New Zealand coped with most of the reading tasks they were given at both age levels; U.S. and Italian pupils coped equally well at age 9, but less well at 14 years.

- At the low end of the distribution of test scores in each country, there were a number of students who scored less than 25%. The test committee judged this score to be a rough indicator of nonreading status. By this index, Finland had only 1% nonreaders at age 9 years; the developing countries had over 30%.

- On a question requiring students to fill in their names, date of birth, and other simple details on a travel form, New Zealand 14-year-olds averaged 94% correct; in contrast, only 34% of Botswana pupils could manage this.

• On a question requiring students to read a timetable, French students averaged 87%, whereas Nigerian students averaged 33%.

• In the United States, 75% of students could read a technical report on the dangers of smoking, and infer the author's aim correctly; in Botswana, only 16% could.

• In New Zealand, 80% of 9-year-olds could read a short story about an old man whose family was unkind to him, and could infer how he must have felt. In Venezuela, only 30% could.

• An analysis of the common reading tasks attempted by both age groups showed that the average score for the 14-year-olds in developing countries was almost identical to the average score of 9-year-olds in developed countries on those questions. In other words, by the middle of high school in Third World countries, typical students have attained the same level of reading ability as students in middle primary school in richer countries.

In short, the evidence is clear that, in spite of the increased enrolments in Third World schools in recent years, the quality of their school learning still leaves much to be desired. Their students spend the same amount of time in school, and work toward ostensibly similar goals in reading, but the outcomes are consistently disappointing. Wherein lies the cause of these discrepancies?

What Factors Make a Difference?

At least some of the variance between countries lies in the societies' attitudes in reading, in the strength of their literacy traditions. According to literacy historians (Graff, 1981; Hebrard, 1990), Finland, Sweden, and France have all had impressive levels of literacy for over a century, and there is no shortage of libraries, bookshops, newspapers, and well-educated adult models to support the reading habit in the next generation. However, there is little that developing countries can do in the short run to change this state of affairs. So we must look elsewhere for alterable variables to focus on.

Several factors that are often considered important gained little or no support from the IEA survey. Although the phonic regularity of the language may help to explain how Finnish students achieved so well after only 2 years at school, it appeared to have little effect elsewhere, at least after the beginning stages of reading acquisition. Again, smaller class sizes may be a factor in the early years of school (and in other subjects), but they did not correlate with better reading in the IEA surveys. Likewise, we found no advantage for a longer school year, or a longer school day, or multigrade classes, and only ambiguous support for an earlier age for starting formal instruction in reading. Even the number of textbooks per student was less important than expected. No doubt it would have shown up as more important if more developing countries had participated in the survey.

On the positive side, what did stand out was a class of variables associated with access to an abundant supply of reading materials—in the home, the school, and the community. Here is a set of variables that differentiated between good and poor readers in virtually every country, and very clearly across countries. Moreover, it is something that can be changed in every country. This matter deserves closer scrutiny.

Access to Reading Materials.

• Access to books in the home: Student estimates of the number of books in their homes correlated clearly with student reading ability. In the developed countries of Europe and North America, about half the students typically reported over 100 books in their homes, much more than those in developing countries. Nationally, the figures ranged from a mean of 174 books per home in Sweden, to 25 in Indonesia. Over all countries, students who reported over 100 books were found to be reading well, on a mean score of 514; those with less than 10 scored 458, and those with none scored only 430—virtually nonreader status (Elley, 1994).

• Access to public libraries: In most Western countries virtually all students had access to public libraries in the local area. However, low-scoring countries such as Botswana, Phillipines, Thailand, and Zimbabwe reported relatively low access, and the correlation between level of access and mean achievement levels across countries was .72 for 9-year-olds and .86 for 14-year-olds (Elley, 1994). Clearly, this high correlation coefficient cannot be interpreted as a cause–effect relationship, but it is consistent with a growing body of experimental studies that show that students do not read well unless they have regular access to suitable reading materials.

• Access to bookstores: A parallel question about access to bookstores showed a similar finding. Level of access showed correlations of .57 and .82 with reading ability, across nations, for 9-year-olds and 14-year-olds, respectively.

• Access to reading materials at school: Table 11.3 shows the relative importance of several other book-related variables that differ markedly between countries. Thus, some countries boast large school libraries (over 7,000 books), whereas other systems have many schools without libraries. Further analysis showed that the 10 high-scoring nations had much larger libraries, on average, than the 10 low-scoring countries. However, this variable is clearly influenced by the relative wealth of the country.

In an effort to remove the influence of a country's socioeconomic status in such analyses, a composite development index (CDI) was calculated for each country. This index was derived from two indicators of wealth (GNP per capita and expenditure per pupil); two indicators of health status (life expectancy and percent low birth weight); and two indicators of community literacy (adult literacy rates and newspaper circulation). When these six indicators were combined, with equal weight, for each country, they generated the composite development index (CDI), which ranged from 4.29 for Switzerland, to 1.63 for Botswana (see Elley, 1992).

Then, to remove the effects of the differences in socioeconomic development of each country, as reflected in this index, the 10 top-scoring countries, relative to their CDI, were compared with the 10 lowest achieving countries, relative to their CDI. Any variable that differentiated between countries, when contrasted this way, was felt to be worthy of attention. The book-related variables listed in Table 11.3 are presented in this manner. They show the effect sizes (differences between the mean of the 10 high-achieving nations, relative to their CDI, and the mean of the 10 lowest achievers on that criterion, divided by the overall standard deviation).

Inspection of Table 11.3 shows that countries that provide better access to books and other reading materials have more students achieving at high levels on the IEA reading tests, regardless of their national socioeconomic status. Thus, pupils read well if they attend schools in countries with policies of investing in large school libraries, and in classroom libraries; they read well too if they borrow more often from their libraries, and if they have teachers who allot more time for silent reading in class, and who read aloud regularly to them. Clearly, access to reading materials is a key factor in raising literacy levels.

Captioned Television. Another somewhat unexpected finding from the IEA survey emerged from the questions on TV viewing. Students in Western countries typically watch more than 2 hours of TV, or videos, per day, and substantial numbers watch more than 5 hours. Generally, those students who watch most read less well than those who watch little. These figures

TABLE 11.3
Selected School-Level Variables That Differentiate Between High- and
Low-Achieving Countries, Relative to Their CDI (for 9-Year-Olds)

School Variable	Effect Size	Mean of High-Achieving Countries	Mean of Low-Achieving Countries
Large school library	0.82	3.50[a]	2.06[a]
Percent class libraries	0.51	55.10	43.50
Frequency of silent reading	0.78	3.58	2.86
More library borrowing	0.31	3.06	2.90
More teacher reading to class	0.25	2.59	2.30

[a]Number of books (thousands).

are surely cause for concern. However, in Scandinavia the pattern was reversed. The best readers reported that they watched TV for 3–4 hours per day. Further inspection showed that these countries frequently show imported films with subtitles (captions) in the home language. So the frequent viewers were getting regular practice at rapid reading, under highly motivating conditions, with lots of picture cues, and assistance from the original language (see also van der Voort, chap. 5, this volume). Such children received large amounts of enjoyable, comprehensible input, a situation that some linguists claim is the main key to language learning (Krashen, 1982). It is a situation that could easily be replicated in other countries. A number of experimental studies have recently confirmed the potential value of captioned television (e.g., Meek & Elley, 1996; Neuman & Koskinen, 1992).

Pupils' Views.   Another approach to identifying key factors in creating more engaged readers is to ask the students themselves. When asked "How do you become a good reader?" most 9-year-olds in the IEA survey stressed such factors as "liking reading," "having lots of time to read," and "being able to concentrate well." As some 9-year-olds were thought not to be sophisticated enough to understand the metacognitive factors involved in such a question, a further analysis was conducted on the highest scoring 5% of pupils in each country (Elley, 1992). For such pupils (who scored at quite similar levels across countries), a contrast between the 10 highest achieving nations and the 10 lowest was revealing. Good readers in the top countries stressed much more than those in low achieving countries:

- Having many good books around.
- Having a lively imagination.
- Learning many new words.

The style of pedagogy reflected in such responses contrasts markedly with that shown by the good readers in the low achieving countries, who emphasized lots of drills, sounding out, and self-discipline. Such a contrast provides additional support for a policy of providing many good books in the school.

Home Language.   Numerous other findings of interest to policy makers in particular countries emerged from the IEA survey of 1991, and some have proved useful to World Bank and OECD officials. However, we report only one more result, of particular interest in developing countries. This is the match between the language of the home and that of the school. In many countries, large numbers of students are taught and tested in a nonnative tongue, for example, in the Philippines (89.6%), Zimbabwe (83.2%), Singapore (74.1%), Indonesia (72.5%), Botswana (61.5%), Nigeria (41.2%), and Thailand (38.7%). These students are expected to master the mainstream language. As expected, students tested in their second language performed relatively poorly. Only in Singapore did the nonnative speakers score above 500, the international mean. This particular finding raises some interesting questions about the conventional wisdom of ensuring that students should acquire literacy first in their native language, before switching to the mainstream language. Most Singapore children arrive at school speaking only Chinese, Malay, or Tamil. However, they are taught from the outset in English. After 3 years at school, using an enriched, book-based approach, with lots of shared reading and silent reading, they achieve at relatively high levels. The Singapore reading program appears to be unusually effective with second-language pupils.

Such a finding should not be passed over. Millions of pupils in Africa and Asia are expected to become literate in a language to which they have little exposure, which they have only fragile incentives to learn, and for which many of their teachers provide only indifferent models. Coupled with these disadvantages, such pupils are typically taught in overcrowded classrooms, with few resources, by poorly educated, underqualified teachers. It is not surprising that their progress is sluggish. Can the findings of this survey point to some useful directions to explore? I am optimistic enough to think so.

BOOK-BASED PROGRAMS IN THIRD WORLD SCHOOLS

We have established so far that:

- Adult literacy figures are unacceptably and persistently low in developing countries, especially in Africa and much of Asia.
- Surveys of school reading levels reflect the same discrepancies between rich and poor nations.
- Access to books and reading materials in the school years is a strong differentiating factor in explaining differences between nations in reading ability over and above socioeconomic factors.
- A discrepancy between home and school language is another major disadvantaging factor for many children in developing countries.

How can we use the findings of literacy research to lift the reading levels in these many countries where resources are poor, teachers are underqualified, and pupils are struggling to learn in a foreign language? For me, the IEA finding that access to a plentiful supply of books was correlated with better literacy in these situations was not new. We had established the same relationship in surveys conducted in Fiji and Indonesia in the 1970s (Elley & Mangubhai, 1979). However, such findings rarely lead to policy changes, even if they can be afforded, as correlational outcomes are prone to other interpretations. For instance, the correlation may mean that the best reading teachers are good at teaching children to read, and that they also like their pupils to have ample supplies of books to read, so they spare no effort to build up their libraries. The presence of books may be only an unnecessary frill.

We faced this situation in Fiji, when we showed clearly that the most successful reading programs were found in schools with large libraries (Elley & Mangubhai, 1979). Policymakers were not impressed. So we took the next step, and decided to clarify the finding experimentally, by flooding a set of bookless schools with an abundant supply of books, and assessed their impact on the pupils. The results were dramatic. Pupils doubled their rate of growth in reading, and the effect spread clearly to other school subjects (Elley & Mangubhai, 1983). The rationale for the study—known as the "Fiji Book Flood"—was that an enriched supply of high-interest, illustrated storybooks, properly handled, would increase the pupils' exposure to the target language, provide them with much comprehensible input, and provide better incentives to hook them on to the reading habit.

These propositions are consistent with the findings of the IEA survey, quoted earlier, and they have been recently tested experimentally in a number of other developing countries where pupils are learning in a second or foreign language and where books are scarce. All produced impressive results. All helped large numbers of pupils to become independent readers, interested in reading and writing, and capable of learning on their own. These studies are summarized here, as I believe they do point a way forward in poorer contries, especially when children are expected to learn in a nonnative tongue.

Fiji Book Flood

In 1981 eight rural disadvantaged schools in Fiji were given 250 high-interest books (mostly fiction) per classroom, and their teachers, in Years 4 and 5, were trained in a short workshop to read them aloud to their pupils and to use the shared reading approach. This method involves sharing a book with a class several times, acting it out, discussing it, drawing and labeling favorite parts, studying words and sentences, rewriting the story, and silent reading—until everyone is familiar with the language of the book. The pupils in these schools had already learned to read in their mother tongue, and were just beginning to use English as the medium of instruction.

After only 8 months, the pupils' English reading was found to be improving at twice the rate of matched control groups, who used an audiolingual approach, with associated reading textbooks produced by the South Pacific Commission. After 20 months, the gains had increased further, and spread to all language areas—reading, writing, listening, grammar, vocabulary— and were found to have affected all areas of the curriculum. Improved reading meant improved science, social studies, and vernacular language as well (Elley & Mangubhai, 1983). Most pupils in the book flood classes had become fluent readers and writers, provided the teachers ensured daily contact with them. A few classes had disappointing results, as their teachers did little or nothing to ensure that the children interacted with the books frequently.

Singapore Reading and English Acquisition Program (REAP)

The Singapore REAP Program was designed in 1984, for Years 1–3, by the Singapore Ministry of Education (Kee, 1984; Ng, 1984), and followed the model of the Fiji Book Flood in several respects. Teachers received 60 books for shared reading, plus 150 books for silent reading later, and were given short courses in using the books constructively. In addition to shared reading, and associated activities, they adopted a language experience method, another child-centered approach, designed to help young children into writing and reading. I served as external consultant to the ministry.

Again, the rich diet of high-interest reading and related practical language activities produced consistent learning gains. Of the 65 language test comparisons made in the 3 years 1985–1987, 53 showed significant gains in relation to matched controls. Teachers and pupils also showed considerable enthusiasm for REAP (see Elley, 1991; Ng, 1987). The program started in 30 schools in 1985, and spread to all schools by 1989. Singapore students now show literacy levels among the best of the OECD countries, and were outstanding in the latest IEA surveys in mathematics and science. Yet most are learning in a second language.

Sri Lanka "Books in Schools" Program

During 1995, the National Institute of Education in Sri Lanka instituted a book flood of 100 high-interest illustrated books per school in 20 small disadvantaged primary schools, at Years 4 and 5. Half the schools were urban and half were in remote rural areas. The books were donated by Wendy Pye Ltd, New Zealand, and I served as one of the external consultants. Teachers were given 4 days of workshops, mostly on the shared reading method and story reading techniques. As the normal English program still had to be followed, the classes were restricted to 15 or 20 minutes per day for using the books.

Nevertheless, after only 6 months of contact with the books, language tests showed that the pupils in the project had progressed in reading at three times the rate of the control groups, who followed the normal textbooks in English. There were similar gains in writing, listening, and attitudes to reading (see Elley & Foster, 1996). The teachers were very enthusiastic about the approach, and the government plans to extend it to all schools in Sri Lanka. More than 200 schools have already moved to a book-based program.

South African READ Program

READ Education Trust is a nongovernment organization (NGO) that has been operating in South African Black schools since 1979 and has now donated over 4 million good quality books to schools and trained over 7,000 teachers in methods similar to those adopted in other book floods. Each class typically receives 60 high-interest books, which are stored in a book box in the classroom, plus another 60 books in duplicate sets for group reading. Teachers are trained in short workshops in story reading, shared reading and writing, group reading, and related methods, and reading is promoted through book fairs, readathons, and festivals.

There is widespread agreement in the schools that the program is very effective in improving children's reading and language skills in English, and in assisting them to become independent learners. Enrollment increases and attendance patterns are healthy indirect indicators of success. In 1996, I assisted the READ researchers to collect more empirical data in five provinces. Comparisons of the achievement means of READ pupils in Grades 3, 4, and 5 with those of similar pupils in schools of the same socioeconomic status in the same districts showed large benefits in reading and writing, which increased systematically as pupils moved up through the school. Thus, by late primary school, READ pupils were typically 2 years ahead of their counterparts in reading, and more in writing (Le Roux & Schollar, 1996).

Further supporting data have recently been collected in an experimental study with Wendy Pye's "Sunshine" books in six provinces at younger age levels (Grades 2 and 3). Again, South African Black students, working on a book-based program under READ supervision, progressed at twice the normal rate in reading, with similar gains in listening and writing (Elley, Le Roux, & Schollar, 1998).

Several more book-based programs have been evaluated and found successful in other countries and in other languages. For instance, studies similar to those just summarized have been reported in Niue, Israel, New Brunswick, Arizona (in Spanish), and Fiji (see Elley 1991); in Brunei (Ng, 1995); and in Thailand (Walker et al., 1992).

CONCLUSIONS AND DISCUSSION

Campaigns dedicated to creating a more literate world have clearly been unsuccessful to date. When one in every four adults is unable to read, with all that this implies about ignorance and dependency, we cannot expect to reduce global inequalities in wealth and knowledge in the short term. Indeed, as we move inexorably into an information-rich era, the gaps seem to be becoming larger. Judged on many criteria, we are losing the battle to attain universal literacy.

The studies cited here, however, have the potential to make a real difference in those countries where children have little access to books, and especially where they are learning in a second or third language. Such children represent a large proportion of the low literates in the Third World. Children who interact daily with high-interest illustrated storybooks make rapid progress in all their literacy skills. The IEA data quoted here are consistent with these findings. Children appear to need regular access to books if they are to become hooked on the reading habit. Once it is established, they are in a position to become independent learners and critical thinkers.

Traditional methods of teaching such pupils, with a single textbook and rote learning drills, are clearly much less effective than a book-based approach. With only two suitable books per pupil, and daily immersion in the books, pupils in Third World schools do learn to read and write fluently in the target language. After two or three years of an enriched program they become independent readers, capable of reading textbooks, reference books, and fiction, and can thus learn much by themselves.

Two arguments are commonly raised against a book flood approach. First is the cost. For a class of 40 pupils, 80 different titles and a teacher handbook can achieve a great deal, and cost no more than 40 standard textbooks, according to the costings we produced in the Sri Lanka project (Elley & Foster, 1996). Moreover, the potential for durable literacy is much greater. Training of the teachers can be undertaken in short workshops, with follow-up monitoring visits in the schools. Our experience is that most primary teachers catch on quickly, even when their own educational levels and fluency in the language are only modest, and the enjoyment and progress shown by the pupils encourage the teachers to persist. Other methods, which often assume higher levels of education in the teachers, normally take longer to implement and are often less appealing to teachers.

A second question relates to the cultural suitability of books published in foreign countries. None of the countries where our own studies were conducted had an indigenous children's literature, and books had to be imported from New Zealand, the United States, Britain, or elsewhere. Some of them are universal favorites, with themes about animals or nature or children of indeterminate race and culture. Others again have been produced by publishers deliberately for Asian or African audiences. However, there is a clear need for more locally produced books, to help children become attracted to the reading habit, and to avoid charges of cultural imperialism.

Two points should be made in this context. First, the shared reading method promotes the practice of pupil rewriting of books, with different characters, backgrounds, or endings. So books about cows and horses intended for those familiar with them can be rewritten by children, with help from their teachers, to include monkeys and elephants. Characters' names, places, fruits, vegetables, and customs can be changed to be more locally familiar. Walker et al. (1992) have many suggestions for building up a supply of homemade books in the classroom. Second, a pool of potential writers can be built up after more teachers and other adults are exposed to a rich diet of books. Workshops for authors of children's books have been conducted in several of the countries listed, and a small supply of locally published books is now emerging. Book floods should increase the demand for more.

Book-based programs at the school level will not solve all the problems of Third World literacy, as there are still more than 130 million chidren who never go to school. However, the evidence is mounting that the cycle of disadvantage can be broken at the primary school level with a practical strategy that is popular with teachers and pupils alike. For national policymakers, the solution may seem expensive at first glance, but the cost of doing nothing is surely greater in the long term.

REFERENCES

Elley, W. B. (1991). Acquiring literacy in a second language: The effect of book-based programs. *Language Learning, 41*(3), 375–411.

Elley, W. B. (1992). *How in the world do students read?* The Hague: IEA.

Elley, W. B. (Ed.). (1994). *The IEA Study of Reading Literacy: Achievement and instruction in 32 school systems.* Oxford: Pergamon.

Elley, W. B., & Foster, D. (1996). *Books in Schools pilot project. Final report.* London: International Book Development.

Elley, W. B., Le Roux, N., & Schollar, E. (1998). *Sunshine in South Africa: Evaluation of the Research Project on Teaching Children to Read.* Johannesburg: READ Education Trust.

Elley, W. B., & Mangubhai, F. (1979). A research report on reading in Fiji. *Fiji English Teachers Journal, 15,* 1–7.

Elley, W. B., & Mangubhai, F. (1983). The impact of reading on second language learning. *Reading Research Quarterly, 19,* 53–67.

Graff, H. J. (Ed.). (1981). *Literacy & social development in the West: A reader.* Cambridge: Cambridge University Press.

Greaney, V. (1996). Reading in developing countries: Problems and Issues. In V. Greaney (Ed.), *Promoting reading in developing countries* (pp. 5–38). Newark, DE: International Reading Association.

Hebrard, J. (1990, October). *Changes in systems for teaching children to read: The situation in France.* Paper presented at UNESCO Conference on Literacy and Basic Education in Europe, Hamburg.

Kee, L. (1984). *Concept paper on REAP.* Singapore: Ministry of Education.

Krashen, S. D. (1982). *Principles and practice in second language acquisition.* New York: Pergamon.

Le Roux, N., & Schollar, E. (1996). *A survey report on the reading and writing skills of pupils participating in the READ programs.* Johannesburg: READ Education Trust.

Lundberg, I., & Linnakyla, P. (1993). *Teaching reading around the world.* The Hague: IEA.

Meek, B., & Elley, W. B. (1996). *The magic box: An evaluation of captioned television as an aid to reading instruction* (SET 1). Wellington, NZ: New Zealand Council for Educational Research.

Neuman, S. B., & Koskinen, P. (1992). Captioned television as comprehensible input: Effects of incidental word learning from context for language minority students. *Reading Research Quarterly, 27*(1), 94–106.

Postlethwaite, T. N., & Ross, K. N. (1992). *Effective schools in reading. Implications for educational planners.* The Hague: IEA.

Ng, S. M. (1984). Reading acquisition in Singapore. *Singapore Journal of Education, 6,* 15–19.

Ng, S. M. (1987). *Annual report of the Reading and English Acquisition Program.* Singapore: Ministry of Education.

Ng, S. M. (1995, January). *New reading program for Brunei Darussalam.* Paper presented at South Pacific Conference on Reading, Suva.

Organization for Economic Cooperation and Development & Statistics Canada. (1995). *Literacy, economy & society: Results of the first international adult literacy survey.* Paris: Author.

Summers, L. (1994). *Investing in all the people: Educating women in developing countries* (Economic Development Institute Paper Ser. No. 45). Washington, DC: World Bank.

Thorndike, R. L. (1973). *Reading comprehension education in 15 countries.* Stockholm: Almquist & Wiksell.

UNESCO. (1995). *Compendium of statistics on illiteracy.* Paris: Author.

Wagemaker, H. (Ed.). (1996). *Are girls better readers? Gender differences in reading literacy in 32 countries.* The Hague: IEA.

Walker, R., Rattanavich, S., & Oller, J. W. (1992). *Teaching all the children to read.* Buckingham, UK: Open University Press.

CHAPTER

12

Cultural Dimensions of Literacy Promotion and Schooling

Robert Serpell
University of Maryland, Baltimore County

In this chapter I propose a culturally contextualized conception of literacy development and discuss its implications for the design of educational practices. In the first section I contend that becoming literate involves acquiring membership in a community of practice, and by implication acquiring a sense of ownership of the cultural meaning system that informs the literate activities of that community. I then suggest that the process through which an individual becomes literate is illuminated by considering development as participatory appropriation (cf. Rogoff, 1993; Rogoff, Baker-Sennett, Lacasa, & Goldsmith, 1995; Serpell, 1998). In Western middle-class society, children acquire a sense of ownership of literacy by participating in routines such as joint storybook reading that are built into the pattern of their everyday life. Such packaged routines are a highly efficient means of socializing literacy, but they are also deeply rooted in one particular subculture. A number of different literacy cultures and subcultures have been documented, each of which reflects a particular language and writing system and includes distinctive sociocultural practices.

How does the coexistence of such contrasting literacy practices within a single society impact on subcultural variations in literacy development? Reflecting on our findings in the Baltimore Early Childhood Project, I propose that we recognize the existence of a level of sociocultural organization intermediary between such categories as language group, social class, ethnic group, or neighborhood, and the life experience of an individual. Smaller social constellations such as the family, the peer group, or the classroom may each be said to have their own intimate culture. The filter of intimate culture determines which elements of various cultural traditions are able to influence a given child's literacy development in particular ways.

Turning to the close association between schooling and literacy, I argue that stepwise mastery of the curriculum is too often treated as a proxy for an individual's progress from immaturity toward sociocultural competence. Both early educational tracking and credentialism in the labor market are accompanied by meritocratic rationalization, which tends to perpetuate Western cultural hegemony and political oppression of marginal groups in Western societies and the people of Third World countries. The staircase model of extractive education involves a form of indoctrination that is often socially alienating for students who succeed in mastering advanced levels of the curriculum, and demoralizing for those who do not.

Finally, I consider several strategic alternatives to the dominant educational paradigm for fostering appropriation of literacy, including programs designed to enhance the effectiveness of cooperative home–school communication, and the promotion of peer support and cooperative learning. If schooling is to be reformed in such a way as to empower the majority of students by giving them access to functional literacy for their subsequent lives, a wider range of activities needs to be acknowledged as valued outcomes of education, with greater emphasis on local accountability of schools to the communities they aspire to serve.

MEMBERSHIP AND OWNERSHIP

The process of becoming literate includes two complementary facets: induction into membership of a community of practice (Lave & Wenger, 1991), and subjective appropriation of a cultural meaning-system (D'Andrade, 1984). Full membership of a community implies an entitlement to ownership of its cultural resources (Serpell, 1993b), which, in the case of a literate community, includes both the technology of writing and the meaning system that informs literate practices.

The cognitive activities of literacy are often portrayed as private: the flow of ideas from a printed page into the consciousness of an individual reader, or from a writer's intentions into the text he or she is composing. Even these silent person–text interactions, however, are profoundly sociocultural processes (Bruner, 1986; Lotman, 1988; Wells, 1990; Wertsch, 1991). The language, the script, and the conventions of textual organization, through which any reading or writing is performed, all derive their legitimacy from the existence of a community of people committed to the use of script for communication among its individual members. Literacy, in this societal sense ("l'usage de l'écrit"), is a characteristic of a social formation.

And the cognition that it sustains is socially distributed (Reder, 1987, Serpell, 1994).

The cultural practice of literacy includes a range of recurrent activities and associated technological artifacts (Scribner & Cole, 1981). In the contemporary Western world, some of its salient constituent activities are scanning a text in a newspaper or on a TV screen, correspondence and note taking with a ballpoint pen and paper, completion of precoded, multiple-choice questionnaires, evaluation of commercially marketed consumer goods, information retrieval from directories, composing text on a computer, and reading a novel for entertainment. In other phases of Western history, and in some contemporary, non-Western, literate cultures, salient constituent activities have included writing on a chalkboard or slate, group recitation of a religious text in unison, and calligraphy with a brush or pen and ink. Each of these literate activities is governed by a set of constitutive rules (Searle, 1965) that specify not only the correspondence between a written text and the ideas that it represents, but also the purposes and entitlements of participation in written communication.

Consider the case of completing a tax return. The attribution of individual literacy to an actor in this socially defined configuration involves not only technical competence to fill out a form, but also an understanding of the activity of "paying one's taxes" as a general obligation incurred as an adult member of a bureaucratized, literate society. Very similar arrangements exist for the payment of taxes in most of the countries of western Europe. And the activity of tax paying takes a similar form within the cultural practice of Japanese literacy, despite the very different language and script in which that literacy is couched. Yet in a Zambian village, most adults will never encounter such forms or be required to fill them out, despite the fact that all the Zambian languages are encoded in the same Roman alphabet used for writing English, and that English is the principal medium of instruction in public education in Zambian society.

In the United States, performing the activity of completing tax returns is generally regarded as a difficult task, and a large team of specialists has emerged to assist ordinary citizens with it. Much as scribes sit outside the post office and other public buildings in West Africa, little offices open up every year in American cities during the months of February, March, and April to offer for a modest fee to help the general public to fill out their tax returns. The activity in the offices involves an expert sitting across the table from a customer and interrogating the customer regarding what should be entered in each box. The entries are negotiated through an elaborate exchange of information designed to map the actual economic activities of the client onto an abstract matrix of categories of entitlements and liabilities. The client brings to the exchange a knowledge of his or her economic activities, and the expert a knowledge of the matrix, and together they work out a way of representing the former in terms of the latter. Both parties share an understanding of the process, but neither could perform it independently of the other: The literate, cognitive activity of completing the tax return is thus socially distributed between them.

Appropriation of a cultural practice involves not only the adoption of resources that were created by earlier generations, such as the language, the script, and the law, religion, and science embodied in the corpus of the culture's accumulated wisdom. It also involves reflective application of these preexisting resources to the individual's own personal experience, and the gradual crafting of a personal perspective on the world, utilizing (and to some extent accepting domination by) the constraints of that culture. When two cultural insiders engage in debate about how best to interpret the behavior of a particular individual in a specified context, one of them praising his or her behavior as appropriate, the other condemning it, they focus initially on the behavior, not on the language they are using. The implicit claim that each of them makes is that they know what it means to be honest, intelligent, or kind, to be unfair, stupid, or cruel, and that other, older members of the community do not have unlimited power to interpret these cultural constructs on their behalf. It is this authority to interpret the application of a meaning system to particular instances that I wish to characterize as "a sense of ownership."

By conceptualizing membership and ownership as complementary and mutually implicative facets of the same developmental dimension, I wish to avoid the absolute progressivist connotations of most developmental models. I do not wish to deny that it is advantageous to the individual to become literate, but rather to relativize that advantage to the particular community of practice within which it is embedded. Moreover, I contend that if true membership of the community is denied to the individual, ownership of its meaning system is frustrating rather than empowering.

DEVELOPMENT AS PARTICIPATORY APPROPRIATION

How does the sense of owning a cultural meaning system come about? Novices to the activities of literacy learn not only from explicit instruction in the techniques of reading (qua extracting meaning from print) and writing, but also by sharing in the processes of planning, problem solving, bargaining, entertainment, and so on that are mediated by literacy. As they participate in social activities, they come to understand the relevance of text to these cognitive processes, and become able to use reading and writing as resources for achieving goals that are more their own than someone else's.

One literate activity that appears to be fine tuned for the socialization of individual literacy in Western society is that of joint storybook reading. It has achieved the status of a "packaged" cultural routine (Serpell, Baker, Sonnenschein, & Hill, 1991) that can be advocated under its label without much explanation, because competent members of the society are expected to know the content without "unpacking" it. The inner workings of this activity have received considerable attention in the research literature over the past two decades (Heath, 1983; Wells, 1986, 1990). One dimension of its effectiveness is its "affordance" (Gibson, 1982) of opportunities for assisted performance within the child's "zone of proximal development" (Vygotsky, 1978). A more highly literate mentor is thought to play a critical role in mediating the text for the child (Teale & Sulzby, 1987). In particular, "scaffolding" by the adult participant can be detected that generates a sense of authentic participation by the child even before the child is able to decode any script (Ninio & Bruner, 1978). This gives rise to such charming anomalies of emergent literacy as a 5-year-old pretending to "read aloud" a story while actually inventing a narrative. Gee's (1989) in-depth, qualitative analysis of one such event shows how much of the literate culture the child has already appropriated, including the formulaic opening of a narrative, "This is a story about . . .", and the use of metaphor to symbolically foreshadow doom in human affairs with ominous changes in the weather.

The routine activity of joint adult–child storybook reading has a two-faceted architecture. Facing inward, its structure consists of a set of constitutive rules that specify the range of legitimate moves available to participants. Facing outward, the structure defines the package as one element of a repertoire of alternative activities, each with a range of requirements (apparatus, timing, location, qualifications of participants, compatibility with other concurrent activities, etc.) and social functions, such as having fun, spending "quality time" with one's child, settling a child down in the evening at bedtime, promoting an apprentice's literacy development, displaying the emergent competence of the apprentice to another expert, and so forth.

Once such a routine is acknowledged by a community of practice as an identifiable element of its cultural repertoire, it acquires certain properties that facilitate (as well as constrain) communication. As a familiar, higher order category, it can be used to "chunk" or recode information (Miller, 1956). Teachers and parents can thus easily refer to it and build on it to advance new propositions in relation to it, such as:

- "You should read more often to Johnny."
- "Try including some more advanced (more entertaining, other language, smaller print, etc.) books in your bedtime story reading sessions."
- "She really loves our storybook sessions."
- "Have you thought of getting her father to read her stories sometimes?"

- "We're reading some stories about travel (friendship, animals, music, etc.) in class (at home, at his grandma's, etc.)."

A packaged routine connects with other elements of the cultural repertoire in ways that make it possible to reconstrue the activity in many different ways. For instance, in the earliest phases of the developmental trajectory envisaged by the socialization package of joint storybook reading, the focus is on language acquisition using pictures, rather than on elements of script as cues for speech-production. This usage provides one rationale for the concept of *pictorial literacy* (a branch of visual literacy). Arising from this particular subcultural literacy practice, most of the children of middle-class families in Western industrialized societies between 1950 and 1970 appropriated the conventions of pictorial representation in their early childhood years, before they were enrolled in school, whereas most children of low-income families in sub-Saharan Africa in the same period only began to learn about those conventions toward the end of their elementary schooling, as they approached adolescence. This striking cross-cultural disjunction in learning opportunities gave rise to some significant differences in perceptual response to pictorial illustrations, with implications for psychological testing and curriculum development (Duncan, Gourlay, & Hudson, 1973; Jahoda, Cheyne, Deregowski, Sinha, & Collingbourne, 1976; McBean, Kaggwa, & Bugembe, 1980; Serpell & Deregowski, 1980).

As Heath (1983), Teale and Sulzby (1987), and Wells (1990) pointed out, the activity of joint storybook reading can be conducted by an adult in a number of different ways, some of which are more conducive to eliciting the child's exercise of imagination than others. Wells (1990) embedded his advocacy of the prototype just outlined within an elaborate theoretical framework of alternative modes of engagement with text, arguing that the most educationally productive mode of storybook reading is one that fosters the apprentice's "epistemic" engagement with the text. As with the process of "instructional conversation" advocated by Tharp and Gallimore (1988), there may indeed be optimal strategies for achieving certain educational outcomes with this cultural resource. From one cultural "insider's perspective," dramatizing the story seems to be an excellent opportunity to foster the child's interest in reading. As a Baltimore mother put it to us, "Why make reading boring?!" (Serpell, Baker, Sonnenschein, & Hill, 1993). Some of our preliminary analyses of data collected in the Baltimore Early Childhood Project suggest that a general orientation toward the socialization of literacy as a source of entertainment, rather than merely as a set of skills to be learned, is predictive of more rapid development by the child on several indexes of emergent literacy (Sonnenschein et al., 1996).

However, it is probably unwise to suppose that the paradigm that appears most effective from the perspective of the middle-class subculture (within which the activity has become standardized as a packaged routine) holds a monopoly on the socialization of literacy. Many of the world's most articulate writers today appear to have achieved their appropriation of the medium through quite different sequences of experience (Akinnaso, 1993; Serpell, 1991). In the research literature, the activity of joint book reading has been so frequently adopted as a unit of analysis that two surveys recently attempted to assess its significance relative to other "variables" as a predictor of literacy development (Bus, van Ijzendorn, & Pellegrini, 1995; Scarborough & Dobrich, 1994). Note that in contemporary educational circles in the West, such reviews further elaborate the cultural repertoire and inform some expert and less expert thinking about the activity. Other examples of such interactions between professional, "expert" ideas and what Moscovici (1981) called the "collective representations" of the culture are specification of what is meant by intelligence, with reference to IQ tests; and the practices of demand versus scheduled feeding and leaving babies to cry themselves to sleep, with reference to authoritative texts on parenting, such as Dr. Benjamin Spock's handbook.

The recent history of Western culture includes a number of changes in received wisdom on these topics, which are reflected in the pronouncements of authorities. Thus, parents are no longer warned by all "baby books" against "spoiling" an infant by feeding on demand or by providing body-contact comfort as a preparation for falling asleep.[1] Likewise, popular texts about intelligence no longer all endorse unquestioningly the validity of IQ tests as measures of intelligence. The historically shifting status of such routinized activities in the culture of a society transforms the previous generation's "ideals to be emulated" into a set of "moving targets." The concept of *appropriation* (especially when combined with that of intimate culture, discussed later) can accommodate this phenomenon more readily than the concept of *internalization*, which seems to posit only two alternatives: outright rejection of cultural tradition or absolute orthodoxy. Over the next few decades, as various cultural groups appropriate and transform the activity, it is more than likely that joint storybook reading will become differentiated into a variety of different genres, each of which will receive recognition within the community of experts on reading promotion as effective instruments of early literacy socialization.

In the field of sociolinguistics, it has long been recognized that distinctive speech varieties (Gumperz, 1968) serve not only to facilitate intragroup

---

[1]As a long-term resident of Africa, I find it tempting to interpret this cultural shift as reflecting a process of cross-cultural diffusion of ideas and practices from Africa to the Western world, along with the Snugli (brand of baby sling) and other types of adaptation of traditional African technology for maintaining continuous body contact with infants. Shweder, Jensen, and Goldstein (1995) provided a fascinating analysis of the cultural myopia that often informs authoritative statements by contemporary pediatricians in the West.

communication, but also to exclude nongroup members from in-group discourse, and to affirm group membership by validating the individual's sense of ownership. Within the English-speaking world, it is now widely recognized that distinct Englishes have evolved in India and the Caribbean, as well as the more closely allied British and American variants (cf. Pride, 1982). In recent decades, the field of literacy research recognized the existence of a parallel phenomenon of social differentiation among distinct subcultural literacies. In Scribner and Cole's (1981) seminal study of literacy practices in Liberia, the three different scripts used to write in the Vai, Arabic, and English languages were found to be used in different types of context, each of which placed a premium on different psychological functions, which were differentially affected in predictable ways by the individual's level of proficiency in each literacy.

In Heath's (1983) study of literacy practices in three socioculturally different communities in the U.S. Piedmont Carolinas, each community's "ways with words" were found to include a distinctive pattern of literacy events that gave rise to a correspondingly adaptive set of literacy skills in the children as they entered school. Schoolteachers, however, were only well attuned to the one of these patterns familiar to them in their own homes, and therefore found many more opportunities to foster the skills of the middle-class children whose experience and skills matched their own subcultural orientation than they did for the children of the other two subcultural groups. This type of "mismatch" between the cultures of home and school provides one widely recognized line of explanation for the grim statistics about social class differences in average levels of educational attainment within the settled, local population of industrialized societies. Yet, as a number of researchers have noted, some cultural groups whose home culture and language are even more radically disjoined from those of the American mainstream appear to fare rather better in American public education than the nation's longer term minorities (Laosa, 1984; Ogbu, 1990; Pang, 1990). How can this paradox be resolved ?

THE FILTER OF INTIMATE CULTURE

Levinson (1996, p. 215) cited Lomnitz-Adler's (1992, p. 28) usage of the concept of *intimate cultures* to refer to the "real, regionally differentiated manifestations of class culture" in "the Mexican national space," and pointed out that it "allows us to appreciate the diversity and complexity of cultural sensibilities which exist within regions, while not losing sight of common class- and race-based identities shared across these same regions." Likewise, in the United States within the city of Baltimore, we may find it useful to distinguish the intimate cultures of African American and European American low-income social groups, while also recognizing commonalities in their predicament, arising from such ostensible phenomena as inadequate public services to their residential neighborhoods.

The concept of an intimate culture appears to me to have at least three important theoretical uses.[2] First, it can help us to elaborate the notion of cultural-group membership beyond the notion of a social address (Bronfenbrenner & Crouter, 1983). An intimate culture may be defined as the nexus of cultural parameters actually experienced by a specified group of persons. Within this framework it becomes apparent that several levels of grouping can be distinguished, and recognizing this is a second useful property of the concept. Not only can we identify regional variants of social class, and ethnocultural group distinctions within a particular regional instantiation of a class. But even within an ethnically and economically homogeneous social group in a particular region, such as the predominantly low-income, African American inner city of Baltimore, there remain cultural parameters that differentiate among particular neighborhoods. Furthermore, within a neighborhood, the cultural context experienced by a particular child differs from one family to another. And within a particular neighborhood school, the experienced intimate culture of one peer group is different from that of another, as are the intimate cultures of particular classrooms. Nevertheless, the larger, less precise categories of African American or middle-class or American do have some explanatory power for the interpretation of culture. Any particular intimate culture will typically include traces of those larger, incorporating social formations, but will filter them selectively.

A third theoretical use of the concept is as a way of conceptualizing a unifying cultural frame of reference for encounters among people originating from a diversity of ethnocultural formations within a transcendent social organization such as a classroom, a school, a neighborhood, or a profession. These transcendent organizations (as D'Amato, cited by Jordan, 1992, argued) have their own emergent, cultural properties that coexist with, rather than challenging the validity of, older cultural traditions. To recapitulate, intimate cultures are interpersonally negotiated subsystems of the macroculture's system of meanings, constrained by the larger system but often substantially deviant from it. Moreover, when we look at them from the outside, we may become aware that certain cognate collections of such subsystems (classifiable as professional guilds, or as "caste-like" social classes; Ogbu, 1990) can be detected that have greater mutual intelligibility than exists between those of one caste and another.

In order to appreciate the significance of this dimension of mutual intelligibility, it is necessary to delve inside these intimate cultures and examine their architecture. Since Heath's (1983) landmark study, a number of other

---

[2]I am aware that in this analysis I may be extending the concept beyond the original intentions of Lomnitz-Adler (1992).

investigators have generated rich, descriptive accounts of the literate practices of subcultures other than the middle-class subculture that is so well
known to the majority of literacy researchers and educational professionals
(e.g., Anderson & Stokes, 1984; Goldenberg, Reese, & Gallimore, 1992; Moll &
Greenberg, 1990; Neumann, Hagedorn, Celano, & Daly, 1995; Purcell-Gates,
1996; Taylor & Dorsey-Gaines, 1988). It is not sufficient to demonstrate that
the lives of these subcultures are rich with literacy events. It is important
also to show that each of them constitutes a coherent form of literacy. We
need to understand the organizing themes around which such activities are
interpreted by their actor-participants, and this thematic organization has
not often been articulated for a wider public (but cf. Gwaltney, 1980, and a
number of autobiographies cited by Ladson-Billings, 1992).

Although the concept of *local knowledge* (Geertz, 1983) has proven a
powerful tool for demystifying "high culture" formulations of expertise, it
may be necessary to emphasize that in the modern world saturated with
telecommunication, *local* does not quite capture the restricted, in-group
quality of what mediates between a developing individual and the
macroculture. The metaphor of concentric circles (or Russian dolls) often
used to depict Bronfenbrenner's (1979) conception of the ecology of human
development, although helpful in some respects, is misleading in others, because of the "excess meaning" that it carries (cf. Reese & Overton, 1970;
Serpell, 1990). The implicitly spatial relationship between the macroculture
and a particular neighborhood is violated in many ways by reality. Not only
does TV programming penetrate into the sitting rooms of every family, but
families use commercially standardized products to clean their carpets,
brush their teeth, read bedtime stories to their children, and so on. When
they travel around the city they use public transport, with schedules that
are bureaucratically determined; buy their daily food and household supplies from stores organized in terms of the macroculture's taxonomy of
commodities, packaging, pricing, and so on; and bring them home to organize their daily lives.

In the Early Childhood Project in Baltimore we tried to characterize this
complex set of relationships as they impact on personal development and
enculturation with special reference to the emergence of literacy. Our sample comprises some 80 children growing up in several contrasting types of
neighborhood in one large, American city. The design of our longitudinal
study affords us several windows into the intimate culture of each family.
An ecological inventory was conducted with each primary caregiver during
the course of a visit to the home. Its main organizational categories represent a typology of recurrent activities in the everyday life of the focal child:
games and play activities; mealtime activities; TV, video, and music activities; recurrent outings; and reading, writing, or drawing activities. Our analysis of the children's home environments in the first 2 years revealed that

prekindergartners in low- and middle-income, African American and European American families had frequent opportunities to engage in activities with the potential to foster development in several domains conducive to literacy: orientation toward print, phonological awareness, knowledge of the world, and narrative competence (Baker, Sonnenschein, Serpell, Fernandez-Fein, & Scher, 1994). Sameroff and Fiese (1992) provided an insightful taxonomy of ways in which a family may coconstruct and maintain its own unique intimate culture within the broader constraints of cultural group membership, through a set of paradigms, myths, stories, and rituals, and offered striking evidence of the significance of rituals for child development. Theoretically, they suggested, "family rituals may contribute to the family code by providing meaning to patterned interactions" (p. 364). In the Baltimore Early Childhood Project, we replicated their measure of the ritualization of dinner time as a family routine and extended the same approach to the recurrent activities of reading aloud and doing homework assigned by the school.

A complementary strand of our approach to the description of each family's intimate culture has been a series of questions designed to elicit statements from our informants about the system of evaluative meanings that informs their socialization practices. For each of a sample of activities identified as recurrent by the caregiver, we asked:

What do you think this activity means to _____ (the focal child) ?

What does it mean to you as her/his parent (Caregiver)?

From their interpretations of the meanings of these recurrent shared activities in their child's life, we derived preliminary formulations of several socialization goals that appeared to be salient to each parent, and, in a subsequent interview, invited the parent to confirm, reject, or reformulate these goals, as well as adding others. These goals were then rank ordered by the informant. Subsequently, we asked about the relative importance and complementarity of the contributions of home and school to the child's development in five domains: learning to read and write, learning about numbers, learning about the physical world, learning to communicate, and learning about right and wrong. Parents were also asked to identify optimal ways to help their children learn in each of these domains.

Both low- and middle-income parents of preschoolers in Baltimore, whether African American or European American, tended to regard their child's social and moral development as more important socialization goals than intellectual and academic outcomes, including literacy (Serpell, Sonnenschein, Baker, Hill, Goddard-Truit, & Danseco, 1997). They regarded the cultivation of literacy as more the responsibility of school, and morality as more the responsibility of home, a point on which teachers and other literacy professionals in the United States agreed with them (Commeyras, DeGroff, Stanulis, & Hankins, 1997). Parents showed little intraindividual consistency in their conceptions of the optimal form of intervention to promote the development of literacy and to nurture moral development. With respect to literacy, however, preliminary indications suggest that the lower income families were more inclined to favor proactive intervention, consistent with their focus on literacy as a set of skills to be learned, whereas more of the middle-income parents favored a reliance on the child's experience, or a strategy of in-flight responsiveness. When the various facets of a family's implicit model of child development and socialization are integrated within an idiographic profile, few generalizations appear to be possible. Although certain trends have been detected, such as the greater emphasis on explicit skills instruction among less educated parents and on the fostering of pleasure in reading among the more educated, it seems clear that much of the "unexplained variance" arises from the uniqueness of each caregiver's conceptualization of her relationship with a particular child in a particular set of circumstances.

The Case of E-Mail

Another illustration of the inadequacy of spatial descriptors to capture the constraints defining community membership and the associated ownership of culture is the emergent cultural practice of electronic mail, which includes the activities of Internet correspondence, listserv newsgroups, and web surfing. This set of cultural activities displays many similar patterns of gradual appropriation of the medium by novices. For instance, Hermann (in preparation) provided an insightful "anatomy of on-line communication" in an academic newsgroup, perhaps better termed a *computer-mediated conference*, that straddles several nations as well as a diverse set of academic disciplines, highlighting many of its distinctive features relative to other communities. It is evident from her analysis (which has high face validity for me as an insider) that most of the participants were engaged in a developmental process of increasing competence, as well as negotiating a set of emergent ground rules for interpreting the interventions in a kaleidoscopic flux of contestation of ideas.

One of the more interesting phenomena is that of "lurkers," registered subscribers to the listserve who seldom if ever post any messages. Another is the peculiar status of humor as a vehicle for subversion of authority by peripheral participants, a topic noted in other contexts as one of the few "weapons of the weak" (Scott, 1985; cf. Luykx, 1996).

Using this medium for graduate education at University of Maryland, Baltimore County, I have found it to offer several unique opportunities. Novices to the medium often draw insightful analogies between their own experiences in coming to terms with the constraints of the medium and the frustrations experienced by second-language users of English when attempting to communicate within the mainstream of American education, and draw on these analogies for empathetic understanding of the social and instructional needs of such students. Shy students, and second-language speakers of English in my classes, on the other hand, often manage to express their point of view more effectively on e-mail than they do in the flow of oral discourse in a graduate seminar. The opportunity to pace one's input at a rate commensurate with one's interpersonal confidence and one's information-processing capacity enables such students to place their ideas alongside those of more confident and/or linguistically competent students, ideas that in the course of an animated oral debate would not have received a hearing.

The most striking benefit of the newsgroup for my classes has been a collective one. The freedom to respond to one another, writing at their own pace, often in the evenings from a remote terminal at their home, drawing on their extracurricular experiences, and exploring possible fields of application of the ideas presented in the course readings and class presentations, gives rise to a sense of community much more intense than the class meetings themselves. Whether such a short-term community of practice can be regarded as having its own intimate culture is debatable, because the participants appear to be relatively independent and have the freedom to detach themselves at will. But the loyalties and conflicts that develop within an e-mail community such as XLCHC (latterly known as XMCA) certainly contain striking parallels with those that occur in longer term communities.[3] As the children and youth of the coming generation begin to participate with increasing frequency in such electronically mediated, virtual communities, we may discover new forms of instructional design that can afford enhanced opportunities for the appropriation of technological literacy.

THE STAIRCASE MODEL OF EXTRACTIVE EDUCATION

Many societies in the modern world expect individual literacy to be acquired primarily through the medium of formal education. The instructional practices of this context are intimately linked to the social structure of the institutions known as schools. By and large, these were not established in the first instance as special places for children, but evolved over

---

[3]The X in these acronyms refers to the network, the remaining letters to Laboratory of Comparative Human Cognition (at the University of California, San Diego), and to *Mind, Culture and Activity* (a journal published by LCHC).

the course of history from practices designed to train a cadre of expert specialists (Goody, 1986; Serpell, 1993a). In recent decades, however, a major trend has occurred toward the standardization of institutionalized public basic schooling (IPBS). Two distinctive characteristics of IPBS, "relative to the full range of culturally structured settings devised by human societies for child development," are an emphasis on "advance preparation as against on-the-spot assistance," and "authorized competence as against practical competence" (Serpell & Hatano, 1997, pp. 367–368). Both of these distinctive features tend to divorce contemporary basic education from the everyday lives of the students it is designed to empower, a phenomenon that poses a well-known and enduring challenge for teachers.

The core of educational orthodoxy in IPBS can be traced conceptually and historically to a relatively narrow strand of Western cultural history. Some elements of this have to do with the invention of printing (Eisenstein, 1979; Ong, 1958), whereas others have more to do with the institutional structure of schools as social organizations (Aries, 1962; Serpell, 1993a). The dominant conception of the educational process for the individual within this tradition is one of cumulative empowerment through acquisition of knowledge and expertise. The child's growing literacy competencies are closely monitored through a stepwise sequence of grades, each of which is associated with a specific prescribed age.

In the earliest phase, Anderson-Levitt's (1996) critical ethnography shows how the preschools and early elementary schooling of children both in France and in the United States generate a spurious orthodoxy about the age and time of year at which particular steps in the development of literacy should occur, and gradually stigmatize those who do not conform to these normative expectations as ahead or behind schedule, with the deeper implication that they are precocious or retarded. The technology of age-based developmental assessment thus fades into intelligence testing on the one hand and into the allocation of educational resources on the other. Teachers set more complex cognitive goals for some children than others, scaffolding their mastery of them on the grounds that they are working within the child's zone of proximal development (or matching instruction to the child's development stage). In this way the educational process tends to accentuate and widen the gap between groups of children, many of whose initial aptitudes reflect their social origins, because of the uneven degree of match between the intimate culture of their homes and that of the school. In the later years, students who do not complete the full sequence of higher education, and especially those who do not become functionally literate, are stigmatized as developmentally incomplete (Cook-Gumperz, 1986; Serpell, 1993a).

In many Third World countries, the metaphor of formal education as climbing a staircase is used not only to represent the notion of cumulative cognitive growth, but also to symbolize the social superiority that is contingent on its completion (Serpell, 1999). This mapping of educational achievement onto a hierarchical organization of society provides the basis for a meritocratic rationalization of literacy as that which entitles the elite to dominate the conceptualization of experience for the rest of society. Bourdieu (1974) elaborated the thesis that an educated elite in Western societies has accumulated "cultural capital" in such a way that their ideas hold greater social legitimacy than they deserve. In societies where a great deal of public debate takes place about how best to conceptualize social problems and the best ways of addressing them, critical analysis may serve to constrain the degree to which such political domination serves to distort the everyday understanding of the world by ordinary citizens, as well as dictating the priorities of public policy. But in societies where access to higher education is severely restricted, the opportunities for systematically distorted communication (Habermas, 1971) are greatly enhanced.

Furthermore, over the last two centuries, the multistranded historical processes of international expansion of Western culture, through missionary evangelization, commercial intrusion, and military conquest, has given rise to a pattern of hegemonic imposition of the Western model of education over indigenous practices in many parts of the world (Serpell & Hatano, 1997). As a result, the Western powers and those that have appropriated their cultural perspective on science and technology have accumulated overwhelming power to dictate to other nations how they should define both individual and societal development as a unilinear progression toward certain outcomes (or, as Greenfield, 1976, ominously termed them, "end-points" of development). Historical progressivism, technological and bureaucratic efficiency criteria (Berger, Berger, & Kellner, 1973), and educational quality criteria are thus all compounded in the "modern world" under the integrative concept of *civilization*. Goody (1977) neatly epitomized this phenomenon in his characterization of the historical rise of literacy as "the domestication of the savage mind"—a choice of phrase that he resentfully noted has not always been understood as intended ironically (Goody, 1986)!

In communities other than those comprising the educated elite, an implicit consensus is established among teachers, students, and their families on an "extractive definition of success" (Serpell, 1993a). Children of low-income families who obtain an educational certificate that enables them to obtain a formal-sector job are regarded as having succeeded educationally, whereas those who remain in the communities into which they were born are characterized as "failures" or "drop-outs." This extractive separation of a cohort into a cream of upwardly mobile successes and a residue of static failures is particularly visible in marginalized, Third World, rural communities. Those who remain in these communities to engage in subsistence agriculture are said to be "loafing" or "just sitting" (Hoppers, 1967) rather than doing productive work. Because the structural economic constraints on opportunities for secondary and tertiary education ensure that the majority of students do not proceed beyond the basic tier of the school system, the result of this ideological orientation is that most students are by definition denied the possibility of considering their years of basic schooling as valuable learning opportunities.

The individual who "drops out" of such a stratified system of education, or who graduates from a low level with insufficient grades to progress to the next step on the staircase, emerges with a stigma of incompleteness that not only disqualifies the person from many economically powerful occupations but also carries with it a strong sense of personal inadequacy. In my study of schooling in a rural community in Zambia (Serpell, 1993a), many of the young men and especially women who withdrew from schooling without completing the basic curriculum attributed their "failure" to their own lack of intelligence, despite ample evidence of intelligence in their everyday lives. Luttrell (1996) described the same phenomenon among her sample of working-class American women who had emerged from their basic schooling unable to read and write. Many of the cultural resources of literacy are known to such an individual only at a distance, as things that other people read, but not as part of a cultural legacy that belongs to her (*son patrimoine*). Her status in society is defined as a person underqualified to interpret, let alone enjoy, such texts. Engagement with such alien resources is therefore highly unlikely, and is discouraged by those members of the society who claim authoritative knowledge of them.

This exclusive, disempowering outcome of education is not readily acknowledged by teachers and school administrators, because one of the ideological premises of public education is equality of opportunity (McLeod, 1987/1995). Those who fail to appropriate enough of what is on offer in the school curriculum are deemed to have denied themselves the opportunity, either due to some intellectual deficiencies or due to obstructively motivated behavior. Indeed, the ideology of education tends to assert that the process is designed to support and direct the personal development of each student. Moreover, the extractive definition of educational success only applies to those students coming from homes and communities where the literate culture of the mainstream has not been appropriated. The child of a highly literate family thus never encounters this problem of self-definition. Such a child is easily able to draw connections between the culture of his or her home and that of the school. Schooling for that child represents a natural extension of the socialization practices of her home community. Hence educational success is a natural and comfortable goal for such a child to aspire to, and indeed comes much more easily to such children than to those for whom educational success involves extraction and alienation from their community of origin.

What then are the prospects of modest empowerment through literacy for the majority of the world's citizens, born into conditions where the schooling offered by the establishment is radically discontinuous with the intimate culture of their home community? In a longitudinal follow-up of children born into a rural community of eastern Zambia in the 1960s, I examined the literacy outcomes for a cohort required by government policy to learn to read and write at school in the medium of a language scarcely spoken at all in their homes (Serpell, 1993a). English, the language of the former colonial power, continues to serve many significant functions in Zambian society, as an instrument of legislation and state administration, of international commerce, of technical research, and of tertiary-level formal education. Yet despite explicit attempts to use it as a vehicle of national integration, it remains unquestionably secondary to the indigenous Bantu languages for the vast majority of the population as a psychocultural resource for the expression of self, community, and religious values, and in most of the transactions of everyday life. Nevertheless, such is the power of political advocacy for the English language in Zambia (as in many other African nations) that the national government decided soon after achieving political sovereignty in 1964 to introduce a nationwide policy of English-medium instruction in public schooling through immersion starting in the first grade (Serpell, 1978). It was thus no surprise, when I asked the assembled teaching staff of a rural primary school to predict the levels of literacy in English and in the local indigenous language, Chi-Chewa, among those of their former students who did not go on to secondary school, that they unanimously expected them to be more literate in English than in Chi-Chewa.

The reality revealed by our individual testing, however, was quite the opposite. Most of the young people we interviewed were manifestly more literate in Chi-Chewa than in English, and were fully aware of this fact, mentioning it as a matter of uncontroversial fact (Serpell, 1993a, chap. 5). Comparable findings have been reported by Eisemon (1988) from a rural sample in Kenya, where a similar English-medium policy has been adopted for basic education. In one case study, we were able to reconstruct in some detail the process through which this had taken place. Gillian stopped attending her local primary school in 1979, claiming: "I could see I didn't know how to read and yet I'm in Grade 5. So that's why I said 'I'm leaving school, I won't go back' . . . money would just be wasted on me going to school." Three years later, she reiterated in another interview: "School was too tough for me . . . personally, I didn't learn anything at school," and then added, as an afterthought, "The one who taught me to read Chi-Chewa is my Mum."[4]

---

[4]These translated excerps are reproduced from Serpell (1993a), chapter 5. All interviews were conducted in Chi-Chewa.

Some years later, we were able to confirm in an interview with Gillian's mother that she had indeed taught her daughter to read at home some time between 1980 and 1983, using Chi-Chewa books she had kept from her own school days. Thus a low-literacy, rural mother achieved in a matter of a few weeks the educational outcome that professional teachers had failed to produce in more than 4 years. Her rationale for this intervention was revealing: She was embarrassed that her daughter was unable to read the prayer book when they attended church together on Sundays. This locally meaningful, constituent literate activity of her intimate culture made it important enough for Gillian with the support of her family to appropriate the technology of script that had eluded her in the context of factitious exercises at school.

Findings such as these are quite incompatible with the traditional orthodox conception of schools as specialized conduits for the flow of information and values from one generation to the next. The instructional paradigm institutionalized in the staircase model of extractive education carries the implication that the desired outcome is a specifiable change in the behavior of students, which constitutes adaptation to a world of which adults have already achieved mastery. Increasingly, however, educationists of all ideological persuasions have begun to acknowledge publicly that the pace of social change, both in the industrialized, affluent, and powerful countries of the world and in the Third World countries that fail to meet several of those criteria, is so rapid that almost anything we old-timers may decide to build into the curriculum of IPBS in the 1990s is likely to be seriously inadequate to the demands of the ecosystem in which its graduates will have to operate in the 21st century. The best we can hope for under these circumstances is that education will cultivate an active process of transformation of our existing cultural practices into a future set of practices that are adaptive to that future world. To the extent that mankind's accumulated wisdom is relevant, it will need to be transformatively appropriated, not passively absorbed or compliantly imitated.

FOSTERING APPROPRIATION

In the preceding sections of this chapter, I have argued that the development of individual literacy is best conceived as a process of participatory appropriation that takes place within a community of practice, and that the key to engagement with literacy practices such as book reading lies in ensuring full membership of the community, from which flows a subjective sense of ownership of its cultural meaning system. I have also proposed that we think of the cultural capital that an individual brings to the challenge of appropriating literacy not simply in terms of a social address, but rather in terms of an intimate culture, defined as the nexus of cultural parameters actually experienced by a specified group of persons. These intimate cultures, I contend, are open to negotiated modification and expansion, as schools connect with children's homes.

The disheartening pattern of alienation described earlier, between communities and the schools purporting to serve them, has given rise to a number of attempts to design alternative programs that address in innovative ways the challenges of supporting human development in low-income, disempowered communities. Thompson, Mixon, and Serpell (1996, pp. 54–55) identified four different and complementary approaches that have attempted to enhance the quality of home-school connections with a view to engaging students in reading among American minority-culture groups: "(a) enriching the cultural repertoire of the family, (b) recruiting caregivers through their own literate engagement, (c) mobilizing indigenous cultural resources, and (d) empowering the community in the organization of schooling."

Goldenberg and his colleagues (Gallimore & Goldenberg, 1993; Goldenberg et al., 1992) described a sensitive, contemporary version of cultural enrichment intervention in a low-income, Latino community in California. These researchers compared the impact of two types of material assigned for "homework" to first-grade students: *libros*, designed to be read as entertaining literature, and workbooks containing basic skills exercises. The workbooks were more popular with parents than the *libros*, and direct observation in a sample of families revealed that they generally used the *libros* in a more formal, didactic manner than the designers of these curricular materials had intended. Consonant with the skills orientation attributed by Delpit (1988) to low-income, inner-city African-American communities, these parents appeared to believe that mastery of letter-sound correspondence rules through repetitive rehearsal holds the key to becoming literate. Goldenberg and his colleagues offered an intriguing discussion of alternative interpretations for their findings. Should the use of literacy materials designed to be read as entertainment by some families for drilling their children be regarded as maladaptive abuse or as adaptively syncretic appropriation?

McNamee (1990) and Shockley (1993) described the successful experiences of kindergarten teachers who entered into regular correspondence with each of their students' primary caregivers at home about the child's progress through the basic literacy curriculum. Parents who participate in such programs not only receive encouragement to pay attention to and support their child's emerging literacy, but through their own writing generate an intimate cultural ambience that values literate activities. Moll and Greenberg (1990) and Heath (1983) described curricular strategies that involve more ambitious mobilization of the funds of cultural knowledge in low-income communities, including their indigenous languages or dialects, by inviting community elders into the classroom as expert resources and assigning students extramural projects to observe and interview relatives and neighbors. The KEEP project in Hawaii (Jordan, 1992; Tharp et al., 1984) represents one of the most systematic and sustained attempts to build cultural compatibility into the schooling of early literacy, by searching in the indigenous culture for patterns of activity, linguistic forms, and symbolic content and integrating them into the curriculum. An explicit focus on sharing power with the local community was adopted by Comer (1988) in an attempt to enhance local accountability to a community that had lost faith in its local school.

These and other exemplary studies were presented to a small sample of teachers from the inner-city Baltimore schools sampled by our Early Childhood Project for reflective discussion in preparation for launching their own, action-research, inservice teacher inquiries. Despite numerous constraints, their experience overall was positive if only in deepening their awareness of the importance of cooperative communication between teachers and parents for fostering young children's early appropriation of literacy (Serpell, Baker, Sonnenschein, Gorham, & Hill, 1996). On the other hand, some of the parameters of these interventions in the United States are very difficult to extrapolate to a Third World country, where the history of educational provision, the range of trained personnel, the administrative mechanisms, and the material resources for implementing applied research are very different. Moreover, the nature of public expectations from the school system can only be understood in relation to the local culture and economy. A more useful source of inspiration for educational innovation in Third World countries may therefore be to examine projects undertaken under Third World conditions.

In the small rural town of Mpika in northern Zambia, a group of innovative teachers have for a number of years been pursuing a curricular strategy of focusing children's learning around practical activities in the community, a strategy that deviates sharply from the mainstream of the nation's schooling practices, introducing the topic of monitoring and nurturing the healthy growth of infants into the curriculum of a government primary school (Mwape & Serpell, 1996). The stimulus for this innovation came from a program designed explicitly to build linkages between child health and education, which places a unique emphasis on collaborative learning, known as Child-to-Child. Building on the work of David Morley and his colleagues (Morley & Woodland, 1979), the Child-to-Child Trust in London has for a number of years promoted the idea of involving schoolage children in the monitoring of younger children's weight and other indices of health (Hawes & Scotchmer, 1993; Otaala, 1978; Young & Durston, 1987).

Consider the following scenario, which is acted out every day in thousands of clinics around the world. A mother helps a nurse to strap an infant into a harness suspended from a weighing scale. When the needle points to a number on the scale, the nurse enters the child's weight as a cross on a growth chart, which is printed on a health record card. Mother and nurse then communicate about the child's rate of growth, depicted as the slope of a line graph plotting the child's weight for age over the span of a series of measurements made on successive occasions. The graph is known as the *growth curve* and is a shared literate cultural resource for monitoring the health status of children under 5 years old (Grant, 1984; Morley & Woodland, 1979). It provides a common index of a complex phenomenon, individualized to fit the particularities of each child and each clinic, yet possessing certain abstract properties that enable it to serve a reliable function for all of them. Much of the scientific research that guarantees the validity of this literate resource is inaccessible to the vast majority of its users. Yet collectively, the community of practice using growth charts may be regarded as having appropriated the technology grounded in that research.

Gibbs and Mutunga (1991) insightfully explained for teachers how this and several other health-related activities involve the application of basic mathematical principles. And Paul Mumba (1996) complemented and extended this text with a number of exercises for his primary school students in Mpika. During our visits to the school, Gertrude Mwape and I observed third graders weighing themselves and measuring one another's heights in class, and beginning to interpret graphs of weight for age plotted on the chalk-board. Sixth graders were writing essays based on their own growth charts, and monitoring the growth of siblings and neighbors under the age of 5 years, escorting them to the local clinic for monthly checkups, and in some cases administering oral rehydration therapy and/or nutritional supplements to infants who experienced acute diarrhea and/or significant weight loss.

The children in these classes are engaged in authentically literate activities, applying the technology of script and mathematics to the interpretation and solution of real problems in their everyday lives as members of their local community. Their appropriation of health science and technology through participation in these activities gives rise to a sense of personal efficacy and social responsibility, which is often expressed in their own literate productivity. The curriculum provides many opportunities for performance of dramas, poetry, and songs, as well as more analytical, reflective writing. One boy in a Grade 7 class wrote the following in an essay:

> The most important things that we were doing, was to adopt our young brothers and sisters and we were giving them the balanced diets because at school we learnt many things about nutritious foods. When we adopted some children some of the parents refuse to adopt their babies because of ~~ignorance~~ been ignorant as a result their children were not growing well because of not

knowing the weight. At the same time we took toddlers to the under five clinic and thereafter we taught them how to write and counting. This was what we were doing on child monitoring and growth of younger child in our community"[5]

The class teacher noted:

Victor is 14 years old. They are seven in his family and he is the second born. He has recently developed much interest in child monitoring. The father has only reached grade eight level of education while the mother has reached grade seven. The first born has only reached grade nine level of education. The parents struggle to make ends meet and sometimes Victor works for other people to pay for his fees and buy his own school uniform. He has interest in his education.[6]

Not only does the literate activity in which they are engaged connect ostensibly with the local world inhabited by these Mpika students. It incorporates two important socialization values of the indigenous culture with respect to middle childhood and adolescence: a nurturant attitude toward younger children, and cooperative relations among peers. Many studies of child rearing in Africa have drawn attention to these values and the practices informed by them (Harkness & Super, 1992; Nsamenang, 1992; Serpell, 1992; Whittemore & Beverly, 1989). Given the processes of dynamic change underway in new conurbations such as Mpika, however, we considered it important to investigate the intimate culture of families in the local community served by this innovative educational program.

In our interviews with a stratified sample of the families of enrolled students, most parents indicated that they regard the practice of involving children of primary school age in caring for younger children as part of an old Zambian tradition, that they themselves were expected to do this in their own childhood, and that they require such participation of their children at home. Only about half of them reported that this had been a theme in their schooling, but several of them went on to reason that its extension in this way was valuable. On the question of what benefits the older child derives from such activity, parents of both boys and girls cited growth of a nurturant attitude, a sense of responsibility and preparation for parenthood, and also intrinsic pleasure and sense of personal worth. These subjective benefits were especially apparent to parents of low-achieving pupils. Only a minority of the parents we interviewed were fully aware of the specific educational activities being organized by the school around growth charts. They were all willing, however, to express an opinion about the po-

[5]Victor Chisanga (unpublished essay, reproduced with permission).
[6]Personal communication from Paul Mumba, May 1996.

tential value of such activities. Many regarded it as useful general knowledge (especially for boys), and as preparation for future parenthood (of both genders). Several parents of girls (but only of one boy) thought this might enhance their child's immediate ability to help with infant health care at home, and some (mainly parents of boys) also felt the program would serve indirectly to improve the infant health care practices of some students' parents. The gender bias reflected by this distribution of attitudes is not surprising, but was a source of debate within the Grade 7 classrooms, where a new generation of more egalitarian gender roles appeared to be being successfully cultivated.

Another noteworthy aspect of the instructional practices we have observed in these classes is the extensive use by teachers of the main local indigenous language, ici-Bemba, and a high tolerance of code switching among their students. The student Gillian whose experience was described earlier would have found it less plausible to claim that she was learning nothing useful or relevant in these classes. Indeed, many of the students we interviewed were enthusiastic about their schooling. The staircase model of extractive education does not disappear in the face of such innovative, local educational practices. It was therefore gratifying for the pioneering teachers at this school to find that their students performed relatively well in 1996 on the national selection examination for admission to secondary schooling. In the future, however, it will be important to evaluate the enduring consequences of their health-related education for the life journeys of students who do not enter secondary school as well as for those who do. The connection forged by the curriculum between the texts and techniques of basic science and mathematics and the real-life task of raising children in an ecosystem fraught with biological and socioeconomic hazards to their survival and healthy development should be a source of empowerment for their functional literacy across a wide range of socioeconomic contexts.

In 1999, we made a small beginning in this direction, and found some indications of lasting benefits experienced by some of the graduates from the Child-to-Child curriculum in Mpika who, like the majority of Africa's children, did not continue their schooling beyond the end of primary school. One young woman of 18 we interviewed in a very low-income neighborhood, almost 3 years after leaving the school, was now married and nursing her first child. Asked what she remembered learning at school, she mentioned growth-monitoring and oral rehydration. So we pressed her for an example of how this had been of value to her community. She then recounted advising one of her friends, who also had a baby, on how to handle an episode of diarrhea by means of oral rehydration using the home-made solution of sugar, salt, and water they had learned about at school. Our interview schedule was carefully designed to pose strictly open-ended questions without any suggestions of appropriate content for the replies. Conventionally, most Zambian primary school-leavers, when asked about the benefits of their schooling, tend to emphasize their basic literacy and numeracy. Moreover, if pressed for examples of how they used those skills, many of them are at a loss to give convincing examples. I was impressed therefore that this young woman singled out the topics of growth-monitoring and oral rehydration therapy, and readily produced an example of their practical application to a substantive issue in the life of her community.

POLICY IMPLICATIONS

At the level of public policy and institutional planning, the greatest challenge posed by the analysis I have advanced in this chapter is how to enable, support, and legitimate creative innovations at the local level without either swamping them with administrative responsibilities, or stifling them with standardization.

The possibilities of fostering the appropriation by individual children of the cultural resources of literacy demonstrated in the various intervention programs considered in this section are real, but their prospects for "going to scale" (Myers, 1992) are frequently challenged. Rather than advancing a "blueprint" for replication at other sites, I favor Korten's (1985) "learning process" approach to dissemination, in which social scientists strive to support the construction of "organizations with a well developed capacity for responsive and anticipatory adaptation—organizations that (a) embrace error; (b) plan with the people; and (c) link knowledge building with action" (p. 498). With particular reference to educational planning in Africa, I have advanced elsewhere a number of tangible, administratively feasible proposals for ways of restructuring the existing pattern of IPBS to reduce the extractive, alienating impact of formal schooling by promoting local accountability (Serpell, 1999).

The strategy most directly relevant to the present analysis is that of acknowledging parallel tracks to various valued outcomes. At the local level, the school needs to expand its public criteria of what constitutes a successful outcome of several years of enrolment: Instead of defining the only index of success as passing an exam to proceed to the next level of the curriculum, schools and the communities they serve need to acknowledge, as highly valued, alternative indices of educational success, such outcomes as a student nursing a young child back to health following a spell of serious weight loss arising from malnutrition. Recording and evaluating such events for purposes of recognition would depend crucially on intensive local consultation. If the development of literacy is to give rise to that sense of ownership from which authentic engagement flows, it needs to be understood by the developing individual as a process of participatory appropriation of cultural resources. Parents, teachers, and educational planners can foster this awareness by according developing individuals opportunities to use those resources in creative ways in the service of their community.

Some guiding principles for policy development in the field of literacy promotion implicit in the preceding discussion are as follows.

Cooperative Communication. Teachers and parents should make every effort to communicate cooperatively about the developmental goals and needs of the children for whom they share responsibility, and to coconstruct opportunities for the children to appropriate the cultural resources of literacy.

Bicultural Mediation. Teachers should be trained to consider as one of their major responsibilities the mediation of intellectual connections between the cultures of their students' homes and the macrosocietal culture of the educational establishment. Such bicultural mediation should be construed as a bidirectional process of mutual enrichment.

Syncretic Curriculum Development. Curriculum developers should work with researchers and teachers to identify resources indigenous to the cultural traditions of minority groups that can be integrated within the mainstream of educational provision, through the design of texts and instructional activities, the recruitment and training of teachers, and continuous interaction between students' intramural and extramural domains of experience.

Local Accountability. Public elementary schools should be mandated to regard the local community from which they draw their student population as a primary constituency to which they are accountable for the educational services they provide.

Devolution and Diversification. Centrally based public policymakers and educational authorities should explicitly legitimate local accountability by treating schools as nodes in their planning models. They should actively promote diversification of the functions of elementary school buildings to include serving as a lending library, as a community forum for discussion of public affairs, and as the base for continuing education activities for parents.

REFERENCES

Akinnaso, F. N. (1993). Literacy and individual consciousness. In A. C. Purves & E. M. Jennings (Eds.), *Literate systems and individual lives: perspectives on literacy and schooling* (pp. 73–94). Albany, NY: SUNY Press.

Anderson, A. B., & Stokes, S. J. (1984). Social and institutional influences on the development and practice of literacy. In H. Goelman, A. A. Oberg, & F. Smith (Eds.), *Awakening to literacy* (pp. 24–37). London: Heinemann.

Anderson-Levitt, K. M. (1996). Behind schedule: Batch-produced children in French and U.S. classrooms. In B. A. Levinson, D. E. Foley, & D. C. Holland (Eds.), *The cultural production of the educated person: Critical ethnographies of schooling and local practice* (pp. 57–78). Albany, NY: SUNY Press.

Aries, P. (1962). *Centuries of childhood* (R. Baldick, Trans.). London: Cape.

Baker, L., Sonnenschein, S., Serpell, R., Fernandez-Fein, S., & Scher, D. (1994). *Contexts of emergent literacy: Everyday home experiences of urban pre-kindergarten children* (Reading Research Rep. No. 24). Athens, GA: National Research Reading Center, Universities of Georgia and Maryland College Park.

Berger, P. L., Berger, B., & Kellner, H. (1973). *The homeless mind*. New York: Random House.

Berrien, F. K. (1967). Methodological and related problems in cross-cultural research. *International Journal of Psychology, 2*, 33–44.

Bourdieu, P. (1974). The school as a conservative force: Scholastic and cultural inequalities. In J. Eggleston (Ed.), *Contemporary research in the sociology of education* (pp. 32–46). London: Methuen.

Bronfenbrenner, U. (1979). *The ecology of human development*. Cambridge, MA: Harvard University Press.

Bronfenbrenner, U., & Crouter, A. C. (1983). The evolution of environmental models in developmental research. In W. Kessen (Ed.), *History, theory and methods, Vol. I, Handbook of child psychology* (P. H. Mussen, Ed., pp. 357–414). New York: Wiley.

Bruner, J. (1986). *Actual minds, possible worlds.* Cambridge, MA: Harvard University Press.

Bus, A. G., van Ijzendoorn, M. H., & Pellegrini, A. D. (1995). Joint book reading makes for success in learning to read: A meta-analysis on intergenerational transmission of literacy. *Review of Educational Research, 65*, 1–21.

Comer, J. P. (1980). *School power*. New York: Freedom Press.

Commeyras, M., DeGroff, L., Stanulis, R., & Hankins, K. (1997). *Literacy professionals' ways of knowing: A national survey.* (Reading Research Rep. No. 86). Athens, GA: National Reading Research Center, Universities of Georgia and Maryland College Park.

Cook-Gumperz, J. (1986). Literacy and schooling: An unchanging equation? In J. Cook-Gumperz (Ed.), *The social construction of literacy* (pp. 16–44). Cambridge: Cambridge University Press.

D'Andrade, R. G. (1984). Cultural meaning systems. In R. A. Shweder & R. A. Levine (Eds.), *Culture theory: Essays on mind, self and emotion* (pp. 88–119). Cambridge: Cambridge University Press.

Delpit, L. (1988). The silenced dialogue: power and pedagogy in educating other people's children. *Harvard Educational Review, 58*, 280–298.

Duncan, H. F., Gourlay, N., & Hudson, W. (1973). *A study of pictorial perception among Bantu and White primary school children in South Africa*. Johannesburg: Witwatersrand University Press.

Eisemon, T. O. (1988). *Benefiting from basic education, school quality and functional literacy in Kenya*. Oxford: Pergamon.

Eisenstein, E. L. (1979). *The printing press as an agent of change: Communications and cultural transformations in early-modern Europe*. Cambridge: Cambridge University Press.

Gallimore, R., & Goldenberg, C. (1993). Activity settings of early literacy: Home and school factors in children's emergent literacy. In E. Forman, N. Minick, & A. Stone (Eds.), *Contexts for learning: Sociocultural dynamics in children's development* (pp. 315–335). New York: Oxford University Press.

Gee, J. P. (1989). Literacy, discourse and linguistics: Introduction. *Journal of Education, 171*, 5–25.

Geertz, C. (1983). *Local knowledge: Further essays in interpretive anthropology.* New York: Basic Books.

Gibson, E. J. (1982). The concept of affordances: The renascence of functionalism. In A. Collins (Ed.), *The concept of development: The Minnesota Symposia on Child Development* (Vol. 15, pp. 55–81). Hillsdale, NJ: Lawrence Erlbaum Associates.

Gibbs, W., & Mutunga, P. (1991). *Health into mathematics.* London: Longman/British Council.

Goldenberg, C., Reese, L., & Gallimore, R. (1992). Effects of literacy materials from school on Latino children's home experiences and early reading achievement. *American Journal of Education, 100,* 497–536.

Goody, J. (1977). *The domestication of the savage mind.* Cambridge: Cambridge University Press.

Goody, J. (1986). *The logic of writing and the organization of society.* Cambridge: Cambridge University Press.

Grant, J. P. (1984). *The state of the world's children.* Oxford: Oxford University Press/UNICEF.

Greenfield, P. M. (1976). Cross-cultural research and Piagetian theory: Paradox and progress. In K. F. Riegel & J. A. Meacham (Eds.), *The developing individual in a changing world* (Vol. 1, pp. 322–333). The Hague: Mouton.

Gumperz, J. J. (1968). The speech community. In *International encyclopaedia of the social sciences* (pp. 381–386). New York: Macmillan.

Gwaltney, J. (1980). *Drylongso.* New York: Vintage Books.

Habermas, J. (1971). *Knowledge and human interests* (J. J. Shapiro, Trans.). Boston: Beacon Press.

Harkness, S., & Super, C. (1992). Shared child care in East Africa: Sociocultural origins and developmental consequences. In M. E. Lamb, K. J. Sternberg, C. P. Hwang, & A. Broberg (Eds.), *Child care in context* (pp. 441–459). Hillsdale, NJ: Lawrence Erlbaum Associates.

Hawes, H., & Scotchmer, C. (Eds.). (1993). *Children for health.* London: Child-to-Child Trust/UNICEF.

Heath, S. B. (1983). *Ways with words: Language, life, and work in communities and classrooms.* Cambridge: Cambridge University Press.

Hermann, F. (in preparation). *Electronic academia: An anatomy of on-line communication.* Unpublished manuscript.

Hoppers, W. (1967). The aftermath of failure: Experiences of primary school leavers in rural Zambia. *African Social Research, 29,* 709–739.

Jahoda, G., Cheyne, W. B., Deregowski, J. B., Sinha, D., & Collingbourne, R. (1976). Utilization of pictorial information in classroom learning: A cross-cultural study. *AV Communication Review, 24,* 295–315.

Jordan, C. (1992). The role of culture in minority school achievement. *Kamehameha Journal of Education, 3*(2), 53–67.

Korten, D. (1985). Community organization and rural development: A learning process approach. *Public Administration Review, 40*(5), 480–511.

Ladson-Billings, G. (1992). Culturally relevant teaching: the key to making multicultural education work. In C. Grant (Ed.), *Research and multicultural education: From the margins to the mainstream* (pp. 106–121). Washington, DC: Falmer.

Laosa, L. (1984). Social policies toward children of diverse ethnic, racial and language groups in the United States. In H. W. Stevenson & A. E. Siegel (Eds.), *Child development research and social policy* (Vol. 1, pp. 1–109). Chicago: Chicago University Press.

Lave, J., & Wenger, E. (1991). *Situated learning: Legitimate peripheral participation.* Cambridge: Cambridge University Press.

Levinson, B. A. (1996). Social difference and schooled identity at a Mexican secundaria. In B. A. Levinson, D. E. Foley, & D. C. Holland (Eds.), *The cultural production of the educated person: critical ethnographies of schooling and local practice* (pp. 211–238). Albany, NY: SUNY Press.

Lomnitz-Adler, C. (1992) *Exits from the labyrinth: Culture and ideology in the Mexican national space.* Berkeley: University of California Press.

Lotman, Y. M. (1988). Text within a text. *Soviet Psychology, 26*(3), 32–51.

Luttrell, W. (1996). Becoming somebody in and against school: Toward a psychocultural theory of gender and self making. In B. A. Levinson, D. E. Foley, & D. C. Holland (Eds.), *The cultural production of the educated person: Critical ethnographies of schooling and local practice* (pp. 93–118). Albany, NY: SUNY Press.

Luykx, A. (1996). From Indios to professionales: Stereotypes and student resistance in Bolivian teacher training. In B. A. Levinson, D. E. Foley, & D. C. Holland (Eds.), *The cultural production of the educated person: Critical ethnographies of schooling and local practice* (pp. 239–272). Albany, NY: SUNY Press.

MacLeod, J. (1995). *Ain't no makin' it: Aspirations and attainment in a low-income neighborhood.* Boulder, CO: Westview. (Original work published 1987).

McBean, G., Kaggwa, N., & Bugembe, J. (Eds.). (1980). *Illustrations for development.* Nairobi, Kenya: Afrolit Society.

McNamee, G. D. (1990). Learning to read and write in an inner-city setting: A longitudinal study of community change. In L. C. Moll (Ed.), *Vygotsky and education: Instructional implications and applications of sociohistorical psychology* (pp. 287–303). Cambridge: Cambridge University Press.

Miller, G. A. (1956). The magical number seven, plus or minus two: Some limits on our capacity for processing information. *Psychological Review, 63,* 81–97.

Moll, L. C., & Greenberg, J. B. (1990). Creating zones of possibilities: combining social contexts for instruction. In L. C. Moll (Ed.), *Vygotsky and education: Instructional implications and applications of sociohistorical psychology* (pp. 319–348). Cambridge: Cambridge University Press.

Morley, D., & Woodland, M. (1979). *See how they grow: Monitoring child growth for appropriate health care in developing countries.* London: Macmillan.

Moscovici, S. (1981). On social representations. In J. P. Forgas (Ed.), *Social cognition: Perspectives on everyday understanding* (pp. 181–209). London: Academic Press.

Mumba, P. (1996). *Child-to-Child twinning project and community study pairs.* Unpublished report, Kabale Primary School, Mpika, Zambia.

Mwape, G., & Serpell, R. (1996, August). *Participatory appropriation of health science by primary school students in rural Zambia.* Poster presentation at the International Conference of the International Society for the Study of Behavioural Development (ISSBD), Quebec, Canada. (ERIC document ED 41791)

Myers, R. (1992). *The twelve who survive.* London: Routledge.

Neumann, S. B., Hagedorn, T., Celano, D., & Daly, P. (1995). Toward a collaborative approach to parent involvement in early education. *American Educational Research Journal, 32,* 801–827.

Ninio, A., & Bruner, J. (1978). The achievement and antecedents of labelling. *Journal of Child Language, 5,* 1–15.

Nsamenang, A. B. (1992). Early childhood care and education in Cameroon. In M. E. Lamb, K. J. Sternberg, C. P. Hwang, & A. Broberg (Eds.), *Child care in context* (pp. 419–439). Hillsdale, NJ: Lawrence Erlbaum Associates.

Ogbu, J. U. (1990). Cultural model, identity, and literacy. In J. W. Stigler, R. A. Shweder, & G. Herdt (Eds), *Cultural psychology: Essays on comparative human development* (pp. 520–541). Cambridge: Cambridge University Press.

Ong, W. J. (1958). *Ramus: Method, and the decay of dialogue.* Cambridge, MA: Harvard University Press.

Otaala, B. (1982). The child-to-child program in the context of educational problems in Africa. *Botswana Educational Research Journal, 1*(1), 39–51.

Pang, V. (1990). Asian-American children: A diverse population. *Educational Forum, 55,* 49–65.

Pride, J. B. (Ed.). (1982). *New Englishes.* Rowley, MA: Newbury House.

Purcell-Gates, V. (1996). Stories, coupons, and the TV guide: Relationships between home literacy experiences and emergent literacy knowledge. *Reading Research Quarterly, 31*(2), 406–428.

Reder, S. M. (1987). Comparative aspects of functional literacy development: Three ethnic American communities. In D. A. Wagner (Ed.), *The future of literacy in a changing world* (pp. 250–270). New York: Pergamon.

Reese, W. H., & Overton, W. F. (1970). Models of development and theories of development. In L. R. Goulet & P. Baltes (Eds.), *Lifespan development psychology* (pp. 116–145). New York: Academic Press.

Rogoff, B. (1993). Children's guided participation and participatory appropriation in sociocultural activity. In R. Wozniak & K. Fischer (Eds.), *Development in context: Acting and thinking in specific environments* (pp. 121–153). Hillsdale, NJ: Lawrence Erlbaum Associates.

Rogoff, B., Baker-Sennett, J., Lacasa, P., & Goldsmith, D. (1995). Development through participation in sociocultural activity. *New Directions for Child Development, 67, Cultural Practices as Contexts for Development* (J. J. Goodnow, P. J. Miller, & F. Kessel, Eds.), pp. 45–65.

Sameroff, A. J., & Fiese, B. H. (1992). Family representations of development. In I. E. Sigel, A. V. McGillicuddy-DeLisi, & J. J. Goodnow (Eds.), *Parental belief systems: the psychological consequences for children* (pp. 347–369). Hillsdale, NJ: Lawrence Erlbaum Associates.

Scarborough, H. S., & Dobrich, W. (1994). On the efficacy of reading to preschoolers. *Developmental Review, 14,* 245–302.

Scott, J. C. (1985). *Weapons of the weak: Everyday forms of peasant resistance.* New Haven, CT: Yale University Press.

Scribner, S., & Cole, M. (1981). *The psychology of literacy.* Cambridge, MA: Harvard University Press.

Searle, J. R. (1965). What is a speech act? In M. Black (Ed.), *Philosophy in America* (pp. 221–239). Ithaca, NY: Cornell University Press.

Serpell, R. (1978). Some developments in Zambia since 1971. In S. Ohannessian & M. E. Kashoki (Eds.), *Language in Zambia* (pp. 424–447). London: International African Institute.

Serpell, R. (1990). Audience, culture and psychological explanation: A reformulation of the emic–etic problem in cross-cultural psychology. *Quarterly Newsletter of the Laboratory Comparative Human Cognition, 12*(3), 99–132.

Serpell, R. (1991). Exaggerating the significance of text. *Curriculum Inquiry, 21*(3), 353–362.

Serpell, R. (1992). African dimensions of child care and nurturance. In M. E. Lamb, K. J. Sternberg, C-P. Hwang, & A. Broberg (Eds.), *Child care in context* (pp. 463–476). Hillsdale, NJ: Lawrence Erlbaum Associates.

Serpell, R. (1993a). *The significance of schooling: Life-journeys in an African society.* Cambridge: Cambridge University Press.

Serpell, R. (1993b). Interface between socio-cultural and psychological aspects of cognition. In E. Forman, N. Minick, & A. Stone (Eds.), *Contexts for learning: Sociocultural dynamics in children's development* (pp. 357–368). New York: Oxford University Press.

Serpell, R. (1994). Beyond the mirage of enlightenment through literacy: Curricular ideologies versus contextualized practices. In U. Frith, G. Ludi, & M. Egli (Eds.), *Proceedings of the Workshop on Contexts of Literacy* (Vol. III, pp. 17–45). Strasbourg, France: European Science Foundation.

Serpell, R. (1998, July). *Participatory appropriation in sociocultural context: A multilevel strategy for applied developmental science.* Paper presented at the 4th Regional African Workshop of International Society for the Study of Behavioural Development (ISSBD), Windhoek, Namibia.

Serpell, R. (1999). Local accountability to rural communities: A challenge for educational planning in Africa. In F. Leach & A. Little (Eds.), *Education, cultures and economics: Dilemmas for development* (pp. 107–135). New York: Garland.

Serpell, R., Baker, L., Sonnenschein, S., Gorham, L., & Hill, S. (1996). Cooperative communication among teachers and parents about the emergence of literacy in sociocultural context. *Final Project Report to the National Reading Research Center* (University of Georgia, University of Maryland College Park). (*ERIC document* ED 414566)

Serpell, R., Baker, L., Sonnenschein, S., & Hill, S. (1991, July). *Caregiver ethnotheories of children's emergent literacy and numeracy.* Paper presented at the 11th Biennial Meetings of the International Society for the Study of Behavioral Development, Minneapolis, MN.

Serpell, R., Baker, L., Sonnenschein, S., & Hill, S. (1993, June). *Contexts for the early appropriation of literacy: Caregiver meanings of recurrent activities.* Paper presented in the Symposium on Learning and Development in Cultural Context, at the Conference of the American Psychological Society, Chicago.

Serpell, R., & Deregowski, J. B. (1980). The skill of pictorial perception: An interpretation of the cross-cultural evidence. *International Journal of Psychology, 15,* 145–180.

Serpell, R., & Hatano, G. (1997). Education, literacy and schooling in cross-cultural perspective. In J. W. Berry, P. R. Dasen, & T. M. Saraswathi (Eds.), *Handbook of cross-cultural psychology* (2nd ed., Vol. 2, pp.+ 345–382). Boston, MA: Allyn & Bacon.

Serpell, R., Sonnenschein, S., Baker, L., Hill, S., Goddard-Truitt, V., & Danseco, E. (1997). *Parental ideas about development and socialization of children on the threshold of schooling (Reading Research Report No. 78).* Athens, GA: National Reading Research Center, Universities of Georgia and Maryland College Park.

Shockley, B. (1993). Extending the literate community: Reading and writing families. *New Advocate, 6,* 11–24.

Shweder, R. A., Jensen, L. A., & Goldstein, W. M. (1995). Who sleeps by whom revisited: a method for extracting the moral goods implicit in practice. *New Directions for Child Development, 67, Cultural Practices as Contexts for Development* (J. J. Goodnow, P. J. Miller, & F. Kessel, Eds.), pp. 21–39.

Sonnenschein, S., Baker, L., Serpell, R., Scher, D., Fernandez-Fein, S., & Munsterman, K. (1996). *Strands of emergent literacy and their antecedents in the home: Urban preschoolers' early literacy development* (Reading Research Rep. No. 48). Athens, GA: National Reading Research Center, Universities of Georgia and Maryland College Park.

Taylor, D., & Dorsey-Gaines, C. (1988). *Growing up literate: Learning from inner-city families.* Portsmouth, NH: Heinemann.

Teale, W. H., & Sulzby, E. (1987). Literacy acquisition in early childhood: The roles of access and mediation in storybook reading. In D. A. Wagner (Ed.), *The future of literacy in a changing world* (pp. 111–130). Oxford: Pergamon.

Tharp, R. G., & Gallimore, R. (1988). *Rousing minds to life: Teaching, learning, and schooling in social context.* Cambridge: Cambridge University Press.

Tharp, R. G., Jordan, C., Speidel, G. E., Av, K. H.-P., Klein, T. W., Calkins, R. P., Sloat, K. C. M., & Gallimore, R. (1984). In M. E. Lamb, A. L. Brown & B. Rogoff (Eds.), *Advances in developmental psychology* (pp. 9–141). Hillsdale, NJ: Lawrence Erlbaum Associates.

Thompson, R., Mixon, G., & Serpell, R. (1996). Engaging minority students in reading: Focus on the urban learner. In L. Baker, P. Afflerbach, & D. Reinking (Eds.), *Developing engaged readers in school and home communities* (pp. 43–64). Mahwah, NJ: Lawrence Erlbaum Associates.

Vygotsky, L. S. (1978). *Mind in Society: the development of higher psychological processes* (M. Cole, V. John-Steiner, S. Scribner, & E. Souberman, Eds.). Cambridge, MA: Harvard University Press.

Wells, G. (1986). *The meaning makers: Children learning language and using language to learn.* Portsmouth, NH: Heinemann.

Wells, G. (1990). Talk about text: Where literacy is learned and taught. *Curriculum Inquiry, 20*(4), 369–405.

Wertsch, J. V. (1991). *Voices of the mind.* Cambridge, MA: Harvard University Press.

Whittemore, R. D., & Beverly, E. (1989). Trust in the Mandinka way: The cultural context of sibling care. In P. Zukow (Ed.), *Sibling interaction across cultures: Theoretical and methodological issues* (pp. 26–53). New York: Springer.

Young, B., & Durston, S. (1987). *Primary health education.* Harlow, Essex, UK: Longman.

CHAPTER

13

Historical Perspectives on Promoting Reading: The Early Soviet Effort

Rose-Marie Weber
University at Albany, SUNY

In the 1920s the popular Soviet writer Mikhail Mikhaylovich Zoshchenko wrote a story called "The Woman Who Could Not Read." The woman was married to a Soviet official and, although both had come to the city from the country, he had educated himself whereas she remained illiterate. He urged her to learn to read and write and even brought her home a primer. But she protested that studying was for young children and she put the primer away. That was until she discovered a scented envelope in her husband's jacket, noticed the inordinate attention he was giving to his moustache, and contemplated returning to her peasant village. Ashamed to show the letter to anyone, she asked her husband to teach her to read. After months of studying syllables, words, and sentences, she was able to read the letter that was, as she had suspected, addressed to her husband by a woman. It said:

> I am sending you the primer I had promised to get for you. I think that your wife will be able to master the art of reading and writing in two or three months. Do promise, dear man, to make her do it. Talk to her, explain to her how disgraceful it is, in fact, to be an illiterate peasant woman. Just now, preparing for our anniversary, we are liquidating illiteracy over the whole of the Union by every means, and yet somehow we tend to forget our own families. Please promise me to carry this through.
> With Communist greetings. (p. 152)

Zoshchenko's narrator closed the story slyly: "This I call a surprising case of liquidation of illiteracy" (Zoshchenko, 1940/1973).

To liquidate illiteracy was the goal of a campaign to bring literacy to everyone between the ages of 8 and 50 years in what came to be the Soviet Union after the October Revolution of 1917. The campaign was successful in spreading literacy to millions who could neither read nor write, who had little use for literacy, and who had not defined a place for it in their lives. This was a truly extraordinary effort in the history of literacy, unparalleled in the ways that it was mobilized, sustained, and accomplished on such a vast scale. Although the circumstances of world economies, political ideology, and technology differ from our times, the condition of literacy is not unfamiliar (Elley, chap. 11, this volume). The Russian Empire was home to sophisticated writers and receptive readers, as well as the marginally literate and the entirely unlettered. Its peoples spoke myriad languages and lived out their days in varying cultures and levels of material wealth. The many facets of the Soviet literacy campaign and its outgrowth remind us of the complexity that any individual, agency, or state may face in promoting literacy as a practical, political, and humanistic endeavor.

My goal in these few pages is to describe the efforts that the early Soviet government made to further the revolution by bringing literacy to the entire population of the former Russian Empire and so raise it to the levels found in the prosperous industrialized West. Against the background of growing involvement by the West in schooling for literacy in the 19th century, I sketch the mobilization of the campaign as an aspect of the Soviet political agenda. I go on to present the practicalities that the new state faced in developing literacy across the diverse languages, with their various writing systems and written traditions, and to give examples of the instructional strategies and materials that were devised by sophisticated educators for the unlettered. Finally, I note the attention given the New Reader by the state and the well read, who were concerned about what newly literate readers with little education would like to read and should read. A notable figure in this regard was the writer Zoshchenko, whose stories had appeal for his literary colleagues as well as the new generations making literacy their own.

To take up these aspects of the literacy effort in the early years of the Soviet Union, I draw on the rich sources on Soviet history available in English and concentrate on the first 10 years or so after the October Revolution of 1917. This was a period of vitality and idealism in many quarters. Ideas from progressive education were influential; Vygotsky was coming into his own; the arts were caught up in modernism. But it was also a time of great turmoil. The initiatives to promote literacy were carried out against the tremendous dislocation caused by civil war, foreign intervention, widespread famine, and the economic chaos that led to the New Economic Policy of 1921–1927. Schools for children were in disarray as internal political struggles wore on. In the 1920s, nevertheless, the campaign for adults took shape. Not only did it introduce literacy to many people across the nation, but it put in place mechanisms for extending itself into the future. Its political and institutional force was so unrelenting that by the end of the 1930s it could be abandoned. Under Stalin, when massive brutality accompanied the collectivization of agriculture, unprecedented industrialization, and the centralization of Russian power, illiteracy was essentially liquidated in the Union of Soviet Socialist Republics (USSR) (Eklof, 1987; Kenez, 1982).

Historically, the nation-state appears as the primary agent for promoting widespread literacy, with its role culminating in campaigns such as the one initiated by the Soviets. The state's involvement, however, was an innovation of the last two centuries in the industrialized West. Before that, knowing how to read and write spread among those who found and created value in the written word: churchmen, nobility, professional classes, entrepreneurs, city folk. It came about largely by the creation, use, and availability of print to serve the interests of the respective groups; schooling was not necessarily the primary agency (Maynes, 1985; Venezky, 1991). "Then, beginning mostly in the 19th century, governments found it within their best interests to provide a basic education to all their citizens as a necessity for productive participation in civic, economic, and military affairs" (Venezky, 1991, p. 58).

As republican governments were consolidated in the 19th century, they took on the responsibility for basic education by building schools, with reading at the core of the curriculum. In the United States, for instance, families and communities came to depend on the publicly funded schools to teach literacy; the provision of schools and an ideology of literacy were fostered by growth in nation building, in economic development, and in population density (Kaestle, Damon-Moore, Stedman, & Trollinger, 1991). In France, the regional linguistic minorities sought French literacy in schools as their peasant ways were changing through emigration to the cities, easier transportation, military service, and their interest in popular literature that would bring greater cultural unity to the country (Weber, 1976). As schools became more widespread throughout the 19th century, control over them by the nation-state expanded. In many places the state came to define the literacy curriculum by preparing or authorizing instructional materials. Through public financing it set up ministries of public instruction to certify, prepare, and pay teachers, to construct buildings, and to set standards through examinations. At the same time, of course, schools were established and maintained by parallel agencies, especially religious groups, and many of these have challenged governments as the primary educator of the young (e.g., DelFattore, 1992). But it was the state that imposed compulsory schooling for all. By the turn of the 20th century, almost all children in the industrialized countries of the West attended at least primary school and learned to read and write well enough to expand their literate skills as they needed in their adult life. The state as the main agency for promoting literacy through schools has been the hallmark of literacy promotion in the 20th century all around the world.

What is notable, however, is that schools and ideas about their value were institutionalized for the young. As Graff (1998) said of the 19th century, schools became "a regular feature of the young's life course. Many . . . leaders and social reformers grasped the uses of schooling and the vehicle of literacy for promoting the values, attitudes, and habits deemed essential to order, integration, cohesion, and certain forms of progress" (p. 17). It was in the 20th century that concern rose sharply for adults who may have missed out on learning to read and write, whether they had attended school without success or never attended school at all. With some important exceptions, however, literacy instruction for adults has been marginal as compared to instruction for children, hardly receiving the dedication from the state in the way of materials, teachers, space, or long-term instructional time (Bhola, 1989; Lind & Johnston, 1994). Among the exceptions have been the campaigns that have engaged the illiterates of an entire nation in acquiring literacy, setting goals embedded in ideology for rapid social and political change, mobilizing resources and motivating learners, and setting the context for the give and take of teaching and learning to read and write (Arnove & Graff, 1987). And so we come to the case of the Soviet Union.

Literacy had begun to spread across the Russian Empire, especially after the freeing of the serfs in 1861. Even so, near the end of the 19th century, a third of the population of St. Petersburg was reported to be illiterate, compared to 4% of Paris, and nearly three-quarters in the Empire, compared to under 20% in France (Cipolla, 1969). When the Bolshevik revolutionaries took power, they were too impatient to wait another generation for literacy to reach the workers and peasants in whose name they had taken power. They wanted to overcome the backwardness of the country and the disgrace of illiteracy, as they saw it, and to prepare the masses of the population for a future free of domination. At the same time, they needed to consolidate their control over a vast expanse of territory and diversity of peoples if they were to realize their political ambitions. They decided to invest unparalleled energies and resources in a massive campaign to bring literacy to adults in all reaches of what was soon to become the USSR.

THE CAMPAIGN

Lenin himself appears to have taken the importance of reading and writing seriously when the Bolsheviks came to power. Twenty years earlier, he had expressed disdain for the earnest efforts by private organizations to bring literacy and culture to the peasants. It was when the revolutionary government needed the support of the peasantry to remain in power that he saw basic literacy as a foundation for educating the people to the revolution. He remarked on one occasion, "As long as there is a such a thing in the country as illiteracy, it is rather hard to talk about political education. [To overcome illiteracy] is not a political task, it is a condition without which one cannot even talk about politics." On another occasion, he said, "The illiterate person stands outside of politics. First it is necessary to teach him the alphabet. Without it there are only rumors, fairy tales, prejudices, but not politics" (Kenez, 1982, p. 175).

The Bolsheviks' ideas for eliminating illiteracy among the unschooled were brought together in the Decree on Illiteracy of December 26, 1919, a date that in subsequent years was marked as a national anniversary. The decree was drawn up in the Commissariat of the Enlightenment (Narkompros), issued by the Council of People's Commissars (Sovnarkom), and signed by Lenin. Literacy was to be sought, in the words of the decree, "for the purpose of allowing the entire population of the Republic to participate consciously in the political life of the country" (Kenez, 1982, p. 180). The intent, in other words, was to create a world of readers engaged as citizens of the revolutionary state.

The decree was framed in such comprehensive terms that it served as a viable blueprint for carrying out the literacy campaign through its existence. Narkompros was to coordinate the overall effort, whereas the Red Army was to advance literacy within its own structure. Mass organizations such as trade unions and Komsomol (Youth Communist League) were directed to participate. Illiterates between 8 and 50 years of age were obliged to study and to be released from work for as much as 2 hours a day without loss of pay in order to do so. Local literacy centers, what came to be called *likpunkty*, were to be set up and states were to provide necessary teaching materials. Teachers were to be paid at the same level as schoolteachers. The decree made it a criminal offense to refuse to teach or study, although no citizen was ever prosecuted for not complying (Eklof, 1987; Kenez, 1982).

Later Soviet educators described the range of actions that the various agencies took to implement the law. The special unit responsible for the literacy campaign in Narkompros trained teachers, set up the literacy centers, carried out publicity work, registered low-literate students, and drafted textbooks and teaching methods, coordinating the activities of comparable units at regional and local levels across the union. Trade unions registered students and, especially in outlying regions, provided premises for the literacy centers, keeping them heated and lit. Komsomol played an enormous role in adult literacy, often in connection with other political action. Groups of 5 to 30 persons were organized into "shock brigades" to keep track of attendance, recruit students, collect contributions, and, among other activities, set up play centers for mothers attending the literacy centers. The Down with Illiteracy Society, founded to promote the government's program, organized volunteer teachers and published single issues of newspapers by the thousands for distribution to literacy centers (Ivanova & Voskresenky, 1959; Koutaisoff, 1952; Nar, 1957). The difficulties in carrying out these activities down to the local level can be imagined. The committee of a local literacy center reported, "The main reasons for delaying the liquidation of illiteracy are the typhus epidemic, the road corvée, and the dire shortages of readers and paper" (Eklof, 1987, p. 133).

The campaign had its ups and downs through the years. At times, interest waned within the agencies. Tensions often arose over conflicting or overlapping jurisdiction. And potential learners resisted, especially in the 1920s, personally and politically. Like the woman in Zoshchenko's story who at first saw no use for literacy in her life, many avoided learning to read or just put their primers away in a drawer. At literacy centers in the countryside, people came to spend time but did not necessarily pay attention to instruction. A teacher reflecting on her experiences in Ukraine described how peasants and workers at a sugar-beet refinery were generally aimless in their studies. Furthermore, they objected to the content of what they were given to read as being absurd ("Our Hut") or childish ("Grandfather, please make me a whistle") or too weighted down with political messages ("Workers of the world, unite!"). But among her better students were wives of ambitious party members concerned that their husbands might leave them for more educated women (Nar, 1957), once again reminding us of Zoshchenko. The government had defined the social and political significance of reading on its terms, but not everyone listened nor was everyone interested. Although there was always an undercurrent of coercion, even in the early years of the literacy campaign, it most probably surfaced in connection with other violations of individuals' dignity.

MINORITY LANGUAGES AND ALPHABETS

Promoting literacy in the early Soviet years required giving attention to a diversity of languages and their writing systems. The Bolsheviks had taken control of an empire that included not only speakers of Russian and closely related Slavic languages, but speakers of many other languages as well. From the beginning, the regime adopted a pluralistic policy, proclaiming the rights of nationalities to flourish and continue in their languages and life ways, while it took measures to consolidate its power through members of the local populations. The literacy decree in fact called for illiterates to learn to read and write in their native language or in Russian, as they preferred, breaking with the Tsarist imposition of Russian in the preceding years (Isayev, 1977). Accordingly, when Narkompros distributed books for the literacy campaign, about a third of the more than 6 million produced by 1920 were printed in languages other than Russian (Kenez, 1982).

Some of these languages, such as Ukrainian, were written in the Cyrillic script, like Russian; other languages, such as Armenian, were written in their own traditional script; and other languages, especially those of the Turkic language family such as Uzbek, were written in Arabic script; still other languages, such as Chukchee, had no traditional written form. Many of the languages had literary varieties that flourished; others were made up of diverse dialects that awaited a unifying written variety. Given its twin commitment to recognize this diversity and to abolish illiteracy, the early government embarked on an immense language planning effort. Committees of scholars with linguistic expertise were formed to work on revising and creating alphabets. On the surface, the practical issue was central: how to provide new literates with a script that fit their spoken language reasonably well, that was relatively easy to learn, and that was convenient to use and reproduce in printed materials. For many cases, resolving the issue required linguistic research on phonology, morphology, and dialect variation; in fact, a good deal was initiated by scholars at the time. But details about writing systems were not only technical matters. Like the promotion of literacy itself, they were embedded in the ideological complexities of the times, not to mention the realities of sustaining the revolution. At the same time that the regime proclaimed the rights of minority peoples within the new socialist order, it needed to prevent them from breaking away in the face of economic and social instability (Weinreich, 1953).

It is striking that the Soviets chose the Roman alphabet to create new writing systems for the minority languages in the early years of the literacy campaign. At the very beginning of the revolution, the regime initiated several small reforms to existing scripts. The Cyrillic system was slightly changed for Russian itself, when several characters were dropped and the spellings of some words were simplified. In the minority regions, the Arabic script was revised for the Turkic languages of Central Asia. These changes were implemented quickly, because the regime had control over the press and publishing. It was not long, however, before the committees turned to the Roman alphabet to replace the Arabic script and to create writing systems for the languages without literate traditions.

The choice of the Roman alphabet was in line with Bolshevik hopes that the revolution would spread to Europe. It had the potential to unite the many languages of the union with the West symbolically, foreshadowing a more advanced culture founded on science. At the same time, it had the potential to break down cultural and religious ties among those using the Arabic script. The work propelled by this ideology was no small effort. During the 1920s about 40 languages were set to the Roman alphabet, some formerly written, mainly in Arabic script, some written for the first time. There were even proposals to cast Russian into the Roman alphabet (Comrie, 1996; Weinreich, 1953).

Through these changes in writing systems, many people learned to read, and others extended their literate abilities as opportunities arose. In the literacy centers of Uzbekistan, for instance, successive generations of learners first saw the Uzbek language in varieties of Arabic script, then in Roman script that incorporated the rural dialect feature of vowel harmony, then in Roman script corresponding to the urban Uzbek without vowel harmony that came to be favored by the speakers of the region. Even though the adoption of the Roman scripts in schools, the press, and other materials was in a sense required by the government, it was often slow to come for Uzbek. For one thing, there was lack of type and scarcity of qualified typesetters. Further, there was reluctance to give up the Arabic script, as shown by the periodicals that appeared over several years in a mix of Roman and Arabic (Fierman, 1991).

It was not long, however, before all of the newly devised Roman scripts for the various languages were dropped and replaced with the Cyrillic script of Russian. With the consolidation of Russian hegemony over the Soviet Union in Stalin's time, the Russian language was spreading with tremendous authority throughout the union. The Cyrillic script reflected the centralization of power and the disintegration of regard for the national minorities through the 1930s. Although the minority languages held their own as mother tongues and as languages of instruction, periodicals, and books, Russian became a required school subject in 1938. In the case of the Uzbek language, the Cyrillic script was adopted in 1940, requiring readers and writers, by now a majority in the republic, to adjust once more to a new writing system. Along with the script came the requirement that the many words from Russian borrowed into Uzbek had to be spelled as in Russian, no matter the pronunciation in Uzbek, a policy imposed for the minority languages in general. Adoption of the Cyrillic script across the Soviet Union allowed for easy transfer of literate skills to Russian as a second language and symbolically united the republics as a distinctive world force (Comrie, 1996; Fierman, 1991; Isayev, 1977; Weinreich, 1953). (Now that the republics went their separate ways in the 1990s, issues about writing systems have arisen again, with the Turkic languages like Uzbek looking to an all-Turkic alphabet using Roman letters [Comrie, 1996].)

MATERIALS AND METHODS

From the outset of the literacy campaign, the government made plans to train and remunerate teachers, prepare materials, and validate methods of instruction that would be consistent with its reasons for bringing literacy to all citizens. This was so expensive, given the economic and social turmoil of the times, that the record of various activities, such as it is, testifies to the seriousness of the commitment. Many teachers received special training, but volunteers using their own experience often did the teaching. Materials were developed and paper bought, but there were constant shortages. Methods were articulated, but how widely they were applied, at far distances from the source of the ideas, across language and cultural boundaries, is in question.

Two instructional facets of the campaign are worth noting, namely, the nature of the materials and the approach to instruction. The teaching materials for beginners were mainly primers and, especially when these were unavailable, placards and posters. The primers were designed to be educationally sound, that is, to introduce letters gradually and limit the length of sentences and texts. At the same time, the primers were designed to express direct political messages. The educator Dora El'kina described her experience of discovering the value of materials that would have political force. As a teacher in the Red Army, she made the students snicker with the sentence "Masha ate the kasha," but she made them sit up when she decided to ask why kasha was so scarce and their Mashas so distant. Then she wrote the sentence for them that later appeared in millions of primers and became emblematic of the Soviet literacy effort, "My ne raby, ne raby my" ["We are not slaves, slaves we are not"] (Kenez, 1982). But of course the ideas that may be stirring in some settings can be estranging in others. The teacher Nina Nar recalled that in the Ukraine of the early 1920s the slogans to be read from placards, such as "We are poor because we are ignorant," held little interest for the learners and turned them away (Nar, 1957). Yet in spite of the content of the primers and placards, there is nothing in the record to suggest that the teachers, formally educated or not, were responsible for political agitation rather than for the specifics of reading and writing instruction.

Various approaches were taken to introduce the basics of reading. These included, at one extreme, the ancient alphabetic approach, requiring the learner to name off the letters of each word before pronouncing it. At the other extreme was the whole word approach, a facet of the progressive curriculum that for a while was adopted in Russian schools (Eklof, 1987). The favored one was the analytic–synthetic approach that alternated between speech and print, reading and writing. To begin, a text was to be broken up into sentences, sentences into spoken words, and words into syllables—the basic working unit in Russian—and so into constituent sounds. Then the direction was to be reversed. Syllables and words were to be built with cardboard letters representing the sounds. Words were to be read, then written. Then came further reading with repetitions of the sentence and text. After the gradual introduction of all the letters of the alphabet, more effort was placed on word building, reading of the primer, and writing. Novice readers were guided through three stages of fluency. In the primer, they were to read the first half or so syllable by syllable, then the second half with attention to fluent delivery. Further on, they were to read silently for comprehension as evaluated through questions, and also to recapitulate what they had read (Ivanova & Voskresensky, 1959; Koutaisoff, 1952; Nar, 1957).

In a detailed overview of approaches taken to teach reading in the literacy effort, the Soviet educators Ivanova and Voskresensky (1959) underlined how the analytic–synthetic approach called on both learners and teachers to apply themselves thoughtfully. For learners, a skill like word building from cardboard letters was important in that it gave them the opportunity to link speech to print "consciously, with understanding" (p. 167). For teachers to be effective, they had to give explanations, carefully track and guide learners' responses, and read aloud to stimulate learners' interest. It is no wonder, then, that Ivanova and Voskresensky attributed some of the failure in the literacy campaign to poor teaching by other methods, especially by volunteer teachers.

Low literates were identified for instruction through a canvas carried out by the trade unions, the government teachers, and members of other agencies. They came to be divided into the illiterates, those who could not read or write, and the semiliterates, those who could read and write either Russian or their native language fairly well, possibly as a result of the literacy program. In the earliest years, instruction in basic reading and writing was intended to last 3 months, but was extended to 6 or 10 months. The goal became to cover the equivalent of the first two grades of elementary school; for semiliterates, it was the fourth-grade equivalent and included arithmetic. In spite of the political rationale underlying the promotion of literacy and the explicit content of much of the material, the instruction itself appears to have focused on breaking into the writing system and developing a modicum of fluency with basic comprehension.

THE NEW READER

The achievement of the revolutionary government in bringing literacy to peasants and workers was remarkable for its speed and comprehensiveness. But it rested to no small degree on the advance of literacy under the Tsars after the liberation of the serfs in 1861. Jeffrey Brooks's (1985) book titled *When Russia Learned to Read* refers not to the 50 years after the revolution, but to the 50 years before it. Local governments and the church had built and supported schools for children. Peasants had created informal village schools for the unschooled among them. With increasing concern for the backwardness of Russia as the 19th century ended, the central government had expanded its commitments to education, and private elite organizations had invested themselves in numberless activities to enlarge the significance of the printed word for new literates.

By the time of the revolution about a third of the people were literate. Among them were not only the highly educated, but also the many with little or no schooling who had just recently come into literacy, being only the first or second generation with the opportunity to read. These new readers, as they have been called, were avid consumers of printed material in their search for entertainment and knowledge (Brooks, 1982; Eklof, 1987; Scatton, 1996).

Under the Tsars, commercial publishers, the church and the state had provided a vast array of print for the growing numbers of new readers from among peasants and recent peasants. Cheap materials such as tales in booklet form, novels serialized in newspapers, and adventure novels sold in installments were available through peddlers and small shops. Materials for self-improvement, for practical matters, and for enrichment were promoted through libraries and public readings by private organizations such as local committees of enlightenment—the literacy volunteers of the period. Notably, detailed surveys of readers' interests were taken to support these efforts (Brooks, 1982).

When the Bolsheviks embarked on their literacy campaign, they recognized the importance of having materials to read that would engage the newly literate and yet serve revolutionary thinking. They interrupted the established production and distribution of materials for new readers when, shortly after the October Revolution, they took over control of the press and publishing, even destroying the existing copies of popular literature. They embarked on ambitious publishing schemes, but soon found it difficult to produce material that they had envisioned. When they adopted the New Economic Policy (NEP) in 1921 in order to selvage an economy sinking from years of war and famine, publishing was an industry that was allowed to participate in the market in a limited way (Brooks, 1982; Robin, 1991).

Believing in the potential of print to create new socialist citizens, the Soviets persisted in their efforts to control the content and distribution of materials, especially to the newly literate. Like their predecessors promoting literacy under the Tsars, they initiated studies of reader preferences, at first through questionnaires to soldiers, workers, and peasants. They collected such information so as to narrow the gap between what was to be published and what readers could and would read, now that the market forces of Tsarist times were no longer in play. One enormous study surveyed nearly 12,000 members of the Red Army. The soldiers were asked about their favorite materials, their favorite authors, whether they preferred to listen to others read or read themselves, and whether they preferred the truth (*pravda*) or tales (*skazky*). And, in a test of a favorite idea, they were explicitly asked whether their political views changed as a result of reading. (Most preferred truth, and many skipped the political questions or gave hostile responses.) Other sources of information were comment sheets that readers of a book could send to the publisher and trial oral readings in worker and peasant halls (Brooks, 1982; Scatton, 1996).

Another ambitious study was concerned to explain why newspapers did not attract subscribers or readers in the provinces, though many people there could read at a basic level. It became clear that new readers could not understand terms like *USSR, ultimatum, class enemy*, or the written syntax of the urban intellectuals. They had not internalized the requisite knowledge or discourse that would allow them to be wholly engaged readers, never mind the interest. This sort of difficulty touched off discussions among writers, some maintaining that the language of the press should be made more comprehensible to workers and peasants by keeping the language close to everyday speech, and others maintaining that the masses of new readers needed to be further educated in language and culture so as to be able to comprehend (Robin, 1991; Scatton, 1996).

It was in this period, still the 1920s, that Mikhail Zoshchenko, the author of "The Woman Who Couldn't Read," began his career as a writer. He was a member of a sophisticated writer's group and wrote stories that appealed to their sensibilities. At the same time, his stories engaged the interests of the less schooled readers struggling with the place of literacy in their lives, recent products of the literacy campaign among them. He chose themes of getting along in the everyday of the new society, created vivid characters with recognizable emotions, and offered transparent turns of events with sly satire, all the while using direct vocabulary and straightforward sentence structure. He maintained that he wrote in the language of the street to fill the gap, at least temporarily, between literature and the street. He had his stories published in formats that made them cheap and accessible, choosing paperback anthologies, humor magazines, and pocket editions to be sold at railway stations (Scatton, 1993).

Zoshchenko's immense popularity and connectedness with new readers were such that they wrote to him about his stories. He received thousands of letters, some readers requesting copies of his books, some expressing an ambition to be a writer, some wanting him to write a story just for them. Many showed their naiveté as readers in equating him with the narrator of his stories, even asking for the money his narrator offers if they don't like his stories. But most of the time they expressed why they liked him: He was simple to read and understand, but he was sensitive to the complexity of human souls and to the cares of everyday life. He published these as *Letters to a Writer* in 1929, turning his readers into writers to the world (Scatton, 1996). The publication of the letters to Zoshchenko accorded with other practices that engaged new readers in many regions as the literacy campaign spread. Newspapers solicited contributions from writers in local communities, encouraging nonprofessionals to write—and their friends and families to read. Furthermore, in remote regions with essentially no written traditions, folklore was collected and edited so as to provide materials that would engage people in the stories of their heritage through print (Ivanova & Voskresensky, 1959; Koutaissoff, 1952).

CONCLUSIONS AND DISCUSSION

The Soviet literacy campaign was embedded in the creation of a new political order, but one that ironically came to impose greater and greater controls on what could be read and written. In the barbarity of the Stalinist regime from the 1930s onward, it is true that many millions were taught to read and write, technically speaking. Cultural leaders who had contributed to the early literacy efforts for adults were among those who suffered in the purges. Zoshchenko himself was denounced as anti-Soviet and expelled from the Writers' Union in 1946, to be reinstated only after Stalin's death (Scatton, 1993).

The Soviet campaign to bring literacy to all citizens 80 years ago nevertheless has relevance for the promotion and significance of reading in our times, especially with respect to its complexity and its comprehensiveness. In its complexity, the Soviet campaign reminds us that any effort to promote literate skills and ideas about their value requires grappling with a range of problems, both large and small. In this case, the effort was propelled by an explicit ideology, planned by sophisticated educators, and implemented by agencies within and entwined with the government. It addressed the everyday details that preoccupy literacy educators—the immediate objectives, the materials and instructional practice, the progress and recalcitrance of learners. It recognized the diversity of languages and cultures, the various writing systems and literary languages, and the perspectives on literacy to be found throughout the territory. At the same time, the climate for literacy in those early years of the Soviet Union fostered a cultural ideal of readers engaging with print for a range of purposes, encouraged publishing for new readers, and supported writers who, as in the Russian literary tradition, were set on creating a literature that addressed our most serious human struggles. The particular complexities of the times and situation are of course unique, but the issues that arose are comparable to many that we face today, in spite of our experience, our research, and our resources.

With respect to its comprehensiveness, the Soviet effort can hardly be matched. In only the first decade following the revolution, the Soviets estimated that 10 million people of the population of about 170 million received

instruction, a little more than half of these in the Russian Republic. This is a
disputed figure on many counts, and its significance darkens in the face of
the decline of school enrollments by children in those difficult times (Eklof,
1987; Kenez, 1982). Nevertheless, it gives an idea of the breadth of the un-
dertaking to organize the literacy centers and provide instruction in a technologically simpler era.

The campaign mobilized the population on a massive scale in a brief period of time, propelled by enormous political will. In the light of its apparent
success, it served as a model for political movements later in the 20th century eager to promote literacy for all citizens as part of a national agenda, in
particular, in Cuba and Nicaragua. The Soviet campaign engaged urban and
rural populations. It cut across European and Asian life ways, languages,
and traditions of literacy. The commitment expressed in the Decree on Illiteracy was not an empty one. Rather, enormous resources were brought to
plan and carry it out on the day to day. Its comprehensiveness contrasts
with the selective small-scale efforts that have been initiated in many areas
of the world since the World War II, even as world populations have increased. It reminds us that our desire for comprehensive, universal literacy, however defined and intended, remains with us as a myriad of agencies have engaged in literacy projects, the nation-states have continued
their efforts in basic education, and wealthy nations have taken stock of the
failure of their educational programs to reach all citizens. Further, as we
recognize education as a human right for all in these times (Haggis, 1992), it
reminds us that we must take into account what the woman in Zoshchenko's
story showed, that one defines the uses and significance of literacy for oneself.

REFERENCES

Arnove, R. F., & Graff, H. J. (1987). *National literacy campaigns: Historical and comparative perspec-
tives.* New York: Plenum.
Bhola, H. S. (1989). *World trends and issues in adult education.* London: Jessica Kingsley/UNESCO.
Brooks, J. (1982). Studies of the reader in the 1920s. *Russian History, 9*(Pts. 2–3), 187–202.
Brooks, J. (1985). *When Russia learned to read: Literacy and popular literature, 1861–1917.* Prince-
ton, NJ: Princeton University Press.
Cipolla, C. M. (1969). *Literacy and development in the West.* London: Penguin.
Comrie, B. (1996). Script reform in and after the Soviet Union. In P. T. Daniels & W. Bright (Eds.),
The world's writing systems (pp. 781–784). New York: Oxford University Press.
DelFattore, J. (1992). *What Johnny shouldn't read: Textbook censorship in America.* New Haven, CT:
Yale University Press.
Eklof, B. (1987). Russian literacy campaigns, 1861–1939. In R. F. Arnove & H. J. Graff (Eds.),
National literacy campaigns: Historical and comparative perspectives (pp. 123–145). New
York: Plenum.
Fierman, W. (1991). *Language planning and national development: The Uzbek experience.* Berlin:
Mouton de Gruyter.

Graff, H. J. (1988). Whither the history of literacy? The future of the past. *Communication, 11,* 5–22.

Haggis, S. (1992). *Education for All: Purpose and context* (World Education for All Monograph I). Paris: UNESCO.

Isayev, M. I. (1977). *National languages in the USSR: Problems and solutions.* Moscow: Progress Press.

Ivanova, A. M., & Voskresensky, V. D. (1959). Abolition of adult illiteracy in the USSR (1917–1940). *Fundamental and Adult Education, 11,* 131–192.

Kaestle, C. F., Damon-Moore, H., Stedman, L., & Trollinger, W. V., Jr. (1991). *Literacy in the United States: Readers and reading since 1880.* New Haven, CT: Yale University Press.

Kenez, P. (1982). Liquidating illiteracy in revolutionary Russia. *Russian History, 9*(Pts. 2–3), 173–186.

Koutaisoff, E. (1952). Literacy campaigns in the USSR. *Fundamental and Adult Education, 4*(4), 11–16.

Lind, A., & Johnston, A. (1994). Adult literacy programs in developing nations. In T. Husén & T. N. Postlethwaite (Eds.), *International encyclopedia of education* (2nd ed., pp. 169–176). Tarrytown, NY: Pergamon/Elsevier.

Maynes, M. J. (1985). *Schooling in western Europe: A social history.* Albany, NY: SUNY Press.

Nar, N. (1957). The campaign against illiteracy and semiliteracy in the Ukraine, Transcaucasus, and Northern Caucasus, 1922–1941. In G. L. Kline (Ed.), *Soviet education* (pp. 139–159). New York: Columbia University Press.

Robin, R. (1991). Popular literature of the 1920s: Russian peasants as readers. In S. Fitzgerald, A. Rabinowitch, & R. Stites (Eds.), *Russia in the era of NEP: Explorations in Soviet society and culture* (pp. 253–267). Bloomington: Indiana University Press.

Scatton, L. H. (1993). *Mikhail Zoshchenko: Evolution of a writer.* Cambridge: Cambridge University Press.

Scatton, L. H. (1996). Writing for the new reader: Mikhail Zoshchenko in the 1920s. In N. Lukar (Ed.), *After the watershed: Russian prose 1917–1927* (pp. 93–106). Nottingham: Astra Press.

Venezky, R. L. (1991). The development of literacy in the industrialized nations of the West. In R. Barr, M. L. Kamil, P. B. Mosenthal, & P. D. Pearson (Eds.), *Handbook of reading research* (Vol. II, pp. 46–67). New York: Longman.

Weber, E. (1976). *Peasants into Frenchmen: The modernization of rural France, 1870–1914.* Stanford, CA: Stanford University Press.

Weinreich, U. (1953). The Russification of the Soviet minority languages. *Problems of Communism, 2*(6), 47–57.

Zoshchenko, M. (1973). *The woman who could not read and other tales* (E. Fen, Trans.) Westport, CT: Hyperion Press. (Original translation published 1940)

14

Literacy Empowerment in Developing Societies

Brian V. Street
Kings College, London

Contemporary literacy programs make frequent claims to be "empowering" their subjects. Women in particular, but also other groups perceived by national and international agencies to be oppressed and disempowered, are encouraged to attend literacy classes and projects on the promise of "empowerment." Frequently, however, very little really changes, and although the learners may (sometimes) emerge from the program with increased literacy skills, this does not necessarily lead to increased social or material power. What precisely we mean by *power* in such contexts is, of course, problematic. The aim of this chapter is to make explicit some of the assumptions about power and literacy that prevail in the world of agencies concerned with programs and also perhaps among practitioners and researchers. This requires a brief statement of the current state of awareness regarding major debates around power and around literacy: I indicate some of the key concepts in both fields, with particular reference to their application to development literacy programs and projects. My aim is to help myself and I hope others to recognize the meanings implicit in our own usages so that we will be in a position to question and challenge them when we see them in practice and/or operationalize them ourselves.

Although this chapter mainly refers to Third World so-called "development" programs and the debates around them, I argue that similar issues of power, and ambiguities in the meaning of *empowerment*, apply also to debates about literacy and reading in "developed" societies. There is, however, one significant difference between the two contexts that I think points up just what is taken for granted in the latter. The development debate tends to be about "literacy" in general rather than reading in particular, although in practice the focus is usually on reading rather than writing. However, in this context "reading" is seen as "functional" (see Verhoeven, 1994, for the multiple meanings of this term), often in the sense of everyday decoding of messages, whether in development agency literature on health, agriculture, financial management, and so on, with reference to commercial products, or for travel and movement and the "reading" of signs (Wagner, Venezky, & Street, 1999). In developed countries, I would suggest, the term *reading*, as it is used by agencies interested in promoting reading, frequently refers to reading of books—and these in turn are often taken to be "literature," frequently in the high sense of culturally valued fiction (cf. Hirsch on cultural literacy, 1987). Stierer and Bloome (1994) refer to the "bookworm" model of teaching reading in English schools, which suggests the cultural idea of inculcating in young pupils the pleasure and desire to curl up with a book (cf. National Literacy Trust, 1997). The notion of silent, sole reading also underpins some of the psychological research on reading (cf. Oakhill, Beard, & Vincent, 1995). The "empowerment" envisaged in this model of literacy is different in many ways than that of development agency projects, indexing in developed societies class differences and levels of reading rather than the "functional" skills indicated in the developing world. There is no space here to pursue further these interesting differences, but their existence reinforces my main point: that what is meant by literacy varies with cultural context; that literacy is often taken to mean "reading," whether functional or literary; and that in both cases there is an assumed link between literacy/reading and empowerment. It is this latter link on which I wish to focus here, attempting to spell out the different models of power on which it is based and raising questions regarding literacy empowerment in developing societies that, I believe, have profound implications for the promotion of reading in developed societies.

MODELING POWER DIMENSIONS OF LITERACY

There are, of course, many different meanings associated with the concept of power, but I suggest two major and conflicting models of power, to characterize some of their features and to suggest how these operate within literacy fields.

A Quantitative Model of Power

Many accounts of the power dimension of literacy (and other development) work suggest that power may be seen as a quantity, a property to be possessed, an object: If someone has a quantity of power, then others need to "take it away from them" in order to become "empowered" themselves. If men have all the power, then empowerment of women needs men to give up some power; men will then finish up with a lesser quantity. This is a theory of power that lies beneath many debates on empowerment and is probably the dominant "commonsense" view.

However, once we think about it more closely, check it against experience, and consider what some of the major theorists of power have had to say, then the "quantity" theory of power begins to look less useful as a starting point. This is particularly the case when we are considering power in relation to literacy. The quantity theory of power, for instance, is often thought of in terms of technical control, competence, skill: If someone achieves a particular competence, say in literacy (it could be in health, agriculture, or any field), then, so the theory goes, they increase their power in the world—they become empowered. However, with regard to literacy we already know that literacy is more than just a skill: The last decade of research and practice in literacy has made it apparent that literacy is a social practice that varies from one context to another and is part of cultural knowledge and behavior, not simply a technical competence to be added on to people as though they were machines being upgraded (cf. Barton, 1994; Street, 1993a, 1993b, 1995). Similarly, the old idea of illiteracy as a kind of disease, to be cured by injections of literacy teaching in programs designed like health campaigns or agriculture programs (with their military metaphors), has proved too simplistic (Verhoeven, 1994). Literacy practices are now seen as social and cultural practices, related to people's cultural identity, their sense of self, their knowledge and world view, their epistemology. These aspects of literacy lie much deeper in people's minds and cultures than just technical skills, so that learning a particular literacy involves a much larger commitment and very often significant shifts in self-concept and ideas. One explanation for the failure of many literacy campaigns in the past was that they failed to realize this cultural and conceptual nature of literacy and so may have alienated many prospective learners, or simply failed to convince them of its value for them. Treating literacy as a technical skill, then, as a quantity of competence to be instilled in people, was never likely to give them much "power": the claims to empowerment of technicist literacy programs have turned out to be ill-founded.

Freirean theories of literacy suggested a fuller and richer view, focusing on self-development and -realization, on "conscientization" and on real shifts in political power in society (Freire, 1972, 1985; Freire & Macedo, 1987; Mclaren & Lankshear, 1994; Mclaren, 1993). Here too, though, expectations were raised that probably could not be met: that literacy alone would bring enlightenment (as though people without literacy were not already intelligent, critical, and thoughtful!). Where the Freirean theory of literacy is associated with the quantity theory of power, it comes up against the same problems as the narrower "functional" theory it is attempting to replace. Again the question is raised of which literacy is being taught, with what cultural associations and meanings. Many literacy practices can be used for control and to deny empowerment, so just increasing the literacy statistics is not on its own going to lead to empowerment. Making "more literacy" available does not necessarily mean that there is "more power" available to the newly literate. Even if their new literacy means some self-development, at a personal level, it does not necessarily relate to any shifts of power at a larger level. Within the literacy program itself, Freirean approaches have also proved problematic.

> One of the greatest weaknesses of the Freirean approach in practice has been the immense difficulty faced by literacy facilitators seeking to generate "dialogue." Time and again, when it comes to the classroom situation, facilitators side-step dialogue (or any effective discussion) and fall back on what they see as the "meat" of teaching literacy. The cases where this is not true tend to be those highly politicised literacy programmes where there is more of a tendency to impose a new consciousness on learners than to generate a truly critical consciousness. (Archer, 1994, p. 11)

The idea of literacy as a technical skill or as political consciousness-raising has given way recently to literacy as personal self-development. This depends on a model of power as entrepreneurial, as enhanced individual agency within existing institutions rather than as an attempt to change those institutions. Conservative governments of the 1980s have sought to define power as an individual matter, related to choice and to personal effort: Each individual, in this view, has the potential to "get to the top," and if they don't, then it is their own fault, through lack of effort or skill. Thus those who lack literacy skills will also lack power, and those who acquire literacy can expect to gain power—in this sense of the term. I would also suggest that in the context of promotional campaigns for reading in the developed world, it is power as personal self-development that is the focus. In this case, the emphasis may be on acquiring the skills necessary for the new work order (cf. Gee, Hull, & Lankshear, 1996), or it may be reading as literary and cultural knowledge (cf. Hirsch, 1987; National Literacy Trust, 1997). In both cases, power is seen as a quantity, although its content may be different.

These views of power as a quantity, then, have been linked with views on literacy: Literacy has been seen as a technical skill, as political consciousness, and as self-development and individual achievement. The more you have of one, the more you can expect to have of the other. Literacy programs and international and national agency funding in the past decade have been based on these theories. What I wish to raise is whether this is an adequate view of the issue—or are these theories themselves responsible for the vast failures in both literacy programs and in "empowerment" that have disillusioned so many activists in this field? I suggest alternative theories of literacy and of power that might both explain the past and, more importantly, provide a sounder basis for future action.

A Process Model of Power

The process model considers power as always contested and in dialogue; it is also always being changed and transformed. This model is therefore less static than the quantity model. It assumes that power varies between sites and contexts rather than remaining the same "thing." Power in this sense is thought of as being exercised in a number of different ways. For instance, it may be thought of as exercised through force—the use of military power or individual strength—or through discourse—the use of language, social institutions, or words to control others. According to this model, such exercise of power is often treated as though it were natural, rather than being always socially and culturally created in different contexts. For instance, those exercising power may claim that what they are doing—through bureaucratic institutions, aid agencies, education, and so on—is simply technical, neutral, and "functional." A closer analysis, however, would inicate how they have created and are maintaining their power over others through those practices. With respect to educational practice, the process view of power forces us to analyze not only the powerful institutions that education and literacy programs are trying to give people access to (military, economic, state institutions) but also the processes of education itself; the very situation of learning, in classes between facilitators and student learners, within schools, programs, projects, are imbued with power relations about which the participants are often unaware (Rogers, 1992). Power, then, is not simply something to be acquired out there, as an outcome of literacy learning, but is already involved in the process of learning itself (for an attempt to take account of this in the area of literacy assessment, see Holland & Street, 1994). One aim of this chapter is to help clarify and make explicit these hidden power relations in our own pedagogy.

Many who adopt the power as process model argue for the revolutionary transformation of subjects and of institutions. Michel Foucault, for instance, one of the major contemporary thinkers about power in society, describes power in terms of "disciplinary" procedures, or "regimes of truth" (Foucault, 1979). Within institutions, such as those of the academic world, disciplines operate, through their language, social authority and institutional force to establish what kind of person we can be and what truths we should adhere to; in social domains, institutions, such as asylums, police the distinction between the sane and the insane by restricting the latter to buildings where they are under continual close surveillance. One of

Foucault's most devastating critiques of modern society has been to argue hat the buildings and disciplines of the educational world are in fact very similar to the buildings and disciplines of the mental asylum—both involve close and powerful surveillance over dominant truths and over people who may disagree with them (Foucault, 1984). Foucault also argued that all forms of discipline are also associated with resistance: "Power is employed and exercised through a netlike organization . . . individuals circulate between its threads; they are always in a position of simultaneously undergoing and exercising power. They are not only its inert or consenting targets: they are always also elements of its articulation" (in Gordon, 1980, p. 98). Activists, creative thinkers, academics, and revolutionaries work to oppose dominant disciplines and the ideas that legitimate them (although they are often treated as "mad" themselves, rather than praised as innovators; Freire can be seen as a classic example of the latter, a "resistant" thinker and activist in the field of literacy whose counterideas have been taken seriously and have become powerful themselves).

The problem with Foucault's model of power is that it appears mainly negative, as though power was always a bad thing, a coercive force exercised by some human beings on others who then struggle to resist it. Pierre Bourdieu, one of the other leading theorists about power in Western critical research, also tended to see power as mainly negative and oppressive, although he linked it more to the nature of the dominant modern economic system, capitalism. Just as there is economic capital, which its holders can use to acquire material resources and political power for themselves, so there is cultural capital, said Bourdieu; forms of language, dress, social manners, institutions such as museums and schools, and so on provide some members of society with capital of this kind that others lack access to (Bourdieu, 1977). For many, the promotion of reading means the acquisition of cultural capital in this sense, involving the learning of a culture's major texts and the ways of reading them (Hirsch, 1987). According to Luke's (1996) reading of Bourdieu, however, the most powerful form of capital is not economic capital or cultural capital in themselves, but symbolic capital—the means to convert or transform these kinds of capital into real, material resources and social authority. If you have cultural capital without symbolic capital, then you may still find yourself excluded from the vital resources of society, access to which in their material and discursive senses lies at the heart of the model of power being put forward here (Bourdieu, 1979). You may learn to read the high literary texts of a culture, or you may learn to read the functional texts in which agency messages are inscribed, but in both cases the reading alone and the knowledge associated with that reading do not lead to empowerment, unless one also has the ability to transform that knowledge into a currency that is powerful in that social context.

In certain educational circles, for instance, it is argued that children and nonliterate adults should be given the "genres" of power—taught to read and write and use discourse in the ways exercised by dominant groups, on the ground that this will give them cultural capital and thereby access to power (Luke, 1996; see also Cope & Kalantzis, 1993). This approach, then, assumes that power is simply about rules, which everyone could learn (rules of pronunciation, spelling, writing, etc.), and it is simply the job of educators to teach these to their students. The argument against this is that if too many of the poor and oppressed learn the rules of the game, then those in power will simply alter the genres or conventions ("move the goalposts" in football jargon, shift the "discourse" in Foucault's sense). From this perspective, the genre approach is a classic example of the limitations of trying to give children cultural capital alone: They may still lack symbolic capital, the power to turn their learning (language, dress, literacy) into real value in that society. Even when acquired by the poor, the cultural capital of literacy does not on its own guarantee wealth, jobs, and political power, as it does for those of the dominant group in society, who have the symbolic capital to turn it to account (Gee, 1990). That symbolic capital does not derive simply from being literate (indeed Graff, 1979, has shown how powerful groups can remain dominant without literacy).

Recently it has been suggested that power could be thought of in a more positive way than that of either Foucault or Bourdieu, while retaining the process model of power that they put forward. For educationalists concerned with "productive" power (cf. Kress, 1997; Lankshear, 1997; Luke, 1996; Street, 1995), the question is not "how can a few gain access to existing power" nor "how can existing power structures be resisted," but rather "how can power be transformed"; this involves a transformation from the disciplinary and coercive forms it has taken on in modern society, so that it works instead in a positive way to bring out human potential and to harness creative energy. Constructing an educational and a literacy agenda that accomplishes this without simply imposing our own disciplines and coercive power on others is a major question at the heart of contemporary society. I believe that a reflective and open discussion, in the context of real case studies of attempts in literacy projects to achieve productive power, can make a major contribution to implementing such a project. With respect to the present concern with promotion of reading, this approach sees reading not just as functional, not just as curling up with a book, not just as cultural capital, not just as a Freirean "reading" of the world, but as a reflexive and culturally self-conscious articulation of the meanings of reading in a given context, allied with a reflexive and culturally self-conscious articulation of the meanings of power in that context. The association of these two strands of reflexivity—about reading/literacy and about power—suggests a different view of either than that conveyed by dominant agencies' discourses.

One reason for putting so much weight on reflexivity is that it focuses attention on the daily lived reality of power relations and helps us recognize how we are all involved in both control and resistance; rather than assuming that power always lies somewhere else, this view assumes that power lies in each of us and our immediate personal and social relations, as well as in institutional formations. A problem with the debates on power cited earlier is that literacy and power are often represented at a level of abstraction and of distance that fails to take account of this concrete nature of oral and written language in everyday social practice. Although Foucault and Bourdieu are generally concerned with the relationship between everyday practices and sociohistorical and economic conditions that shape them, there is no accounting for how these day-to-day practices come about. The daily practices and routines of teaching, learning, and interacting with others as we read and write represent the concrete reality of how we exercise and maintain power through literacy practices. Attempts to transform power relations as they work through literacy practices must take account of this reality, rather than simply "resisting" other people's power.

CONCLUSIONS AND DISCUSSION

I conclude by summarizing the assumptions on which this chapter has been based and suggesting directions for future activity in this area. First, I have argued that in considering how to create a world of engaged readers we need to take account of the same issues of identity and of power relations that have been raised by studies of literacy more generally. From this broader perspective, it follows that, as with literacy so with reading, "engagement" does not automatically give rise to empowerment. The daily practices and routines of teaching, learning, and interacting with others as we read and write represent the concrete reality of how we may both exercise and maintain power and at the same time be subject to the exercise of power by others. And finally, reading as a social practice involves more than either reading books (as envisaged in some high cultural promotions in developed societies) or "functional" uses (as in many development campaigns); it engages with multiple identities and multiple cultural practices that are embedded in relations of power through culturally specific literacy practices. For recent ethnographies of such literacy practices, see Aikman (1999); Doronilla (1996); Hornberger (1998); Kalman (1999); King (1994); Prinsloo and Breier (1996).

To consider a world of engaged readers, then, is to consider a world in which power relations are always present. But this attention to power is not simply the same as a traditional static concern with hierarchy, status, or "access." The model of power that I am putting forward, rather, attempts to be a "process" model that believes in transformation. Power in this model is not simply a matter of access to cultural resources or resistance to others' control of them; power as process recognizes how we are all looking both ways when it comes to being powerful and powerless. Just learning to read on its own will not ensure that we become more powerful; it may lead to us being subject to the power of others, or to us exercising power in limited arenas over others who remain powerless. From the point of view of both policy and practice, understanding the relationship between literacy and power requires research that focuses on the concrete everyday lived reality of literacy practices, as for instance in the recent ethnographic studies of literacy in different social contexts—what has come to be termed the New Literacy Studies (Barton, 1994; Gee, 1990; Street, 1995). It is in these lived realities and the ethnographic descriptions of them that we can come to see and to understand the ways in which literacy generally and reading more particularly may transform relations of power. Critical readers may disagree with this approach. They may, for instance, see the New Literacy Studies as ethnocentric, rooted in Western academic traditions and theories, or as too theoretical and not sufficiently practical in approach, or as unrealistic in addressing transformation rather than access, or as idealist in asserting that critical reflection can affect social transformation. I look forward to such discussion and disagreement. This chapter will have served its purpose if it helps us to think more critically and more carefully about the relation between reading and power and their implications for creating a world of engaged readers.

ACKNOWLEDGMENT

Parts of this chapter were originally published as "Literacy and Power" in *BALID Bulletin and Newsletter*, 1994, *10*(1), 33–36, although the chapter has been subject to considerable revision.

REFERENCES

Aikman, S. (1999). *Intercultural education and literacy: An ethnographic study of indigenous knowledge and learding in the Peruvian Amazon.* Amsterdam: Benjamins.
Archer, D. (1994). Participatory rural appraisal and adult literacy. *Ngoma.* (CODE Europe's semi-annual newsletter); *2*(1), 11.
Barton, D. (1994). *Literacy: An introduction to the ecology of written language.* Oxford: Blackwell.
Bourdieu, P. (1977). *Outline of a theory of practice.* Cambridge: Cambridge University Press.
Bourdieu, P. (1979). Cultural reproduction and social reproduction. In J. Karabel & A. H. Halsey (Eds.), *Power and ideology in education* (pp. 487–510). Oxford: Oxford University Press.
Cope, B., & Kalanztis, M. (1993). *The powers of literacy: A genre approach to teaching writing.* Brighton: Falmer.

Doronilla, M. L. (1996). *Landscapes of literacy: An ethnographic study of functional literacy in marginal Philippine communities.* Hamburg: UIE.

Foucault, M. (1979). *Discipline and power.* London: Penguin.

Foucault, M. (1984). What is an author? In P. Rabinow (Ed.), *The Foucault reader* (pp. 101–120). London: Penguin.

Freire, P., & Macedo, D. (1987). *Literacy: Reading the word and the world.* New York: Bergin & Garvey.

Freire, P. (1972). *The pedagogy of the oppressed.* London: Sheed & Ward.

Freire, P. (1985) *The politics of education: Culture, power and liberation.* New York: Bergin & Garvey.

Gee, J. (1990). *Social linguistics and literacy: Ideology in discourses.* London: Falmer.

Gee, J., Hull, G., & Lankshear, C. (1996). *The new work order: Behind the language of the new capitalism.* NSW, Australia: Allen & Unwin.

Gordon, C. (Ed.). (1980). *Foucault: Power/knowledge: Selected interviews and other writings.* New York: Partheon.

Graff, H. (1979). *The literacy myth.* New York: Academic Press.

Hirsch, E. D., Jr. (1987). *Cultural literacy: What every American needs to know.* Boston: Houghton Mifflin.

Holland, D., & Street, B. (1994). Assessing adult literacy in the United Kingdom: The progress profile. In C. Hill & K. Parry. (Eds.), *The test at the gate: Cross-cultural perspectives on English language assessment* (pp. 229–250). London: Longmans.

Hornberger, N. (Ed.). (1998). *Language planning from the bottom up: Indigenous literacies in the Americas.* Berlin: Mouton de Gruyter.

Kalman, J. (1999). *Writing on the plaza: Mediated literacy practices among scribes and clients in Mexico City.* Creskill, NJ: Hampton Press.

King, L. (1994). *Roots of identity: Language and literacy in Mexico.* Palo Alto, CA: Stanford University Press.

Kress, G. (1997). *Before writing: Rethinking the paths to literacy.* London: Routledge.

Lankshear, C. (1997). *Changing literacies.* Milton Keynes: Open University Press.

Luke, A. (1996). Genres of power? Literacy education and the production of capital. In R. Hasan & G. Williams (Eds.), *Literacy in society* (pp. 308–338). London: Longman.

Mclaren, P. (1993). *Paulo Freire: A critical encounter.* London: Routledge.

Mclaren, P., & Lankshear, C. (1994). *Politics of liberation: Paths from Freire.* London: Routledge.

National Literacy Trust. (1997). *Literacy Today, 10.*

Oakhill, J., Beard, R., & Vincent, D. (Eds.). (1995). The contribution of psychological research [Special issue]. *Journal of Research in Reading, 18*(2).

Prinsloo, M., & Breier, M. (1996). *The social uses of literacy.* Amsterdam/Sacched: S. Africa.

Rogers, A. (1992). *Adults learning for development.* London: Cassell Educational Ltd.

Stierer, B., & Bloome, D. (1994). *Reading words.* Sheffield: NATE.

Street, B. (Ed.). (2001). *Literacy and development: Ethnographic perspectives.* London: Routledge.

Street, B. (Ed.) (1993a). The new literacy studies [Special issue]. *Journal of Research in Reading, 16*(2).

Street, B. (Ed.). (1993b). *Cross-cultural approaches to literacy.* Cambridge: Cambridge University Press.

Street, B. (1995). *Social literacies: Critical approaches to literacy in development, ethnography and education.* London: Longmans.

Verhoeven, L. (Ed.). (1994). *Functional literacy: Theoretical issues and educational implications.* Amsterdam: John Benjamins.

Wagner, D., Venezky, L., & Street, B. (Eds.). (1999). *Literacy: An international handbook.* New York: Garland.

Conceptual Dichotomies and the Future of Literacy Work Across Cultures

Daniel A. Wagner
University of Pennsylvania

One of the strongest assertions that can be made in the study of reading, and in the practice and politics of improving reading worldwide is that children's reading and their parents' reading behavior are intimately linked. Whether one is studying the nature of children's bedtime storytelling behavior, or considering demographic trends in literacy rates in developing countries, or creating new programs in intergenerational literacy, there is no doubt that the nature and extent of reading activities of children and their parents are highly correlated as demontrated by the chapters in the first section of this volume. Thus, the continuing problem of low levels of adult literacy may be considered to be one of the gravest continuing threats to poor and non-reading among children worldwide.

Adult literacy statistics—both in developing or industrialized countries—remain shocking as we begin the 21th century. UNESCO estimates that there are still about one billion adult "illiterates" in the world today, most of whom are located in the world's poorest countries. Furthermore, in the International Adult Literacy Survey (OECD/Statistics Canada, 1995), which actually assessed literacy skills of adults in a household survey, it was found that there are large numbers (perhaps as high as 25% or more) of adults in industrialized countries like Great Britain, Germany, and the United States who have inadequate literacy skills. Thus, although differing standards are employed to define "illiteracy" in contemporary society, most countries agree they have serious problems with adults who are not literate enough to function well in modern society.

There are many in the political world, and in the media, who claim that these statistics, from all parts of the world, constitute an "educational and social crisis." And, many educational specialists see these literacy and illiteracy statistics as among the best reasons to invest larger sums into the primary school system as a way to staunch the influx of low literates coming into adulthood. So, we regularly hear the well-known "faucet" metaphor—if you can't turn off the faucet (of non-reading children) then the cycle of illiteracy will be maintained. The other side of the coin, of course, represents those who advocate more resources for adult literacy programs and adult education. The list of reasons for these investments runs the gamut from human rights arguments, to helping children do their homework, or the need for better skilled workers in a competitive global marketplace.

Although most of these arguments seem understandable and straightforward, the field of adult literacy education has often been bedeviled by what one might call a conceptual minefield—where specialists, teachers, and policymakers fear to tread, or tread at the risk of getting into seemingly endless debates. This issue—addressed in the remaining sections of this chapter—concerns the nature of this conceptual minefield, and how we can move beyond it. The debates engendered provide useful focal points for both discussion and action in literacy work. I maintain that these debates have (like politics itself) often taken the form of debilitating conceptual dichotomies, which tend to polarize the field. Of course, science (including social science and education) are filled with dichotomies that help by focusing paradigmatic investigations (cf. Kuhn, 1968)—such as light being composed of waves versus particles. But, as with this latter example, educational reality—combining real-world activities with real people—is almost always a mix of both sides of a given continuum. In the literacy field, it is maintained, the dichotomy debates reign to such a degree that common ground has often been difficult to find. This chapter is an attempt to shed light both on the nature of some key dichotomies, and ways to move beyond them.

SEVEN CONCEPTUAL DICHOTOMIES

I. Literacy–Illiteracy Versus Scale of Skills. This dichotomy has both conceptual and practical dimensions, and is tied to the fundamental issue of defining literacy itself (Venezky, Wagner, & Ciliberti, 1990; Wagner, 1992). Historically, and especially before World War II, it was possible to make an arbitrary distinction between those who had been to school and those who had not; this was especially obvious in the newly independent countries of the Third World, which were just beginning to provide public schooling beyond a relatively small elite. As the 21st century begins, this situation has changed dramatically. Although there are still millions of adults who have never attended school, in even the poorest countries of the world the majority of the population (up to about to about age 40) has had some schooling. Although this leaves open the serious question of the level of literacy of this often-minimally schooled population, it nonetheless points to a world with a much more variegated landscape of literacy skills, levels of achievement, and degree of regular use.

The key issue here is that many countries still report data (then picked up by UNESCO and other agencies) in the dichotomous fashion of "literates" versus "illiterates," often based on little more information than the number of children who have entered primary school. We have substantial information on the inaccuracy of such statistics. One need only to mention the recent national surveys in industrialized countries, undertaken in the United States (Kirsch, Jungeblut, Jenkins, & Kolstad, 1993), and OECD countries (OECD/Statistics Canada, 1995) to show that an application of learning achievement data can provide a much more nuanced approach to this dichotomy. The bottom line here is that the previous dichotomy is not only inaccurate and of little use today, but is also misleading in terms of the types of policies that need to be put into place. Yet it is a dichotomy that is dying a relatively slow death, and has yet to find its way into the international data analyses of UNESCO and the UNDP, among others. By the year 2000, it seems that this particular dichotomy has finally begun to cede to the much more useful concept of literacy as a broader concept, encompassing not only a range of skills, but also concern about the meanings and practices that embed literacy in social contexts around the world.

2. Literacy Versus Literacies. A current debate has begun to take shape over the use of the singular term *literacy* versus the multiple term *literacies*. As far as this author has been able to determine, the first contemporary usages appeared almost simultaneously in the works of Brian Street (Street, 1984) and Wagner (Wagner & Spratt, 1984); curiously, each author made reference to the same basic phenomenon, that of the interesting contrast between Muslim religious literacy on the one hand and secular literacy on the other—Wagner in Morocco, and Street in Iran. The intent of each author was to describe the multifaceted differences in context, use, and meaning of literacy that contrast the secular and Muslim traditions in those two different societies.

However, over time, the term literacies began to take on a life of its own, partly due to the increased use of the term literacy to represent "expertise" in such areas as computer literacy, geographical literacy, statistical literacy—a veritable host of *literacies*. In addition, in the writings of Street and others (see chapters in this volume by Street and Barton), a turning toward a new theoretical approach to literacy which sought in the term *literacies* an opportunity to break—both conceptually and practically—with what was thought to be a much more skill-driven and restrictive notion of literacy. The intention by such scholars seems to rely on the discourse of sociolinguistics—on the diversity of languages, dialects, registers, and so forth, which describes the world of speech—to formulate a new way to think about literacy. As Street (1995) states "literacy is not a single, essential thing, with predictable consequences for individual and social development. Instead there are multiple literacies that vary with time and place and are embedded in specific cultural practices."

Embedded within this issue is an additional dichotomy advanced by Street (1984, 1995), that of "autonomous" vs. "ideological" models of literacy. This distinction follows from the former, but suggests that those who posit a single literacy often do so because they view reading or literacy as a singular or "autonomous" skill that can be applied in any context. Street argued that an ideological model makes more sense because it would allow for a more patterned view of literacy or literacies in culturally and linguistically diverse contexts. This is a philosophically appealing argument, and it has had a significant impact on both scholars and practitioners in recent years.

Yet, the literacy—literacies and autonomous—ideological dichotomies of Street, although attractive on some levels, also contain the seeds of confusion for the literacy field. Although the term *literacies* conveys diversity better than the single word *literacy*, the term also suggests that all literacies are both equivalent and distinct from one another. In a recent attempt to clarify what is meant by literacies, Street (1997) suggested that the term would be better employed when referring to literacy practices (in the plural) than to literacies alone. The conceptual danger here is that both learners and policymakers will misunderstand the intent of literacies, and assume (falsely, in this writer's view) that any composite set of skills (even well beyond the domain of conventional definitions of literacy) constitutes a sufficient level of literacy for particular purposes. In sum, whereas Street's critical perspective of the traditional literacy terminology has been useful to many, the creation of such fluid standard leaves the field in danger of becoming unable to know just what it is talking about. One way to be convinced that this is so is to ask how, with the term *literacies*, would practitioners begin to determine how to measure *success* in learning—no single standard could be developed.

3. Supply Versus Demand. The supply and demand equations for adult literacy instruction are complicated by, among other factors, the changing demands for basic skills in the workplace, the limited awareness on the part of those with low reading and writing ability that their skills are not sufficient for everyday literacy needs, and in the varied policies of countries toward support for basic skills instruction (Venezky & Wagner, 1996). For adult education, and particularly for adult literacy instruction, considerable attention has been given in countries like the United States to the mismatch between worker skills and projected workplace skill needs (Johnston & Packer, 1987), but few supply–demand studies in adult literacy have gone beyond enumerating service providers or measuring in detail the barriers to further participation (i.e., demand). Furthermore, as Mishel and Teixeira (1991) have demonstrated, a projected mismatch between worker skills and the skill demands of the U.S. workplace may be highly exaggerated.

Nonetheless, literacy sponsors (at local and national levels, whether in the U.K. or India) often say that they are "oversubscribed" and simply do not have the resources to fill "long waiting lists" of learners who want to learn. This claim has rarely been challenged, both due to the dearth of data, and due to the political sensitivities of funding support. For example, in the United States, in 1991, a little over 3.7 million persons were enrolled in federally funded literacy and basic education programs. This represents about 8% of the 45.4 million U.S. residents who were 16 years of age or older who were both out of school and without a high school certificate. This 8% is within the range of 5%–10%, which is often cited for the percentage of those in need who actually participate in literacy programs (Wikelund, Reder, & Hart-Landsberg, 1992). Furthermore, a comprehensive study showed that nearly 50% of such federally funded programs were operating under their capacity and only 25% reported having clients on a waiting list (Development Associates, 1992). This finding suggests that the perceived demand for programs may be substantially overestimated by sponsors (i.e., policymakers and programs). Similar misrepresentation of the demand for literacy has been observed in many developing countries as well (Wagner, 1995).

4. Campaigns Versus Programs. Supply can also be overestimated, which has been noted in mass literacy campaigns in numerous developing countries (see also Weber, this volume). For example, in countries such as Cuba and Tanzania, where literacy campaigns used an "each one teach one" philosophy, the theory was that any literate person (often determined by a person having a primary or secondary school certificate) could rapidly make a literate person out of an illiterate peasant. Because virtually no evaluations were undertaken, governments went on to proclaim "total success" (cf. Arnove & Graff, 1987). In such campaigns, there remains an emphasis on massive supply-side programming (irrespective of demand), which puts political capital and political support behind the programs in question (Wagner, 1989). This is a risky political strategy because, as political winds change, literacy campaigns can disappear as quickly as they were created.

As far as this author knows, there has been no comprehensive review of literacy campaigns, but the balance of evidence suggests that the politics of campaigns often (and perhaps always) obscures the issues of effectiveness. It is rare to find a campaign that has undertaken a serious review of its own effectiveness (but see Gillette, 1999, for an interesting critique of UNESCO's Experimental World Literacy Programme).

Of course, community based literacy programs may be seen as smaller instances of campaigns, usually more diverse and with less political support at higher levels of authority. Some advantages of work at the program level include a better capacity for adaptation to local needs and the ability to utilize local talent more effectively; disadvantages include difficulties of maintaining a strong professional staff with limited funding, problems of building an adequate physical infrastructure (including technology), and so forth. In sum, both campaigns and program level work have their share of difficulties, and part of the dichotomy here is in the matter of degree. However, the political imperative that is enveloped within the campaign mode cannot be ignored. The fact that campaigns exist for and are largely determined by political forces—rather than by educational professionals—is one of the key reasons for poor performance and short-lived impact.

5. Volunteers Versus Professional Teachers. Volunteers are a common feature in literacy programs worldwide, but they are relatively more prevalent in industrialized countries where government funding comprises a smaller percentage of support than in developing countries. Although volunteers can supplement the work of professional teachers, the American empirical research in this area does not support the assumption that an expanded volunteer teaching or tutoring effort can make a major impact on the literacy needs of adult learners. A recent review of tutoring research (Jain & Venezky, 1996) suggests that tutoring can be effective in various learning contexts, but is especially sensitive to the match between the tutor and the student. In voluntary literacy programs, according to Tenenbaum and Strong (1992), tutor–student matches are usually determined by geographic proximity, rather than by other factors (ethnicity, age, gender) which seem to be most important for effective learning.

The substantial use of volunteers also makes it difficult for programs to engage in sustainable staff training and development. In the United States, a beginning volunteer tutor typically remains active for less than one year, so that investments in the improvement of teaching are often not seen to be cost effective. The same situation is paralleled in the use of volunteers in many other countries as well, where there is rarely support available for any professional development of literacy teachers. All of the above is not to say that volunteerism in adult literacy should be discouraged, as volunteer organizations can and do play an important part in many national literacy efforts. Rather, the point here is simply that major improvements in literacy work are unlikely to be achieved through volunteer services, as attractive as the idea of volunteerism may be in industrialized or developing countries.

Overall, there is a serious need to enhance professional development that will enable administrators, teachers, and tutors to take advantage of training as an ongoing process within programs and to link staff development more closely with program improvement and evaluation. Teachers and administrators should have more opportunities to investigate local problems and to invent local solutions. Increasing the proportion of full-time professional instructors is an essential element of enhanced staff development; indeed, without more full-time staff, programs have little incentive to spend scarce resources on teacher development. Such changes will require policymakers to change their attitude toward literacy programs, which are still considered to be "nonformal" and even nonessential to the educational system. Thus, although the debate over volunteers versus professionals can be seen as one of balance, contemporary fiscal pressures continue to push the former at the expense of the latter.

6. Mother-Tongue First Versus Second Language. Most countries have formulated an explicit language policy stating which language or languages have official status for education. The decision on national or official language(s) is usually based on such factors as major linguistic groups, colonial or postcolonial history, and the importance of a given language to the concerns of economic development. The use of mother tongue instruction in adult education remains a topic of continuing debate, with mother tongue literacy favored by most experts from the 1950s (Unesco, 1953) until the early 1990s (cf. Wagner, 1992). However, with the advance of universal primary schooling, there appears to be growing diversity of views, especially among adult learners in many countries where access to the economic marketplace drives motivation for particular (often colonial) languages, even if pedagogical evidence suggests that learning to read in a second literacy is a more difficult learning task.

The issue of language of teaching has remained complex in part due to three competing levels of analysis: the ideological level (what appears to be best policy from a political perspective), the planning level (what fits best with national or regional plans in principle), and the individual level (what learners say they want, and what they exhibit in terms of learning achievement). Each of these levels may produce a somewhat different answer as to which language ought to be taught to which individual or groups of individuals. For example, in Senegal, from an ideological level, the government has alternated between African languages and the colonial language (French) over recent decades, both in formal and nonformal education (NFE) programs. In the late 1990s the government seems to be opting for French in most primary schools, but African languages in most NFE programs. These choices seem derived from a political analysis. Yet, from a planning level, it remains to be seen as to whether the language mix will provide the needed levels of skills in the various languages for both economic and social goals. Finally, at the individual (or empirical) level, there is little in the way of hard evidence that any of these choices is better than another. The data are simply not available.

7. Quantity Versus Quality. Although all areas of education have had to cope with the trade-off between quantity and quality, the literacy area has found this dichotomy to be particularly nettlesome. In part, this is due to some of the definitional issues mentioned earlier, such as how literate is a literate person. If a person can be made literate very easily, then mass campaigns would seem to be a good strategy. There are economic temptations of quantity approaches like campaigns, such as the reduction of unit cost as in the mass production of literacy primers, or the use of mass media for publicity or for distance education. In a parallel fashion, volunteers are seen to be a quick and cheap way to dramatically expand the literacy teacher corps, especially if the training of these volunteers is kept to a minimum. And, there are also quantity issues implicated in language choice issues, where one can argue that indigenous languages give greater educational access to the most disadvantaged, or that a metropolitan (colonial) language gives more potential access to a wider world (beyond the confines of the indigenous language).

In each of these examples, however, there remains a serious concern that quality has been sacrificed. Campaigns have been found to deliver far less than their proclamations, volunteers rarely stay long enough in programs to become expert instructors, and language choice issues are more often dominated by the politics of the moment rather than the empirical impact of one program over another. Overall, it may be reasonably concluded that too much has been promised in terms of quick gains by large numbers of adult learners, and much too little delivered. This is true even in wealthy countries, like the United States, where there is growing evidence that, on average, adults learn relatively little in federally funded adult basic education programs, either due to poor attendance or poor quality programs (Development Associates, 1992; Wagner & Venezky, 1999).

CONCLUSIONS AND DISCUSSION

Dichotomies can be useful, indeed liberating, when the occasion is to reflect on how things ought to be. The use of oppositional thinking is at the heart of innovation and creativity. Yet, in some contexts, dichotomies can also be debilitating and polarizing. In this chapter, an attempt was made to show how such conceptual dichotomies have, to some extent, held the literacy field hostage to a variety of polar opposites as sketched above. This is not to say that such dichotomies cannot live in peaceful coexistence within a field of inquiry, but rather that in literacy the field seems to be unusually constrained by this set of classic issues. This need not be the case, in my view, as many of the dichotomies can and will be resolved by researchers over time.

Based on recent research, and a collation of the conceptual dichotomies enumerated earlier, this chapter provides several new directions required to guide future work in the literacy field. This would include, first, moving away from a "one size fits all" approach, to one focused on quality achievement. The lowest unit cost dimension of literacy work, and the historical perspective that adult education is something that is helpful but not central to ministries of education, and must be changed. Literacy should not be seen as *only* a human right or even an educational right, but rather as part of a national (and international) strategy to improved education and human development for all, for a more literate world. Second, the field needs to move away from a search for politically palatable sound bites to a greater emphasis on "truth in advertising." Based on an improved research and evaluation base, we need to provide better indices for learners, teachers, and policymakers as to what can and should be achieved in literacy work. These data need to be provided in user friendly ways to consumers. Finally, we need to shift our thinking away from the idea that illiteracy is "easy to eradicate," to one where standards, and long-term training and development are central to program improvement. Literacy work, even when we agree on which way to go, is not something that is easy to accomplish quickly, contrary to common public opinion.

In sum, this chapter has elucidated some of the ways in which literacy work is hard work, and made harder still by the kinds of classic dichotomies that have rendered discussion so difficult among the field's practitioners and researchers. There are areas of common ground that can be found, on which new consensus can be built and extended. No doubt other dichotomies will surface along the way, but finding ways through conceptual minefields of today can (it is hoped) build the skills needed to address those we shall confront tomorrow.

REFERENCES

Arnove, R. F., & Graff, H. J. (Eds.). (1987). *National literacy campaigns.* New York: Plenum.

Development Associates (1992). *Profiles of service providers.* NEAEP: First interim report.

Development Associates (1995). *National Evaluation of Adult Education Programs: Final report.* Washington, DC: U.S. Department of Education.

GED Testing Service (1992). *1991 Statistical report.* Washington, DC: American Council on Education.

Gillette, A. (1999). The Experimental World Literacy Programme: A unique international effort revisited. In D. A. Wagner (Ed.), *The future of literacy in a changing world* (2nd ed.). Cresskill, NJ: Hampton.

Jain, R. & Venezky, R. L. (1996). *Tutoring: A research review* (Tech. Rep. No. 1). READ*WRITE* NOW Initiative, Planning and Evaluation Service Division. U.S. Department of Education, Washington, DC.

Johnston, W. B., & Packer, A. E. (1987). *Workforce 2000: Work and workers for the 21st century.* Indianapolis, IN: Hudson Institute.

Kirsch, I. S., Jungeblut, A., Jenkins, L., & Kolstad, A. (1993). *Adult literacy in America: A first look at the results of the National Adult Literacy Survey.* National Center for Educational Statistics, U.S. Department of Education.

Kuhn, T. (1968). *The structure of scientific revolutions.* Chicago: University of Chicago Press.

Mishel, L., & Teixeira, R. A. (1991). *The myth of the coming labor shortage: Jobs, skills, and incomes of America's workforce 2000* (EPI Study Series). Economic Policy Institute, Washington, DC.

Street, B. V. (1984). *Literacy in theory and practice.* London: Cambridge University Press.

Street, B. V. (1995). *Social literacies: Critical approaches to literacy in development, ethnography and education.* New York: Longman.

Street, B. V. (1999). The meanings of literacy. In D. A. Wagner, R. L., Venezky, & B. V. Street (Eds.), *Literacy: An international handbook* (pp. 34–42). Boulder, CO: Westview.

Tenenbaum, E., & Strong, W. (1992). *The major national adult literacy volunteer organizations: A descriptive review.* U.S. Department of Education, Washington, DC: Government Printing Office.

Unesco. (1953). The use of vernacular languages in education. *Monograph on fundamental education, No. 8.* Paris: Unesco.

U.S. Congress, Office of Technology Assessment (1993). *Adult literacy and new technologies: Tools for a lifetime* (Final Report No. OTA-SET-550). Washington, DC: U.S. Government Printing Office.

Venezky, R. L., & Wagner, D. A. (1996). Supply and demand for literacy instruction in the United States. *Adult Education Quarterly, 46,* 197–208.

Venezky, R. L., Wagner, D. A., & Ciliberti, B. S. (Eds.). (1990). *Toward defining literacy.* Newark, DE: International Reading Association.

Wagner, D. A. (1989). Literacy campaigns: Past, present and future. *Comparative Education Review, 33,* 256–260.

Wagner, D. A. (1992). *Literacy: Developing the future.* Paris/Geneva: UNESCO.

Wagner, D. A. (1995). Literacy and development: Rationales, myths, innovations, and future directions. *International Journal of Educational Development, 15,* 341–362.

Wagner, D. A., & Spratt, J. (1984, November). *Religious and secular literacies: Conflict and integration in Moroccan education.* Annual Meetings of the American Anthropological Association, Denver.

Wagner, D. A., & Venezky, R. L. (1999). Adult literacy: The next generation. *Educational Researcher, 28*(1), 1–9.

Wikelund, K. R., Reder, S., & Hart-Landsberg, S. (1992). *Expanding theories of adult literacy participation: A literature review* (Tech. Rep. No. TR92-1). National Center on Adult Literacy, University of Pennsylvania, Philadelphia, PA.

Author Index

Subject Index

mobilization of the campaign,
276-280
speed and comprehensiveness,
284-287
Vygotsky and, 276

T

Teacher training, 130-133
Teacher's role, 5-8
  see Prevention of reading difficulties
Teaching
  learner-centered approach, 8
  teacher-directed approach, 8
  see Scaffolding
Technology, 35, 36
  see Media, Digital environments
Television
  audio comparisons, 104-106
  concentration-deterioration
   hypothesis, 104
  correlational research, 100-103,
   108, 109
  decoding skills, 95
  impact of, 15
  psychological and social dimensions, 206
  quantitative displacement
   hypothesis, 112-114

reading attitude, 103
reading decline, 96, 98, 103, 106-116
reading-depreciation hypothesis,
103, 113, 114
restriction/deprivation studies,
99, 110, 114-116
socialization/competence
hypotheses, 98, 99
subtitled programming, 15, 96,
110, 112, 234, 235
time-use diaries, 96-99
type of programming watched,
110, 111
Thinking, 4, 7, 73
Third World countries, 17, 18
Third World schooling, 256-260
Third World Intervention programs
  see Global perspectives, Intervention programs, Health-related programs

V

Vernacular (everyday) practices,
23-37
  dominant literacies, 30, 31, 33, 34
  voluntary vs. self-generated, 31
Visual processing, 3
Vygotskiian approach to
development, 16

LITERACY AND MOTIVATION

Reading Engagement in Individuals and Groups

The central question in this volume is how to create a society of "engaged readers" in today's world, where reading is increasingly overruled by other media such as television and personal computers. Engaged readers, as the term is used in this book, means readers who are socially interactive, strategic, and motivated.

In this state-of-the-art review of research on integrating cognitive, social, and motivational aspects of reading and reading instruction, the chapter authors argue that coming to grips with the notion of engagement in literacy requires redefining literacy itself to acknowledge the degree to which it is not only a cognitive accomplishment, but a social activity and an affective commitment as well. Promoting literacy acquisition thus requires interventions that address attitudes and beliefs as much as those that assure cognitive changes in learners.

Equally important, the authors posit that literacy engagement involves the integration of cognitive strategies and motivational goals during literate activities. This necessary link between literacy and motivation is addressed from a variety of perspectives.

Acknowledging the value of cross-national and cross-cultural comparisons, the book features chapters on the promotion of literacy in different regions around the world.

EDITED BY

LUDO VERHOEVEN
CATHERINE SNOW

ISBN 0-8058-3194-0

90000

9 780805 831948
ISBN 0-8058-3194-0